SHORT ESSAYS

—◆—

SIXTH
EDITION

GERALD LEVIN
Professor Emeritus of English,
University of Akron

Harcourt Brace Jovanovich College Publishers
Forth Worth   Philadelphia   San Diego   New York   Orlando   Austin   San Antonio
Toronto   Montreal   London   Sydney   Tokyo

Aquisitions Editor: Karen Allanson
Manuscript Editor: Sarah Helyar Smith
Production Editor: Socorro P. Gonzalez
Designer: Linda Cable
Production Manager: Suzanne Rogers

Preface

The Sixth Edition of *Short Essays* follows earlier editions in presenting concrete, contemporary essays of interest to students. Most of the essays in this edition are three to five pages long—about the length assigned in many composition courses. The book also contains longer essays by Wendell Berry, Arthur L. Campa, Robert Coles, Joan Didion, Nathan Irvin Huggins, Paul Lancaster, Noel Perrin, L.E. Sissman, and Lewis Yablonsky. The range of subjects is again wide. Changing values in American life, growing up in America, discovering the world of nature, threats to the environment, and the effect of stereotypes continue to be important themes in the book. New subjects include America as a multicultural nation, liberal and conservative values, using animals in research, and testing for drugs on the college campus. Of the 75 essays, 21 are new to the book. Among the new writers are John Gould, Meg Greenfield, Nathan Irvin Huggins, Elizabeth Janeway, Paul Lancaster, Faith McNulty, Pat Mora, Anna Quindlen, William Raspberry, David Updike, and Virginia Woolf. New essays by Annie Dillard, Joan Didion, and Sydney J. Harris complement their essays retained from the Fifth Edition.

As in the Fifth Edition, Part 1 discusses strategies for organizing and developing the essay. These strategies now include example, process, comparison and contrast, cause and effect, definition, and classification and division—methods usually associated with exposition and presented as methods of exposition in previous editions. Part 1 shows how these methods may be used to organize and develop essays of all kinds. Part 2 discusses strategies for expressive writing, with a focus on narrative, descriptive, and reflective ssays. Part 3 discusses strategies for exposition—returning to example, process, and other methods discussed in Part 1 to show

how they combine in various essays. Part 4 discusses strategies of argument and persuasion and contains a new section presenting contrasting articles on two controversial issues. Finally, Part 5 discusses sentence style and diction at various levels of usage. Six topics are discussed: emphasis, parallelism and sentence variety, concreteness, figurative language, tone, and usage. The discussion of sentence and diction now concludes the Sixth Edition. Except for this change from the Fifth Edition, the organization of the new edition is the same.

Each of the five parts of the book opens with an introductory discussion of the rhetorical or logical topic and an analysis of a representative essay in light of the specific topics that follow. Part 5 contains separate introductory analyses of an argumentative and a persuasive essay. Each essay in the book is followed by a comment on the rhetorical principles introduced at the beginning of each section. The Questions for Study and Discussion explore the content and rhetoric of the essay, developing points in the general comment. The Vocabulary Study supplements these questions in teaching the uses of the dictionary and emphasizing the importance of context in reading and writing.

A thematic table of contents appears at the beginning of the book. Since each essay addresses topics other than the one it illustrates in the book, instructors may want to switch essay and rhetorical topic or group essays on a single theme. The Suggestions for Teaching and Suggestions for Writing in the Instructor's Manual often suggest alternatives for teaching.

Again I wish to thank Andrea A. Lunsford, Ohio State University, and Ann Raimes, Hunter College of the City University of New York, for their advice on the first edition. Eben W. Ludlow originally suggested the book, helped to plan it, and as always gave me strong encouragement and support. I owe thanks also to former colleagues at the University of Akron, as well as to many teachers who made suggestions for earlier editions. I owe special thanks to those who produced this book: to my acquisitions editor, Karen Allanson, for her useful comments on this edition; to Eleanor Garner, the permissions editor, for again arranging for use of the essays; to Linda Cable, for the design of the book; to Pat Gonzalez, the production editor; and to Sarah Helyar Smith, the manuscript editor. My debt to my wife, Lillian Levin, is always a great one.

Gerald Levin

Contents

PART I
Strategies for Organizing and Developing the Essay

PART III
Strategies for Exposition

PART IV
Strategies for Arguing and Persuading

PART V
Effective Sentences and Diction

Thematic Table of Contents

Growing Up

Education

Goals and Personal Values

Social Character and Values

Urban Experience

Science, Technology, and Social Values

Work

Sports

Language and Thought

Contemporary Social Issues

Introduction

This book is concerned with essays of personal expression, information or exposition, and persuasion, and it shows how they each serve particular purposes. The purposes for which we write are so numerous that no one classification can account for all of them, but one recent classification distinguishes four purposes: personal expression, reference or giving information, creating literary effect, and persuasion. But these purposes are not exclusive of one another. Thus, an essay may express one's personal feelings or beliefs, and it may also give information about a particular subject, as in a textbook, or generate laughter or pathos as in a play or novel, or seek to change opinion on an issue as in a political speech. A piece of writing may have several purposes. For example, a satirical essay may amuse and inform us about a contemporary issue while it seeks to persuade the audience to change their minds about the issue.

Part One of this book presents various strategies for organizing and developing essays. One strategy is to develop a central impression or central idea or thesis for the essay as a whole. The individual paragraphs of the essay would also contain a topic sentence or statement of the subject or guiding idea. In turn, the paragraphs would have some kind of organization or order of ideas, held together by transitional words and phrases. Other strategies or means of development include narration and description. In writing home about your first week at college, you might use narration to give a chronological account of the events of the week and description to give details about your room, new friends, or classes. Still other means of developing the essay include example, process, comparison and contrast, cause and effect, definition, and classification and division. In your letter you might use the registration of classes as an example of why college life can be frustrating, give details of the registration process, compare and contrast a college class with a high school class, give reasons for differences you find, define a new interest or activity you have taken up, or classify the various friends or teachers encountered during the week.

Part Two of the book describes two important kinds of expressive writing—autobiography and reflection. Part Three shows how various methods of development such as definition and comparison and contrast work together to give information. Part Four describes strategies for developing arguments and making them persuasive. Persuasive essays use narration, description, and other means of development such as definition, classification, and comparison and contrast, but they chiefly use argument. Argument is concerned with establishing the truth of statements; persuasion, with getting readers to accept these statements and perhaps take action that the statements support. Part Five describes ways of making sentences and diction serve the various purposes of the essay.

The questions and suggestions for writing that follow each selection will give you practice in achieving various objectives through various means or strategies. Although an understanding of purposes and strategies alone will not make you a better writer, knowledge of how other writers develop their experiences and ideas will help you in drafting and revising your own essays. You will become a better writer only through constant writing and revision. The essays presented here are examples of proven ways of organizing and developing essays. They show how a wide range of writers who differ in background and interest achieve their various purposes.

PART 1

Strategies for Developing and Organizing the Essay

Accurate though my story had been, and based on a public record, it had nevertheless exploited human unhappiness for the amusement or titillation of others.

— Tom Wicker

The word *essay* has various meanings. To many writers the word describes a short, carefully organized composition that develops a single idea or impression. To other writers the word describes a beginning or trial attempt, in which the central idea or impression is explored rather than developed or analyzed completely. Thus, Samuel Johnson, the great eighteenth-century essayist and lexicographer, referred to the essay as "an irregular undigested piece."

Johnson's definition fits many essays that have the informality of a rough draft—those that contain loosely organized ideas and impressions. Informal letters and journal entries sometimes are essays in this sense of the word. Like journal entries, trial essays help writers discover what they want to say. Much of your writing in your composition course may be trial essays of this kind.

Of course, upon revision the trial essay may become a carefully organized composition that focuses upon a single idea or impression. Although many essays in newspapers and magazines merely explore a topic, others contain a central idea or thesis and a careful organization or order of supporting ideas and details. A newspaper editorial that argues for energy conservation is one kind of essay; an extended magazine article describing methods of energy conservation is another; a newspaper column that describes personal experiences with energy-saving devices is yet another. The purpose of each essay is different and so may be the organization. The editorial is persuasive in intent, the magazine article informative. Both organize the argument or exposition in ways that will best persuade or inform the readers of the essay. The personal column on energy-saving devices that expresses amusement or frustration about electrical devices may organize the description or narration to generate laughter or some other response from the reader.

Edward Hoagland's essay on stuttering is neither persuasive nor informative, though Hoagland tells us something about changes in telephoning and banking that create discomfort in a person who stutters. Hoagland's purpose is to express his interest in the discomfort of his friend and the increasing problems these changes create in others without handicaps. He concludes the essay with the statement that he has "no solutions to offer."

Hoagland builds to the central idea or *thesis* of his short essay—stated at the end of paragraph 3:

> And inevitably, as we all become known more and more by
> account numbers, doing business will become still more im-
> personal, and any voice that doesn't speak as plainly as digits·
> entering a computer will cause problems.

He restates his thesis in the concluding paragraph, in noting
that an increasing number of people will be discomforted by the
changes described in the essay. The word *thesis* is perhaps an
inexact word to describe the central idea of this kind of essay
because Hoagland is not arguing a proposition in a formal way.
Observation is probably the better word. Nevertheless, the observation, like the central idea or thesis of a persuasive essay,
organizes the details and gives direction. Hoagland might have
presented only a series of details or observations from which
readers could make inferences or draw conclusions. Had he
done so, we might refer to this sense or impression as an *implied thesis*.

When writing your own essays, remember that few readers
see the world exactly as you do. They may, indeed, see different
things and have different ideas and feelings about them.
Whether your purpose is chiefly to express your feelings or
beliefs, to give information about the world, or to persuade
readers to accept a belief of yours, you must help them see the
world as you do. You must also help them follow the flow of
your observations and thoughts. The sections that follow discuss
ways of doing so.

Edward Hoagland

STUTTERING TIME

Edward Hoagland has published numerous essays in *The New
Yorker*, *The New York Times*, and other periodicals. His books
include *The Courage of Turtles* (1970), *Red Wolves and Black Bears*
(1976), *The Tugman's Passage* (1982), and *Seven Rivers West* (1986).
Hoagland writes on a wide range of subjects—from circuses to the
changing seasons, animal life, and changes in American life.
"Stuttering Time" discusses changes in our telephone system.

We have a friend who stutters; and while he notices no 1
increase in rudeness or sarcasm from people in person,
he does hear more impatience from telephone operators,
secretaries, businessmen, switchboard personnel, and
other strangers whom he must deal with over the phone.
As he stands at a phone booth or holds on to the devilish
device at home, the time allotted to him to spit out the
words seems to have markedly shrunk; perhaps it has
been halved in the past half-dozen years. This alarms him
because at the same time the importance of the telephone
in daily transactions has zoomed. Indeed, many people
use answering machines to consolidate their calls, and
soon voiceprinting may become a commonplace method
of identification. Imagine, he suggests, stuttering into a
voiceprinting machine.

Bell System operators, who used to be the most patient 2
people he encountered, now often seem entirely unfamiliar
with his handicap. They either hang up or switch him to
their supervisors as a "problem call" after listening for only
a few seconds, interrupting a couple of times to demand
that he "speak clearly, please." They seem automated
themselves, as if rigged to a stop clock that regulates how
long they will listen to anything out of the ordinary,
though twenty years ago, he says, they practiced their
trade with a fine humanity.

But it is not just individuals in individual occupations 3
who have changed. The division between personal life and
business life has deepened, and the brusqueness of business gets worse all the time. At the bank, one can no
longer choose one's teller but must stand in a single line.
(The tellers seem to work more slowly, having less responsibility individually for the length of the line.) And inevitably, as we all become known more and more by account
numbers, doing business will become still more impersonal, and any voice that doesn't speak as plainly as digits
entering a computer will cause problems.

We have no solutions to offer. We have brought up 4
the subject only because our friend sometimes feels like

the canary that miners used to carry into a mine. He believes his increasing discomfort foretells a worsening shortness of breath in other people—even those who started out with no handicaps at all.

Questions for Study and Discussion

1. What is meant by the title of the essay "Stuttering Time"? How is the title related to the thesis of the essay?
2. How does Hoagland show that he is moving from a specific example—the experience of his friend who stutters—to general experiences and then to ideas?
3. Would Hoagland's observation or thesis be clear without examples? Or could Hoagland have discussed the idea abstractly rather than concretely?
4. What example can you give of the problem discussed by Hoagland? Can you offer a solution to the problem?

Vocabulary Study

Explain the difference between the words in each pair. Then explain why Hoagland chose the first word and not the second.

1. *zoomed* (paragraph 1), risen
2. *consolidate* (paragraph 1), combine
3. *automated* (paragraph 2), robotized
4. *brusqueness* (paragraph 3), rudeness

Suggestions for Writing

1. Present your own example of the problem discussed by Hoagland or another problem created by modern invention. Discuss a solution to the problem if you have one to offer.
2. Hoagland suggests that occupations change individuals. Explain what he means and give examples from your own working experience. Draw a conclusion from your discussion.

Unity and Thesis

In a unified essay all ideas and details connect to the thesis or controlling idea, or sometimes to a controlling impression. The reader sees their connection at every point and experiences them as a unit. The central idea that organizes the many smaller ideas and details of an essay is called the *thesis*. Occasionally the thesis appears in the first sentence or close to the beginning, as in many newspaper articles and editorials. The effect is likely to be dramatic, as in these opening paragraphs of a newspaper aticle:

> "Don't you want to be one of the Now people?" asks an ad for a new soft drink, going on to urge, "Become one of the Now generation!"
> The only thing I can think of that is worse than being one of the Now people is being one of the Then people. As a member of civilization in good standing, I reject both the *nowness* and the *thenness* of the generations. I opt for the *alwaysness*.
> —Sydney J. Harris, "Now People and Then People"

In fact, the newspaper or magazine reader *expects* to find the main ideas or details of the editorial or column in the opening sentences.

Beginning an essay or article directly with the thesis can seem abrupt, however, and often the thesis may not be clear to the reader without background. So the essayist frequently builds to the thesis, sometimes through details of a controversy or issue, as in the following opening paragraphs:

> Over the past weeks, the nation's colleges have taken a beating because of loudmouths who shouted down invited speakers. Eldridge Cleaver at Wisconsin, Ambassador Jeane

Kirkpatrick at Berkeley and Sheik Ahmad Zaki Yamani at Kansas were the speakers, and the noise raised in their defense is only slightly less deafening than the shouts that drowned their speeches. No one in the academy approved or condoned the shouting: the clearest defense of the university as an open forum has come from university people themselves through the national associations that represent presidents, faculty members and students.

Whether or not they are aware of it, our critics misread our vulnerability to disruption. They seem to think that universities are orderly places, and if they aren't, presidents and trustees ought to make them so, even by force. Force is, however, our last and least resource, and order in the universities has seldom been more than skin-deep [*thesis*]. We order our planning, our upkeep, our payroll and the lawns. But where our most serious work is done, messiness, not to say a kind of anarchy, is part of our nature [*restatement of thesis*].
—Rev. Timothy S. Healy, S.J., "In Defense of Disorder"

Such introductory comments and details before the statement of the thesis help to place the reader in the world of the writer.

Sometimes the thesis is stated toward the end of the essay rather than toward the beginning. One reason for this delay is that the reader may not understand the thesis without examples and considerable explanation. Another reason is that the writer may need to make the reader receptive to a controversial thesis before stating it. Also, a thesis is highlighted when it appears toward the end, particularly if the writer builds to it gradually but steadily.

In some essays—especially those that are mainly narration (that recount a series of events) or description—the thesis may be implied rather than explicitly stated, or the essay may contain a central impression rather than a thesis. In these instances, a carefully planned accumulation of details, rather than any single statement in the essay, conveys the main idea or impression the writer wishes to share with the reader. In the absence of a stated thesis, it is especially important that the writer maintain a clear sense of purpose and a consistent point of view in presenting the details.

You will find that you can produce unified, well-developed essays of your own if you take time to formulate a clear preliminary thesis statement after an initial draft. The act of writing is often an act of discovery—of finding meanings and ideas you could not anticipate at the start. In the course of writing, you may discover that your details and discussion suggest another thesis. When you do state a thesis that you find completely satisfactory, you need to review what you have written to be certain that the details develop it and not another idea. This review is particularly necessary if you decide not to state the thesis explicitly in the essay.

Susan Walton

THE CAUTIOUS AND OBEDIENT LIFE

Susan Walton received her B.A. in anthropology from Carleton College and an M.A. in journalism from the University of Wisconsin—Madison. Walton has done scientific and technical writing for the National Academies of Science and Engineering and various federal agencies, and she has written on science and education for numerous periodicals including *BioScience*, *Education Week*, and *Psychology Today*. Her essay on living an obedient life originally appeared in the *The New York Times*.

Little herds of people mill around intersections in the   1
morning, waiting for the lights to change. Washington is full of traffic circles, so sometimes you have to wait through several lights, standing on narrow islands of concrete while traffic comes at you from unexpected directions.

Not everyone waits. Some people dash, even when   2
they see the No. 42 bus bearing down on them or some squirrel of a driver running every red light for blocks. The particularly daring ones make the cars stop for them.

I seldom walk until the light turns green. It is part of   3
being obedient, a manifestation of the misbegotten belief that you must do what people tell you to to do, and if you do, you will be rewarded. This syndrome of behavior is characterized by a dedication to form at the expense of spontaneity and substance. It is turning papers in on time and expecting to receive better grades than those who turn

them in late, even if theirs are superior. It is believing your mother—who probably didn't believe it herself—when she says that boys prefer nice girls. This toe-the-line mentality is not confined to women; men, too, lie awake wondering how things ended up so wrong when they so carefully did everything right. Which is exactly the problem.

Some people are born to follow instructions. They are 4 quiet children who always finish their homework, are never caught being bad, never sneak off and do undetected wicked things. They never figure out that it is possible to ignore what others want you to do and do whatever you like. The consequences of deviation are usually minimal. Nobody really expects you to be that good. If you are born this way, you acquire a look of puzzlement. You are puzzled because you can't figure out how or why these other people are doing outrageous things when the rules have been so clearly stated. Nor do you understand why people are not impressed with your mastery of those rules.

Puzzlement may turn to smugness. At first, when peo- 5 ple asked me whether I had completed an assignment, I was surprised: of course I had; didn't the teacher *tell* us to? After I realized that punctuality was not all that common, I became smug. Yes, of course I turned my paper in on time. I did not see that the people who got noticed were likely to be erratic and late, rushing in explaining that their thesis had not fallen into place until 4 a.m. of the third Monday after the paper was due. Us punctual types did not wait for theses to fall into place. Whatever could be knocked into shape in time was what got turned in. The thing was due, wasn't it?

The message did not sink in for years, during which I 6 always showed up for work, double pneumonia and all. I wandered into a field—journalism—mined with deadlines and populated by more missed deadlines, per capita, than any other. I repeated the process—first the assumption that you had to make the deadline, or why did they call it a deadline? Then I realized that this behavior was not universal. By the time I began working for a weekly, I had deluded myself into thinking that reliability was the way to success.

And it was, sort of. At this job, however, I encoun- 7
tered one of those people apparently sent by life as an object lesson. For every deadline I made, he missed one. Stories that everyone was counting on failed to materialize for weeks, as he agonized, procrastinated and interviewed just one more person. Everyone was annoyed at the time, but when the work was completed, mass amnesia set in. Only the product mattered, and the product, however late it was, was generally acceptable.

We advanced together, but what I gained with pro- 8
motion was the opportunity to meet more deadlines per week and to hang around waiting to edit the copy of those who were late. What he got was the opportunity to linger over ever more significant stories. In my case, virtue was its own punishment. The moral of this story is that you should stop to think whether being good is getting you anywhere you want to go.

The most common and forgivable reason for the cau- 9
tious, obedient life is fear. It is true, something terrible could happen if you stray. Something terrible could also happen if you do not stray, which is that you might be bored to death. Some people are lucky; what they are suppposed to do is also what they like to do. They do not need to muster their nerve. I do not consider myself a nervy person. Rather, I think of myself as a recovering coward. Cowardice, like alcoholism, is a lifelong condition.

The James boys, William and Henry, are instructive on 10
the subject of following too narrow a path. William James wrote in a letter to Thomas Ward in 1868 that the great mistake of his past life was an "impatience of results," which, he thought, should not be "too voluntarily aimed at or too busily thought of." What you must do, he believed, is to go on "in your own interesting way." Then the results will float along under their own steam. Henry left the classic record of the unlived life in "The Beast in the Jungle." It is the story of a man convinced that fate has

something momentous in store for him, and he sits around carefully waiting for it to arrive. Consequently, his fate turns out to be that of a man to whom nothing ever happens. Better for him had he not listened quite so earnestly to the inner voice murmuring about fate. Better had he been distracted from his mission.

Be bold, my graduate school adviser, Mr. Ragsdale, used to say—his only advice. I see now that he was right. Think again of your future self: the little old lady sitting on the porch of the old folks' home. When she thinks back on opportunities, will she regret the ones that passed unused?

Or find some other device. Myself, I keep a dumb postcard in my desk drawer. It is light purple, with a drawing of a cowering person standing on the edge of a diving board. Beneath the drawing it says, ''If you don't do it, you won't know what would have happened if you had done it.'' Think about the possible headline: ''Cautious Pedestrian Squashed by Bus While Waiting on Traffic Island—Should Have Jaywalked, Police Say.'' Then look both ways, and go.

Comment

Susan Walton echoes the advice given by the nineteenth-century American writer Ralph Waldo Emerson in ''Self-Reliance'': ''The virtue in most request is conformity. Self-reliance is its aversion. It loves not realities and creators, but names and customs.'' In his sermon-like essay, Emerson advises us to be nonconformists; the advice is unqualified—Emerson does not suggest exceptions to being a nonconformist. Like Emerson, Walton ranges widely over the subject; but her essay is not a loosely organized series of ideas. Walton states a thesis about the cautious and obedient life early in the essay and supports it through her personal experience, observations of other people, and ideas of the American philosopher William James and his brother Henry James, the novelist and short story writer.

Questions for Study and Discussion

1. What is Walton's thesis, and how does she introduce it? How does she keep the thesis before the reader as the essay proceeds?
2. Is Walton one of the people "born to follow instructions," or is she describing other people?
3. What did Walton learn from her experiences as a journalist?
4. Walton states that the commonest reason for the cautious and obedient life is fear. What other reasons does she give? In what order does she present these reasons?
5. Is Walton reflecting upon her character and that of others, or is she writing to persuade cautious and obedient readers to change their lives? How do you know?
6. Do you agree with Walton that the "most common and forgivable reason for the cautious, obedient life is fear"? If you disagree, what explanation seems a better one, and why?

Vocabulary Study

1. Would substitution of *groups* for *herds* change the meaning of Walton's statement that she sees "little herds of people mill around intersections in the morning"?
2. What does Walton mean by "a dedication to form at the expense of spontaneity and substance" (paragraph 3)? What is a "syndrome of behavior"? Is it the same thing as a "pattern" of behavior?
3. What is the dictionary meaning of "erratic" (paragraph 5)? What images or feelings does the word connote or bring to mind? Is an erratic person necessarily eccentric or odd?
4. Walton states in paragraph 8: "In my case, virtue was its own punishment." What does she mean by *virtue*? What dictionary meanings of the words are inapplicable to the sentence?
5. Explain the word *distracted* in the closing sentence of paragraph 10.

Suggestions for Writing

1. Discuss the extent to which you live "the cautious, and obedient life." Then discuss why you act as you do.
2. Discuss your agreement or disagreement with Walton on the issue of conduct, referring to your own habits and experiences.
3. Describe how you meet deadlines at school or at work. Then discuss what your habits reveal about your character, attitudes, or way of living.

James Thurber

THE PRINCESS AND THE TIN BOX

James Thurber (1894–1961) worked as a journalist on the *Columbus Dispatch* and *Chicago Tribune* before beginning his long association with *The New Yorker* in 1925, the year it began publication. Most of his stories, sketches, and cartoons appeared in that magazine. Thurber was a humorist and a satirist of many aspects of American life. His many books include *My Life and Hard Times* (1933), *Fables for Our Time* (1943), *The Thurber Carnival* (1945), and *Thurber Country* (1953).

Once upon a time, in a far country, there lived a king   1
whose daughter was the prettiest princess in the world. Her eyes were like the cornflower, her hair was sweeter than the hyacinth, and her throat made the swan look dusty.

From the time she was a year old, the princess had   2
been showered with presents. Her nursery looked like Cartier's window. Her toys were all made of gold or platinum or diamonds or emeralds. She was not permitted to have wooden blocks or china dolls or rubber dogs or linen books, because such materials were considered cheap for the daughter of a king.

When she was seven, she was allowed to attend the   3
wedding of her brother and throw real pearls at the bride

instead of rice. Only the nightingale, with his lyre of gold, was permitted to sing for the princess. The common blackbird, with his boxwood flute, was kept out of the palace grounds. She walked in silver-and-samite slippers to a sapphire-and-topaz bathroom and slept in an ivory bed inlaid with rubies.

On the day the princess was eighteen, the king sent a   4 royal ambassador to the courts of five neighboring kingdoms to announce that he would give his daughter's hand in marriage to the prince who brought her the gift she liked the most.

The first prince to arrive at the palace rode a swift   5 white stallion and laid at the feet of the princess an enormous apple made of solid gold which he had taken from a dragon who had guarded it for a thousand years. It was placed on a long ebony table set up to hold the gifts of the princess's suitors. The second prince, who came on a gray charger, brought her a nightingale made of a thousand diamonds, and it was placed beside the golden apple. The third prince, riding on a black horse, carried a great jewel box made of platinum and sapphires, and it was placed next to the diamond nightingale. The fourth prince, astride a fiery yellow horse, gave the princess a gigantic heart made of rubies and pierced by an emerald arrow. It was placed next to the platinum-and-sapphire jewel box.

Now the fifth prince was the strongest and handsom-   6 est of all the five suitors, but he was the son of a poor king whose realm had been overrun by mice and locusts and wizards and mining engineers so that there was nothing much of value left in it. He came plodding up to the palace of the princess on a plow horse and he brought her a small tin box filled with mica and feldspar and hornblende which he had picked up on the way.

The other princes roared with disdainful laughter   7 when they saw the tawdry gift the fifth prince had brought to the princess. But she examined it with great interest and squealed with delight, for all her life she had been glutted with precious stones and priceless metals, but she had never seen tin before or mica or feldspar or horn-blende. The tin box was placed next to the ruby heart pierced with an emerald arrow.

"Now," the king said to his daughter, "you must   8
select the gift you like best and marry the prince that brought it."

The princess smiled and walked up to the table and   9
picked up the present she liked the most. It was the platinum-and-sapphire jewel box, the gift of the third prince.

"The way I figure it," she said, "is this. It is a very   10
large and expensive box, and when I am married, I will meet many admirers who will give me precious gems with which to fill it to the top. Therefore, it is the most valuable of all the gifts my suitors have brought me and I like it the best."

The princess married the third prince that very day in   11
the midst of great merriment and high revelry. More than a hundred thousand pearls were thrown at her and she loved it.

Moral: All those who thought the princess was going to   12
select the tin box with worthless stones instead of one of the other gifts will kindly stay after class and write one hundred times on the blackboard "I would rather have a hunk of aluminum silicate than a diamond necklace."

Comment

As in "The Princess and the Tin Box," Thurber's humor often arises in his fables and stories from incongruities between what we expect to see in people or expect to happen to them and what does happen. Another incongruity is found in Thurber's language. Disparities of this sort are a major source of irony—the sardonic discovery that life is different from what we expect it to be, that appearances deceive. Many authors do not comment on what they show; they allow truths and ironies to emerge from the details of the story—from the setting, happenings, statements of characters. Thurber does comment in the moral he attaches to his story. But this moral by no means expresses all the truths contained in what the princess does and says.

Questions for Study and Discussion

1. How do the details of the first six paragraphs lead you to believe that the princess will choose the fifth prince? Is the order of these details important?
2. At what point do you discover the real character of the princess? What does her manner of speaking or choice of words contribute to this discovery?
3. Thurber, in his moral, talks to us in a language different from that of the story. What exactly is this difference, and what humor arises from it?
4. What idea or attitude is Thurber satirizing? Is he also satirizing the princess or the reader of the essay or possibly both? Do you find other truths in the story?
5. Do you find Thurber's moral pertinent to the world today?

Vocabulary Study

Look up the following words: *parable, fairy tale, fable, allegory.* How closely does "The Princess and the Tin Box" fit the definitions you found?

Suggestions for Writing

1. Write a fairy tale or fable or parable of your own that develops an idea or truth about people.
2. Write a non-satirical essay that examines the idea or values Thurber writes about from your point of view and experience. If you take a different view of these values, compare your view with Thurber's.

Topic Sentence

The phrase *topic sentence* usually describes the main or central idea of the paragraph—the idea that organizes details and subordinate ideas:

> Having listened to both Chinese and English, I also tend to be suspicious of any comparisons between the two languages [*topic sentence*]. Typically, one language—that of the person doing the comparing—is often used as the standard, the benchmark for a logical form of expression. And so the language being compared is always in danger of being judged deficient or superfluous, simplistic or unnecessarily complex, melodious or cacophonous. English speakers point out that Chinese is extremely difficult because it relies on variations in tone barely discernible to the human ear. By the same token, Chinese speakers tell me English is extremely difficult because it is inconsistent, a language of too many broken rules, of Mickey Mice and Donald Ducks.   —Amy Tan, "The Language of Discretion"

Many paragraphs open with a statement of the topic idea, restrict the statement to an aspect of the subject, and then illustrate the restricted idea:

> Members of the barrio describe the entire area as their home [*topic*]. It is a home, but it is more than this. The barrio is a refuge from the harshness and the coldness of the Anglo world [*restriction*]. It is a forced refuge. The leprous people are isolated from the rest of the community and contained in their section of town. The stoical pariahs of the barrio accept their fate, and from the angry seeds of rejection grow the flowers of closeness between outcasts, not the thorns of bitterness and the mad desire to flee. There is no want to escape, for the

feeling of the barrio is known only to its inhabitants, and the material needs of life can also be found here [*illustration*].
—Robert Ramirez, "The Woolen Sarape"

Occasionally a paragraph opens with a descriptive statement that introduces a series of details, as in the following paragraph describing a journey through western Scotland:

> The train bucked and turned north at Arisaig. The bays were like crater crusts filled with water. And offshore islands: Rhum, Eigg, Muck, and Canna—names like items from a misspelled menu. The Scour of Eigg was a hatchet shape against the sky. And now beneath the train there was a basin of green fields for three miles to the Sound of Sleat—and above the train were mountains of cracked rock and swatches of purple heather. Suddenly a horse was silhouetted in the sun, cropping grass beside the sea.   —Paul Theroux, *The Kingdom by the Sea*

Placed at the beginning of the paragraph, the topic sentence guides the reader's attention. However, the topic sentence may appear anywhere in the paragraph—at the beginning, the middle, or the end. The following paragraph is typical of those that open with a series of details and end with a generalization, which is the central idea of the paragraph:

> The first transcontinental New Year's excess occurred in 1894—95 when Amos Alonzo Stagg took his University of Chicago team to Los Angeles to play Stanford. The trip served as a multifaceted precedent for intercollegiate football. The distance travelled (6,200 miles), the duration (three weeks) and the trip's national publicity all served to demonstrate the possibilities of such intercollegiate games. When the teams from the two young universities met at the turn of the year far from either campus and for no discernible educational purpose, the modern bowl concept was established [*topic sentence*].
> —Robin Lester, "The Bowl as Cathedral"

When a paragraph ends with the central idea, the succeeding paragraph may open with a transitional sentence:

> Before coming to Bellevue, in the course of my medical school training, most of my meager experience had been with patients in private hospitals, well-to-do people who cooperated with us medical students at the request of their private doctor. It didn't take me long to see that there was an enormous

sociological gap between Bellevue patients and private patients. Our Bellevue patients didn't think like private patients [*topic sentence*].

Take their attitude toward hospitalization [*transition*]. Most private patients have absolutely no desire to be hospitalized. They'd rather be in their nice, comfortable, warm homes, drinking martinis, eating steak, surrounded by their families. The most luxurious of hospitals can't offer the comforts of home.

But what if you have no home? [*transition*] What if you sleep in doorways in the warm weather and in a flophouse in the cold? What if you never know where your next meal is coming from and have no family to solace you? What, then, is your attitude toward hospitalization? —William A. Nolen, *The Making of a Surgeon*

Beginning your paragraphs with the topic sentence will help you organize the details and the many ideas coherently. In writing or in revising the paragraph, you may decide to restate the topic idea because new details and ideas may occur to you as you record your experiences and think about their meaning.

Anna Quindlen

MELTING POT

A journalist and essayist, Anna Quindlen wrote about herself, her family, and life in New York in a regular column for the *New York Times*, "Life in the 30's." Quindlen now writes a column on social and political issues for the *Times*. *Living Out Loud* (1988) is a collection of her writings on a broad range of topics, including life in a multicultural world, the subject of the essay reprinted here. Quindlen is also author of a novel, *Object Lessons* (1991).

My children are upstairs in the house next door, having dinner with the Ecuadorian family that lives on the top floor. The father speaks some English, the mother less than that. The two daughters are fluent in both their native and their adopted languages, but the youngest child, a son, a close friend of my two boys, speaks almost no

Spanish. His parents thought it would be better that way. This doesn't surprise me; it was the way my mother was raised, American among Italians. I always suspected, hearing my grandfather talk about the "No Irish Need Apply" signs outside factories, hearing my mother talk about the neighborhood kids, who called her greaseball, that the American fable of the melting pot was a myth. Here in our neighborhood it exists, but like so many other things, it exists only person-to-person.

The letters in the local weekly tabloid suggest that 2 everybody hates everybody else here, and on a macro level they do. The old-timers are angry because they think the new moneyed professionals are taking over their town. The professionals are tired of being blamed for the neighborhood's rising rents, particularly since they are the ones paying them. The old immigrants are suspicious of the new ones. The new ones think the old ones are bigots. Nevertheless, on a micro level most of us get along. We are friendly with the Ecuadorian family, with the Yugoslavs across the street, and with the Italians next door, mainly by virtue of our children's sidewalk friendships. It took awhile. Eight years ago we were the new people on the block, filling dumpsters with old plaster and lath, drinking beer on the stoop with our demolition masks hanging around our necks like goiters. We thought we could feel people staring at us from behind the sheer curtains on their windows. We were right.

My first apartment in New York was in a gritty ware- 3 house district, the kind of place that makes your parents wince. A lot of old Italians lived around me, which suited me just fine because I was the granddaughter of old Italians. Their own children and grandchildren had moved to Long Island and New Jersey. All they had was me. All I had was them.

I remember sitting on a corner with a group of half 4 a dozen elderly men, men who had known one another since they were boys sitting together on this same corner, watching a glazier install a great spread of tiny glass panes to make one wall of a restaurant in the ground floor of an old building across the street. The men laid bets on how long the panes, and the restaurant, would last. Two years later two of the men were dead, one had moved in with his married daughter in the suburbs, and the three remaining sat and watched dolefully as people waited each night for a table in the restaurant. "Twenty-two dollars for a piece of veal!" one of them would say, apropos of nothing. But when I ate in the restaurant they never blamed me. "You're not one of them," one of the men explained. "You're one of me." It's an argument familiar to members of almost any embattled race or class: I like you, therefore you aren't like the rest of your kind, whom I hate.

Change comes hard in America, but it comes constantly. The butcher whose old shop is now an antiques store sits day after day outside the pizzeria here like a lost child. The old people across the street cluster together and discuss what kind of money they might be offered if the person who bought their building wants to turn it into condominiums. The greengrocer stocks yellow peppers and fresh rosemary for the gourmands, plum tomatoes and broad-leaf parsley for the older Italians, mangoes for the Indians. He doesn't carry plantains, he says, because you can buy them in the bodega.

Sometimes the baby slips out with the bath water. I wanted to throw confetti the day that a family of rough types who propped their speakers on their station wagon and played heavy metal music at 3:00 a.m. moved out. I stood and smiled as the seedy bar at the corner was transformed into a slick Mexican restaurant. But I liked some of the people who moved out at the same time the rough types did. And I'm not sure I have that much in common with the singles who have made the restaurant their second home.

Yet somehow now we seem to have reached a nice mix. About a third of the people in the neighborhood think of squid as calamari, about a third think of it as sushi, and about a third think of it as bait. Lots of the single people who have moved in during the last year or two are easygoing and good-tempered about all the kids. The old

Italians have become philosophical about the new Hispanics, although they still think more of them should know English. The firebrand community organizer with the storefront on the block, the one who is always talking about people like us as though we stole our houses out of the open purse of a ninety-year-old blind widow, is pleasant to my boys.

Drawn in broad strokes, we live in a pressure cooker: 8
oil and water, us and them. But if you come around at exactly the right time, you'll find members of all these groups gathered around complaining about the condition of the streets, on which everyone can agree. We melt together, then draw apart. I am the granddaughter of immigrants, a young professional—either an interloper or a longtime resident, depending on your concept of time. I am one of them, and one of us.

Comment

Anna Quindlen introduces her thesis at the end of her opening paragraph and reminds us of it in succeeding paragraphs, often in her topic sentences. Mixing ideas with personal recollection, she uses these sentences also to unify the essay. Notice that Quindlen provides just enough detail to support her ideas; too much detail would have blurred the focus. Writing an essay is much like taking a photograph: author and photographer must find the proper distance from the subject if the subject is not to disappear into a mass of details. The photographer frames the picture by eliminating as much of the background as necessary to focus attention on the subject; the author does the same in reporting just those details that illuminate the subject or explain the idea and eliminating needless details in the course of revision.

Questions for Study and Discussion

1. Quindlen uses the concluding topic sentence of paragraph 1 to state her thesis. How does she introduce the topic and build up to her thesis statement?

2. Each of the opening sentences in paragraphs 2–5 states the subject or topic of the paragraph. Which of these sentences also states an idea? How is that idea related to the thesis, stated in paragraph 1?

3. How do the details of paragraph 6 explain the opening statement, "Sometimes the baby slips out with the bath water"? How does paragraph 6 develop the idea introduced in paragraph 5? How do paragraphs 5 and 6 develop the thesis of the essay?

4. What are the topic sentences of paragraphs 7 and 8, and what is their function?

5. Does Quindlen conclude the essay with a restatement of her thesis or with final explanatory details or reflections?

Vocabulary Study

1. How do the details of paragraph 2 help you to understand the phrases "macro level" and "micro level"?

2. What is a goiter, and how is the word used in paragraph 2?

3. How does the context, or surrounding statement and details, help to explain the following words:
   a. *glazier, dolefully* (paragraph 4)
   b. *gourmands, bodega* (paragraph 5)
   c. *interloper* (paragraph 8)

4. In what sense do the people of the neighborhood think of squid as calamari, sushi, and bait?

Suggestions for Writing

1. Discuss the extent to which your own experiences in your college dormitory or in a neighborhood confirm the thesis that Quindlen develops in her essay.

2. Discuss the extent to which Quindlen agrees with Margaret Mead and Rhoda Metraux (in Part 4) on neighborliness in America.

Pat Mora

CONNECTED TO THE BORDER

A graduate of the University of Texas at El Paso, Pat Mora held several positions in the administration of that institution between 1981 and 1989, including Director of the University Museum. Mora is the author of numerous children's stories and essays on Hispanic culture, as well as several collections of poetry. Awards for creative writing include the Harvey L. Johnson Award from the Southwest Council of Latin American Studies.

Last September, I moved away from the United States–Mexico border for the first time. Friends were sure I'd miss the visible evidence of Mexico's proximity found in cities like my native El Paso, Texas. Friends smiled that I'd soon be back for good Mexican food, for the delicate taste and smell of fresh cilantro, for fresh, soft tortillas. There was joking about the care packages that would be flying to the Midwest.

Although most of my adult home and work life had been spent speaking English, I was prepared to miss the sound of Spanish weaving in and out of my days like the warm aroma of a familiar bakery. I knew I'd miss the pleasure of moving back and forth between two languages —a pleasure that broadens one's human flexibility.

When I hear a phrase in Spanish in a Cincinnati restaurant, my head turns quickly. I listen, silently wishing to be part of that other conversation—if only for a few moments, to feel Spanish in my mouth. I think Hispanics who become U.S. citizens need to speak English in order to participate in public life, but I think it's equally important to value native languages, to value the rich range of options for communicating. In my apartment, I'm reading more books in Spanish, sometimes reading the sentences aloud to myself, enjoying sounds I don't otherwise hear.

I smile when my children, who never had time for learning Spanish when they were younger, now as young adults inform me that when they visit they hope we'll be speaking Spanish. They have discovered as I did once that languages are channels, sometimes to other people, sometimes to other views of the world, sometimes to other aspects of ourselves. So we'll struggle with irregular verbs, laughing together which is such a part of Mexican homes.

Is it my family that I miss in this land of leaves so   5
unlike my bare desert? Of course, but although they are miles away, my family is with me daily. The huge telephone bills and the steady stream of letters and cards are a long-distance version of the web of caring we would create around kitchen tables. Our family web just happens to stretch across these United States, a sturdy, flexible web steadily maintained by each in his or her own way.

I miss the meals seasoned with that phrase, "remem-   6
ber the time when. . . ." But I've learned through the years to cherish our gatherings when I'm in the thick of them, to sink into the faces and voices, to store the memories like the industrious squirrel outside my window.

I've enjoyed this furry, scurrying companion as I've   7
enjoyed the silence of bare tree limbs against an evening sky, updrafts of snow outside our third floor window, the ivory light of cherry blossoms. I feel fortunate to be experiencing the part of this country which calls itself the heartland. If I'm hearing the "heart," its steady, predictable rhythms, what am I missing from its Southern border, its margin?

Is it other rhythms? I remember my mixed feelings as   8
a young girl whenever my father selected a Mexican station on the radio, feelings my children now experience about me. I wanted so to *be* an American—which to me, and perhaps to many on the border, meant (and means) shunning anything from Mexico.

As I grew, though, I learned to like dancing to those   9
rhythms. I learned to value not only the rhythms but all that they symbolized. As an adult, I associated such music with celebrations and friends, with warmth and the showing of emotions. I revel in a certain Mexican passion not

for life or about life, but *in* life, a certain intensity in the daily living of it, a certain abandon in such music, in the hugs, sometimes in the anger. I miss the *chispas*, sparks which spring from the willingness, the habit, of allowing the inner self to burst through polite restraints. Sparks can be dangerous but, like risks, are necessary.

I brought cassettes of Mexican music with us when we   10
drove to Ohio. I rolled my car window down and turned the volume up, taking a certain delight in sending such sounds across fields and into trees—broadcasting my culture, if you will.

On my first return visit to Texas I stopped to hear a   11
group of mariachis playing their instruments with proud gusto. I was surprised and probably embarrassed when my eyes filled with tears not only at the music, but at the sight of wonderful though often undervalued Mexican faces. The musicians were playing for some senior citizens. The sight of brown, knowing eyes which quickly accepted me with a smile, and the stories in those eyes were more delicious than any *fajitas* or *flan*.

When I lived on the border, I had the privilege of daily   12
seeing the native land of my grandparents. What I miss about that land is its stern honesty. The fierce light of that grand, wide Southwest sky not only filled me with energy, it provided unsoftened viewing, a glare of truth.

The desert is harsh, hard as life, no carpet of leaves to   13
cushion a walk, no forest conceals the shacks on the other side of the Rio Grande. Although a Midwest winter is hard, it ends, melts into rich soil yielding the yellow trumpeting of daffodils. But the desert in any season can be as relentless as poverty and hunger. Oddly, I miss that clear view of the difference between my comfortable life as a U.S. citizen and the lives of my fellow human beings who also speak Spanish, value family, music, celebration. In a broader sense, I miss the visible reminder of the difference between my economically privileged life and the life of most of my fellow humans.

Comment

Pat Mora describes two worlds that she lives in daily. Topic sentences in the essay focus our attention on this central subject or topic. Some of these sentences state the central topic of paragraph, sometimes in the form of a question; some state the central idea. At the end of the essay, Mora broadens her focus by introducing another topic or idea—one that she cannot explore within the limits of her short essay but one she can at least suggest to the reader.

Questions for Study and Discussion

1. What are the two worlds that Mora describes in her essay? How many aspects of these worlds does she refer to or describe?
2. What points does Mora make about these worlds?
3. Which topic sentences state these points or ideas? Which of them merely state the topic of the paragraph?
4. What contrast does Mora develop in paragraph 13? How does this contrast pick up contrasting themes and details of earlier paragraphs?
5. What new subject or theme does Mora introduce at the end of the essay? How is this subject or theme related to the point or thesis of the whole essay?

Vocabulary Study

Use an unabridged or Spanish dictionary to explain the following terms:

1. *cilantro, tortilla* (paragraph 1)
2. *mariachi, fajita, flan* (paragraph 11)

Suggestions for Writing

1. Describe two worlds in which you live, and develop a point of your own about them, perhaps one related to different values or personal attitudes toward people or life.
2. Mora states that "languages are channels, sometimes to other people, sometimes to other views of the world, sometimes to other aspects of ourselves." Illustrate this statement, drawing on your own experience with a language other than English, perhaps one that you or your parents or friends speak, or a language you have studied.

✧ Order of Ideas

Ideas in the paragraph as well as in the whole essay can be presented or ordered in various ways. We saw in the previous section that paragraphs commonly open with a general idea which is then developed through specific details. But, as in Robin Lester's paragraph on bowl games (p. 19), some paragraphs move from the *specific* to the *general*—building up to the central or topic idea.

Certain kinds of writing have their own order. Descriptions are *spatial*—perhaps moving from foreground to background or from earth to sky:

> Once we even saw a giraffe, but miles, miles away from us, alone under the clear sky among the thorn trees on the horizon, and we could see its silhouetted head and long neck turned to watch us; it seemed very lonely, very small, and very far away on the yellow flats; when the noise of our trucks reached it, it was frightened and began to run, heaving itself up and down. It ran away from us for a long time and got even smaller but never out of sight. At last it reached the horizon.   —Elizabeth Marshall Thomas, *The Harmless People*

Narrative, in contrast, presents events chronologically—in the order of *time*. The paragraph just quoted combines spatial description with chronological narrative: the writer presents the sighting of the giraffe, the movement of the trucks, and the flight of the animal in their temporal order. In reporting an experience or explaining a process, the facts or steps are also presented as they occur. To a person learning to drive, you would not explain how to turn corners until you explained how to brake and steer.

In expository and persuasive writing ideas may be presented in numerous ways. The author considers the reader's knowledge of the subject, the purpose of the paragraph or essay, and the subject itself in organizing the paragraph. For example, in describing the care of an automobile you would probably describe simple procedures before complex ones, especially if your readers are owners of new models. In training mechanics to repair a new kind of engine, you might proceed from the most common to the most unusual problems mechanics are likely to encounter.

In the following definition of the potlatch, a ceremony in which Indians of the Northwest dispose of property, the author clearly has his readers in mind in presenting details of the ceremony in the order of *importance:*

> A proper potlatch involved prodigious displays of eating, since it was a point of honor with the host to provide much more food than his guests could consume. The eating would last for days, interspersed with singing, belching, speechmaking, dramatic performances and the ceremonial conferring of honorific names. But the vital part of the occasion was the bestowing of gifts—bowls, boxes, baskets, blankets, canoes, ornaments, sculptures—that the chief had collected among his people, from each according to his ability, and now distributed among his guests, to each according to his rank. —Frederic V. Grunfeld, "Indian Giving"

The greater the drama of the event, the greater our sense of *climax*—of increasing importance or intensity as the paragraph or essay moves to the end.

As Pat Mora's essay shows, some paragraphs (and essays) move from *question* to *answer:*

> How wide is the scope of physical law? Do life, thought, history fall within its orderly domain? Or does it describe only the inanimate, the remote and the very tiny? It is the claim of contemporary physics that its laws apply to all natural things, to atoms, stars and men. There are not two worlds: the cold, precise mechanical world of physics, and the surprising, disorderly and growing world of living things or of human existence. They are one. —Philip Morrison, "Cause, Chance and Creation"

A related order is the movement from *problem* to *solution.* The following paragraph states a problem in biology and then presents a tentative solution:

How either whales or seals endure the tremendous pressure changes involved in dives of several hundred fathoms is not definitely known [*problem*]. They are warm-blooded mammals like ourselves. Caisson disease, which is caused by the rapid accumulation of nitrogen bubbles in the blood with sudden release of pressure, kills human divers if they are brought up rapidly from depths of 200 feet or so. Yet, according to the testimony of whalers, a baleen whale, when harpooned, can dive straight down to the depth of half a mile, as measured by the amount of line carried out. From these depths, where it has sustained a pressure of half a ton on every inch of body, it returns almost immediately to the surface. The most plausible explanation is that, unlike the diver, who has air pumped to him while he is under water, the whale has in its body only the limited supply it carries down, and does not have enough nitrogen in its blood to do serious harm [*solution*]. The plain truth is, however, that we really do not know since it is obviously impossible to confine a living whale and experiment on it, and almost as difficult to dissect a dead one satisfactorily [*qualification*].   —Rachel Carson, *The Sea around Us*

As Elizabeth Marshall Thomas's paragraph on giraffes shows, paragraphs can combine various orderings of ideas and details—in this case, the spatial arrangement of details with the chronological presentation of events. A paragraph may, in addition, show that the events increase in importance or intensity. In writing your own paragraphs and essays, you may discover better ways of presenting your details and ideas as you see the paragraph or essay take shape.

Harold Krents

DARKNESS AT NOON

Harold Krents graduated from Harvard College and later studied law at Oxford University and Harvard Law School. He practiced law from 1971 until his death in 1986. Krents was the prototype for the blind boy in Leonard Gershe's play (and the later film) *Butterflies Are Free*. His experiences at Harvard are the basis of the film *Riding on the Wind*. Krents was long active in organizations and government agencies concerned with the employment of handicapped people.

Blind from birth, I have never had the opportunity to   1
see myself and have been completely dependent on the
image I create in the eye of the observer. To date it has
not been narcissistic.

There are those who assume that since I can't see, I   2
obviously also cannot hear. Very often people will converse with me at the top of their lungs, enunciating each
word very carefully. Conversely, people will also often
whisper, assuming that since my eyes don't work, my ears
don't either.

For example, when I go to the airport and ask the   3
ticket agent for assistance to the plane, he or she will invariably pick up the phone, call a ground hostess and
whisper: "Hi, Jane, we've got a 76 here." I have concluded that the word "blind" is not used for one of two
reasons: Either they fear that if the dread word is spoken,
the ticket agent's retina will immediately detach, or they
are reluctant to inform me of my condition of which I may
not have been previously aware.

On the other hand, others know that of course I can   4
hear, but believe that I can't talk. Often, therefore, when
my wife and I go out to dinner, a waiter or waitress will
ask Kit if *"he* would like a drink" to which I respond that
"indeed *he* would."

This point was graphically driven home to me while   5
we were in England. I had been given a year's leave of
absence from my Washington law firm to study for a
diploma in law degree at Oxford University. During the
year I became ill and was hospitalized. Immediately after
admission, I was wheeled down to the X-ray room. Just
at the door sat an elderly woman—elderly I would judge
from the sound of her voice. "What is his name?" the
woman asked the orderly who had been wheeling me.

"What's your name?" the orderly repeated to me.   6

"Harold Krents," I replied.   7

"Harold Krents," he repeated.   8

"When was he born?"   9

"When were you born?"   10

"November 5, 1944," I responded.   11

"November 5, 1944," the orderly intoned.   12

This procedure continued for approximately five min-   13
utes at which point even my saint-like disposition deserted
me. "Look," I finally blurted out, "this is absolutely ridiculous. Okay, granted I can't see, but it's got to have become
pretty clear to both of you that I don't need an interpreter."

"He says he doesn't need an interpreter," the orderly   14
reported to the woman.

The toughest misconception of all is the view that be-   15
cause I can't see, I can't work. I was turned down by over
forty law firms because of my blindness, even though my
qualifications included a cum laude degree from Harvard
College and a good ranking in my Harvard Law School
class.

The attempt to find employment, the continuous frus-   16
tration of being told that it was impossible for a blind person to practice law, the rejection letters, not based on my
lack of ability but rather on my disability, will always remain one of the most disillusioning experiences of my life.

Fortunately, this view of limitation and exclusion is   17
beginning to change. On April 16, [1978] the Department
of Labor issued regulations that mandate equal-employ-
ment opportunities for the handicapped. By and large, the
business community's response to offering employment
to the disabled has been enthusiastic.

I therefore look forward to the day, with the expecta-   18
tion that it is certain to come, when employers will view
their handicapped workers as a little child did me years
ago when my family still lived in Scarsdale.

I was playing basketball with my father in our back-   19
yard according to procedures we had developed. My father
would stand beneath the hoop, shout, and I would shoot
over his head at the basket attached to our garage. Our
next-door neighbor, aged five, wandered over into our
yard with a playmate. "He's blind," our neighbor whispered to her friend in a voice that could be heard distinctly
by Dad and me. Dad shot and missed; I did the same.

Dad hit the rim: I missed entirely: Dad shot and missed the garage entirely. "Which one is blind?" whispered back the little friend.

I would hope that in the near future when a plant 20 manager is touring the factory with the foreman and comes upon a handicapped and nonhandicapped person working together, his comment after watching them work will be, "Which one is disabled?"

Comment

Krents states a problem and proceeds to a solution: this is the general organization of the essay. But Krents wishes to do more than state a solution; he wishes his readers to fully understand the difficulties of being blind and, through understanding and sympathy, provide the solution by changing the way they talk to and behave with blind people. Krents organizes the three misconceptions about blindness with this purpose in mind. He might have presented these misconceptions in a different order; the order he chooses helps us appreciate the bizarre situation he describes. A notable quality of the essay is the proportion of examples to discussion—just enough are provided to illustrate each of the ideas. Krents selects his details carefully. Leonard Kriegel describes a different handicap and its effect on his life on p. 125.

Questions for Study and Discussion

1. In what paragraph does Krents state the basis for his ordering of the three misconceptions? How does this order help you to appreciate the bizarre situation created by blindness? How does the change in tone in paragraph 15 accord with the order of ideas?
2. What is his thesis? Does he state it directly, or is it implied?
3. What are the implied causes of the problems described? What is the solution? Does Krents state or imply this solution?
4. What attitudes and feelings does Krents express in the final anecdote?

5. Do you find the organization of ideas successful, or would you have organized them in a different way?

Vocabulary Study

Use your dictionary to distinguish the differences in meaning in the following series of words. Write a sentence using each of the words according to its dictionary meaning. The first word in each series is Krents's:

1. *narcissistic* (paragraph 1), vain, conceited, proud
2. *enunciating* (paragraph 2), pronouncing
3. *graphically* (paragraph 5), sharply, starkly, vividly
4. *disillusioning* (paragraph 16), disappointing, frustrating

Suggestions for Writing

1. Discuss the effect that a permanent or temporary handicap or disability has had on your life, or discuss problems you have observed in the life of a disabled, or handicapped, friend or relative. You may want to organize your essay as Krents does—working from a problem to a solution. Note that the solution need not be complete or permanent; you may want to discuss the extent to which the problems described can be solved.
2. Krents writes about his blindness with humor. Discuss how he achieves that humor and what it tells you about his view of himself and people in general.
3. Describe an embarrassing experience of your own—how it came about, the persons involved in it, its outcome. Then discuss its causes, focusing on the most important of them.

Coherence

In a unified essay all of the details and ideas connect to a central idea or thesis. To emphasize the unity, these details and ideas must obviously fit together into a whole: the reader must see how they cohere, or hold together. The ideas and details must seem to follow naturally.

Using pronoun reference and repeating key words and phrases are important ways to obtain coherence—ways that we depend upon with little if any thought. In the following paragraph, examples of key words have been italicized:

> In the 40's my parents and I moved from Hillside Homes to a neighborhood in the Bronx that is now dominated by what was then known as the Einstein–Jacoby medical center. *It* was bordered by hundreds of acres of undeveloped land. What I remember most distinctly about *that land*, beyond a huge, flat-topped rock studded with a lifetime supply of mica chips, are the many hills that were covered by tiger lilies in the spring, poison sumac in the summer and perfect snow for sledding after any reasonable winter storm. Early on there were a few squatters farming land near *those hills*; later *they* disappeared. And early on I was content to stay in our beautiful new neighborhood, while later there wasn't enough *there* to hold me. —Judith Rossner, "The Dyre Avenue Shuttle" [emphasis added]

Another important means of achieving coherence is through the use of parallel structure, the arrangement of similar words, phrases, and clauses to highlight similar ideas (again, examples have been italicized):

> Though perhaps Brooklyn is not quite a refuge anymore where sheep may safely graze, *there are places* there where you can listen in the dark of winter to the wind attacking from the

Atlantic as moon-whitened waves break against the beach. *There are neighborhoods* of nations so alien and incredible that crossing into them mobilizes beyond any expectation both distance and time. *There are streets* where, on January nights, fires burn on every floor of every house, sending fragrant smoke through the cold black trees. *There are meadows and fields, long rows of old oaks, bridges that sparkle from afar, ships about to leave for Asia, lakes, horses and islands in the marsh.*
—Mark Helprin, "Brooklyn's Comforting Infinitude" [emphasis added]

Where the natural course is clear through pronoun reference, repetition of key words and phrases, questions and parallel structure, no helping words or formal connectives are necessary. Sometimes, however, you will need transitional words and phrases when the connection of ideas or details is not immediately clear. If the steps of a process are presented chronologically and each step requires explanation, you may introduce the words *first, second,* and *third* to keep the steps distinct. You may also add the phrases *less important, just as important, more important* to show that you are presenting ideas in the order of importance. Connectives such as *thus, therefore, however, moreover,* and *nevertheless* show the logical relation of ideas. *Thus* and *therefore* show that one idea is the consequence of another or that certain conclusions can be drawn from the evidence presented. *However* and *nevertheless* show that one idea qualifies or contradicts another. *Moreover* shows addition.

L. E. Sissman

THE OLD FARMER'S ALMANAC, 1872

The poet and essayist L. E. Sissman was born in Detroit, Michigan, in 1928. After graduating from Harvard University he worked in advertising. His poems are collected in *Hello, Darkness* (1978); his personal essays for *The Atlantic Monthly* are collected in *Inner Bystander* (1975). Sissman died in 1976. In the essay reprinted here, Sissman compares our world today with the world described in an issue of a nineteenth-century farmer's almanac.

The homely publications of a hundred years ago have   1
a message for us. The *Official Railway Guide* of June, 1868,
for example, tells me the disheartening news that my
regular twenty-seven-mile commute took ten minutes less
one hundred and four years ago than it does today. And
the 1872 *Old Farmer's Almanac*, which I picked up in a New
Hampshire secondhand store some years ago, bears even
odder tidings.

If you consult the *Almanac* today, you know that be-   2
hind its familiar yellow cover is a thick pack of oddments
—snippets of astrology, weather prognostications, old
rhymes and jokes, a spate of small-space ads for trusses,
roach-killer, and fish lures, and on pages that deal with
the months of the year ahead, a series of nostalgic, neatly
written "Farmer's Calendars."

Things were different in 1871. The *Almanac* was thin—   3
a mere fifty-two pages—and the only ads inside its peach
covers (the original yellow was dropped for a time in the
middle of the nineteenth century) touted Hallet & Davis
pianos (endorsed by "F. Liszt, the First Pianist in the
World"), Webb & Twombly's Premium Chocolates (which
"have taken the highest award at every Fair in which they
have been exhibited"), Wheeler & Wilson's Sewing
Machines, Worcester's Quarto Dictionary (with a testi-
monial from Edward Everett), and the wares of Hency C.
Sawyer, whose Waltham Book Store also sold stationery,
wallpaper, silverplate, luggage, desks, Bibles, brushes,
combs, perfumery, soap, pocket knives and scissors, fans
for ladies, umbrellas, picture frames, and, of course, the
Almanac.

But it is the editorial matter of the old *Almanac* that   4
startles the modern reader. Beginning soberly with a table
of Meetings of Friends in New England and a list of
salaries of executive officers of the United States ("Ulysses
S. Grant, Ill., Pres., $25,000; Hamilton Fish, N.Y., Sec.
State, $8,000"), it goes on through a page of astronomical
data and rosters of New England colleges and registers
in bankruptcy to an early crescendo: the spreads for the

months of the year. Each is laid out much as it is today: a table of astronomical calculations on the left, a rather sketchy forecast and the "Farmer's Calendar" on the right. But these "Farmer's Calendars" are nothing like the rather bland, pleasant little essays of today. Each of them preaches and rails at the farmer to keep a better farm and live a better life; the Protestant ethic rears its minatory head in January and harangues the reader through the waxing and the waning year. The nameless scourge of slothful husbandmen begins the cycle, after a terse New Year's greeting, well into his evangelical stride: "Make up your mind therefore to be better and to do better, to aim higher and to have nobler ends in view. . . . Let us sit down by the crackling fire and lay out plans for the year. I suppose you have done the chores, of course, fed the cattle and the pigs, and cleaned up the barn. No use to sit down till the chores are done. . . ." In February, he has progressed a step further in his righteous indignation at his captive parishioners; now he begins by berating them: "Snug up about the barn this winter. Shut the door and the windows. Cold won't make cattle tough. . . . I wouldn't give a fig for a man who can't turn his mind to little things. All your luck in farming hangs on the chores at this season."

In March, he is quick to turn on the hapless, snow-   5
bound farmer who grouses about the weather. "No use to fret about the storm and the snow. Keep your temper is a good rule on the farm. This way of finding fault with heaven and earth won't do. . . . It's a pity you don't raise more roots. Hadn't you better look about for a spot to put in an acre of mangolds and another of swedes?"

The Old Farmer takes the offensive early and keeps the   6
pressure up; the shiftless reader won't get a breather, even in springtime: "All plant life is on the spring now, and animal life too, as to that matter. And so you'd better spring around, John, if you want to see your barn well filled in the fall. Yoke up and go at it with your fine and sprightly team. . . . The fact is, there is no end to the work

this month, and no time to lose in standing around or lean-ing over the wall with a gossiping neighbor." And "It is of no use to find fault with work. We ought to thank our stars that we are able to work."

As the summer ends, the taskmaster's lips are thinner   7
than ever: "Now that the dog star rages, why don't you give the dog a bullet [presumably a pill of dog-days medicine], the boy a hoe, the girl the knitting needles. No work, no eating, is the rule, you know. Can't afford to keep drones on the farm." In September, to keep the ener-vated farmer on the qui vive, the *Almanac* lays out an im-pressive list of chores, including removing stones from fields to be tilled. 'I hope you got out those rocks. . . . It is a shiftless way to lay down a lot with the bushes growing along the walls. Why don't you dig them out, and clean up the lot?" In October, he notes, with relish, that "there is enough to do to keep us on the jog all this month"; in November, after a peremptory reference to Thanksgiving, he's off again about stalling the cattle every night, fall sowing and plowing, and trimming the grape-vines. Even in December—notably, there's no mention of Christmas—he's harping about the grapevines again, as well as pruning the fruit trees, making an inventory of stock and tools on the farm ("the sooner you set about it, the better you will be off"), and generally preparing for the worst: "Spruce up and get ready for a hard winter."

The rest of the *Almanac* is similarly grim; it dispels a   8
number of common notions among farmers about cabbage, kitchen gardens, grass for horses, and food for stock, calls attention to the adulteration of commercial fertilizers, cau-tions the reader about transplanting evergreens ("it is a mistake to suppose that the same rules apply to evergreens as to deciduous trees"), and sagely discusses the pitfalls of stockbreeding farms. Then a little light relief: three pages of poetry, anecdotes, and puzzles, most of them not so light, at that. One poem, a tearjerker, was "found under the pillow of a soldier who died in a hospital near Port Royal, South Carolina." "Selections" includes Scott's

"O, what a tangled web we weave/When first we practise to deceive"; the jokes include this epitaph: "I was well—wished to be better—read medical books—took medicine—and died."

The 1872 *Almanac* ends there, with the exception of a few population tables (according to the census of 1870, there were 38,555,983 people in the United States, of whom 942,292 lived in New York City and 4,382,759 in New York State; California could boast a mere 560,247), weather tables, tide tables, and post office regulations (first-class letters, 3 cents per half ounce). It ends with a sort of a whimper and a curious feeling of oppression in the reader, as if he had just been through that exhausting year with the poor, bone-weary farmer. It ends, finally, with a question forming in the modern reader's mind: Were the good old days that bad? In an age when we are daily and sorely tried by all sorts of mind-boggling disasters and injustices, when we daily repair to the past for reassurance and refreshment, is it possible that we are really better off than our forebears, and that our carefully cultivated nostalgia is founded on a mirage? On the evidence of the 1872 *Almanac*, that could well be. The stern preachments of the anonymous author of the "Farmer's Calendar" are not mere mouthings; it seems clear that the struggling farmer of a century ago really needed these appeals to his pride and his sense of duty in order to get on with the backbreaking, dawn-to-dusk job of cultivating his garden. It was a savage life of imponderables—blizzards, floods, crop failures, insect plagues, human and animal diseases for which there were no known cures—and only the most bitterly Calvinistic outlook could prepare one to compete in what had, eventually, to be a losing race. There was no social security in those days, no government price supports, no anesthesia, and above all no leisure. The farmer had literally nothing to look forward to except the fruits of a job well done and another day, week, month, and year of unremitting toil to keep ahead of a hostile nature.

To us, seated in our warm houses on our choreless days off from work, knitted to all our friends by the telephone, possessed of cars to take us across the county or across the country as the whim strikes us, disposing of a hundred diversions to beguile our leisure, protected by effective medical care (for those, at least, who can afford it), assured of a cash competence in our retirement, this stark world of a hundred years ago is hard indeed to believe in—which is one of the reasons why we believe in a gilded age when all the world was young, when cares were few, when love was true, when, over the river and through the woods, grandmother's house was filled with goodwill, provender, and jollity. What a shame the truth was otherwise.

Comment

Sissman depends on a number of devices to hold together the various details and ideas. The opening sentences of some of the paragraphs make transitions to a new consideration or new stage of the analysis of the almanac. For example, the opening sentence of paragraph 4 marks the turn from advertisements to the editorial matter; the opening sentence of paragraph 6 shifts the discussion to the attitude of the Old Farmer toward his readers. The long paragraphs require careful transitions to mark turns of idea—for example, in the following transitional sentence in paragraph 4: "But these 'Farmer's Calendars' are nothing like the rather bland, pleasant little essays of today." Sissman is describing a publication and a world unfamiliar to his readers, and he keeps his many details in focus through his much longer paragraphs, each devoted to one idea or feature of the almanac.

Questions for Study and Discussion

1. How do the topic sentences of paragraphs 1–8 keep our attention focused on the central topic of the essay?
2. How late in the essay does Sissman state his thesis? What is gained by not stating it in the opening paragraph?

3. How are paragraphs 1–8 organized? Does Sissman describe the almanac cover to cover, or does he present the contents in a different order?

4. The "Protestant ethic" (paragraph 4) is the ideal of hard, unremitting work which exercises the virtues of the upright person. How is this ideal related to the "Calvinistic outlook," referred to in paragraph 9? How does the discussion of the farmer's life throughout the essay explain these phrases?

5. Do you agree with Sissman's explanation of our romantic view of the American past? What additional or different reason would you cite?

Vocabulary Study

Give the dictionary meanings of the following words. Then write an explanation of how the word is used in the particular sentence:

1. *homely, tidings* (paragraph 1)
2. *snippets, prognostications, spate, nostalgic* (paragraph 2)
3. *touted* (paragraph 3)
4. *bland, minatory, harangues, scourge, evangelical* (paragraph 4)
5. *peremptory* (paragraph 7)
6. *anesthesia, unremitting* (paragraph 9)
7. *beguile, competence, provender* (paragraph 10)

Suggestions for Writing

1. Examine an issue of a magazine published in the 1940s or the 1950s, and describe some of its contents. Organize your description to develop a thesis—perhaps a conclusion about the world of your parents or grandparents based on the evidence of the magazine.

2. Discuss how true a recent movie or newspaper or magazine article describing teenagers is to your own experiences and observations. Restrict your discussion to one or two characters or episodes; don't try to discuss the whole movie or article. Use your discussion to state a general conclusion —a thesis suggested by the similarities or differences you have discussed.

Narration

You are familiar with narration through works of fiction that present a series of events chronologically or weave past and present events into complex narratives or plots that explore the connection of events. Narratives are also basic in expository, persuasive, and expressive essays. An essay tracing historical events may do so through narrative. The following paragraph describing the first landfall of Christopher Columbus in the Bahamas shows how narration serves historical exposition:

> As the sun set under a clear horizon October 11, the northeast trade breezed up to gale force, and the three ships tore along at 9 knots. But Columbus refused to shorten sail, since his promised time was running out. He signaled everyone to keep a particularly sharp watch, and offered extra rewards for first landfall in addition to the year's pay promised by the Sovereigns. That night of destiny was clear and beautiful with a late rising moon, but the sea was the roughest of the entire passage. The men were tense and expectant, the officers testy and anxious, the Captain General serene in the confidence that presently God would reveal to him the promised Indies.
> —Samuel Eliot Morison, "First Crossing of the Atlantic"

Narration is also important in persuasive writing. In the legal brief it is essential in providing the background of the case—the events at issue. A simple argument may contain a supporting narrative of an event. A plea for a change in public policy may trace the consequences of present policy through a narrative illustrating them. We will consider examples in a later section.

Narration is important, too, in expressive writing. Gloria Emerson's account of her parachute jump in Part Two is a simple narrative. Here, Sue Hubbell begins her essay on woodcutting with a narrative of her experiences:

This morning I finished sawing up a tree from the place where I had been cutting for the past week. In the process I lost my screwrench, part screwdriver, part wrench, that I use to make adjustments on my chain saw. I shouldn't carry it in my pocket, but the chain had been loose; I had tightened it and had not walked back to the truck to put the wrench away. Scolding myself for being so careless, I began looking for another tree to cut and found a big one that had recently died.

In narration the amount of detail you present depends on the knowledge of your readers. Since you usually cannot know how much knowledge each reader possesses about a subject, you will do best to include essential facts and to introduce those nonessential facts that give the reader details about the world and the characters in your essay. It is important, however, not to give excessive detail that diverts the reader from the central event. In his paragraph on Columbus, Morison gives a necessary though brief description of the sailors and officers of the ship. To have described each of their reactions in detail would lessen the suspense and divert attention from Columbus himself, who is the actual focus of the narrative.

Edward Rivera

THE SOCIOLOGY FINAL

Born in Orocovia, Puerto Rico, Edward Rivera grew up in New York City, attending school in Spanish Harlem, and at nineteen entered evening school at City College. He returned to college after army service, graduating from City College in 1967 and later from Columbia University. Rivera describes the very different worlds of Puerto Rico and New York in his semi-autobiographical book *Family Installments: Memories of Growing Up Hispanic*. The experience described in this excerpt—taking a final exam in a college course—will be familiar to many students.

I took a cab up to school, but I was still late. On the way there, I reviewed the "material" in my head: almost total confusion, a jumble of jargon, ordinary things passed off as profundities with the aid of "abstractionitis." ("The home then is the specific zone of functional potency that grows about a live parenthood . . . an active interfacial membrane or surface furthering exchange . . . a mutualizing membrane between the family and the society in which it lives. . . .'')

The classroom was packed for the first time since the   2
opening day of classes, and filled with smoke. Over forty students were bent over their examination booklets, most of them looking confused by the questions. The professor, puffing an immense pipe, was at his desk (manufactured by Vulcan), reading Riesman on *The Lonely Crowd*, casually, as if it were a murder mystery whose ending he had figured out back on page one. He didn't look pleased when I stepped up to his desk: another pair of lungs in a roomful of carbon dioxide and cigarette smoke.

"Yes?"   3

I asked him for a question sheet and an examination   4
booklet. They were on the desk, weighted down with the eighth edition of his anthology.

"Are you registered in this course?" he asked.   5

Yes, I was. He wanted to know my name. I told him.   6
He looked me up in his roll book. Had I been coming to class regularly? Every time. How come I never spoke up in class? Because I sat in the back. It was hard to be heard from back there. I might try sitting up front, he said. I said I would. He said it was a little late for that. For a moment I'd forgotten what day this was. *Dies irae*, according to my paperback dictionary of foreign phrases. Do-or-die day.

There were no empty chairs, so I walked to the back of   7
the room and squatted in a corner, keeping my coat and scarf on.

"Answer one from Part A, one from Part B, and one   8
from Part C." I had no trouble understanding that much. But my mind blanked out on the choices in Parts A, B, and C. There was something about "group membership as the source of individual morality and social health" (Durkheim? I couldn't remember). I must have slept through that lecture, and I couldn't remember any mention

of it in the eighth edition. Another one asked for something or other on Weber's contention that "minorities in 19th-century Europe—the Poles in Russia, the Huguenots in France, the Nonconformists in England, and the Jews in all countries—had offset their socio-political exclusion by engaging in economic activity whereas the Catholics had not." This one had to be explained in fifteen minutes. I got around it by drawing a blank.

The easiest choice in Part C asked for "a sociological autobiography, demonstrating your command of certain relevant aspects in this course, as well as the terminology of sociology."

"Terminology of sociology." That wasn't even a good rhyme. It was also asking too much for fifteen minutes. It wasn't even enough time for my nerves to calm down. Too bad. I got up and left the room. No one noticed.

I went down to the student cafeteria for a cup of coffee, and while I drank it, I read the opening chapter of Dr. A. Alonso's *El Gibaro*, a Puerto Rican classic which I'd brought with me to reread on the subway back home. "I am one of those," it went, "and this can't matter much to my readers, who are in the habit of not sleeping without first having read something"—another one, I thought, nineteenth-century version—"and this something must be of the sort that requires more than usual seclusion, order and meditation, since I think that at no time other than the night's silence can one withdraw from the real world, to elevate oneself into the imaginary; above all when the day has been spent without affliction, something that a young man achieves from time to time, before he becomes the head of a family, or while he does not have to govern, on his own, the vessel of his future."

In the examination blue book, which I hadn't bothered returning, I translated some of these long, rhythmic sentences as best I could (no dictionary on me, for one thing), just for practice, and then, when I'd finished a second cup of coffee, I shoved the Alonso and the blue book back inside my coat pocket and left for the subway.

Comment

"Let me tell you what the final was like," a friend says to you. The story she tells expresses various feelings—perhaps joy or anger or frustration. It may even develop a thesis—either an explicit or implicit point that your friend wants to make. You discover the implicit thesis largely through the tone of the narrative and the stress given particular details. Tone is an essential consideration, because it conveys the attitude of the narrator (see p. 484). These are matters to consider in Rivera's narrative of his sociology final.

The effectiveness of Rivera's narrative arises from the exactness of his detail. He does not tell us everything about the professor of the exam, but rather he selects the details that best convey the atmosphere of the classroom and that explain why he leaves without completing the exam. The episode is a small one, but it tells us much about the feelings of the outsider—of a Puerto Rican youth facing numerous barriers.

Questions for Study and Discussion

1. What are Rivera's feelings in arriving for the exam, in talking to the professor, in reading the questions, and in leaving the building? To what aspects of the experience does Rivera give the most attention in his narrative?
2. How do the details of the professor and the exam help you to understand Rivera's feelings? What may be the significance of the title of the book the professor is reading? What is the general tone of his description?
3. What does the quotation from Alonso's *El Gibaro* tell you about Rivera's attitude? What is the general tone of paragraph 11?
4. Is Rivera merely expressing his feelings about the sociology exam, or is he in addition making a point? If so, what is that point or thesis?

Vocabulary Study

1. How do Rivera's examples explain the word *abstractionitis?*
2. The *Dies irae* ("Day of Wrath") is a hymn describing Judgment Day, sometimes included in masses for the dead. What is the point of the reference?
3. Read the entry on *Vulcan* in a dictionary of classical mythology. Then explain the reference to Vulcan in paragraph 2.

Suggestions for Writing

1. Describe an exam you took, or a similar experience, and convey your feelings through your details and the tone of your description. Remember that your tone need not be the same throughout the essay.
2. Rivera shows how language, like the jargon or the directions quoted, sometimes creates barriers or difficulties in everyday situations. Discuss a barrier or difficulty that jargon or unclear directions created for you.
3. Narrate an episode in your life in which you felt and acted like an outsider. Let the details of your narrative reveal why you did.

Description

Usually a narrative contains description of people and places—a drawing in words of what they look like. The narrator may pause to draw this picture, sometimes doing so in a few words and sometimes at greater length. Description is always spatial—the scene observed from a particular angle of vision. This angle may remain fixed or may change.

Robert Ramirez (p. 259) describes a barrio as most observers would see it, walking or driving through it at different times. Toward the beginning of his essay, he shows us the barrio as a whole—from a distant point of observation:

> Leaning from the expressway or jolting across the tracks, one enters a different physical world permeated by a different attitude. The physical dimensions are impressive. It is a large section of town which extends for fifteen blocks north and south along the tracks, and then advances eastward, thinning into nothingness beyond the city limits. Within the invisible (yet sensible) walls of the barrio, are many, many people living in too few houses. The homes, however, are much more numerous than on the outside. —"The Woolen Sarape"

This observation point changes in the course of the essay. In the following passage Ramirez shows us a neighborhood of the barrio at evening:

> In the evenings, the porches and front yards are occupied with men calmly talking over the noise of children playing baseball in the unpaved extension of the living room, while the women cook supper or gossip with female neighbors as they water the *jardines*. The gardens mutely echo the expressive verses of the colorful houses. The denseness of multicolored plants and trees gives the house the appearance of an oasis or a tropical island hideway, sheltered from the rest of the world.

The point of observation is closer to the scene than in the first passage. We are closer to the houses of the barrio—close enough to see what the people are doing. Ramirez is showing us the barrio as any observer would see it if sensitive to the special qualities of the barrio world.

Description is an essential part of every kind of writing. An expository essay on auto repair may include a description of some of the tools or the workplace. A persuasive essay may give us a picture of the people the writer wants us to help. The expressive essay centers on the writer primarily; a descriptive passage may therefore be colored by the writer's personal feelings. For example, not every student entering the classroom described by Edward Rivera would see it as Rivera does (see p. 46). The point of view in a descriptive passage may be an objective one, as in the Ramirez paragraphs, though no two observers will notice or stress the same details. Or, as in Rivera, the point of view may be a subjective one, shaped by and expressive of personal feelings.

Maya Angelou

PICKING COTTON

Maya Angelou was born Marguerite Johnson in 1928. When her parents separated, the three-year-old girl traveled with her brother from California to Stamps, Arkansas, to live with her grandmother. The woman Angelou called "Momma" owned the only black general store in town. Angelou and her brother later returned to California to live with their mother. During her long career, Angelou has worked in the theater and television as a dancer, an actress, and a producer. She served as Northern Coordinator of the Southern Christian Leadership Conference, traveled in Africa, and taught school and wrote for newspapers in Egypt and Ghana. On her return to the United States, she wrote for television. Angelou has written several autobiographies and several volumes of poetry, collected in *Maya Angelou: Poetry.* Her description of black cotton pickers in Stamps is a self-contained section from her first autobiography, *I Know Why the Caged Bird Sings* (1969).

Each year I watched the field across from the Store   1
turn caterpillar green, then gradually frosty white. I knew
exactly how long it would be before the big wagons would
pull into the front yard and load on the cotton pickers at
daybreak to carry them to the remains of slavery's
plantations.

During the picking season my grandmother would get   2
out of bed at four o'clock (she never used an alarm clock)
and creak down to her knees and chant in a sleep-filled
voice, "Our Father, thank you for letting me see this New
Day. Thank you that you didn't allow the bed I lay on
last night to be my cooling board, nor my blanket my
winding sheet. Guide my feet this day along the straight
and narrow, and help me to put a bridle on my tongue.
Bless this house, and everybody in it. Thank you, in the
name of your Son, Jesus Christ, Amen."

Before she had quite arisen, she called our names and   3
issued orders, and pushed her large feet into homemade
slippers and across the bare lye-washed wooden floor to
light the coal-oil lamp.

The lamplight in the Store gave a soft make-believe   4
feeling to our world which made me want to whisper and
walk about on tiptoe. The odors of onions and oranges
and kerosene had been mixing all night and wouldn't be
disturbed until the wooded slat was removed from the
door and the early morning air forced its way in with the
bodies of people who had walked miles to reach the
pickup place.

"Sister, I'll have two cans of sardines."   5

"I'm gonna work so fast today I'm gonna make you   6
look like you standing still."

"Lemme have a hunk uh cheese and some sody   7
crackers."

"Just gimme a coupla them fat peanut paddies." That   8
would be from a picker who was taking his lunch. The
greasy brown paper sack was stuck behind the bib of his
overalls. He'd use the candy as a snack before the noon
sun called the workers to rest.

In those tender mornings the Store was full of laugh-   9
ing, joking, boasting and bragging. One man was going
to pick two hundred pounds of cotton, and another three
hundred. Even the children were promising to bring home
fo' bits and six bits. The champion picker of the day before
was the hero of the dawn. If he prophesied that the cotton in today's field was going to be sparse and stick to
the bolls like glue, every listener would grunt a hearty
agreement. The sound of the empty cotton sacks dragging
over the floor and the murmurs of waking people were
sliced by the cash register as we rang up the five-cent sales.

If the morning sounds and smells were touched with   10
the supernatural, the late afternoon had all the features of
the normal Arkansas life. In the dying sunlight the people
dragged, rather than carried their empty cotton sacks.
Brought back to the Store, the pickers would step out of
the backs of trucks and fold down, dirt-disappointed, to the
ground. No matter how much they had picked, it wasn't
enough. Their wages wouldn't even get them out of debt
to my grandmother, not to mention the staggering bill that
waited on them at the white commissary downtown.

The sounds of the new morning had been replaced   11
with grumbles about cheating houses, weighted scales,
snakes, skimpy cotton and dusty rows. In later years I was
to confront the stereotyped picture of gay song-singing cotton pickers with such inordinate rage that I was told even
by fellow Blacks that my paranoia was embarrassing. But
I had seen the fingers cut by the mean little cotton bolls,
and I had witnessed the backs and shoulders and arms
and legs resisting any further demands.

Some of the workers would leave their sacks at the   12
Store to be picked up the following morning, but a few
had to take them home for repairs. I winced to picture
them sewing the coarse material under a coal-oil lamp with
fingers stiffening from the day's work. In too few hours
they would have to walk back to Sister Henderson's Store,
get vittles and load, again, onto the trucks. Then they
would face another day of trying to earn enough for the
whole year with the heavy knowledge that they were

going to end the season as they started it. Without the money or credit necessary to sustain a family for three months. In cotton-picking time the late afternoons revealed the harshness of Black Southern life, which in the early morning had been softened by nature's blessing of grogginess, forgetfulness and the soft lamplight.

Comment

Angelou combines narration with description, beginning with her grandmother's rising at four o'clock in the morning and ending with a picture of workers mending their sacks under coal-oil lamps at night. Descriptive details at the beginning suggest the "soft make-believe feeling": "The odors of onions and oranges and kerosene had been mixing all night and wouldn't be disturbed until the wooded slat was removed from the door"; the sounds and smells of morning "were touched with the supernatural," she tells us in a later passage. In contrast to the morning, the late afternoon is harsh and ordinary, and she gives details of that world in the remaining paragraphs. The concluding sentence of the essay combines these impressions.

Questions for Study and Discussion

1. What details in the essay suggest "nature's blessing of grogginess, forgetfulness and the soft lamplight"? Why are these a blessing? What other details suggest the "features of the normal Arkansas life"?
2. How does Angelou suggest the influence of that world on her feelings about her race?
3. How do the details contradict a stereotype of the Southern black? How does Angelou remind us of that stereotype? What other stereotypes is she possibly criticizing?
4. Is her main purpose in writing to challenge this stereotype?
5. What personal qualities does Angelou stress in her description of her grandmother? What does this description contribute to the picture of Southern black life?

6. What mistaken picture or stereotype of a group—perhaps teenagers or high-school athletes—could you correct through a similar description?
7. What impression do you get of Angelou as a person, judging from the qualities of people she writes about and the things in her world that catch her eye?

Vocabulary Study

1. Which words in the essay are colloquial (words used conversationally and informally)?
2. What is *paranoia*, and how does Angelou use the word in paragraph 11?

Suggestions for Writing

1. Describe an aspect of your childhood or adolescence that tells the reader something important about your upbringing. Build your details to a statement of your controlling idea as Angelou does.
2. Describe one of your childhood or adolescent experiences from two points of view—that of the child and that of the young adult remembering the experience. Then comment on the differences between what the child or adolescent remembers and what the young adult understands. Use these differences to state a thesis.
3. Discuss a stereotype that shaped your view of other people or of yourself. Explain how you came to hold the stereotype, and how you discovered its falseness.

Example

An example is a picture or illustration of an idea. In explaining ideas, we fit our examples to the knowledge and experience of our readers or listeners. In explaining to a child that points of light in the night sky are really very large distant objects, we first have to explain why large objects can appear small. An example suited to the child's experience might be a ball that seems to get smaller as it flies through the air. In explaining to college physics students why the space of the universe is said to be "curved," a professor draws on mathematical formulas and scientific observations, but for the person who knows little or nothing about science, the professor would look for comparisons or analogies in everyday experience.

The word *example* carries the meaning of typical: that is, the example represents the many occurrences or forms of the idea. Examples are essential in exposition, particularly to the explanation of complex ideas. For instance, it would be difficult to explain the following idea without an example:

> The attitude that produces the pseudo-technical tone is made up of a desire to dignify the subject and the writer, coupled with the belief that important matters require a special vocabulary. —Jacques Barzun, *Simple and Direct*

Barzun provides this example of pseudo-technical tone:

> I am sorry not to be able to accept the experience of more intensive interaction with your group and its constituency.

No amount of definition and descriptive detail can replace an effective example such as this. At the same time, many examples do require explanation or analysis, particularly when the idea is a complex one.

Tom Wicker

"COURT DAY" IN MOORE COUNTY, NORTH CAROLINA

Tom Wicker was born and raised in Hamlet, North Carolina, and studied journalism at the University of North Carolina, graduating in 1946. He worked as a sports editor, feature editor, and correspondent for several Southern newspapers, including the *Nashville Tennessean,* and in 1960 began working for *The New York Times.* From 1964 to 1968 he was the *Times* Washington bureau chief, and he has been associate editor of the newspaper since 1968. Wicker's novels include *The Judgment* (1961) and *Facing the Lions* (1973); his nonfictional books include *JFK and LBJ: The Influence of Personality Upon Politics* (1968), *A Time to Die* (1975), on the Attica prison uprising, and *On Press* (1978), from which this essay is reprinted.

Monday was "court day" in Moore County, North Carolina, in 1949, and I regularly spent it at the county seat, Carthage, as correspondent for the *Sandhill Citizen,* of Aberdeen, North Carolina (population 1603). I reserved most of the afternoon for peddling ads—another of my duties—to the Carthage merchants, in keen competition with the county seat weekly, the *Moore County News.* On first arrival at the courthouse in the morning, I checked with the register of deeds, the clerk of court, the sheriff, and other officials for suits newly filed, big property transfers, scandalous foreclosures, heinous crimes, and the like; then I laboriously copied down births, deaths, and marriages of note. Later I hastened to the courtroom, where County Judge Leland McKeithen dispensed even-handed justice, or something as close to it as anything I've seen since.

That courtroom was rank with the enduring follies and foibles of mankind. It was segregated still, and in the summer months sweltering in the harsh dry heat of the North Carolina Sandhills in the days before universal air conditioning. But it provided a generous education in human nature, lawyers' tricks, oratory, and the law itself—in roughly that order. I witnessed court actions involving murders, manslaughters, crimes of property too numerous to define, vagrancies, seductions, desertions, auto offenses of every variety, bitterly disputed wills, breaches of promise and peace, recoveries of damage, alienations of affection, assaults, rapes, batteries, break-ins, reckless endangerments, ad infinitum. It seemed natural enough to me in the South of the 1940s that most defendants, and most victims, were black.

One divorce case—that of a white couple—had a particular impact on me, although I scarcely recall its details. They involved one party futilely chasing the other with an ax. The story plaintively related from the witness stand by the complainant, a worn-out woman with a ZaSu Pitts voice, haggard eyes, and hair just beginning to go gray, was the human comedy at its most ribald and perverse— Moore County transported to Chaucer's time and *The Canterbury Tales*. The spectators scattered around the courtroom, the press—another reporter and I—at its privileged table, even occasionally Judge McKeithen, rocked with laughter. The conclusion was foregone—divorce granted, with a fine crack of the gavel.

That was Monday. That afternoon, I hawked the *Citizen*'s ad space, probably to no better effect than usual. The next day, armed with copious notes, I turned out a humorous account of the divorce case for my long lead over the agate type that summed up the other court cases ("Lonzo McNair, Star Route, Carthage, failure to observe stop sign, costs of court"; "A. C. Overby, Vermont Avenue, Southern Pines, aggravated assault, continued to Superior Court") and sent it back to the *Citizen*'s ever-clacking Linotype machine (in a small shop in the days before offset printing, it was mandatory to keep "the machine" running, both to make the thing pay and to keep the lead pot from "freezing").

On Thursday, putting on my editor's hat, I wrote a two-column head for my court story and scheduled it for page one, above the fold—top play in the *Citizen* as in any other newspaper. We went to press routinely that night, got the mail copies to the post office in the nick of time, and went off for a few late beers.

Working late justified sleeping late; and when I drag-   6
ged myself into the *Citizen* office about noon the next day,
I had a visitor: a worn-out looking woman with a ZaSu
Pitts voice, but whose once-haggard eyes were blazing,
whose fluttering hands were clenched into fists, and whose
graying hair—I suddenly saw at range closer than that of
the witness stand—was that of a woman not too many
years older than I, who not too long before probably had
been considered a peach by the boys in her high school
class.

"Mr. Wicker," she said without preamble, "why did   7
you think you had the right to make fun out of me in your
paper?"

I have never forgotten that question—and I still can't   8
answer it. In 1949 I doubt if I even tried. I remember thinking I had not bargained for such awful moments when
I had landed my first reporter's job a few months before.
Accurate though my story had been, and based on a public
record, it had nevertheless exploited human unhappiness
for the amusement or titillation of others. I had made the
woman in my office something less than what she was—
a human being possessed, despite her misfortunes, of real
dignity.

Seeing that, I saw too that I had not only done her an   9
injury but missed the story I should have written. This
is one of the besetting sins of journalism—sensationalism
at the expense of the dignity and truth of the common
human experience. I have been fortunate to have worked
mostly for publishers and editors who sought to avoid that
sin—not always successfully. And reading some of the
more lurid journals, I've often thought that sensationalism
and gossip columns tend to be techniques employed
mostly by big-circulation publications for an anonymous
audience. Not many editors and reporters would be callous
or unseeing enough to engage in them if they had to face
the victims the next morning over a battered desk in an
office not much bigger than a closet.

Comment

Our understanding of the concluding paragraph depends on the example Wicker develops: without it the "sensationalism" that he refers to would be a vague term. In developing his example, Wicker gives us the setting as well as some of the important details—enough of them to make his point. Had he given all of them, the focus would have shifted from his own experience as a young reporter to the woman and the divorce hearing.

Questions for Study and Discussion

1. What information about the divorce does Wicker include, and what details show why he found it funny? What other aspects of the case might he have included had he wished to focus on its humor?
2. How does the episode reveal the "sensationalism" that Wicker refers to in the final paragraph?
3. What personal qualities does Wicker reveal in his account of the episode? Which of these qualities does he want to stress?
4. Is Wicker saying that the divorce was not newsworthy and should not have been reported?

Vocabulary Study

Use your dictionary to explain how Wicker uses the following words:

1. *heinous, dispensed* (paragraph 1)
2. *foibles, sweltering, vagrancies* (paragraph 2)
3. *ribald, perverse* (paragraph 3)
4. *copious, Linotype* (paragraph 4)
5. *exploit, titillation* (paragraph 8)
6. *lurid, callous* (paragraph 9)

Suggestions for Writing

1. The character of a newspaper is often revealed by its front page—by what news, what pictures, what headliness the front page includes. Analyze the front page of a paper you read regularly to define its character. Do not try to describe everything on the page. Focus on key details.
2. We have all had experiences like Wicker's in which we made important discoveries about ourselves. Discuss one such experience of your own, giving enough details to let the reader discover what you did. Draw a conclusion from your example.

Process

Another important method of developing ideas is process analysis. A *process* is any activity or operation that contains steps which are usually performed in sequence. It may be a mechanical one, like changing a tire, or a natural one, like the circulation of the blood. The process referred to in the following statement is a natural one:

> Just as human individuals and populations undergo continual alteration in response to infectious disease, so also the various infectious organisms that provoke disease undergo a process of adaptation and adjustment to their environment.
> —William H. McNeill, *Plagues and Peoples*

These are two common types of process analysis.

A third type deals with a historical process—one that occurred in the past, and can occur again, according to identifiable causes and effects:

> At all times famines have led to social disturbances. In mere self-preservation people took food wherever they could find it, or stole the money to buy it. Criminality, brigandage, and prostitution were well known symptoms of famines. Families were torn apart and children grew up without guidance, as in the Russian famine of 1921, when the hordes of vagrant children presented a serious problem. Exasperated by starvation, people were ready to rise against the authorities. The sight of rich families indulging in luxuries while they were deprived of the bare necessities made them acutely aware of class distinctions. Hunger was one factor that contributed to unleash revolutionary forces in France in 1789. The Roman emperors well knew that the best way to keep the masses quiet was to give them *panem et circenses*, food and entertainment— and usually, the more entertainment, the less food. In the 2nd

63

century after Christ about 500,000 inhabitants of Rome lived on public charity. The emperors' example has been followed by all dictators. —Henry E. Sigerist, *Civilization and Disease*

Whether mechanical, natural, or historical, the steps of a process are usually described chronologically. In mechanical processes, you may have a choice of procedures or tools, and you may decide to describe more than one of these—for example, you may discuss several kinds of tire jacks and how they work. In the course of explanation, you may have to define and illustrate key terms, make comparisons, and comment on the uses of the process.

Many processes are complex: they contain several related processes, each of which must be carefully distinguished. For example, the instruction book that gives directions for wiring a stereo receiver and a tape deck to a turntable and speakers describes each process step by step. Assembling a receiver from a kit is even more complex a procedure.

Faith McNulty

HOW TO RAISE A WOODCHUCK

Faith McNulty has written about nature and wildlife in numerous articles and books, including *The Whooping Crane* (given the Dutton Animal Book Award in 1966), *The Great Whales* (1974), *Wildlife Stories* (1980), and *Must They Die?*—on the prairie dog and the black-footed ferret. Many of her articles have appeared in *The New Yorker*. In the following essay, McNulty describes her experience raising a woodchuck.

I have faith that for every piece of information there 1 is someone somewhere who wishes to receive it. In that spirit I am putting down a few notes on the topic, "How to raise a woodchuck." Admittedly this is not a problem on everyone's mind: but if you live in woodchuck country, which in the East is almost anywhere, it is possible you will find yourself holding a baby woodchuck and wondering what to do with it.

This happened to me on a spring day at the end of 2
May, and I haven't been sorry. It had been years since
I had close contact with a wild animal. I wondered if
possessing it would have any of the thrill it had when I
was ten years old. Then, any creature I encountered was
an individual, as distinct, for better or worse, and as ir-
replaceable as myself. Its death would be as final. This is
a feeling that is often attacked as sentimental by those who
see individual animals as interchangeable digits in a very
large number and point out that while woodchucks come
and go, only the existence of the species need concern us.
This view has its validity, and I don't want anyone to think
I have spent my adult years putting up tombstones for
deceased pets or holding funeral rites over fallen sparrows,
and yet I have never divorced myself from the idea that
individual worth in the animal kingdom is not restricted
to human beings.

On May 29th there was a heavy rain. Our farm near 3
Wakefield, Rhode Island, is in the midst of rolling fields.
They were thoroughly soaked, and the new grass turned
even more brilliant green. There were puddles in the
driveway and on the low spots in our neighbor's potato
field. The next day the sun came out beautifully hot. Driving back from the village, I decided that instead of going
on another errand I would go home and get my bathing
suit. I turned in and pulled the car up short, because a
small woodchuck was traveling along the road, its belly
almost flat to the gravel. It was smaller than any I had
ever seen except the one I had picked up after a similar
rain, so many years ago, when I was ten years old.

I got out of the car, took off my sweater, threw it over 4
the woodchuck and wrapped him in it, then put him on
the floor of the car while I drove the short distance home.
I surmised the rain had washed out his burrow and the
young had wandered off in different directions. If I hadn't
come along he would have gone on in a hopeless search
until he died of starvation. Rescuing him, I felt as large
as Fate. It also occurred to me that by picking him up I
was letting myself in for quite a lot of bother. I wondered

if I really wanted to do it at my age. But by the time I thought of this, the woodchuck was already wrapped in my sweater and it was too late to reconsider.

At home I put him in the bathtub, where he gamely scrabbled against the unyielding porcelain. My husband found a large carton. I put cat litter in the bottom and straw on top of that. I put the chuck in it. He did not try to bite. He gratefully burrowed into the straw.

I put the carton in the bathroom. This is where I always kept animals in my childhood. This also, I must admit, is where my first woodchuck met his end. He somehow climbed up and fell into the toilet, where he stayed for some time with his nose just above the surface. He died later, presumably of pneumonia. Now, faced with my new responsibility, I recalled that first woodchuck. At that time we had a litter of kittens. We brought the mother and kittens into the bathroom. The little chuck shared their bed. The old cat licked him, and the kittens warmed him, but he could get no milk. We fed him with a bottle. I recall that he sat on his haunches like a bear and held the bottle in his paws. I remember, too, that he followed me around making a sound like a tiny outboard motor. He also shared the cat's toilet pan, which was filled with sand. At the time I thought the mother cat had taught him, but I have since learned that this is innate in woodchucks.

In the old days there were doll nursing bottles with real rubber nipples. Now the doll bottles are plastic and no use. Instead I tried a coarse medicine dropper. The chuck sucked noisily and greedily while I squeezed out a mixture of nonfat milk and baby cereal. He accepted me quickly. Within a day or two he was rushing into my hands and making a strange little noise when I came to feed him. Two ounces filled him to bulging. Then he slept, often on his back with legs flung out in an attitude of abandon. Awake, he began to play, rolling around and biting at the straw. If I put my hand in the carton, he nibbled my fingers and wrestled with them, kicking against my hand the way kittens do.

It became clear that I was imprinting the woodchuck   8
and vice versa. When I had first picked him up, I thought
he was homely as a burlap bag. I felt sorry for him for
being what he was—a mere woodchuck. He would never
be graceful or very bright, never swift or surprising or
beautiful. He would just be a chunky brown fellow with
coarse fur and a taste for the depths of the earth. Now,
as I held him, five or six times a day, I began to observe
him closely.

I noticed his hands. They were black, with four very   9
long fingers ending in long curved nails. The thumb was
only a small projection. He could close these fingers to
grasp something—the medicine dropper or my finger. With
these expressive hands he was almost as dexterous as a
squirrel and, of course, a woodchuck is in the squirrel
family. It is the largest of the family Sciuridae, which includes the prairie dog, the squirrel, and the chipmunk.
His coat, coarse against my hands as I held him, was a
mixture of grays and tans and consisted of a thick under-
coat interspersed with long, bristly guard hairs, banded
in black-and-white, giving a tweedy appearance. His front
and hind legs were very short but stout and strong. His
shoulders, upper arms, and lower flanks were covered
with red fur. His tail wasn't much, neither long nor short,
and only slightly bushy. His belly was round and babyish,
with rather sparse dark hair the color of coffee beans. I
noted his ears. They were small, round, squirrel ears, neat
and pretty and appropriate to life spent partly in tunnels.
His eyes were oval and set near the top of his skull to
give good upward vision. They were dark as raisins and
softly shiny. There were bristly whiskers by his nose and
an additional set on his cheeks, I presume for checking
the diameter of tunnels.

All of this, plus the energy and will emanating from   10
him as he struggled mightily in my grasp to get every drop
of milk despite the odd shape of the new teat, added up
to the statement, "I am a woodchuck, and I want to live."
And, by holding him and feeding him, I was allowing

myself to be imprinted with the added message, ''I am *your* little brown woodchuck. My survival is up to you.''

Very shortly the carton seemed too small. I let the   11
woodchuck loose in the bathroom and offered him a nest
made of a covered box, bedded with straw and with a
round doorway cut in the front. He knew instantly that
a hole spells home, and he dashed inside. I put the cat
litter in a dishpan nearby. In the wild, woodchucks are
fastidious, burying their excrement in a special chamber
of the burrow. The woodchuck immediately used the pan
for this purpose.

Now that he was free, his extreme wariness became   12
evident. He was very sensitive to sound. Any sudden
noise sent him flying into his house. At first the sight of
me or my husband walking around scared him, too, but
his fear wore off rapidly. He began to greet me by scrab-
bling at my ankles, trying to climb up my legs, a painful
process. He often followed closely at my heels, making
his funny, urgent little noise. If I offered my hand he
nibbled it eagerly. He possessed four long, curved front
teeth that could easily have punctured me, but his bite
was always restrained. I guessed that wild woodchucks
groom each other with these gentle bites. Together the nibbling and the chuckling sound were very expressive of
emotion.

We have a dog, and a meeting was inevitable. The first   13
few times the woodchuck fled at sight of the dog. Then
he stood his ground. The dog, filled with curiosity, extended her nose, and the woodchuck's nose came up to
meet it. After one sniff the woodchuck turned, hissed as
if he had tasted something disgusting, and withdrew. The
dog's odor must advertise the meat-eater's lethal habits.

At this stage it occurred to me that I really knew little   14
about the lives of woodchucks, and I turned to the library
for some basic data. I found that there are woodchucks
practically everywhere in the United States—including
Alaska, but not in the Deep South—and in Canada. The

species that frequent the West and the high mountains are known as the yellowbelly marmot and the hoary marmot. The proper name of our woodchuck is *Marmota monax,* and there are nine subspecies. My particular woodchuck is *Marmota monax preblorum,* and it must once have been a forest dweller, since before our time dense forests covered the East. With the cultivation of open fields *monax* has found an improved food supply and has prospered.

Woodchucks, the textbook says, have three white nipple-like organs just inside the anus that emit a musky odor when the animal is excited and whose purpose probably is communication. (I have smelled no musky odor on my woodchuck, however.) The woodchuck also is said to whistle. I have not heard mine whistle, either, but in addition to his chuckling plea for attention, I have heard an indignant yip when I dipped his front paws in water. 15

The life of the woodchuck revolves around its burrow. This is a complicated structure that may be from 25 to 30 feet long, with a front door that is obvious because of the dirt heaped around it and a second plunge hole dug from beneath and thus hard to see. Within the hole there is a turnaround near the entrance, a nest chamber lined with soft grass, and a toilet chamber used exclusively for sanitary purposes. The nest chamber is invariably 14 by 16 inches, which is so small that a full-grown woodchuck must sleep curled up. The digging of woodchucks improves the soil by its mixing action and by letting in air and water. An average den requires the moving of nearly 400 pounds of dirt. In New York State, it has been estimated, woodchucks turn over 1.6 million tons of earth each year. 16

An ability for deep hibernation is the woodchuck's most famous characteristic, one it shares with ground squirrels, bats, and jumping mice. The older and fatter woodchucks go to earth first, sometimes before the first frost, followed by the yearlings and juveniles. They sleep in a tightly curled ball. A captive woodchuck was examined once a week during hibernation, and although it was handled its eyes did not open. It was cold to the touch. It 17 took one breath every six minutes, and its heartbeat was equally slow. Its temperature had sunk from 96.8 degrees F. while awake to 50 degrees. Thin woodchucks emerge from hibernation first, sometimes even during winter. Wakening may be either slow or abrupt and accompanied by trembling. Woodchucks do not sleep in their summer dens but move to new dens in woods or brush, where leaves carpet the ground and the frost does not go deep. They prefer a slope safe from flooding. Their weight loss during hibernation ranges from one-third to one-half their body weight, but the newly awakened woodchucks are nonetheless in good condition. While they are asleep their teeth and toenails do not grow.

Woodchucks lead a relatively unsocial life. They live together only briefly during mating, though yearlings not yet ready to mate sometimes consort together and even occupy the same den. Chucks place their dens at a distance from each other whenever they can. They compete for food, but there is no real territoriality. Bigger woodchucks chase off smaller ones, which do not defend their home range. A woodchuck threatens by arching its back, flipping its erect tail up and down, and approaching the adversary with open mouth, but actual fights are few. Woodchucks are notorious eaters, and this is their main occupation. They eat selected succulent plants, particularly clover, chickweed, alfalfa, and dandelion when these are abundant. They love fruit and vegetables, and it is to this that they owe the great hostility of most farmers. Fat woodchucks weight 10 or 12 pounds, but a 15-pound specimen is not unheard of. 18

When the cycle of woodchuck life begins in the spring, the males immediately begin to wander, searching for dens occupied by females. The females stay at home, waiting to be courted. Thus in the spring it is possible to tell the sex of a woodchuck at a distance—a wanderer is a male, a stay-at-home is a female. Females also are warier, especially when pregnant. 19

Tails wagging, the males check each den to see if it is occupied by an agreeable female. If it is, and she accepts 20 him, he usually moves in with her, though sometimes the two live in different burrows while the male visits his mate daily. During this period a mated pair is monogamous, something we tend to read of with approval, but the conjugal period is brief. The gestation of woodchucks is only about 30 days, and as the time of birth approaches, the female drives the male away. He is to be permitted no part in raising the young. It is one of nature's casual cruelties that the male remains sexually ardent after the female has rejected him, and so, for a while, the fields are full of frustrated males wandering lonesomely about. The arrangement, however, ensures that any female coming into heat later than the others will be mated nonetheless.

The young woodchucks are born in the early spring   21
in litters that average four but may be larger. The newborn woodchuck is tiny: blind and hairless, it is only about four inches long and weighs an ounce. At four weeks its eyes are open and it weighs six and one-half ounces. At six weeks young chucks are active, weigh half a pound, and follow their mother into the open, but they don't go far. They sun themselves at the edge of the burrow and wrestle and play. The mother grooms them affectionately. It is at this stage, I was interested to read, that she begins to wean them by going farther from the burrow than they dare to follow so they are forced to eat herbs to stay their hunger.

Sometimes after the young are six weeks old their in-   22
creasing size crowds the nest, and the mother separates them, leading each one to a new den dug nearby. There it must learn to do without the emotional support of the family and prepare for the solitary life that lies ahead. This preparation is gradual. The mother visits each one daily and spends time with it, grooming it and continuing its opportunity to learn from her such survival lessons as wariness and the selection of the proper herbs as food. Young woodchucks sometimes take food from a mother's mouth, and it is thought this is part of learning what is good to eat. They follow her example when she shows alarm and learn to respond to the sight or sound or smell

of danger with a quick dive to safety. As the young wood-chucks become more prepared physically and psychologically to face life alone, the mother's visits taper off. Then, sometime in midsummer, the young will feel an urge to move off and explore the world. They may go a long way or only a few hundred yards before they find new homes, but now they are on their own.

Once I had acquainted myself with the scenario of woodchuck life in the wild, it was clear how I must carry out my role as foster mother, but accomplishing it was not so easy. I brought my woodchuck all sorts of grasses and vegetables, but he merely tasted them and dropped them. I was happy when he consented to eat a cherry and a marigold, but he would go no further. I was also aware that life in my bathroom was not providing the proper lessons about growing plants, damp earth, and the sudden threat of a marauding dog, which would be the most important elements in his adult survival. 23

I took him outside and put him down on the lawn. He showed sheer terror at the sight of the open sky. I brought his box outside. He dashed in and refused to leave it. There seemed nothing to do but bring him back to the bathroom. I continued to leave offerings of grass and flowers, but he allowed them to wilt and clambered into my lap as eagerly as ever for each feeding. He was getting quite big, and my husband remarked that if I didn't do something about it, I would be followed around for the rest of my days by a 15-pound woodchuck begging for milk. 24

At last I decided I must do what mother woodchucks do: put him in a new burrow. I searched along the wall of our orchard and found a small hole. I wasn't sure of its origin, or if it was occupied, but decided I must take a chance. I put the chuck, housed in his box, near the hole and left him, knowing that eventually hunger would drive him out. A few hours later, when his next feeding time came, I went out. The box was empty. I called, and within seconds my woodchuck emerged from the hole and flung himself on my ankle, chuckling gladly. I sat down and 25 fed him. When I finished he tried persistently to follow me back to the house, but I put him on the far side of the wall and escaped.

I continued to visit him several times a day with his milk. Each time he greeted me joyfully and drank greedily, but I felt sure he must be finding food on his own. He also began to accept carrots and cherries and daisies. The final weaning came abruptly. Between breakfast and lunch he forgot how to suck. It was as if a switch had been flipped in his maturing nervous system. I offered milk a few more times, but he was quite unable to suck it in. Clearly, weaning had been accomplished. [26]

Still the emotional ties persisted. I visited him every day bringing carrots. Sometimes he was quite far away, but he would always come at the sound of my voice. He showed more emotion about nibbling my fingers and climbing up my legs and into my arms than he did about the carrots. It is an odd feeling to be desperately embraced by a lonesome woodchuck. I always left him with a slight sense of guilt at rejecting him, and I wondered if wild woodchucks tried as hard to keep their mother's waning interest. [27]

The parting came unexpectedly. I went away on a brief trip. When I came back there were days of rain and I didn't visit the burrow. In truth it didn't seem as important as it once had. When I remembered and went out to call, no woodchuck came. In the past weeks I have seen no sign of him, and I suppose he has moved away as the textbook said young woodchucks do. I hope he has found a safe, dry burrow. When autumn comes I will wish him deep sleep and happy dreams. In the spring when I see a large, handsome woodchuck ambling through the new grass, I will hope that it is he. [28]

Comment

Faith McNulty tells us how to raise a woodchuck and, in the course of doing so, describes the habits and life cycle of woodchucks. Like Rachel Carson, Annie Dillard, and other writers

about nature in this book, McNulty also tells us about herself—
sometimes directly, sometimes indirectly. Specifically, she tells
us about her rural life, her love of animals, her view about
nature. These details are not presented casually, in a rambling,
disconnected narrative; McNulty instead weaves them together,
each detail developing her central topic.

Questions for Study and Discussion

1. What aspects of raising a woodchuck does McNulty stress,
   and why does she? What aspects receive the least attention, and why do they?
2. How does McNulty connect the life cycle and habits of the
   woodchuck to the process of raising one? Why is it important to understand this life cycle and these habits?
3. Does McNulty make a point about raising a wild animal?
   Or is she concerned only with describing the process?
4. What does McNulty state directly about her interests, ideas,
   and life? What does she reveal to us indirectly?

Vocabulary Study

1. What does McNulty mean by the following words and
   phrases?
   a. *interchangeable digits* (paragraph 2)
   b. *imprinting the woodchuck* (paragraph 8)
   c. *dexterous as a squirrel; interspersed with long, bristly guard
      hairs* (paragraph 9)
   d. *fastidious* (paragraph 11)
   e. *nibbling and chuckling sound* (paragraph 12)
   f. *lethal habits* (paragraph 13)
   g. *deep hibernation* (paragraph 17)
   h. *no real territoriality; succulent plants* (paragraph 18)
   i. *gestation; casual cruelties* (paragraph 20)
   j. *ambling* (paragraph 28)
2. Explain the statement: "Rescuing him, I felt as large as
   Fate."

3. What does McNulty mean in paragraph 6 by "innate" behavior in woodchucks, and what other examples of innate
   behavior does McNulty give?

Suggestions for Writing

1. Describe your own experience with a wild or domestic animal, perhaps your own attempt to raise it. In the course
   of your essay, give your reader details about yourself—your
   life, your interests, perhaps your own attitude toward
   animals and nature generally.
2. Describe the pleasures and frustrations of building or
   repairing something. Give enough details about the process to let your readers experience what you did.
3. Describe the same process in enough detail that someone
   who has never performed it can do so. Assume that this
   person is unfamiliar with the tools required.

Comparison and Contrast

Like definition and division, comparison and contrast is an important method of analysis in exposition. *Comparison* deals with similarities, *contrast* with differences. In comparing, you show what two or more people or objects or places have in common; in contrasting, how they are unlike. There are many ways of organizing paragraphs or essays of comparison or contrast. One way is the block listing of the qualities of the first person or place, then the block listing of the qualities of the second—in the same order:

> Chicago, at the southern tip of Lake Michigan, is a port city and an important commercial and industrial center of the Middle West. It is also an important educational, cultural, and recreational center, drawing thousands to its concert halls, art museum, and sports arenas. Cleveland, on the south shore of Lake Erie, is also a port city and a commercial and industrial center important to its area. Like Chicago, it has several important colleges and universities, a distinguished symphony orchestra, one of the fine art museums of the world, and many recreational centers. The location of the two cities undoubtedly contributed to their growth, but this similarity is not sufficient to explain their wide social diversity. (paragraph of comparison)

A second way is an alternating comparison or contrast, point by point:

> Chicago is on the southern tip of Lake Michigan; Cleveland, on the south shore of Lake Erie. Both are important commercial and industrial centers of the Middle West, and both offer a wide range of educational, cultural, and recreational activities.

In developing such paragraphs or essays, transitions like *similarly, likewise, by comparison,* and *by contrast* may be needed to clarify the organization. The purpose of comparison and contrast is usually to provide a relative estimate: we discover the qualities of the first person or object or place through the qualities of the second (or third), and the qualities of the second through the first. If Cleveland and Chicago share these characteristics and have the same history of growth, we are better able to understand the causes that shape cities. A contrast with Atlanta or Omaha—large inland cities—would clarify these causes further through a similar relative estimate.

Sydney J. Harris

OPPOSING PRINCIPLES HELP BALANCE SOCIETY

Sydney J. Harris attended the University of Chicago and later taught in its University College. From 1941 to 1978 he was a drama critic and columnist for *The Chicago Daily News.* His column "Strictly Personal" first appeared in the *Daily News* in 1944. Harris is one of the masters of the journalistic essay. Although his essays are brief (most are between 600 and 1000 words), he deals with important social, political, and philosophical issues in simple, exact, and sometimes eloquent words. His essays are collected in *Majority of One* (1957), *For the Time Being* (1972), *Clearing the Ground* (1986), and other books.

I devoutly wish we could get rid of two words in the   1
popular lexicon: *liberal* and *conservative.* Both are beautiful and useful words in their origins, but now each is used (and misused) as an epithet by its political enemies.

Liberal means liberating—it implies more freedom, more   2
openness, more flexibility, more humaneness, more willingness to change when change is called for.

Conservative means conserving—it implies preserving   3
what is best and most valuable from the past, a decent respect for tradition, a reluctance to change merely for its own sake.

Both attributes, in a fruitful tension, are necessary for   4
the welfare of any social order. Liberalism alone can
degenerate into mere permissiveness and anarchy. Conservatism alone is prone to harden into reaction and
repression. As Lord Acton brilliantly put it: "Every institution tends to fail by an excess of its own basic principle."

Yet, in the rhetoric of their opponents, both *liberal* and   5
conservative have turned into dirty words. Liberals become
"bleeding hearts"; conservatives want "to turn the clock
back." But sometimes hearts *should* bleed; sometimes it
would profit us to run the clock back if it is spinning too fast.

Radical, of course, has become the dirtiest of words,   6
flung around carelessly and sometimes maliciously. Today
it is usually applied to the left by the right—but the right
is often as "radical" in its own way.

The word originally meant "going to the roots" and   7
was a metaphor drawn from the radish, which grows
underground. We still speak of "radical surgery," which
is undertaken when lesser measures seem futile. The
American Revolution, indeed, was a radical step taken to
ensure a conservative government, when every other effort had failed.

Dorothy Thompson was right on target when she re-   8
marked that her ideal was to be "a radical as a thinker,
a conservative as to program, and a liberal as to temper."
In this way she hoped to combine the best and most productive in each attitude, while avoiding the pitfalls of each.

Society is like a pot of soup: It needs different, and   9
contrasting, ingredients to give it body and flavor and last-
ing nourishment. It is compound, not simple; not like wine
that drugs us, or caffeine that agitates us, but a blend to
satisfy the most divergent palates.

Of course, this is an ideal, an impossible vision never   10
to be fully realized in any given society. But it is what we
should aim at, rather than promoting some brew that is
to one taste alone. It may take another thousand years to
get the recipe just right. The question is: Do we have the
time?

Comment

Harris contrasts three words used widely in political discussion—*liberal, conservative,* and *radical*. Because those using these words seldom agree on their meaning, Harris is careful to define them. From his definition of them he leads into a discussion of his thesis. His series of short paragraphs are typical of newspaper articles, editorials, and journalistic essays that often devote each paragraph to a single idea and key supporting details. Harris uses his short paragraphs to contrast meanings and ideas.

Questions for Study and Discussion

1. Does Harris contrast *liberal* and *conservative* in blocks or point by point? Why does he introduce the word *radical* only after contrasting the first two words?
2. What essential differences in meaning between the three words does Harris stress? Why does he?
3. Why does Harris give us the etymology or origin of *radical*? What is a metaphor, and why is *radical* an example?
4. How early in the essay does Harris introduce his thesis? How does his discussion of the three words develop it?
5. Where does Harris finally restate his thesis?

Vocabulary Study

1. What did Lord Acton, the nineteenth-century British political writer, mean by the statement "Every institution tends to fail by an excess of its own basic principle"? What do the words *excess* and *principle* mean?
2. What did Dorothy Thompson, the American journalist, mean by the statement that she wished to be "a radical as a thinker, a conservative as to program, and a liberal as to temper"? What did she mean by *temper*?

Suggestion for Writing

Using the *Oxford English Dictionary, Dictionary of American English, Safire's Political Dictionary,* or other reference sources, trace the meanings of one of the following words or another word used in politics. Then write a short essay explaining how the history of the word illuminates one or more of its current uses:

1. fascist
2. kingmaker
3. maverick
4. mossback
5. mugwump
6. radical
7. scalawag
8. Young Turk

✧

Cause and Effect

Reasoning about *cause and effect* is often a simple matter of connecting two events. When I get wet during a thunderstorm, I know that rain is the cause. But making other connections is usually not this simple. If I catch a cold the same day, I may blame it on the rain. However, I might have caught a cold even if I had stayed indoors; and if I had been in the rain, the rain alone may not have been the single cause or even a condition. A number of conditions together may have produced the cold: a run-down state arising from overwork or lack of sleep, poor eating habits, getting wet—these may have triggered a virus in the body.

The sum of these conditions is generally what we mean by *cause*. We ordinarily speak loosely of one of these conditions as the cause. Except where an immediate action (exposure to the storm) produces a direct consequence (getting wet), reasoning about cause and effect is probable rather than certain. Having identified conditions that produced colds in the past, I cannot be sure that they *must* produce one in the present. The identical conditions may be present, without producing a cold.

All discussions of cause and effect, formal and informal, include hidden or unstated assumptions or beliefs about people, society, the ways things happen in nature—human beings are naturally aggressive, adolescents are naturally rebellious, the Irish have hot tempers, the English are cold and reserved, opposites attract. Many who hold these beliefs unquestioningly seldom think about them, nor do they feel it necessary to test them through observation. In cause-and-effect reasoning such assumptions are hidden in the explanation and may be decisive.

Appletree Rodden

WHY SMALLER REFRIGERATORS CAN PRESERVE THE HUMAN RACE

Appletree Rodden did research in biochemistry at Stanford University and has been a member of the Staatstheater Ballet Company, in West Germany. His essay, first published in *Harper's* in 1974, is as timely today as it was when Americans were becoming aware of the energy crisis.

Once, long ago, people had special little boxes called 1 refrigerators in which milk, meat, and eggs could be kept cool. The grandchildren of these simple devices are large enough to store whole cows, and they reach temperatures comparable to those at the South Pole. Their operating costs increase each year, and they are so complicated that few home handymen attempt to repair them on their own.

Why has this change in size and complexity occurred 2 in America? It has not taken place in many areas of the technologically advanced world (the average West German refrigerator is about a yard high and less than a yard wide, yet refrigeration technology in Germany is quite advanced). Do we really need (or even want) all that space and cold?

The benefits of a large refrigerator are apparent: a sav- 3 ing of time (one grocery-shopping trip a week instead of several), a saving of money (the ability to buy expensive, perishable items in larger, cheaper quantities), a feeling of security (if the car breaks down or if famine strikes, the refrigerator is well stocked). The costs are there, too, but they are not so obvious.

Cost number one is psychological. Ever since the re- 4 frigerator began to grow, food has increasingly become something we buy to store rather than to eat. Few families go to market daily for their daily bread. The manna in the wilderness could be gathered for only one day at a time. The ancient distaste for making food a storage item is echoed by many modern psychiatrists who suggest that such psychosomatic disorders as obesity are often due to the patient's inability to come to terms with the basic transitoriness of life. Research into a relationship between excessive corpulence and the size of one's refrigerator has not been extensive, but we might suspect one to be there.

Another cost is aesthetic. In most of Europe, where 5 grocery marketing is still a part of the daily rhythm, one can buy tomatoes, lettuce, and the like picked on the day of purchase. Many European families have modest refrigerators for storing small items (eggs, milk, butter) for a couple of days, but the concept of buying large quantities of food to store in the refrigerator is not widely accepted. Since fresh produce is easily available in Europe, most people buy it daily.

Which brings to mind another price the large refrig- 6 erator has cost us: the friendly neighborhood market. In America, time is money. A large refrigerator means fewer time-consuming trips to the grocery store. One member of a deep-freeze-owning family can do the grocery shopping once or twice a month rather than daily. Since shopping trips are infrequent, most people have been willing to forego the amenities of the little store around the corner in favor of the lower prices found in the supermarket.

If refrigerators weren't so large—that is, if grocery mar- 7 keting were a daily affair—the "entertainment surcharge" of buying farm fresh food in a smaller, more intimate setting might carry some weight. But as it is, there is not really that much difference between eggs bought from Farmer Brown's wife and eggs bought from the supermarket which in turn bought them from Eggs Incorporated, a firm operated out of Los Angeles that produces 200,000 eggs a day from chickens that are kept in gigantic warehouses lighted artificially on an eighteen-hour light-and-dark cycle and produce one-and-a-half times as many eggs—a special breed of chickens who die young and insane. Not much difference if you don't mind eating eggs from crazy chickens.

Chalk up Farmer and Mrs. Brown as cost number four   8
of the big refrigerator. The small farmer can't make it in
a society dominated by supermarkets and big refrigerators;
make way for superfarmers, super yields, and pesticides
(cost number five).

Cost number six of the big refrigerator has been the   9
diminution of regional food differences. Of course the
homogenization of American fare cannot be blamed solely
on the availability of frozen food. Nonetheless, were it not
for the trend toward turning regional specialties into frozen
dinners, it might still be possible to experience novelty
closer to home.

So much for the disadvantages of the big refrigerator.   10
What about the advantages of the small one? First of all,
it would help us to "think small," which is what we must
learn anyway if the scary predictions of the Club of Rome
(*The Limits of Growth*) are true. The advent of smaller
refrigerators would set the stage for reversing the "big-
thinking" trends brought on with the big refrigerator, and
would eventually change our lives.

Ivan Illich makes the point in *Tools for Conviviality* that   11
any tool we use (the automobile, standardized public
education, public-health care, the refrigerator) influences
the individual, his society, and the relationship between
the two. A person's automobile is a part of his identity.
The average Volkswagen owner has a variety of characteristics (income, age, occupation) significantly different from
those of the average Cadillac owner. American society,
with more parking lots than parks, and with gridded
streets rather than winding lanes, would be vastly different
without the private automobile. Similar conclusions can
be drawn about any of the tools we use. They change us.
They change our society. Therefore, it behooves us to think
well before we decide which tool to use to accomplish a
given task. Do we want tools that usurp power unto themselves, the ones called "nonconvivial" by Illich?

The telephone, a "convivial tool," has remained   12
under control; it has not impinged itself on society or on
the individual. Each year it has become more efficient, and

it has not prevented other forms of communication (letter writing, visits). The world might be poorer without the telephone, but it would not be grossly different. Telephones do not pollute, are not status symbols, and interact only slightly (if at all) with one's self-image.

So what about the refrigerator? Or back to the more 13 basic problem to which the refrigerator was a partial answer: what about our supply of food? When did we decide to convert the emotion-laden threat of starvation from a shared community problem (of societal structure: farm-market-home) to a personal one (of storage)? How did we decide to accept a thawed block taken from a supermarket's freezer as a substitute for the voluptuous shapes, smells, and textures of fresh fruits and vegetables obtained from complex individual sources?

The decision for larger refrigerators has been consistent 14 with a change in food-supply routes from highly diversified "trails" (from small farms to neighborhood markets) to uniform, standardized highways (from large farms to centrally located supermarkets). Desirable meals are quick and easy rather than rich and leisurely. Culinary artistry has given way to efficiency, the efficiency of the big refrigerator.

People have a natural propensity for running good 15 things into the ground. Mass production has been a boon to mankind, but its reliance on homogeneity precludes its being a paradigm for all areas of human life. Our forebears and contemporaries have made it possible to mass-produce almost anything. An equally challenging task now lies with us: to choose which things of this world should be mass-produced, and how the standards of mass production should influence other standards we hold dear.

Should houses be mass-produced? Should education? 16 Should food? Which brings us back to refrigerators. How does one decide how large a refrigerator to buy, considering one's life, one's society, and the world, and not simply the question of food storage?

As similar questions are asked about more and more 17 of the things we mass-produce, mass production will become less of a problem and more of a blessing. As cost begins to be measured not only in dollars spent and minutes saved, but in total richness acquired, perhaps smaller refrigerators will again make good sense. A small step backward along some of the roads of "technological progress" might be a large step forward for mankind, and one our age is uniquely qualified to make.

Comment

If Rodden were trying to persuade West German readers to buy large refrigerators, the benefits they provide would be emphasized. Writing to persuade Americans to give up large refrigerators, he focuses on one cause of their preference for them, the attitude that "time is money." If this attitude is a necessary condition of the American preference—that is, a condition that must be present for this preference to exist—attacking the attitude may help to diminish the incentive. Rodden attacks this attitude by showing the disadvantages of thinking about life in this way; these include the sacrifice of fresh food and the fun of buying it, the gradual disappearance of the small farmer, the use of dangerous pesticides—in general, the limits of choice imposed by technology. There may be other necessary conditions, but Rodden need not identify all of them and does not claim to have done so. The "natural propensity for running good things into the ground" is a necessary condition that would be difficult to eliminate. Writers seldom try to identify all the causes of a situation or attitude—not only because it would be difficult to do so, but because they need not do so to make their point.

Questions for Study and Discussion

1. In what order does Rodden present the cost of large refrigerators?
2. What other causes does Rodden state or imply for the American preference? What is the thesis of the essay, and where is it first stated?

3. Does Rodden explain why Europeans prefer small refrigerators? Is Rodden implying that Americans are more easily captivated by "technological progress"?
4. What in Rodden's comments on storing food and the problem of obesity shows that he is stating only some of the reasons for practices and attitudes, not all of them?
5. Does Rodden assert or imply that the greater efficiency a tool has, the greater control it exerts over people?
6. Do you agree that the telephone is a "convivial tool" and do you agree with Rodden's theory of tools?

Vocabulary Study

Find the synonyms for the following words:

1. *psychosomatic*
2. *transitoriness*
3. *corpulence*
4. *aesthetic*
5. *amenities*
6. *homogenization*
7. *convivial*
8. *usurp*
9. *culinary*
10. *propensity*

Suggestions for Writing

1. Analyze your preference for a certain make or size of automobile, or a comparable product or tool. Discuss as many causes of your preference as you can, and present them in the order of their importance.
2. Discuss your eating habits, or those of your family, with attention to the role of the refrigerator in shaping these habits.
3. Discuss a possible change in American eating or consumption habits or recreation that in your opinion would improve the quality of American life. Explain your reasons as Rodden does.

Definition

There are many ways to define a word, each depending on your purpose in writing and on the knowledge of your readers. In defining a cow for a child, it may be enough to point to one in a pasture or picture book. In a formal discussion you may point to a cow through words: first by relating it to the class *animal*, then stating the *specific differences* between the cow and all other animals: "the mature female of domestic cattle (genus Bos)" (*Webster's New World Dictionary*). Also, you could explain that *cow* can refer to the female elephant or whale and some other female animals.

These definitions are called *denotative* because they point to the object or single it out from all others. *Connotative* definitions by contrast refer to ideas and feelings associated with the word. Denotative definitions are the same for everyone; connotative definitions are not. To some people *cow* suggests laziness, or stupidity; others may associate a cow with feelings of nourishment and contentment.

If you want to explain the origin or derivation of a word, perhaps for the purpose of explaining current meanings, you may state its etymology. The word *coward* derives from the idea of an animal whose tail hangs between its legs. The etymology illuminates one or more connotations of the word. You may, if you wish, propose or stipulate a new word for an idea or discovery. In the thirties Congressman Maury Maverick proposed the word *gobbledygook* as a description for pretentious, involved official writing. Such definitions may gain general acceptance. Some definitions remain in use for years, only to fall into disuse as new discoveries are made and new ideas appear, and better terms are invented to describe them.

How complete the definition is depends on its purpose in the essay, as well as on the reader. For one kind of reader it may not be necessary to point to or single out an object: the writer will assume that the reader knows what the object is, and needs only to be told how it works. Parts of the object (the blade casing of a manual lawn mower) may be defined fully in the course of describing how to care for or fix it; other parts may not be defined because they are unimportant to the process. It may be enough to tell readers of novels written about the 1920s that the Pierce-Arrow is an expensive automobile, or you may give one or two distinctive qualities of the Pierce-Arrow to explain an allusion to it.

August Heckscher

DOING CHORES

August Heckscher, born in 1913 in Huntington, New York, worked for many years as a newspaper editor and as an editorial writer for the *New York Tribune*. He served as director of the Twentieth Century Fund, president of the Woodrow Wilson Foundation, and administrator of recreation and cultural affairs for New York City. His writings include numerous essays and books on public affairs, including *Open Spaces: The Life of American Cities* (1977) and *When LaGuardia Was Mayor: New York's Legendary Years* (1978). His essay on chores is one of several essays in this text concerning the nature of work.

I have been doing chores, being for a brief spell alone   1
in a house that recently was astir with bustle and echoed
with the voices of a gathered family. For those who may
be in some doubt as to the nature of chores, their variety, their pleasures and their drudgery, I am prepared to
deliver a short disquisition.

The first point about chores is that they are repetitive.   2
They come every day or thereabouts, and once done they
require after a certain time to be done again. In this regard
a chore is the very opposite of a "happening"—that
strange sort of event which a few years back was so much

in fashion. For a happening was in essence unrepeatable; it came about in ways no one could predict, taking form from vaporous imaginings or sudden impulse. Chores, by contrast, can be foreseen in advance; for better or worse, I know that tomorrow I must be re-enacting the same small round of ritualistic deeds; and they arise, moreover, from practical necessities, not from poetic flights.

A second point about chores is that they leave no visi-   3
ble mark of improvement or progress behind them. When I am finished, things will be precisely as they were before—except that the fires will have been set, the garbage disposed of, and the garden weeded. In this, they are different from the works which optimistically I undertake. Ozymandias may have been presumptuous, but he was essentially right when he looked about him and said: *"See how my works endure!"* A work, once achieved, leaves a mark upon the world; nothing is ever quite the same again. The page of a book may have been printed or a page of manuscript written; a sketch, a poem, a song composed; or perhaps some happy achievement reached in one of the more evanescent art forms like the dance or cooking. All these have an existence of their own, outside of time, and at least for a little while live on in the mind of their creator and perhaps a few of his friends.

The well-meaning wife, seeing her husband about his   4
chores, will miss the character of his performance. "Henry loves to cut wood," she will say; "he positively dotes on controlling the flow of waste from dinner-table to compost heap." The wife is perhaps trying to appease an unnecessary sense of guilt at seeing her spouse engaged in mundane efforts. The fact is, he doesn't love doing chores. But neither does he feel humiliated or out of sorts for having to do them. The nature of a chore is that it is neither pleasant nor unpleasant in itself; it is entirely neutral— but it is obligatory.

Neutral—and yet I must confess that with their repe-   5
tition, and perhaps because of their very inconsequence, chores can in the end evoke a mild sort of satisfaction.

Here, as in more heroic fields of endeavor, a certain basic craft asserts itself. To do what must be done neatly, efficiently, expeditiously—"without rest and without haste"—lights a small fire deep in the interior being and puts a man in good humor with the world. Santayana described leisure as "being at home among manageable things"; and if he was right we who are the chore-doers of the world are the true leisure classes. At least one can be sure that no chore will defeat us; none will raise insuperable obstacles, or leave us deflated as when the divine muse abandons her devotee.

A man I know became seduced by the minor pleasure 6
of doing chores—or at any rate by the absence of pain which they involve—and could be seen from morning till nightfall trotting about his small domain, putting everything in order, setting everything to rights that the slow process of time had disturbed. He was perhaps going too far. To season chores with work, and to intersperse them with a few happenings, is the secret of a contented existence. Fortunate the man or woman who achieves a just balance between these three types of activity—as I have been able to do by good chance, and for a little space of time.

Comment

Whereas Maya Angelou writes concretely about the experience of work in an Alabama community, Heckscher writes in general terms. His purpose is to define one kind of happiness. That definition, coming in the final paragraph, takes the form of a general comment on the three activities discussed in the essay—chores, work, and happenings: "To season chores with work, and to intersperse them with a few happenings, is the secret of a contented existence." Heckscher builds to this thesis instead of beginning with it, because his point about these activities would not be clear without his having defined and illustrated them.

Questions for Study and Discussion

1. What are the differences between chores and work? Has Heckscher given a meaning to *work* different from your own? Do you ordinarily describe chores as work?
2. How does Heckscher introduce the essay? Does he merely state the subject—or does he also hint at his thesis?
3. Could the second point about chores (paragraph 3) have been discussed before the first?
4. Is Heckscher writing to a general audience or to a special one—perhaps husbands who perform weekend chores? What is his purpose in writing—to reflect on his personal experience, to inform his readers about work and chores, or to persuade them to change their thinking about work or their way of performing it?
5. Do you agree that chores can provide "a mild sort of satisfaction"?

Vocabulary Study

1. Read Shelley's poem "Ozymandias," and in a short paragraph discuss Heckscher's reference to it in his essay.
2. Compare the dictionary meaning of the italicized word with the word following it in parentheses. Be ready to explain how the parenthesized word changes the meaning of the sentence:

   a. *disquisition* (sermon) [paragraph 1]
   b. *ritualistic* (habitual) [paragraph 2]
   c. *presumptuous* (conceited) [paragraph 3]
   d. *evanescent* (changing) [paragraph 3]
   e. *dotes on* (enjoys) [paragraph 4]
   f. *mundane* (ordinary) [paragraph 4]
   g. *neutral* (uninteresting) [paragraph 4]
   h. *expeditiously* (speedily) [paragraph 5]
   i. *deflated* (tired); *devotee* (fan) [paragraph 5]
   j. *domain* (household) [paragraph 6]

Suggestions for Writing

1. Discuss how accurately Heckscher's definitions fit the various kinds of work you perform at home. In the course of your essay, discuss how closely your idea of happiness agrees with Heckscher's.
2. Discuss daily activities at home and at school that you do not consider chores, and explain why.
3. About chores, Heckscher states: "Here, as in more heroic fields of endeavor, a certain basic craft asserts itself." Discuss the "basic craft" of a chore that you perform regularly. Contrast this "craft" with work that you also perform regularly.
4. Write your own definition of a contented existence, comparing your ideas and experiences with Heckscher's if you wish.

✦

Classification and Division

Classification and division are important methods of analysis in exposition. Repair manuals classify various tools into broad groups like drills, then explain the uses of individual drills. When you classify you arrange individual objects into broad groups or classes. Hardware stores, for example, shelve tools according to classes—hammers, drills, wrenches, pliers, and so on.

Division arranges the members of a general class into subclasses according to various principles. The division may be formal or scientific, as in the textbook or dictionary division of fleshy fruits like apples and oranges, drupaceous fruits (those with pits at the center) like cherries and peaches, and dry fruits like peas and nuts. The class to be divided may be as broad as *fruit* or as narrow as *apples* (a member of one of the subclasses of fruit).

The division of the class is made on a single basis or principle. For example, apples can be divided according to color, use, variety, or taste, to cite a few possible divisions:

by color: red apples, green apples, yellow apples, and so on
by use: eating apples, cooking apples, and so on
by variety: Golden Delicious, Jonathan, Winesap, and so on
by taste: sweet, tart, winy, and so on

The principle of division depends on the purpose of the analysis. In instructing people what apples to buy for baking pies, you would divide apples according to variety, then perhaps according to taste. The color of the skin would not be important.

The division need be only as complete as your purpose requires: you might only distinguish tart from sweet and winy apples without naming the varieties. It is sometimes important to note that the division is not exhaustive. You might mention one or two varieties of tart apples like Jonathans and Granny Smiths, noting that other tart varieties are out of season. If you divide apples in more than one way in the course of the essay (for example, dividing according to taste as well as variety), each division should be separate.

Michele Huzicka

ON WAITING IN LINE

Michele Huzicka wrote the following essay in her first year at the University of Akron. She uses informal division simply and effectively, distinguishing types of students and experiences she encountered at various times of the day.

At one time or another, in the course of an average   1
day, all of us must wait in some sort of line. In these lines we can learn much about ourselves and one another before we reach our destination. I wait in line often on campus—most often at meal time in the dining room.

As we all know, there are those who can be called   2
"morning people" and there are those who cannot. Morning people don't mind getting up early. They are cheery, pleasant, organized, and attentive—all without a hair out of place or the least bit of sleep left in their eyes. The non-morning people loathe the morning people for these qualities. When the two come together in a line for breakfast, turbulent feelings may arise. For this reason the breakfast line is relatively quiet, compared to other lines. People would rather not run the risk of sparking ill-feelings so early in the morning. However, if the same people were to meet later in the day, the situation would probably be entirely different.

The lunch line is probably the most pleasant of all the   3
lines we must cope with on campus. The majority of students are now fully awake. The non-morning people no

longer feel muddled or groggy; they are now simply "people"—people waiting in line. Idle chatter about one's next class or one's hometown or mutual friends is a good distraction from what would otherwise be a very boring wait. It is here at lunch that we are forced to break away from our little cliques and explore the possibility that there are people different from ourselves. So we meet new people and learn about different classes on campus and about different towns and cities in Ohio. We even listen to trivial details just for the sake of having something to do.

In the dinner line I can see people once again returning to the security of their friends as I join mine. It is always this line that seems to move the fastest as we recap the day's events, gossip about friends, analyze new boyfriends, and plan for the evening ahead. It is not surprising to look around and see other little groups doing very much the same thing. Talk of this sort is the most entertaining of the day.

Other lines, too, weave their way into our everyday lives. Depending upon their location and the time of day, they can most definitely be quite uncomfortable and dull, or they can be adventurous discoveries about other people. Waiting in line at any time of day, we constantly learn new things about ourselves and other people. We are forced to be with masses of people who share one common goal—getting to the start of the line.

Comment

Michele Huzicka might have chosen another basis of division in her essay. Had she noticed differences in how students wait in different kinds of lines, for instance, she might have divided on that basis. Those waiting to register for classes perhaps behave differently from those waiting in a cafeteria. Huzicka began writing her essay with an observation that she wanted to develop and a sense of college life that she wanted to express. Her thesis occurred to her in the act of reporting that observation. At another time, she might have begun her essay with a general idea or thesis that she wished to illustrate and then searched her experience for examples.

Questions for Study and Discussion

1. How does Huzicka introduce her subject? How early in the essay does she state her thesis?
2. Huzicka writes both informatively and expressively. What does she reveal about her personality and interests in characterizing people and lines?
3. In what other ways might Huzicka have divided students standing in line? What other purposes might such divisions have?

Suggestions for Writing

1. Write an essay of your own on the same topic—on standing in line. Use classification or division at some point in the essay or throughout. Use your discussion to develop an idea as Huzicka does.
2. Write an essay characterizing people on another basis, drawing on your personal experience. Use classification or division to develop your essay.
3. Use classification or division to develop an essay on one of the following topics or another of your choosing:

   a. On writing essays
   b. On sitting in college classes
   c. On first living away from home
   d. On making repairs
   e. On studying for exams

PART 2

Strategies for Expressive Writing

For dinner, Mama
would send me
to the field with
a basket over
my arm to get
a dozen ears
of corn, some
cucumbers, and
tomatos.

—Mary E. Mebane

You have probably scribbled words or made designs in your notebook in an absent moment at home or at school. Perhaps you doodle on the edges of a newspaper or magazine as you listen to the stereo or watch television. Like this absent-minded scrawling, much writing has the purpose of personal expression, the play of the mind for its own sake. For instance, a rambling letter from a friend may jump from one experience to another without obvious transition. Your friend wrote the letter to share feelings and thoughts of the moment, and you may do the same in responding.

Other kinds of expressive writing are more organized. A journal entry, a statement of personal belief, an essay recalling a personal experience, a letter expressing pleasure or anger—these are different kinds of personal expression, and they may be organized in various ways for various purposes. For different audiences, you may choose a different order of ideas and details appropriate to a particular audience.

A journal entry, for example, is written for your own use, and that use determines the order in which you record impressions and ideas. You may keep the journal as a strictly chronological record of a trip or a loose compilation of facts collected for a paper. In contrast, a letter of protest is expressive in voicing anger at an unjust law; the order of ideas and details will be shaped by your feelings of the moment—and would probably be quite different from a letter written to urge a change in the law. The statement of personal belief, too, will be shaped by the thoughts and feelings you want to stress as well as by considerations of audience. Writing to a familiar audience, you might include personal details that an unfamiliar audience might neither understand nor appreciate.

In the following essay, Gloria Emerson's purpose in describing her parachute jump is to share the pleasure and surprise of the experience: "Everyone at the center was pleased; in fact, I am sure they were surprised. Perhaps this is what I had in mind all the time." Her purpose is therefore expressive, though she does give us information about sky diving. She presents enough details about the jump to allow us to imagine the experience. But these details are not presented separately from her description of her feelings. The essay focuses on these feelings throughout. Had Emerson wanted merely to give information about sky diving, the focus of her essay would have been different.

No doubt Emerson discovered new feelings and meanings as she wrote. In writing your own essays, you will probably make similar discoveries; indeed, you may discover a purpose you did not have in mind when you began writing. A piece of writing often changes in focus and organization as you put words on paper. Because expressive writing so often incorporates new discoveries and insights, this form of the essay is sometimes more open and organized more loosely than informative and persuasive essays. The writer of the expressive essay wishes to convey the openness of feeling and thought.

Gloria Emerson

TAKE THE PLUNGE . . .

Gloria Emerson worked as a foreign correspondent for the *New York Times* from 1965 to 1972, reporting on Northern Ireland, on the Nigerian Civil War, and, from 1970 to 1972, on Vietnam. She received the 1971 George Polk Award for excellence in her reporting from Vietnam, and the 1978 National Book Award for her book about the Vietnam War, *Winners and Losers*. Her most recent book is *Some American Men* (1985). The feelings she describes in this essay on sky diving require the most careful mounting of detail, and that is what Emerson gives us.

It was usually men who asked me why I did it. Some were amused, others puzzled. I didn't mind the jokes in the newspaper office where I worked about whether I left the building by window, roof or in the elevator. The truth is that I was an unlikely person to jump out of an airplane, being neither graceful, daring nor self-possessed. I had a bad back, uncertain ankles and could not drive with competence because of deficient depth perception and a fear of all buses coming toward me. A friend joked that if I broke my bones I would have to be shot because I would never mend.

I never knew why I did it. It was in May, a bright and dull May, the last May that made me want to feel reckless. But there was nothing to do then at the beginning of a decade that changed almost everything. I could not wait that May for the Sixties to unroll. I worked in women's news; my stories came out like little cookies. I wanted to be brave about something, not just about love, or a root canal, or writing that the shoes at Arnold Constable looked strangely sad.

Once I read of men who had to run so far it burned   3
their chests to breathe. But I could not run very far. Jumping from a plane, which required no talent or endurance, seemed perfect. I wanted to feel the big, puzzling lump on my back that they promised was a parachute, to take serious strides in the absurd black boots that I believed all generals wore.

I wanted all of it: the rising of a tiny plane with the   4
door off, the earth rushing away, the plunge, the slap of the wind, my hands on the back straps, the huge curve of white silk above me, the drift through the space we call sky.

It looked pale green that morning I fell into it, not the   5
baby blue I expected. I must have been crying; my cheeks were wet. Only the thumps of a wild heart made noise; I did not know how to keep it quiet.

That May, that May my mind was as clear as clay. I   6
did not have the imagination to perceive the risks, to understand that if the wind grew nasty I might be electrocuted on high-tension wires, smashed on a roof, drowned in water, hanged in a tree. I was sure nothing would happen, because my intentions were so good, just as young soldiers start out certain of their safety because they know nothing.

Friends drove me to Orange, Massachusetts, seventy   7
miles west of Boston, for the opening of the first U.S. sports parachuting center, where I was to perform. It was the creation, the passion, of a Princetonian and ex-Marine named Jacques Istel, who organized the first U.S. jumping team in 1956. Parachuting was ''as safe as swimming,'' he kept saying, calling it the ''world's most stimulating and soul-satisfying sport.'' His center was for competitions and the teaching of skydiving. Instead of hurtling toward

the earth, sky divers maintain a swan-dive position, using the air as a cushion to support them while they maneuver with leg and arm movements until the rip cord must
be pulled.

None of that stuff was expected from any of us in the   8
little beginners class. We were only to jump, after brief
but intense instruction, with Istel's newly designed
parachute, to show that any dope could do it. It was a
parachute with a thirty-two-foot canopy; a large cutout
hole funneled escaping air. You steered with two wooden
knobs instead of having to pull hard on the back straps,
or risers. The new parachute increased lateral speed,
slowed down the rate of descent, reduced oscillation. We
were told we could even land standing up but that we
should bend our knees and lean to one side. The beginners jumped at eight a.m., the expert sky divers performed
their dazzling tricks later when a crowd came.

Two of us boarded a Cessna 180 that lovely morning,   9
the wind no more than a tickle. I was not myself, no longer
thin and no longer fast. The jump suit, the equipment,
the helmet, the boots, had made me into someone thick
and clumsy, moving as strangely as if they had put me
underwater and said I must walk. It was hard to bend,
to sit, to stand up. I did not like the man with me; he
was eager and composed. I wanted to smoke, to go the
bathroom, but there were many straps around me that I
did not understand. At twenty-three hundred feet, the
hateful, happy man went out, making a dumb thumbs-
up sign.

When my turn came, I suddenly felt a stab of pain for   10
all the forgotten soldiers who balked and were kicked out,
perhaps shot, for their panic and for delaying the troops.
I was hooked to a static line, an automatic opening device,
which made it impossible to lie down or tie myself to
something. The drillmaster could not hear all that I
shouted at him. But he knew the signs of mutiny and
removed my arms from his neck. He took me to the doorway, sat me down, and yelled "Go!" or "Now!" or
"Out!" There was nothing to do but be punched by the

wind, which knocked the spit from my mouth, reach for the wing strut, hold on hard, kick back the feet so weighted and helpless in those boots, and let go. The parachute opened with a plop, as Istel had sworn to me that it would. When my eyelids opened as well, I saw the white gloves on my hands were old ones from Saks Fifth Avenue, gloves I wore with summer dresses. There was dribble on my chin; my eyes and nose were leaking. I wiped everything with the gloves.

There was no noise; the racket of the plane and wind   11 had gone away. The cold and sweet stillness seemed an astonishing, undreamed-of gift. Then I saw what I had never seen before, will never see again; endless sky and earth in colors and textures no one had ever described. Only then did the parachute become a most lovable and docile toy: this wooden knob to go left, this wooden knob to go right. The pleasure of being there, the drifting and the calm, rose to a fever; I wanted to stay pinned in the air and stop the ground from coming closer. The target was a huge arrow in a sandpit. I was cross to see it, afraid of nothing now, for even the wind was kind and the trees looked soft. I landed on my feet in the pit with a bump, then sat down for a bit. Later that day I was taken over to meet General James Gavin, who had led the 82nd Airborne in the D-day landing at Normandy. Perhaps it was to prove to him that the least promising pupil, the gawkiest, could jump. It did not matter that I stumbled and fell before him in those boots, which walked with a will of their own. Later, Mr. Istel's mother wrote a charming note of congratulations. Everyone at the center was pleased; in fact, I am sure they were surprised. Perhaps this is what I had in mind all the time.

Questions for Study and Discussion

1. What is Emerson's purpose in writing? Does she state her purpose directly, or do you discover it from her approach to the subject and her focus? What were her motives in making the jump?

2. What details does she provide about the operation of the parachute, the descent, and the landing? How are these details fitted to the discussion of her feelings at various stages in her experience? What are these stages?
3. How does she maintain the focus on her feelings throughout the essay? Do these feelings change?
4. Would you have reacted to the parachute jump as Emerson did? What comparable experience aroused similar expectations and feelings in you?

Vocabulary Study

1. Emerson uses a number of technical terms, among them *rip cord, static line,* and *wing strut.* See whether your dictionary—or an unabridged dictionary—contains these. If you do not find them listed, state how the essay clarifies their meaning. Notice that we do not always require a complete definition of a term to understand its purpose or role in the process. Is that true of these terms?
2. Explain the italicized words and phrases:
   a. "The truth is that I was an unlikely person to jump out of an airplane, being neither graceful, daring nor *self-possessed.*"
   b. "That May, that May my mind was as *clear as clay.*"
   c. "Instead of *hurtling* toward the earth, sky divers maintain a *swan-dive position,* using the air *as a cushion* to support them while they *maneuver with leg and arm movements* until the rip cord must be pulled."

Suggestions for Writing

1. Describe an experience with a complex piece of equipment like a parachute. You might discuss the problems encountered in assembling it, or other difficulties it created for you.
2. Describe an experience comparable to the one Emerson describes. Explain your motives in undertaking the experience, and trace the stages of the experience as Emerson does, giving an account of your feelings at each stage.

Autobiography

In the autobiographical essay, the writer seeks to reach personal understanding by recalling vital experiences of the past. Virginia Woolf tells us that the nineteenth-century English writer Thomas De Quincey "understood by autobiography the history not only of the external life but of the deeper and more hidden emotions." Woolf uses this idea to define the art of the autobiographer:

> To tell the whole story of a life the autobiographer must devise some means by which the two levels of existence can be recorded—the rapid passage of events and actions; the slow opening up of single and solemn moments of concentrated emotion. —"De Quincey's Autobiography"

We see this art in the four autobiographical essays that follow. Mary E. Mebane re-creates the world of her North Carolina childhood through a description of daily chores and family life, Annie Dillard narrates girlhood experiences shared with her father, John Gould recalls the ways he used to repair a bicycle, and Leonard Kriegel describes the effort to overcome crippling effects of polio. In the autobiographical essay, authors often reach insights about themselves in concentrating upon central experiences in their past.

The autobiographical essay may serve other purposes in addition to recalling the past and expressing personal feelings and insights. In re-creating the past, Mebane informs us about growing up black in America. Kriegel gives his essay an argumentative edge in questioning values that gave him strength to deal with physical handicaps.

Annie Dillard

MY FATHER

Annie Dillard describes her early life in Pittsburgh in her autobiography *An American Childhood* (1987), from which the following account of her father is taken. Dillard later lived in the Roanoke Valley of Virginia, and she describes her experiences there in *Pilgrim at Tinker Creek* (1974), awarded the Pulitzer Prize for General Non-Fiction in 1975. A chapter from this book appears in Part 4. Dillard is also the author of *Tickets for a Prayer Wheel* (1974), *Teaching a Stone to Talk* (1982), and *Living by Fiction* (1982).

Years before this, on long-ago summer Sundays, be-   1
fore Father went down the Ohio and ended up selling his boat, he used to take me out with him on the water. It was a long drive to the Allegheny River; it was a long wait, collecting insects in the grass among the pebbles on shore, till Father got the old twenty-four-foot cabin cruiser ready to go. But the Allegheny River, once we got out on it, was grand. Its distant shores were mostly wooded on both sides; coal barges, sand barges, and shallow-draft oil tankers floated tied up at a scattering of docks. Father wore tennis shoes on his long feet, and a sun-bleached cotton captain-style hat. He always squinted outside, hat or no hat, because his eyes were such a pale blue; the sun got in them. He was so tall he had to lean under the housetop to man the wheel.

We stopped at islands and swam. There were wooded   2
islands in the river—like Smoky Island at Pittsburgh's point, where Indians had tortured their English and Scotch-Irish captives by night. The Indians had tied the soldiers and settlers to trees, heaped hot coals on their feet, and let their small boys practice archery on them. Indian women heated rifle barrels and ramrods over fires till they glowed, then drove them through prisoners' nostrils or ears. The screams of the tortured settlers on Smoky Island reached French soldiers at Fort Duquesne, who had handed them over to the Indians reluctantly, they said. "Humanity groans at being forced to use such monsters."

Father and I tied up at Nine-Mile Island, upstream   3
from Smoky Island, and I jumped from a high rope-swing
into the water, after poor Father told me all about those
boaters' children who'd been killed or maimed dropping
from this very swing. He could not bear to watch; he shut
his eyes. From the tree branch at the top of the ladder
I jumped onto the swing; when I let go over the water,
momentum shot me forward like a slung stone. I swam
up to find the water's surface again, and called to Father
onshore, "It's okay now."

Our boat carved through the glossy water. Pittsburgh's   4
summer skies are pale, as they are in many river valleys.
The blinding haze spread overhead and glittered up from
the river. It was the biggest sky in town.

We rode up in the locks and down in the locks. The   5
locks scared me, for the huge doors that locked out the
river leaked, and loud tons of water squirted in, and we
sat helpless below the river with nothing to do but wait
for the doors to give way. Enormous whirlpools dragged
at the boat; we held on to the lock walls, clawed, with
a single hand line and a boat hook. Once I dropped the
boat hook, a new one with a teak handle, and the whirlpools sucked it down. To where? Where did the whirlpools
put the water they took, and where would they put you,
all ground up, if you fell in?

Oh, the river was grand. Outside the lock and back   6
on the go, I sang wild songs at the top of my voice out
over the roaring boat's stern. We raced under old steel
bridges set on stone pilings in the river. How do people
build bridges? How did anyone set those pilings, pile those
stones, under the water?

Whenever I was on the river, I seemed to be visiting a   7
fascinating place I had forgotten all about, where physical
causes had physical effects, and great things got done,
slowly, heavily, because people understood materials and
forces.

Father on these boat outings answered my questions at   8
length. He explained that people built coffer dams to set
bridge pilings in a river. They lowered a kind of big pipe,

or tight set of walls, to the bottom, and pumped all the water out of it; then the men could work there. I imagined the men piling and mortaring stones, with the unhurried ease of stone masons; they stood on gasping catfish and stinky silt. They were working under the river, at the bottom of a well of air. Just a few inches away, outside their coffer dam, a complete river of water was sliding downhill from western New York to the Gulf of Mexico. Above the workers' heads, boats and barges went by, their engines probably buzzing the coffer-dam walls. What a life. Father said that some drowned in accidents, or got crushed; it was dangerous work. He said, answering my question, that these workers made less money than the men I knew, men I privately considered wholly unskilled. The bridge pilings obsessed me; I thought and thought about the brave men who built them in the rivers. I tried to imagine their families, their lunches, their boots. I tried to imagine what it would feel like to accomplish something so useful as building a bridge. What a queer world was the river, where I admired everything and knew nothing.

Father explained how to make glass from sand. He explained, over and over, because I was usually too frightened to hear right, how the river locks worked; they ran our boat up or down beside the terrible dams. The concrete navigation dams made slick spillways like waterfalls across the river. From upstream it was hard to see the drop's smooth line. Drunks forgot about the dams from time to time, and drove their boats straight over, killing themselves and everyone else on board. How did the drunks feel, while they were up loose in the air at the wheels of their boats for a split second, when they remembered all of a sudden the dam? "Oh yes, the dam." It seemed like a familiar feeling.

On the back of a chart—a real nautical chart, with shoals and soundings, just as in *Life on the Mississippi*—Father drew a diagram of a water system. The diagram made clear something I'd always wondered about: how water got up to the top floors of houses. The water tower was higher than the highest sinks, that was all; through all those labyrinthine pipes, the water sought its own level, seeming to climb up, but really still trickling down. He explained how steam engines worked, and suspension bridges, and pumps.

Father explained so much technology to me that for a   11
long time I confused it with American culture. If pressed, I would have claimed that an American invented the irrigation ditch. Certainly the coffer dam was American, I thought, and the water tower, the highway tunnel—these engineering feats—and everything motorized, and everything electrical, and in short, everything I saw about me newer than fishnets, sailboats, and spoons.

Technology depended on waterworks. The land of the   12
forty-eight states was an extended and mighty system of controlled slopes, a combination Grand Coulee Dam and Niagara Falls. The water fell and the turbines spun and the lights came on, so steel mills could run all night. Then the steel made cars, millions of cars, and workers bought the cars, because Henry Ford in 1910 had come up with the idea of paying them enough to buy things. So the water rolled down the continent—just plain fell—and everyone got rich.

Now, years later, Father had picked Amy and me up   13
after church. When we got out of the car in the garage, we could hear Dixieland, all rambling brasses and drums, coming from the house. We hightailed it inside through the snow on the back walk and kicked off our icy dress shoes. I was in stockings. I could eat something, and go to my room. I had my own room now, and when I was home I stayed there and read or sulked.

While we were making sandwiches, though, Father   14
started explaining the world to us once again. I stuck around. There in the kitchen, Father embarked upon an explanation of American economics. I don't know what prompted it. His voice took on urgency; he paced. Money worked like water, he said.

We were all listening, even little Molly. Molly, at four,   15
had an open expression, smooth and quick, and fine blond

hair; she was eating on the hoof, like the rest of us, and looking up, a pale face at thigh level, following the conversation. Mother futzed around the kitchen in camel-colored wool slacks; she rarely ate.

Did we know how water got up to our attic bathroom? 16 Money worked the same way, he said, worked the way locks on the river worked, worked the way water flowed down from high water towers into our attic bathroom, the way the Allegheny and the Monongahela flowed into the Ohio, and the Ohio flowed into the Mississippi and out into the Gulf of Mexico at New Orleans. The money, once you got enough of it high enough, would flow by gravitation, all over everybody.

"It doesn't work that way," our mother said. She of- 17 fered Molly tidbits: a drumstick, a beet slice, cheese. "Remember those shacks we see in Georgia? Those barefoot little children who have to quit school to work in the fields, their poor mothers not able to feed them enough"—we could all hear in her voice that she was beginning to cry—"not even able to keep them dressed?" Molly was looking at her, wide-eyed; she was bent over looking at Molly, wide-eyed.

"They shouldn't have so many kids," Father said. 18 "They must be crazy."

The trouble was, I no longer believed him. It was be- 19 ginning to strike me that Father, who knew the real world so well, got some of it wrong. Not much; just some.

Comment

The writer of autobiography may narrate a personal history to make a point or argue a thesis. Other writers give us an account of their lives without developing a thesis, though they usually interpret events and may make comparisons with present-day life. Benjamin Franklin wrote his famous autobiography as a lesson on how to succeed in the world, his "having emerged from the poverty and obscurity in which I was born and bred to a state of affluence and some degree of reputation in the world." By contrast, Mark Twain, in his autobiographical *Life on the Mississippi*, had no intention of making his own life a model for others; he wanted instead to re-create the Missouri river town of his youth and recall his experiences as a cub pilot on the Mississippi. Like Twain, Annie Dillard also describes the river town of her youth and experiences that shaped her life. And like Twain, she is not presenting her life as exemplary; but she does make discoveries that tell us something about family relationships and the world in general.

Questions for Study and Discussion

1. Why does Dillard give us the history of Smoky Island? Does she wish to tell us something about her father, or the Pittsburgh of her youth, or her experiences on the Allegheny River? Or does this history serve another purpose?
2. What do her experiences on Nine-Mile Island and the conversations with her father tell you about their relationship?
3. What does the final episode reveal about her mother and family relaltionships?
4. What did her father get right about the world, and what did he get wrong? Is Dillard referring to the information he gave about dam building, water systems, and other technical matters, or to something else?

Vocabulary Study

1. How do the details of paragraph 4 explain the description of the river as *glossy*?
2. How do the details of paragraph 8 help to explain the term *coffer dam*?
3. What are *shoals* and *soundings* (paragraph 10)?
4. What does the statement "His voice took on urgency; he paced" mean (paragraph 14)?

Suggestions for Writing

1. Write an essay about a discovery you made about someone, giving details of the exprerience. Let your details reveal the discovery to your readers. Interpret the details as little as possible.
2. Describe a place—a river, an island, a neighborhood street, a city building—that has been important in your life. Let your details about the place reveal why it has been important.

Mary E. Mebane

THE RHYTHM OF LIFE

Born in Durham, North Carolina, in 1933, Mary E. Mebane grew up in a segregated world in which her parents struggled to make a living. Her mother worked in a tobacco factory and did housework; her father farmed and sold junk. Mebane tells us at the end of her autobiography, *Mary:* " I made it the main aim of my life to find someone who was understanding and sensitive, and to find an environment in which I could develop and flourish. Beyond me lay the great world, the white world, the world that I had been taught was my implacable enemy. I didn't know how I was going to get out, but I was going to try. I had to." Encouraged by her aunt, Mebane entered college in Durham, receiving a B.A. from North Carolina College. She later received an M.A. and Ph.D. from the University of North Carolina at Chapel Hill. She has taught at various universities in the United States. In this self-contained section from her autobiography, Mebane describes some of the happy experiences of her childhood. Jesse is her older brother, Ruf Junior her younger brother.

Life had a natural, inexorable rhythm. On weekdays,   1
Mama went to work at a tobacco factory. On Saturdays, early in the morning, we washed clothes. We washed clothes outdoors. First Mama and Jesse drew buckets of water from the well and poured it into the washpot. It was a big iron pot that stood on three legs and was very black from soot. Mama put paper and twigs under it and

poured kerosene on them. They blazed up and soon there was blue smoke curling all around the pot. She put all the "white" things in the pot—sheets and pillowcases and underwear—and put Oxydol in with the clothes. I was puzzled because most of the things she put in with the "white" clothes were colored. Our sheets were made from flour sacks and had red or green or blue patterns on them. Some of the underwear was colored, too.

My job was to stand over the pot and "chunk" the   2
clothes down to keep the water from boiling over and putting out the fire. I loved my job. I had a big stick, and sometimes I stood there and "dobbed and dobbed" the clothes up and down all the morning.

Then Mama and Jesse drew water and filled up two   3
large tin tubs. One was to wash clothes in; the other was the first rinse. Then there was a foot tub that was for the second rinse, the one with the bluing in it. Sometimes Mama let me melt the bluing, which came in a long, flat cake.

Then there was an even smaller pot, full of starch—   4
cooked flour and water—with a heavy translucent skim on it. It was my job to skim it and throw the heavy part away. I loved that job, too.

After the clothes boiled and boiled, Mama would get a   5
big stick and carry them a few at a time from the washpot to the washing and rinsing tubs. Then she would put more clothes in the washpot, add water and more Oxydol, and I would dob some more. Sometimes instead of dobbing I "jugged" the clothes—that is, dobbed from side to side.

While the second pot of clothes was boiling, I helped   6
Mama with the wash. There was a big washboard in the first tub and a smaller one in the second tub (that was the first rinse). Mama washed with a big cake of lye soap that she had made, rubbing up and down the washboard. The lye soap sometimes made tiny holes in her fingers. Then I rubbed the clothes up and down in the first rinse, which got the suds out; next I stirred them around and pulled them up and down in the bluing water. Then Mama wrung them out. Some things she starched. She hung

them up high on the clothesline. By that time the second pot of boiling clothes was ready and we started all over again. Later in the morning she put in the "heavy things" to boil—overalls and her blue factory uniforms and the blankets. While they boiled, we ate dinner, the noon meal.

For dinner, Mama would send me to the field with a basket over my arm to get a dozen ears of corn, some cucumbers, and tomatoes. I would shuck the corn, pulling the long green hard leaves off, next the lighter green inner leaves, then the silk in long yellow strands. Ruf Junior helped to silk it; then Mama would go over it again. She would let me slice the tomatoes and put mayonnaise on them, and slice the cucumbers and put vinegar, salt, and black pepper on them. But I didn't want to slice the onions because they made me cry, so Mama would slice them in with the cucumbers herself. She sliced the corn off the cob into a big frying pan, full of hot grease. Then we ate the fried corn with tomatoes and cucumber and onions, and a hunk of corn bread, and a big mayonnaise jar full of buttermilk, and a piece of pork.

Sometimes Mama put on a "pot." It cooked a long time on the back of the wood stove. Sometimes it cooked all day. It cooked all the while we were washing, and when we came in we had a steaming plate of turnip greens with tomatoes and cucumbers and onions. Sometimes it was cabbage, yellow from having cooked so long. (I didn't like the yellowish cabbage or the orangey rutabagas.) Sometimes it was string beans. If we didn't have a pot, we had something quick, like fried squash with onions. Mama put on a pot of meat to go with the pot of vegetables. Often it was neck bones or pig feet or pig ears. Sometimes we had pork slices, swimming in red gravy. She would put on a pie at dinner, blackberry or apple, so it would be ready at suppertime; we had lemon meringue pie only on Sunday. We sometimes had sweet-potato custard through the week, also.

After dinner we went back out in the yard. By then the heavy things had boiled, and Mama took them on a large stick to the washtub. The water in the tub was gray now, with a high meringue of foam on it. But she rubbed and I rinsed, and she hung out the clothes high, but now she gave me the socks and sweaters to hang on the bushes. She sent me to see if any of the clothes were "hard," and I went to the line and lowered the stick that was holding it up. I took down the clothes that had been in the sun so long that they were dry and stiff. I took them in the house and put them on the bed. Then Mama went over to the field to look at her crop, leaving me to churn.

I put the gallon jars of sweet milk into the tall churn,   10 using a stick shaped funny at the bottom. Then I jugged it up and down, up and down, looking every few minutes to see if the butter had come. If it hadn't, I jugged some more. Mama would be over in the field a long time and then she would come and say, "The butter come yet?" And I'd look up and say, "No, ma'am," and churn some more. When the butter came, she scooped it up and shaped it into a cake.

For supper we had what was left in the pot from din-   11 ner, along with a pie Mama had put on then, and a glass of buttermilk, and corn bread.

Before supper, Mama would get out two heavy irons   12 and put them on the hot part of the stove. Then she'd tell me to go sprinkle the clothes. I would take some water and wet the clothes down and then roll them into a ball. That would soften them up some and make the wrinkles come out easier. After supper, Mama would start to iron on a big ironing board that had burned places at the end where the iron stood. I couldn't lift the real heavy iron, but she would let me have the small iron and I would push it up and down a handkerchief or a pair of socks, glad to be a woman like Mama.

She would fold the clothes and put them in a drawer   13 and put the sheets and pillowcases on the beds. By that time the flies and mosquitoes would be buzzing the lamp. When she finished she would go out on the porch and sit in the cool, with the basket of butter beans to be shelled for Sunday dinner. I would take a newspaper and shell right along with her, pausing occasionally to protest when Ruf Junior got a pod that I wanted.

After we finished shelling the beans, my eyes would 14 have sand in them and Mama would tell me to go to bed. I would go into the house and fall asleep while I heard her still moving around.

I helped Mama pick the green tomatoes for chowchow. 15 She cut up the green tomatoes, then a hill of onions while tears ran down her face. She put in green peppers and cup after cup of sugar and a bag of spice. Then she pushed the chowchow far back on the stove and let it cook. In a little while the kitchen and back porch smelled good. It was the chowchow cooking. Mama let it cook and cook until it "cooked down." By nightfall she was ready to put it in the jars that Ruf Junior and I had washed.

She canned vegetables after she came home from 16 work. There were tomatoes, which she put in hot water and scalded, then peeled; peas and corn; corn and okra; and butter beans and string beans. She put down cucumbers in a large stone jar and filled it with brine for pickles. And after we finished eating watermelon, I peeled the rinds, front and back, and Mama cooked them with sugar and we had watermelon preserve.

I washed jars and Ruf Junior washed tops; and row 17 after row of canned goods, looking just like pictures, formed on the shelves, around the sides of the back porch, and under the house.

When the truck came with the peaches, we stopped 18 everything. If it was Saturday, we didn't wash anymore or gather vegetables; if it was during the week we worked until late at night. Everybody had to help because peaches spoiled so fast. Daddy and Jesse and even Aunt Jo helped. The grown folks and Jesse had big knives. Ruf Junior and I had small paring knives. Mama didn't like Ruf Junior and me to peel because she said we left more of the peach in the peel than we put in the pot. But she let us peel, too, because if she didn't we'd holler so loud and beg so hard that she wouldn't have any peace. She picked out the soft ones, near the bottom, that had bad places on them and let us peel those. We peeled and ate and peeled and ate and went to bed full of peaches, sometimes sick.

Slopping the hogs was Jesse's job when Daddy didn't   19
do it. But sometimes if Jesse heard them squealing over
in the pigpen before it was time, he'd let Ruf Junior and
me take them something. We'd get water buckets; I'd take
a full one and Ruf Junior would have half a one, and we'd
carry slops—discarded vegetables cooked with "ship
stuff," a coarse thickening substance about the consistency
of sawdust. We'd pour it through the big spaces between
the railings into the trough and watch them eat. There
would always be four or five, and we'd beat the big ones
away with sticks so the little ones could eat. We were careful not to make too much noise because Daddy would
wonder what was happening to the hogs if he heard them
squealing too much.

Sometimes Mama would get after Ruf Junior and me   20
when she'd hear a chicken squawking and would look out
to see a hen flying across the yard with Ruf Junior and
me running after it. We didn't want to hurt her; we
wanted to play with her; but she didn't understand that
and went running for her life.

Daddy and Jesse plowed in the Bottom in the tobacco   21
and cotton. Mama and Aunt Jo hoed in the vegetables.
I hoed until I started chopping up too many plants and
Mama protested; then I joined Ruf Junior in running up
and down the rows, feeling the hot sun on the dry dirt
under my feet and the cool wet where the plow had just
been. If Ruf Junior and I were good, we could go to the
house and get cold water and bring it to the fields in half-
gallon jars.

Comment

Autobiographical writing usually expresses the writer's feelings
about the past. In this section from her autobiography, Mary
E. Mebane seeks to give us a sense of herself through the details
of her world and also through the experiences of growing up.
Like Maya Angelou, Mebane gives us the details of the everyday world so exactly that we are not likely to forget them. Most

of her readers probably never washed clothes in a pot or cooked chowchow. She is careful, therefore, to give necessary details, at the same time using these details to evoke the qualities and feelings of Southern life in the 1930s. Description and narrative combine in the essay, as they do in Angelou's.

Questions for Study and Discussion

1. What are the qualities and feelings that Mebane evokes in her description of her childhood world? What is her attitude toward that world?
2. How does her description of washing, preparing food, and other activities illustrate the "natural, inexorable rhythm" of life? How does Mebane show that these activities are inexorable?
3. How different is the impression of Southern black life in Mebane's essay from that in Angelou's? Are there significant similarities?
4. How different from Mebane's was your participation in everyday family activities such as preparing food? Did life have the same "natural, inexorable rhythm" in your growing up?

Vocabulary Study

1. Be ready to explain how Mebane helps us to discover the meaning of the following words:
   a. *chunk, dobbed* (paragraph 2)
   b. *bluing* (paragraph 3)
   c. *jugged* (paragraph 5)
   d. *shuck* (paragraph 7)
   e. *"pot"* (paragraph 8)
   f. *"hard"* (paragraph 9)
   g. *chowchow* (paragraph 15)
2. Examine the following reference books to find out how many of the above words are listed with the meaning they have in the essay:
   a. an unabridged dictionary
   b. *Dictionary of Americanisms on Historical Principles*

c. *Dictionary of American Slang*
d. *Dictionary of American English*

Suggestions for Writing

1. Write your own essay on the statement "Life had a natural, inexorable rhythm," drawing on your own childhood experiences. Make all of your details relate to this idea, and give your discussion unity by dealing with one experience at a time.
2. Like Angelou, Mebane tells us much about Southern life in general by focusing on a segment of that life and describing it in detail. Do the same with the world in which you grew up, focusing on a segment of it that you can describe fully in several pages. Define those terms and activities that your audience may not be familiar with.
3. Mebane describes the effect books, magazines, and radio programs had on her in high school: "I lived so intensely what I read in books and what I heard on the radio that even though I knew that it wasn't everyday, it was more real than everyday." Discuss reading and television experiences that had an intense effect on you during high school, and draw a conclusion from these experiences.

John Gould

ALWAYS UPHILL

The essayist and humorist John Gould has written much about New England rural life. His many essays have appeared in the *Brunswick* (Maine) *Record* and in his column for the *Christian Science Monitor*, "Dispatch from the Farm," begun in 1942. His many books include *The Jonesport Raffle* (1969), *Main Lingo* (1975), *Glass Eyes by the Bottle* (1975), and *Stitch in Time* (1985).

A news item tells us the Meddle Department of the   1
United States government has required the J. C. Penney
people to call back a batch of bicycles. Something about

these bicycles can come apart, and Uncle Sam is fearful people might get hurt. This may be a laudable function of today's bureaucratic Omnisciency, but it doesn't make sense in my recollections of boyhood bicycles. If J. C. Penney is putting out a bicycle that threatens the flesh and bones of the kiddos, J. C. Penney should get an A-plus for perpetuating the honest American traditions.

I never had a bicycle that didn't come apart several times a day, always with dire disaster, and if there came a day nothing broke it made talk about the neighborhood. True, this was a bit ago. Just this summer a mother down the road told me she had a deal on with her young son—every dollar he earned she was matching with two dollars, and he was "working" on a bicycle. I never had a deal like that and I never earned a dollar. I earned money, but never a dollar. I mowed the lawn for one sea captain's widder-woman, and she paid me ten cents an hour. I could mow her lawn in an hour. But if I hustled and finished the lawn in fifty minutes, she'd pay me but eight cents. I had quite another way to work on a bicycle.

I found my frame on the town dump. It had a twisted front fork, suggesting it had moved the immovable object, and also explaining why it was on the town dump. There was no problem. I stuck the thing in the big vise at Charlie Dunning's blacksmith shop, and Charlie ran a length of iron pipe over the bent part and yanked back a certain amount of originality. He didn't get it all, as he felt he might break something, so my bike had a list to starboard and I was never able to ride it no-handsies. But he did get the fork so the cones of a wheel would line up, and now I had to go and find a wheel. Thaddy Buker had one with eight broken spokes. It didn't just rub; it bound up. But I could get spokes for it, so I gave Thaddy fifteen cents and took the wheel. Then I had to mow some lawns to get money enough to buy new spokes at the bicycle shop in the city. I tried to stretch the widder-woman's lawn into twelve cents, but she shook her head and said she never paid more than ten cents.

I was lucky with the rear wheel. I found an old kitchen   4
range buried under pine needles in the woods, probably
all that was left of a chopper's camp, and I carried the
pieces home one by one until I had them all. About a mile.
Then Benjy Gartley, who bought junk, took them and gave
me a perfectly good hind wheel, coaster brake and all. It
was perfect, except that it was smaller than my front
wheel, and I always rode uphill.

The frame had a crack, which spread shortly and be-   5
came a break. I couldn't fix it until it broke off, so I rode
around some in the constant expectation of taking a header
when it let go. I did, and then I fixed it. I shoved a piece
of water pipe on over the break, so the break was in the
middle, and then I bored holes for rivets. Charlie Dunning,
good friend of all us boys, gave his approval and said the
job would last for years. Good as new.

Tires were a problem. None, then, had inner tubes,   6
and each was shellacked to its rim. Had to stick them on,
because if they moved on the rim the valvestems would
tear out. When a tire sprang a leak, which every tire did,
it was a major operation to get the wheel out of the fork,
the tire off the wheel, and everything back again. So the
make-do was to wind friction tape around the leak, wheel
and all. This kept the Neverleek from oozing, and a
wound-around tire would hold air sometimes. Neverleek
was a patent product that came in a tube. The tube was
threaded to fit the valvestem of a tire, and the tube of
Neverleek was squeezed in. After that, if a tire leaked, it
leaked Neverleek, and the tape helped stop that. Neverleek
looked like molasses, and may have been. What I saved
on new tires I spent for Neverleek and friction tape.

All of which was attended constantly by the J.C.   7
Penney hazard Uncle Sam is now hoping to abate. Things
did fall apart, and bicycling taught us how to fall at high
speed and slide forty yards on the back of the neck. What
would fine old Uncle Sam know about the abrasive quality
of a cinder sidewalk of my youth, which would shred a
pair of corduroy pants in a split second? And so we boys

would pick ourselves up, and then pick up the separated parts of our bicycles, and we would carry them home in our arms. Now to find replacements, to dicker, to mow some more lawns, and then be back in business for the next disaster.

Funny thing, and probably J. C. Penney and Uncle 8 Sam don't know this, but after the high-wheeled bicycle, the new kind was called a "safety." The safety eliminated the dangers and disadvantages of the old high-wheeler. I still heard the word "safety" for a bicycle when I was a boy, meaning a bike just like mine. And what would Uncle Sam do about the grave dangers of the carbide lamp? A little can of carbide and a drip of water made a gas that burned with bright white light, and on the front of a bicycle this shone enough so night riding was reasonably safe. Marty French's carbide bicycle lamp blew up on him and took the side off his father's barn.

Comment

Prompted by the recall of J. C. Penney bikes, Gould recalls how, as a boy, he repaired his own bicycle. His account is typical of many autobiographical essays that comment on the present world through an account of past experiences. Gould uses process analysis in the course of the essay but gives only those details needed to understand points that he makes. By contrast, a set of instructions on these processes would require details on each step.

Questions for Study and Discussion

1. Is Gould merely recalling boyhood experiences, or is he using these experiences to make a general point or develop a thesis? If the latter, what is that point or thesis?
2. What point is Gould making about repairing a twisted front fork, a frame, and a leaking tire? How do the details on each process support Gould's point?

3. What features of the essay best define Gould's special humor and way of looking at a happening like the bicycle recall?
4. Why does Gould title his essay "Always Uphill"?

Vocabulary Study

1. What does the word *Omnisciency* (paragraph 1) mean, and why does Gould capitalize it?
2. What does Gould mean by the statement that the blacksmith yanked back "a certain amount of *originality* (paragraph 3)?

Suggestions for Writing

1. Write a short essay, perhaps a humorous one, in which you relate a past experience to an event in the present.
2. Write a short essay in which you refer to a mechanical process you have performed. Since you are not writing a set of instructions on how to perform the process, you need only present relevant details, as Gould does.

Leonard Kriegel

TAKING IT

Born in the Bronx, in 1933, Leonard Kriegel contracted polio at the age of eleven and spent two years in a hospital recovering from its effects; he later completed grade school and four years of high school through home instruction. In his book *Working Through* (1972), Kriegel states that, upon entering college, "I was far hungrier for education than [my friends]; I was both more expectant and less skeptical of the college experience. I very much wanted to learn, to read whatever was worth reading. It was obvious to me that I knew very little. I was fortunate since, having survived as a cripple, I suspect that I possessed a stronger sense of self and perhaps a better-developed sense of competitiveness than most of my fellow students." Kriegel relates these experiences to the developed idea in the following essay, published in 1985.

In 1944, at the age of 11, I had polio. I spent the next
two years of my life in an orthopedic hospital, appropriately called a reconstruction home. By 1946, when I returned to my native Bronx, polio had reconstructed me
to the point that I walked very haltingly on steel braces
and crutches.

But polio also taught me that, if I were to survive, I
would have to become a man—and become a man quickly.
"Be a man!" my immigrant father urged, by which he
meant "become an American." For, in 1946, this country
had very specific expectations about how a man faced
adversity. Endurance, courage, determination, stoicism—
these might right the balance with fate.

"I couldn't take it, and I took it," says the wheel-chair-
doomed poolroom entrepreneur William Einhorn in Saul
Bellow's *The Adventures of Augie March,* "And I *can't* take
it, yet I do take it." In 1953, when I first read these words,
I knew that Einhorn spoke for me—as he spoke for scores
of other men who had confronted the legacy of a maiming
disease by risking whatever they possessed of substance
in a country that believed that such risks were a man's
wagers against his fate.

How one faced adversity was, like most of American
life, in part a question of gender. Simply put, a woman
endured, but a man fought back. You were better off struggling against the effects of polio as a man than as a
woman, for polio was a disease that one confronted by
being tough, aggressive, decisive, by assuming that all
limitations could be overcome, beaten, conquered. In short,
by being "a man." Even a vocabulary of rehabilitation was
masculine. One "beat" polio by outmuscling the disease.
At the age of 18, I felt that I was "a better man" than
my friends because I had "overcome a handicap." And
I had, in the process, showed that I could "take it." In
the world of American men, to take it was a sign that you
were among the elect. An assumption my "normal"
friends shared. "You're lucky," my closest friend said to
me during an intensely painful crisis in his own life. "You
had polio." He meant it. We both believed it.

Obviously, I wasn't lucky. By 19, I was already begin- 5
ning to understand—slowly, painfully, but inexorably—
that disease is never "conquered" or "overcome." Still,
I looked upon resistance to polio as the essence of my
manhood. As an American, I was self-reliant. I could create
my own possibilities from life. And so I walked mile after
mile on braces and crutches. I did hundreds of push-ups
every day to build my arms, chest, and shoulders. I lifted
weights to the point that I would collapse, exhausted but
strengthened, on the floor. And through it all, my desire
to create a "normal" life for myself was transformed into
a desire to become the man my disease had decreed I
should be.

I took my heroes where I found them—a strange, dis- 6
parate company of men: Hemingway, whom I would write
of years later as "my nurse"; Pete Reiser, whom I dreamed
of replacing in Ebbets Field's pastures and whose penchant
for crashing into outfield walls fused in my mind with my
own war against the virus; Franklin Delano Roosevelt, who
had scornfully faced polio with aristocratic disdain and
patrician distance (a historian acquaintance recently dis-
abused me of that myth, a myth perpetrated, let me add,
by almost all of Roosevelt's biographers); Henry Fonda and
Gary Cooper, in whose resolute Anglo-Saxon faces Hollywood blended the simplicity, strength and courage a man
needed if he was going to survive as a man; any number
of boxers in whom heart, discipline and training combined
to stave off defeats the body's limitations made inevitable.
These were the "manly" images I conjured up as I walked
those miles of Bronx streets, as I did those relentless push-
ups, as I moved up and down one subway staircase after
another by turning each concrete step into a personal insult.
And they were still the images when, 15 years later, married,
the father of two sons of my own, a Fulbright Professor in
the Netherlands, I would grab hold of vertical poles on a
train in The Hague and swing my brace-bound body across
the dead space between platform and carriage, filled with
self-congratulatory vanity as amazement spread over the
features of the Dutch conductor.

It is easy to dismiss such images as adolescent. Un- 7
doubtedly, they were. But they helped remind me, time
and time again, of how men handled their diseases and
their pain. Of course, I realized even then that it was not
the idea of manhood alone that had helped me fashion
a life out of polio. I might write of Hemingway as "my
nurse," but it was an immigrant Jewish mother—already
transformed into a cliché by scores of male Jewish
writers—who serviced my crippled body's needs and who
fed me love, patience and care even as I fed her the
rhetoric of my rage.

But it was the need to prove myself an American man 8
—tough, resilient, independent, able to take it—that pulled
me through my war with the virus. I have, of course, been
reminded again and again of the price extracted for such
ideas about manhood. And I am willing to admit that my
sons may be better off in a country in which "Manhood"
will mean little more than, say, the name for an after-shave
lotion. It is 40 years since my war with the virus began.
At 51, even an American man knows that mortality is the
only legacy and defeat the only guarantee. At 51, my legs
still encased in braces and crutches still beneath my
shoulders, my elbows are increasingly arthritic from all
those streets walked and weights lifted and stairs climbed.
At 51, my shoulders burn with pain from all those push-
ups done so relentlessly. And at 51, pain merely bores—
and hurts.

Still, I remain an American man. If I know where I'm 9
going, I know, too, where I have been. Best of all, I know
the price I have paid. A man endures his diseases until
he recognizes in them his vanity. He can't take it, but he
takes it. Once, I relished my ability to take it. Now I find
myself wishing that taking it were easier. In such quiet
surrenders do we American men call it quits with our
diseases.

Comment

Kriegel gives us a few details about the onset of his polio and the physical effects of the disease. However, the focus of the essay is on the means by which he learned to cope with the physical effects. Had he given a full account of the onset of the disease and its effects, he would have blurred this focus. He would also have confused the reader about his purpose in writing. Kriegel's style is notable for its vigor and directness. His sentences are often colloquial, but he turns to metaphor in stating important ideas in the final paragraph: "A man endures his diseases until he recognizes in them his vanity." We hear Kriegel speaking to us, but we also get the sense of a person thinking.

Questions for Study and Discussion

1. What ideal of manhood helped Kriegel survive the effects of polio? Does he tell us how he acquired this ideal?
2. How does Kriegel illustrate the effect that this ideal has had upon his character and behavior? What is his attitude toward the ideal? Would a different ideal have also helped him survive?
3. What does Kriegel mean by the final sentence, "In such quiet surrenders do we American men call it quits with our diseases"?
4. What is Kriegel's thesis? What is Kriegel's purpose in writing this essay, and how do you know?
5. Kriegel describes his experiences chronologically but interrupts his account to comment on their effects. Are these comments random, or do they have an order of their own?

Vocabulary Study

Explain the following words and phrases:

1. *orthopedic hospital* (paragraph 1)
2. *stoicism* (paragraph 2)
3. *poolroom entrepreneur* (paragraph 3)

4. *question of gender* (paragraph 4)
5. *inexorably* (paragraph 5)
6. *perpetrated* (paragraph 6)
7. *transformed into a cliché* (paragraph 7)

Suggestions for Writing

1. Kriegel states that when he was growing up the way a man and a woman faced adversity was "like most of American life, a question of gender." Drawing on experiences at home and at school, discuss how you were taught to face adversity and how you do so. State whether your experience suggests that attitudes toward facing adversity have changed from those Kriegel discusses.
2. Discuss your own ideal of manhood or womanhood and how you reached it. Then discuss the effect of this ideal on your relationship with people—perhaps with friends or fellow workers.
3. Write your own essay on the topic, "Taking It." You might focus your essay on experiences at home, at school, or at work. In working out a thesis, you need not draw general conclusions about people or social attitudes. You might draw a specific conclusion about your own ideal of conduct or social attitudes.

Reflection

The reflective essay is more open in its structure than essays bound by the requirements of narration or exposition. For example, it occasionally follows the wanderings of the writer's thought, concluding without tying ideas and details together. This kind of essay comes closest to the journal entry, like those from Virginia Woolf's diary (p. 132), and to the trial essay described in the introduction—the loosely organized essay that explores ideas without necessarily bringing the exploration to completion. The sixteenth-century French essayist Michael Montaigne defended these wanderings and unrevised thoughts in his essays, pointing out that his "understanding does not always advance, it also goes backwards. I do not distrust my thoughts less because they are the second or third, than because they are the first, or my present less than my past thoughts. Besides, we often correct ourselves as foolishly as we correct others."

Sometimes the reflective essay is tightly constructed, its ideas built carefully, without continuous revision or restatement. The structure and language of the essay depend on the writer's personality and characteristic manner of thinking. Montaigne describes his own. Writers like Montaigne think as they put words on paper; they revise and correct as they compose. Other writers choose to revise the whole essay and present only their finished thoughts. The reflective essay, more so than other kinds, takes the shape of the writer's thought and feeling.

Virginia Woolf

EXTRACTS FROM A DIARY: 1918–1919

As a girl of fifteen the English novelist and essayist Virginia Woolf (1882–1941) kept a diary for the year 1897. She did not continue the diary, but in years following she did keep a record of her observations and scraps of writing in a series of notebooks, and for a short period in 1905 she also kept a daily journal. In 1915, Woolf began another diary, recording thoughts and observations on a wide range of topics—her marriage (to the political writer and editor, Leonard Woolf), friends, relatives, the writing of her novels, London and southeastern England where she lived. Woolf maintained this diary, with some interruptions, until shortly before her death. Woolf did not edit her diaries for publication, and the editors of the diary neither added to nor changed Woolf's punctuation. The extracts reprinted here discuss the purpose of the diary and record observations made at the end of World War I. Woolf refers to her husband, Leonard, as "L."

Monday 11 November [1918]

Twentyfive minutes ago the guns went off, announcing peace. A siren hooted on the river. They are hooting still. A few people ran to look out of windows. The rooks wheeled round, & were for a moment, the symbolic look of creatures performing some ceremony, partly of thanksgiving, partly of valediction over the grave. A very cloudy still day, the smoke toppling over heavily towards the east; & that too wearing for a movement a look of something floating, waving, drooping. We looked out of the window; saw the housepainter give one look at the sky & go on with his job; the old man toddling along the street carrying a bag out [of] which a large loaf protruded, closely followed by his mongrel dog. So far neither bells nor flags, but the wailing of sirens & intermittent guns.

Monday 20 January [1919]

I mean to copy this out when I can buy a book, so I omit the flourishes proper to the new year. It is not

.money this time that I lack, but the capacity, after a fortnight in bed, to make the journey to Fleet Street. Even
the muscles of my right hand feel as I imagine a servants
hand to feel. Curiously enough, I have the same stiffness
in manipulating sentences, though by rights I should be
better equipped mentally now than I was a month ago.
The fortnight in bed was the result of having a tooth out,
& being tired enough to get a headache—a long dreary
affair, that receded & advanced much like a mist on a
January day. One hours writing daily is my allowance for
the next few weeks; & having hoarded it this morning,
I may spend part of it now, since L. is out, & I am much
behindhand with the month of January. I note however
that this diary writing does not count as writing, since I
have just reread my years diary & am much struck by the
rapid haphazard gallop at which it swings along,
sometimes indeed jerking almost intolerably over the cob-
bles. Still if it were not written rather faster than the fastest
typewriting, if I stopped & took thought, it would never
be written at all; & the advantage of the method is that
it sweeps up accidentally several stray matters which I
should exclude if I hesitated, but which are the diamonds
of the dustheap. If Virginia Woolf at the age of 50, when
she sits down to build her memoirs out of these books
is unable to make a phrase as it should be made, I can
only condole with her & remind her of the existence of
the fireplace, where she has my leave to burn these pages
to so many black films with red eyes in them. But how
I envy her the task I am preparing for her! There is none
I should like better. Already my 37th birthday next Saturday is robbed of some of its terrors by the thought. Partly
for the benefit of this elderly lady (no subterfuge will then
be possible: 50 is elderly, though I anticipate her protest
& agree that it is not old) partly to give the year a solid
foundation, I intend to spend the evenings of this week
of captivity in making out an account of my friendships
& their present condition, with some account of my friends
characters; & to add an estimate of their work, & a forecast
of their future works. The lady of 50 will be able to say

how near to the truth I come; but I have written enough for tonight (only 15 minutes, I see).

Sunday 20 April [1919]

In the idleness which succeeds any long article, & Defoe[1] is the 2nd leader this month, I got out this diary, & read as one always does read one's own writing, with a kind of guilty intensity. I confess that the rough & random style of it, often so ungrammatical, & crying for a word altered, afflicted me somewhat. I am trying to tell whichever self it is that reads this hereafter that I can write very much better; & take no time over this; & forbid her to let the eye of man behold it. And now I may add my little compliment to the effect that it has a slapdash & vigour, & sometimes hits an unexpected bulls eye. But what is more to the point is my belief that the habit of writing thus for my own eye only is good practise. It loosens the ligaments. Never mind the misses & the stumbles. Going at such a pace as I do I must make the most direct & instant shots at my object, & thus have to lay hands on words, choose them, & shoot them with no more pause than is needed to put my pen in the ink. I believe that during the past year I can trace some increase of ease in my professional writing which I attribute to my casual half hours after tea. Moreover there looms ahead of me the shadow of some kind of form which a diary might attain to. I might in the course of time learn what it is that one can make of this loose, drifting material of life; finding another use for it than the use I put it to, so much more consciously & scrupulously, in fiction. What sort of diary should I like mine to be? Something loose knit, & yet not slovenly, so elastic that it will embrace any thing, solemn, slight or beautiful that comes into my mind. I should like it to resemble some deep old desk, or capacious hold-all, in which one flings a mass of odds &

---

[1]Daniel Defoe, the seventeenth-century journalist and novelist, was the subject of an article that Woolf was writing.

ends without looking them through. I should like to come back, after a year or two, & find that the collection had sorted itself & refined itself & coalesced, as such deposits so mysteriously do, into a mould, transparent enough to reflect the light of our life, & yet steady, tranquil composed with the aloofness of a work of art. The main requisite, I think on re-reading my old volumes, is not to play the part of censor, but to write as the mood comes or of anything whatever; since I was curious to find how I went for things put in haphazard, & found the significance to lie where I never saw it at the time. But looseness quickly becomes slovenly. A little effort is needed to face a character or an incident which needs to be recorded. Nor can one let the pen write without guidance; for fear of becoming slack & untidy like Vernon Lee.[2]

Sunday 20 July [1919]

Perhaps I will finish the account of the peace celebrations. What herd animals we are after all—even the most disillusioned. At any rate, after sitting through the procession & the peace bells unmoved, I began after dinner, to feel that if something was going on, perhaps one had better be in it. I routed up poor L. & threw away my Walpole.[3] First lighting a row of glass lamps, & seeing that the rain was stopped, we went out just before ten. Explosions had for some time promised fireworks. The doors of the public house at the corner were open, & the room crowded; couples walzing; songs being shouted, waveringly, as if one must be drunk to sing. A troop of little boys with lanterns were parading the Green, beating sticks. Not many shops went to the expense of electric light. A woman of the upper classes was supported dead drunk between two men partially drunk. We followed a

---

[2]Woolf had reviewed two books of the early twentieth-century writer Violet Paget, who wrote under the name Vernon Lee.
[3]Woolf was writing a review of the letters of Horace Walpole, the eighteenth-century British author.

moderate stream flowing up the Hill. Illuminations were almost extinct half way up, but we kept on till we reached the terrace. And then we did see something—not much indeed, for the damp had deadened the chemicals. Red & green & yellow & blue balls rose slowly into the air, burst, flowered into an oval of light, which dropped in minute grains & expired. There were hazes of light at different points. Rising over the Thames, among trees, these rockets were beautiful; the light on the faces of the crowd was strange; yet of course there was grey mist muffling everything, & taking the blaze off the fire. It was a melancholy thing to see the incurable soldiers lying bed at the Star & Garter with their backs to us, smoking cigarettes, & waiting for the noise to be over. We were children to be amused. So at eleven we went home, & saw from my study Ealing do its best to rejoice, & indeed one fire balloon went so high that L. believed it a star; but there were none showing. Today the rain has left us in no doubt that any remaining festivities are to be completely quenched.

Comment

The diarist "writes to the moment," recording ideas, impressions, chance thoughts, observations as they occur. Diary entries thus usually come to us unrevised, though Woolf did revise the entry for 20 January 1919, in copying it into a new notebook. At a later time, the diarist may draw on a diary in writing an autobiography or memoir; Woolf considers this possibility in the same extract. In revising an entry, the writer may reconstruct it to illustrate a point or develop a theme. The diarist, indeed, may have a point or theme in mind in writing an entry. Woolf usually begins with an impression or thought that she wishes to explore. The exploration usually remains unfinished, for people and places look different when observed later, and there is always more to say about a topic.

Questions for Study and Discussion

1. What statements or features suggest that Woolf was "writing to the moment," without a preconceived idea in mind? What statements or features show that she is exploring the nature and purpose of a diary and not making definitive statements?
2. What details caught her attention when guns announced the Armistice? Does she convey an attitude toward the event, or is she merely recording her impressions?
3. What details caught her attention at the peace celebration? Does she convey an attitude or express her feelings?
4. What personal qualities stand out for you in these diary entries? Is there a single personal quality that dominates?

Vocabulary Study

State how the following words differ in meaning, and explain why Woolf chooses the italicized word and not the others:

1. *toddling*, tottering, lurching (entry 1)
2. *intermittent*, continual, occasional (entry 1)
3. *flourishes*, announcements (entry 2)
4. *subterfuge*, deception, evasion (entry 2)
5. *slovenly*, carelessly, slipshodly (entry 3)
6. *coalesced*, combined, blended (entry 3)
7. *melancholy*, sad, mournful (entry 4)

Suggestion for Writing

For a week or two, record in a notebook your daily impressions, thoughts, and observations relating to one or more of your classes or other school experiences. At the end of this period, select one or more of your thoughts and observations and use them as a basis for an essay. Think of your notebook as a discovery draft, a basis for exploring ideas and observations that you will later refine into a longer, more coherent piece of writing.

Sun Park

DON'T EXPECT ME TO BE PERFECT

As a sixteen-year-old Korean-American, Sun Park attended
Nottingham High School in Hamilton Township, New Jersey. Her
short essay on how she deals with expectations of parents and
friends appeared in a special issue of *Newsweek* that addressed the
stresses and challenges faced by young Americans in the early
1990s.

I am a 16-year-old Korean-American. My family has 1
been in the United States for six years now. I'll be a junior
next fall.

When I first came to the States, it took two years 2
before I could speak English fluently. By the time I started
middle school, I realized that most of my fellow students
had never met many kids like me before. They had this
idea, probably from TV and movies, that all Asians are
nerds and all Asians are smart. It's true that some are.
I know many smart people. But what about those Asians
who aren't so smart? Having a reputation for brains is nice,
I guess, but it can also be a pain. For instance, sometimes
when my classmates do not know something, they come
to me for the answer. Often I can help them. But when
I can't, they get these weird expressions on their faces.
If I were a genius, I would not mind being treated like
one. But since I am not, I do.

The problem isn't just limited to the classroom. My 3
mother and father expect an awful lot from me, too. Like
so many Korean parents, and many ambitious American
parents, they're very competitive and can't help comparing me with other kids. Mine always say to me, "So and
so is so smart, works so hard and is so good to his or her
parents. Why can't you be more like him or her?" Because
I am the oldest kid in my family, they expect me to set
a good example for my younger sisters and relatives.

They'd rather I concentrate on schoolwork than dating. They want me to be No. 1.

Most of the time I want to do well, too. I'm glad I take all honors classes. But now that I am at those levels, I have to be on my toes to keep doing well. The better I do, the more pressure I seem to place on myself. Because my parents want me to be perfect—or close to perfect—I find myself turning into a perfectionist. When I do a project and make one little error, I can't stand it. Sometimes I stay up as late as 2 a.m. doing homework. 4

I don't think I would be like this if my parents weren't motivating me. But I don't think they know what pressure can do to a teenager. It's not that they put me down or anything. They have plenty of faith in me. But to tell the truth, sometimes I really like to be lazy, and it would be nice just to take it easy and not worry so much about my grades all the time. Maybe my parents know this. Maybe that's why they encourage me to be better. Well, it still drives me crazy when they compare me with others. I wonder if those smart kids have parents like mine. 5

Sure, I'm proud of who I am, and I love my parents very much. But then there are times I just feel like taking a break and going far away from parents and teachers. Of course that's impossible, but it's always nice to dream about it. 6

Comment

Sun Park describes attitudes of her Korean-American parents and many of her friends, and she expresses her feelings about these attitudes and expectations. Since these expectations arise from a positive stereotype of Korean-Americans, Sun Park might have limited the essay to an exploration of this stereotype and a solution to the problems it creates for her and others. Sun Park does discuss problems and solutions. But she needs also to understand her feelings about herself, her parents, and her world, and she focuses on these feelings. Her expressive essay is an effort to reach this understanding.

Questions for Study and Discussion

1. What is the stereotype of Korean-Americans and Asians generally that has created the problem discussed in the essay? Does Sun Park state that the stereotype is wholly false?
2. What effect does this stereotype have upon her life? What feelings does Sun Park express about this stereotype?
3. What in the essay shows that Sun Park is concerned with her feelings rather than with solutions?
4. What is the value of expressing one's feelings about a problem, without proposing a solution?

Suggestions for Writing

1. Write an essay about a problem that you confront daily, and express your feelings about this problem. Give enough details about the problem to allow your reader to share your experience.
2. Rewrite your essay, analyzing the problem and suggesting a solution to it. You may wish to incorporate parts of your original essay. Note that your readers will need more information about the problem in order to understand and consider the solution you are proposing.

Henry Beetle Hough

ON SMALL THINGS

Henry Beetle Hough (1896–1985) was born in New Bedford, Massachusetts, and attended Columbia School of Journalism. For more than forty years he was editor and co-publisher (with his wife) of the *Vineyard Gazette*, in Edgartown, Massachusetts. An early book, *History of Services Rendered by the American Press*, won the Pulitzer Prize in 1917. Hough is also the author of novels and nonfiction including his autobiography, *Mostly on Martha's Vineyard*. The essay reprinted here is an example of the reflective essay in which Hough excels.

August 7

Dear Jack,

When I dressed this morning I inadvertently put on an   1
old green shirt and the bright blue slacks I bought a few
weeks ago at Dave Golart's because my waistline now
rebels at the long-familiar Size 36, and because bright blue
was about as modest a shade as I could find in this
pigment-passionate age. My investment in Size 36 pants
is dropping faster and I fear more permanently than the
value of the stock portfolios of my betters.

I say this morning's color combination was inadver-   2
tent because I think it was, and in that case it was a small
thing. If it was not inadvertent, it was probably a big thing,
dictate of some enormous reason I shall never learn. Green
and bright blue look odd, I know, but they feel all right,
and I shall not change until time for the bank director's
meeting this afternoon. The requirements for that are
obviously severe.

Assuming my vagary in costume to be a small thing,   3
I remembered on my morning walk with Lochinvar something I had not thought of for years. I quote:

> Neglect of small things is the rock on which the great major-
> ity of the human race has split.

I learned this, and the rest of the moral passage, now   4
forgotten, in the Mary B. White School, a red brick building in a graveled yard which stood at the corner of
Maxfield and Pleasant streets in New Bedford long ago.
It was popularly but incorrectly known as the Maxfield
Street School. There were four rooms, two downstairs and
two upstairs, and I had a year's schooling in each room.
The principal's office was in the turret which surmounted
the outside stairs. All public buildings built of brick had
turrets. I saw the principal's office only once, and I have
forgotten the occasion.

The janitor was Mr. Cochrane. He had a red beard and   5
so far as I can remember always wore a business suit and

a derby hat. The boys' urinal in the basement smelled so strong and frightful that I have hardly escaped from it yet, but I suppose Mr. Cochrane considered this normal and acceptable. I tried to hold my breath as I went through, but my lung capacity was usually insufficient.

Once we were let out of school to watch the circus   6
parade pass by on Purchase Street, a block downhill from Pleasant. Across from the school an elderly woman sat on an uncommonly high porch platform attached to the front of a dun-colored house, and just as we were crossing the graveled yard the planks gave way and dropped the elderly woman and her chair ten or twelve feet to the ground. As I remember it, she landed upright, still sitting in the chair. Mr. Cochrane set out on a dead run. I wondered what he was so excited about.

I have forgotten the circus parade in particular; I re-   7
member it only in an amalgamated succession of these wonders, mixed up with seeing the circus come in of an early morning at the Pearl Street railroad yards near the Wamsutta Mills. My brother and I used to see the stakes driven and the big tents raised in a lot at the North End near Brooklawn where Daniel Ricketson lived and where he entertained Henry Thoreau. Later the circus went to the West End or the South End, and I lost interest. When something is completely right and wonderful, it shouldn't be changed.

I remember that in my class at the Mary B. White   8
School there were two boys with the given name of Byron.

These various details I supply because if one is going   9
to write of the importance of little things, he had best show he is himself really attentive to them. Maybe the things I have drawn from memory, though small, may not be small enough to make the desired point. I can't tell. Everything one remembers long enough tends to become fascinating, though not to a wide public.

The passage I was required to learn, the first sentence   10
of which I have quoted, was written by Dr. Samuel Smiles. He has seven lines and a fraction in the *Columbia Encyclopedia*, and I learn for the first time that he was Scottish,

a physician, and that his books were mostly devoted to moral education. I think he is one of the writers of the past century (1812–1904) who has gone out, and I doubt if he will be back. There is no use whatever in putting the usual placard on the door, BACK IN TWENTY MINUTES or even BACK IN A HUNDRED YEARS.

I suppose the small things Dr. Smiles regarded as im-   11
portant were of an order now outdated: picking up odds and ends of string, washing behind the ears, painting the length of fence behind the lilac bush even though no one will see it, lifting one's hat clear from the scalp instead of merely tipping the brim, sweeping out the corners with conscience rather than haste, and so on. It was Dr. Smiles who wrote, "A place for everything and everything in its place," but I never had to learn that. It was in Chapter 5 of a piece called *Thrift*.

This is all I shall say about Dr. Smiles, and it seems an   12
odd beginning for the defense of small things I have set out to make. He was so moral—so stuffy, I say—that I can hardly expect to lean upon him or his lavendered philosophy. I must start out for myself and may as well do so abruptly. I object to my life being portentous, and especially to the requirement that I pretend it to be.

Whatever comes up in the matter of ideas or enter-   13
prise, someone says, "Let's broaden it." I don't want to broaden it. I prefer to narrow it. I can't paint, except for porches, walls, and things like that, but if I could I would not choose to paint on a large canvas. I probably wouldn't be able to reach the top or the sides, and I would only be an overblown, pretending artist, not a real one. Another thing—I don't want to be in the mainstream. The water is muddy, the pollution great, the vision limited, and too many people are trying to swim at once, each hitting another over the head.

I suppose what I am getting at principally is what I   14
hope is the small integrity of my point of view. It has to be small, because it is mine, and because I don't want to look out from way up there or way out yonder. I want to look out from here, and "here" happens to be an

uncrowded place. Besides, if the ground on which I stand is too large or high I will surely be pushed over.

I think the small things now being importantly ne- 15 glected, that it is so much the fashion to neglect as routine and perfunctory, are the things generally that make life itself and in the end give it the meaning out of which new, fresh, or even grand ideas may spring. Information comes by radio, television, newspaper, magazine, and book, but these are not the country's thinking or the people's thinking. They may be stimulating and they may also be conforming. A man still needs his walking or hammering nails or chopping wood or bowling or shooting pool if he is really to find out what he thinks. The sweeping concept is often not much by itself; it's like the wind that blew over last night, leaving a scatter of debris.

Thoreau said that a man was not born into the world 16 to do everything, but to do something. The opportunities of modern times, puffed and inflated by so many prophets, some real, some false, are over-appreciated; the limitations are undervalued a hundredfold, though they are the intimate companionship of our days and nights, our Sundays and our weekdays.

I suppose, too, that although limitations are generally 17 what they seem and no more, there is always a chance that they may nourish some particular fertility. Most great things nowadays are abstractions, and did not Dr. J. Robert Oppenheimer suggest that some of their puzzling relationships might be brought into understandable order through a small specific?

I argue that we, as ordinary people, ought to neglect 18 great things, even at the cost of appearing presumptuous. I am aware that Dr. Samuel Smiles (there he is again), if he could rise up from his serene bit of God's acre among the yews and willows beside the ivy-mantled church, would be bound to insist that this was not what he had in mind. Maybe, though, he could be persuaded.

I remember how David Copperfield, after his life with 19 Dora, declared that trifles make the sum of life. This is not what Dr. Smiles meant, either; his small things were not trifles. Not to him. But I am of David Copperfield's way of thinking. Life's trifles and trifling are not only its sum but its essence.

One small matter of doubt remains, rising from our ex-   20
perience in the newspaper profession. I remember Betty's intent pursuit of trifles: to keep Mrs. Duble's name from appearing in the *Gazette* as Mrs. Deeble, or vice versa; to defeat at all costs that persecuting vulgarity, "Rev. Smith"; to put the apostrophe in exactly and not approximately the correct place. So much of the good health of the paper lay here that, looking backward, I can almost accept the view that there are no minutiae.

As a last word in trying for an understanding or even   21
for a compromise with Dr. Smiles, I suggest that if the great majority of the human race is going to split on the rock of neglect of small things, it will at least be too bad for so many of us to split on the rock of the wrong ones.

Yours, as ever,

Comment

Hough's letter has the openness and loose structure typical of much expressive writing. The miscellany of details that leads into paragraph 9 seems to illustrate Samuel Johnson's definition of the essay as an "irregular undigested piece." But the details have a purpose, as Hough directly states. That purpose is related to the statement of Samuel Smiles—first quoted in paragraph 3. Throughout the essay Hough gives us a sense of the reflective writer turning over the experiences and sayings that have mattered over a lifetime; Hough discovers a special meaning in writing about them. Out of seemingly small details and ideas concerned with everyday experiences come ideas about life itself.

Questions for Study and Discussion

1. What is the purpose of the miscellany of details that leads into paragraph 9?
2. What is the meaning of the quotation from Samuel Smiles in paragraph 3? How does Hough explain the statement in later paragraphs?
3. Hough discusses how people can live meaningful lives. What paragraphs introduce and develop these ideas?
4. Hough addresses his letter to "Jack"—a particular friend and reader of his newspaper. What features of the essay suggest that Hough has a larger audience in mind?
5. What impression do you get of Hough through his letter? What personal qualities most stand out? What kind of sense of humor does he have?

Vocabulary Study

1. Look up the following words and be ready to discuss how Hough uses them:
   a. *inadvertently, inadvert* (paragraphs 1–2)
   b. *vagary* (paragraph 3)
   c. *amalgamated* (paragraph 7)
   d. *attentive* (paragraph 9)
   e. *portentous* (paragraph 12)
   f. *integrity* (paragraph 14)
   g. *routine, perfunctory, concept* (paragraph 15)
   h. *intimate* (paragraph 16)
   i. *presumptuous* (paragraph 18)
   j. *trifles* (paragraph 19)
   k. *minutiae* (paragraph 20)
2. The following words and phrases call a picture or smell to mind. What is that picture, and what does the word or phrase contribute to the meaning of the sentence?
   a. *lavendered* (paragraph 12)
   b. *scatter of debris* (paragraph 15)
   c. *puffed, inflated* (paragraph 16)
   d. *split, rock of neglect* (paragraph 21)
3. The words and phrases in question 2 above are metaphors— implied comparisons which attribute the qualities of one thing to another. In paragraph 13 Hough uses another

metaphor, *mainstream,* and describes it: "The water is muddy, the pollution great, the vision limited, and too many people are trying to swim at once, each hitting another over the head." What is the implied comparison in *mainstream,* and what other comparisons is Hough making in the sentence?

Suggestions for Writing

Hough gives us a picture of himself through a miscellany of details. He draws no conclusion other than to say that he has paid attention to small details in his life:

1. Write down quickly a scattering of details that give the reader a picture of your life and interests.
2. Look carefully at the details, then write down one or two patterns that they suggest. Discuss one of these patterns in a paragraph.
3. Your paragraph probably contains several ideas. Use one of these ideas as the thesis of an essay that incorporates some or all of the details you recorded. You may wish to add others. Remember that a thesis organizes the details of the essay, giving them direction and purpose.

David Updike

THE LITTLE HOUSE

David Updike attended Harvard and Columbia universities and later taught English at Roxbury (Massachusetts) Community College and M.I.T. Updike's writings include *A Winter Journey* (1985); *An Autumn Tale* (1988); and *Out on the Marsh* (1988), a collection of stories. In his essay on building a house, Updike reflects on a recent personal experience.

A few years ago, not long after I had gotten out of 1
college, yet before I figured out how I was going to make my way in the world, I came upon the idea of building a small, one-room house for myself in the woods. I had

recently returned from a tumultuous trip through Italy with my girlfriend and returned home penniless, homeless, unemployed and certainly more confused than I had been when I left, a month or two before.

For the time being, I stayed at my mother's house in ² the country, and during this hiatus, I started reading *Walden*. I was filled with happy notions of self-sufficiency and independence, and I felt that if only I could make a little place for myself, a room to which I could always return, I would be safe, somehow, protected from future hardships.

Having received rather vague, disbelieving permission ³ from my mother, I went out into the woods in search of a place to build. I soon found a treeless rectangle of land, roughly 16 feet by 12, in a deep thicket of woods halfway between the field and the marsh. I returned with a mattock and a hoe and began to clear away the undergrowth, hacking down through the roots and rotting branches, clearing the topsoil until I came to the sandy undersoil on which I would build my footing. It was late fall, almost winter, and it was not until the third day of excavation that I discovered that the plant I had been unearthing was poison ivy. I went to our hospital's emergency room for treatment, and, after several days, I returned to the woods wearing a ski mask and sunglasses and resumed my work undaunted.

At the library, I found several books on house con- ⁴ struction and carpentry. Then, with a shovel, I dug foundation holes, filled them with rocks and cinder blocks, and I began to forage around the house for lumber. Because I was broke at the time, part of my aspiration was to prove that, if one were clever and resourceful enough, money was a necessity that could be done without.

In the barn, I found some old 4 by 4's that had once ⁵ held up the backboard on the tennis court and some heavy boards that had once been the railing of a bridge. My greatest find was an enormous beam, 8 inches by 10 inches by 18 feet long, that had washed up in the marsh.

It must once have been part of a ship or a dock. I sawed off its one pulpy end, and, using a long pole as a lever, raised it a few inches off the marsh so it could dry out. A few days later, I used boards, rollers and a skateboard turned on its back (so the beam rolled on its upturned wheels), and in the style of the ancient Egyptians, I managed with enormous difficulty and satisfaction to roll the beam through the woods to the site. I then raised it up on cinder blocks and made it level. It was to form the structural center, the backbone, of the little house.

Not far from my mother's home, developers had begun to gut my old elementary school in order to turn it into condominiums. After receiving permission from the foreman, I drove up in our family car and began to load it with 2 by 4's and old, bent floorboards that I had trod two decades before.   6

By this time, my project had begun to interest and amuse my family. "So how's Walden Two?" my stepfather would inquire when I came in from a long day in the woods.   7

"It's not Walden Two," I would say indignantly. "If I thought I was Thoreau, I wouldn't build it in my mother's backyard."   8

"Well, that's true," he said. "How is it, anyway?"   9

"Fine," I said, but offered little else.   10

I soon moved back to the city, found an apartment and a job and began to run my life in a reasonably orderly way. But my mind was steadily working, turning, as I contemplated the next phase of construction. And on my visits home, I continued to build. I used the old bridge railing as joists, and built the frame for the floor. I bought some rough pine floorboards from an old man who ran a small sawmill in a nearby town.   11

On one of my visits to my grandmother's farm in Pennsylvania, I studied the construction of her 19th-century barn and spent an afternoon carving oak pegs with which, I plotted, my house would be held together. On my mother's lawn I laid out pieces of the frame, and, using   12 a dull drill and chisels, I began to cut mortise and tenon joints and then peg them together. With my brother's help, I raised the frames for the walls, braced them and made rafters from the boards from my old school. I found some beautiful old windows in the barn. My mother pilfered a small blue door from someone's trash. Last summer, I tar-papered the roof and boarded up the last of the walls.

During the winter, with the help of my stepfather, I installed an old wood stove which, if the day is not too cold, brings the temperature to a reasonable level of warmth. On my visits home, I continued to work— shingling the sides, covering the roof, wondering how better to keep out the cold. 13

Now that it is finished, after two years of sporadic, though persistent, labor, I sometimes wonder what exact purpose I had imagined the house would serve when I began. My mother sometimes paints there, and when I visit I use it as a kind of retreat, a refuge from the familial throng. I light a fire, listen to the sound of wind in the trees, the shouts of the clammers out on the flats, the crunch of a visitor's approaching footsteps. 14

But the function of the little house, I now realize, was less in its finished form than in the making, and its construction served as a kind of catharsis, an agent of transformation. In the very act of scavenging lumber for my creation—from the barn, the house, the marsh, my old school—I assembled the artifacts of a receding past into a cohesive, functional whole. Strangely, all that time I was working alone in the woods, banging nails and sawing boards and wrestling with enormous pieces of wood, something was silently shifting, and, when I finally looked up, it was only to discover that the world had changed in my absence, shifted beneath me, and the place where I was building was no longer my home. In the end, what I constructed, really, was a monument to the past, to childhood—an empty room, absorbing the nights and the days and the seasons, sitting by itself in the trees. 15

Comment

Many reflective essays deal with abstract topics like freedom, truth, and past or present-day values in abstract terms that refer to concepts rather than to concrete experiences. Ralph Waldo Emerson's essays are often typical of this kind of philosophizing:

Illusion, Temperament, Succession, Surface, Surprise, Reality, Subjectiveness—these are threads on the loom of time, these are the lords of life. I dare not assume to give their order, but I name them as I find them in my way.
—"Experience"

Writing about his life at Walden Pond, where he built a cabin on property that belonged to Emerson, Henry David Thoreau often expresses an abstract truth through everyday experiences:

This was an airy and unplastered cabin, fit to entertain a travelling god, and where a goddess might trail her garments. The winds which passed over my dwelling were such as sweep over the ridges of mountains, bearing the broken strains, or celestial parts only, of terrestrial music. The morning wind forever blows, the poem of creation is uninterrupted; but few are the ears that hear it. Olympus is but the outside of the earth everywhere. —*Walden*

Like Thoreau, David Updike explores the experience of building a little house to discover a truth about himself and his world.

Questions for Study and Discussion

1. How does building the house explain Updike's concluding statement that "the function of the little house . . . was less in its finished form than in the making"?
2. With what "artifacts of a receding past" did Updike build the house?
3. How was the building of the house "a kind of catharsis, an agent of transformation"?
4. What was shifting or changing as Updike built the house? What do we discover the word *home* to mean in the course of the essay?

5. Updike might have opened his essay with a statement of his central topic, perhaps even a statement of his thesis. What would have been the advantage and disadvantage of doing so? By introducing the central topic and thesis early in the essay, would Updike have created a different effect?

Vocabulary Study

Paraphrase paragraph 15, putting its substance and such words and phrases as *catharsis, agent of transformation, artifacts of a receding past,* and *a cohesive, functional whole* into your own words.

Suggestions for Writing

1. Rewrite the opening paragraph of Updike's essay, stating the theme of the essay and anticipating (but not stating in full) the main point or thesis. Then rewrite the concluding paragraph, taking account of the revised opening. Be ready to discuss the problems you encountered in this revision.
2. Like Updike, give an account of an unusual experience—perhaps something that you built or assembled. Lead from your account into a reflection on the meaning of your experience.

William Raspberry

LESSONS OF THE WHALES

Born in northeastern Mississippi, William Raspberry after college began his career as a journalist. In 1962 Raspberry joined the staff of the *Washington Post,* first as a reporter and editor, then as a columnist on urban and national affairs. Raspberry has written much about Afro-American life and education and on a wide range of other subjects—including American values and goals. His column on the California gray whales appeared in the *Washington Post* on September 10, 1990.

For three dramatic weeks, the world was able to rise above its divisions of culture, competition, political ideology and even the pursuit of money and join in noble common cause.

The effort paid off. Two California gray whales have been rescued from their arctic prison and are (presumably) on their way to the open sea and freedom.

It was, as President Reagan said, "an inspiring endeavor," involving cooperation from people often at odds with one another: scientists, environmentalists, oil developers, Eskimo whale hunters, American officials, Soviet sailors. And while hundreds of workers participated directly in the tricky—and extremely dangerous—rescue effort, millions of us were involved vicariously, cheering them and wishing them luck.

But I confess that for the whole of the three weeks, I found myself asking a number of rude questions for which I still don't have answers.

The main question is: Why? Why is it that three trapped whales—in a far off place where local residents routinely hunt and kill whales—should evoke such universal sympathy? If they had been bullheads (or whatever species the Eskimos prefer) they would have wound up as dinner, with no more tears than accompany the slaughter of innocent chickens at Frank Perdue's Eastern Shore establishment.

The Eskimos participated in the rescue only because they don't, except in dire circumstances, eat California grays.

Is it because California grays are an endangered species? Because they were innocent victims of circumstance? Because they are huge? Because they seemed so determined to live? Because they are benign animals of above-average intelligence? Because they are fellow mammals?

Certainly it is difficult to imagine a similar effort on behalf of other animals. Dolphins or porpoises or apes or koalas, yes, but not menhaden or snail darters or timber wolves or warthogs.

Even human tragedy often fails to inspire the sort of [9] international response evoked by the trapped whales. The recent slaughter of some 5,000 Hutu in Burundi inspired nothing like the media coverage, or the public response, sparked by three whales.

Where is the concerted outpouring on behalf of Amer- [10] ica's homeless families or AIDS victims? Where was the international ideology-be-damned response to the Southeast Asian boat people? How can a few whales inspire us to action while hungry children and members of the desperate inner-city underclass elicit only helpless shrugs?

Maybe a part of the answer is in the particularity of the [11] whales. Millions who remain unmoved by a generalized Save the Whales campaign were genuinely concerned about these specific whales—just as millions who seem indifferent to the Children's Defense Fund's urgings on behalf of poverty-stricken and hungry children were willing to do whatever was necessary to rescue Jessica McClure from that Texas well a year ago.

Another part of it may be the clear-cut nature, no mat- [12] ter how difficult, of what needed to be done for the whales. Hard work and technology saved the whales; charity can save the victims of an African drought. But no similarly simple action can save Africans from the encroachment of the Sahara, or the Hutu from tribal war, or ghetto youth from drug-induced violence and despair.

And surely part of it is just plain drama. For the Hutu [13] thousands (and a fair number of Burundi's ruling Tutsis), the outcome is not at issue; they are dead already. But with the whales, as with little Jessica McClure, the outcome was very much in doubt. Will they last until the rescue can be consummated? Will the icebreakers arrive in time? Will the well collapse? Tune in tomorrow.

The point is not that the whale rescue effort was silly, [14] or a waste of resources; I'm as glad as the next one that there were people willing to undertake the effort, and that it succeeded.

The point is whether there are lessons in the Arctic [15] rescue that could teach us how to generate concerted action on behalf of the other victims we know about but who seem to hover beyond the reach of our empathy.

Can we learn to respond to the nameless victims of multifaceted problems as generously as we respond to particular victims of specific tragedies? I don't know the answer, but it's a whale of a question.   16

Comment

The reflective essay sometimes opens with a question that the writer answers in the remainder of the essay. This answer often consists of a series of thoughts or speculations rather than the formal thesis or proposition typical of persuasive essays. As in the expository and the persuasive essay, the writer usually takes account of the readers' knowledge and opinions in organizing the essay, particularly where the reflective essay also has an argumentative edge. William Raspberry's reflective essay has an argumentative edge: Raspberry wishes to generate interest in the particular issue discussed and also concern about mass slaughter like that in Burundi, about homelessness, and about AIDS victims. In organizing his essay, he has his readers' knowledge in mind; he also has in mind the fact that his readers hold different opinions on the issue, or perhaps hold no opinion at all.

Questions for Study and Discussion

1. How much knowledge does Raspberry assume his readers possess on the gray whales, the Burundi deaths, Jessica McClure, and other events and situations he refers to? How much detail on these does Raspberry provide?
2. How does Raspberry keep the attention of the reader directed to this central issue and not to important but peripheral matters to this essay, such as homelessness and AIDS?
3. Does Raspberry give a definitive answer to the question of inaction, or instead give a tentative, qualified one?
4. Do you agree with the answer that Raspberry gives to the question? Why or why not?

Vocabulary Study

State the meaning of the following words as Raspberry uses them. Then state how the word immediately following would change the meaning of the sentence:

1. *vicariously* (paragraph 3), indirectly
2. *rude* (paragraph 4), simple
3. *evoke* (paragraph 5), awaken
4. *dire* (paragraph 6), serious
5. *benign* (paragraph 7), gentle
6. *ideology* (paragraph 10), opinion
7. *particularity* (paragraph 11), individuality
8. *generalized* (paragraph 11), general
9. *technology* (paragraph 12), equipment
10. *consummated* (paragraph 13), accomplished
11. *empathy* (paragraph 15), sympathy
12. *multifaceted* (paragraph 16), complex

Suggestions for Writing

1. State your own thoughts on the question discussed. You may wish to state a tentative thesis—that is, a qualified opinion rather than a definitive idea. You might introduce your thesis early in your essay or build up to it, as Raspberry does.
2. State your ideas on a question or issue related to that discussed by Raspberry. Again, you might introduce your thesis early or build up to it.

PART 3

Strategies for Exposition

The shaman's journey through disorder and illness to health has parallels to the surgeon's journey into the body

— Richard Selzer

Much writing that you do is for the purpose of giving information. A recipe, directions on how to repair a tire, an explanation of how mules differ from horses, a definition of a molecule, analysis of how the United States became engaged in Vietnam—all these give information. The word *exposition*, meaning explanation or the unfolding or setting forth of an idea, describes this kind of writing.

Exposition may use one or more of the methods of analysis illustrated in Part One. These include narration, description, example, process, comparison and contrast, cause and effect, definition, and classification and division. In explaining how to repair a tire, you may describe the tire rim and the tire and define and classify the tools needed to do the repair. In explaining Vietnam, you may narrate the events leading to the American engagement, compare the policies of President Kennedy and President Johnson, and trace the effects of these policies. Most of the essays in this section contain more than one method of exposition.

Exposition, in turn, may serve other kinds of writing. Expressive writing often contains information of various kinds; a veteran's personal account of Vietnam probably will include informative details on weapons, terrain, and jungle warfare. Persuasive writing—for example, an essay arguing for or against America's involvement in Vietnam—probably would include details of that involvement as well as an analysis of causes and effects.

The purposes of giving information are obviously many. In the following essay on the need of error in human life, Lewis Thomas is defining the word *human*. Thomas might have developed an abstract definition that a special audience probably would understand without the observations and details he provides in the essay. Instead, he compares humans with computers and thus draws on experiences most readers have had. The technique of proceeding gradually from known experiences to complex and difficult ideas is a common method in exposition. Many essays do begin with abstract statements, but many essayists prefer to lead into abstract ideas gradually through concrete details. These generate interest in the subject, sometimes through historical background unfamiliar to most readers.

Thomas combines some of the methods of exposition illustrated in the sections that follow. He bases his exposition on comparison with computers, using the similarities between computers and humans (in particular the programmed error in computers) to define the kind of error that makes human life possible. And he uses analogy, or a point-by-point comparison between unlike things—here a good laboratory and a good computer—to illustrate why error promotes increased inefficiency and thinking. He also uses contrast between humans and lower animals, which lack the "splendid freedom" of error, to explain why error is essential to human development. Throughout the essay Thomas is concerned with cause and effect—the cause of human progress, the effect of error.

Thomas introduces his thesis early in the essay, following his discussion of computers:

> Mistakes are at the very base of human thought, embedded there, feeding the structure like root nodules. If we were not provided with the knack of being wrong, we could never get anything useful done.

He restates his thesis in the course of his illustration and discussion:

> The capacity to leap across mountains of information to land lightly on the wrong side represents the highest of human endowments.

> What we need, then, for moving ahead, is a set of wrong alternatives much longer and more interesting than the short list of mistaken courses that any of us can think up right now.

In this concluding restatement, Thomas moves from information to persuasion. But he stops short of developing proposals—ways to encourage acceptance of error, the "splendid freedom" that he earlier suggested animals lack.

This analysis shows that Thomas is organizing the essay according to his judgment of his audience. He is writing as you would converse with a friend—pausing to explain and illustrate ideas when you see that you are not being understood. You repeat your main point to give your explanation a frame but also to be persuasive even when your main purpose is informative.

In writing, you must make a judgment about an audience and assess the kind of explanation and information it needs to understand your main point or thesis.

Lewis Thomas

TO ERR IS HUMAN

A graduate of Princeton University and Harvard Medical School, Lewis Thomas has served in a number of medical posts, including chairman of pathology and medicine and dean of New York University–Bellevue Medical Center; chairman of pathology and dean of Yale School of Medicine; and president and later chancellor of Sloan-Kettering Cancer Center in New York City. He has also served as professor of medicine and pathology at Cornell Medical School in New York, and as university professor at State University of New York–Stony Brook Health Sciences Center. Thomas describes his medical career in *The Youngest Science: Notes of a Medicine Watcher* (1983). His essays, most of which first appeared in the *New England Journal of Medicine*, have been collected in *Lives of a Cell* (1974), *The Medusa and the Snail* (1979), and *Late Night Thoughts on Listening to Mahler's Ninth Symphony* (1983). Thomas writes on science and medicine for the specialist as well as the general reader. His lucid style is ideal for the exposition of complex ideas.

Everyone must have had at least one personal experi- 1
ence with a computer error by this time. Bank balances are suddenly reported to have jumped from $379 into the millions, appeals for charitable contributions are mailed over and over to people with crazy-sounding names at your address, department stores send the wrong bills, utility companies write that they're turning everything off, that sort of thing. If you manage to get in touch with someone and complain, you then get instantaneously typed, guilty letters from the same computer, saying, "Our computer was in error, and an adjustment is being made in your account."

These are supposed to be the sheerest, blindest acci- 2
dents. Mistakes are not believed to be part of the normal

behavior of a good machine. If things go wrong, it must be a personal, human error, the result of fingering, tampering, a button getting stuck, someone hitting the wrong key. The computer, at its normal best, is infallible.

I wonder whether this can be true. After all, the whole   3
point of computers is that they represent an extension of the human brain, vastly improved upon but nonetheless human, superhuman maybe. A good computer can think clearly and quickly enough to beat you at chess, and some of them have even been programmed to write obscure verse. They can do anything we can do, and more besides.

It is not yet known whether a computer has its own   4
consciousness, and it would be hard to find out about this. When you walk into one of those great halls now built for the huge machines, and stand listening, it is easy to imagine that the faint, distant noises are the sound of thinking, and the turning of the spools gives them the look of wild creatures rolling their eyes in the effort to concentrate, choking with information. But real thinking, and dreaming, are other matters.

On the other hand, the evidences of something like an   5
unconscious, equivalent to ours, are all around, in every mail. As extensions of the human brain, they have been constructed with the same property of error, spontaneous, uncontrolled, and rich in possibilities.

Mistakes are at the very base of human thought, em-   6
bedded there, feeding the structure like root nodules. If we were not provided with the knack of being wrong, we could never get anything useful done. We think our way along by choosing between right and wrong alternatives, and the wrong choices have to be made as frequently as the right ones. We get along in life this way. We are built to make mistakes, coded for error.

We learn, as we say, by "trial and error." Why do we   7
always say that? Why not "trial and rightness" or "trial and triumph"? The old phrase puts it that way because that is, in real life, the way it is done.

A good laboratory, like a good bank or a corpora-   8
tion or government, has to run like a computer. Almost

everything is done flawlessly, by the book, and all the numbers add up to the predicted sums. The days go by. And then, if it is a lucky day, and a lucky laboratory, somebody makes a mistake: the wrong buffer, something in one of the blanks, a decimal misplaced in reading counts, the warm room off by a degree and a half, a mouse out of his box, or just a misreading of the day's protocol. Whatever, when the results come in, something is obviously screwed up, and then the action can begin.

The misreading is not the important error; it opens the way. The next step is the crucial one. If the investigator can bring himself to say, "But even so, look at that!" then the new finding, whatever it is, is ready for snatching. What is needed, for progress to be made, is the move based on error.   9

Whenever new kinds of thinking are about to be accomplished, or new varieties of music, there has to be an argument beforehand. With two sides debating in the same mind, haranguing, there is an amiable understanding that one is right and the other wrong. Sooner or later the thing is settled, but there can be no action at all if there are not the two sides, and the argument. The hope is in the faculty of wrongness, the tendency toward error. The capacity to leap across mountains of information to land lightly on the wrong side represents the highest of human endowments.   10

It may be that this is a uniquely human gift, perhaps even stipulated in our genetic instructions. Other creatures do not seem to have DNA sequences for making mistakes as a routine part of daily living, certainly not for programmed error as a guide for action.   11

We are at our human finest, dancing with our minds, when there are more choices than two. Sometimes there are ten, even twenty different ways to go, all but one bound to be wrong, and the richness of selection in such situations can lift us onto totally new ground. This process is called exploration and is based on human fallibility. If we had only a single center in our brains, capable of responding only when a correct decision was to   12 be made, instead of the jumble of different, credulous, easily conned clusters of neurones that provide for being flung off into blind alleys, up trees, down dead ends, out into blue sky, along wrong turnings, around bends, we could only stay the way we are today, stuck fast.

The lower animals do not have this splendid freedom. 13 They are limited, most of them, to absolute infallibility. Cats, for all their good side, never make mistakes. I have never seen a maladroit, clumsy, or blundering cat. Dogs are sometimes fallible, occasionally able to make charming minor mistakes, but they get this way by trying to mimic their masters. Fish are flawless in everything they do. Individual cells in a tissue are mindless machines, perfect in their performance, as absolutely inhuman as bees.

We should have this in mind as we become dependent 14 on more complex computers for the arrangement of our affairs. Give the computers their heads, I say; let them go their way. If we can learn to do this, turning our heads to one side and wincing while the work proceeds, the possibilities for the future of mankind, and computerkind, are limitless. Your average good computer can make calculations in an instant which would take a lifetime of slide rules for any of us. Think of what we could gain from the near infinity of precise, machine-made miscomputation which is now so easily within our grasp. We would begin the solving of some of our hardest problems. How, for instance, should we go about organizing ourselves for social living on a planetary scale, now that we have become, as a plain fact of life, a single community? We can assume, as a working hypothesis, that all the right ways of doing this are unworkable. What we need, then, for moving ahead, is a set of wrong alternatives much longer and more interesting than the short list of mistaken courses that any of us can think up right now. We need, in fact, an infinite list, and when it is printed out we need the computer to turn on itself and select, at random, the next way to go. If it is a big enough mistake, we could find ourselves on a new level, stunned, out in the clear, ready to move again.

Questions for Study and Discussion

1. To what extent do computers resemble human beings? How does Thomas distinguish the reasoning of each?
2. What is gained in the exposition by the comparison with computers?
3. What consequences of human reasoning does Thomas explore?
4. What is the thesis of the essay, and where is it stated?
5. Does Thomas explicitly say that nonhuman beings or things cannot possess the human faculty of reasoning?

Vocabulary Study

1. Explain how the italicized words are used in each sentence. Then explain how the word in brackets changes or modifies the meaning:
    a. "The computer, at its *normal* [average] best, is *infallible* [reliable]."
    b. "After all, the whole point of computers is that they represent an *extension* [development] of the human brain. . . ."
    c. "With two sides debating in the same mind, *haranguing* [arguing], there is an *amiable* [mutual] understanding that one is right and the other wrong."
    d. "It may be that this is a uniquely human gift, perhaps even *stipulated* [arranged for] in our *genetic instructions* [brains]."
    e. "[The lower animals] are limited, most of them, to absolute *infallibility* [predictability]."
    f. "I have never seen a *maladroit* [awkward], clumsy, or *blundering* [muddling] cat."
    g. "Think of what we could gain from the near *infinity* [immensity] of *precise* [exact], machine-made *miscomputation* [misconception] which is now so easily within our grasp."
2. Write a paraphrase of paragraph 12, giving particular attention to the metaphors of the final sentence.

Suggestions for Writing

1. Describe an experience of your own with a computer error. Use your description to develop your own conclusions about the impact of machines on our lives or about some other idea.
2. Discuss an important change that occurred in your life as a result of a mistake you made in thinking about people or about action you intended to take.
3. Explain what Thomas means by *unconscious* in paragraph 5. Then illustrate the point Thomas is making from your own experience.
4. Discuss the extent to which your own experience with dogs and cats supports the statements Thomas makes about them.

Louis Inturrisi

ON NOT GETTING THERE FROM HERE

An American, Louis Inturrisi gained his knowledge of Italian life from experiences in Italy, including teaching English at the University of Rome. In his essay on the Italian way of giving instructions, he draws on his American-Italian background in interpreting the attitudes and behavior of Italians. Inturrisi makes his points through example. He brings humor and insight to the subject.

Before my first trip to Europe, my grandfather, who was then a very confident 82 and is now a very opinionated 100, poured me a glass of wine and gave me the following instructions: Over there, don't believe anything until three people have told you the same thing. I not only found this advice invaluable for getting around Europe that summer, it has proven useful for traveling in other parts of the world as well. Nowhere, however, has my grandfather's advice been more useful than in his native Italy, where a remarkable enthusiasm to assist foreigners is sometimes overshadowed by a lack of reliable information.

One must start by realizing that in Italy the phrases ₂
used when giving directions—such as "go straight," "turn
right," "follow this road"—are not to be taken literally.
Most of the time they are only suggestions. For example,
if you inquire about the location of a museum and are told
to go straight—"sempre dritto"—the phrase usually means
"go straight *and then ask again*." Your informant may or
may not add the second part, assuming that you are
already aware of this vital additional step and will not be
dumbfounded or, worse, upset if the museum doesn't appear in front of you in the next 10 minutes.

The trouble comes from thinking that "sempre dritto" ₃
means that by trudging ahead you will see what you are
looking for. What it really means is that you are probably
on the right track, and there is a very good chance that
you might find the museum somewhere in this area.

Likewise, the phrase "segua questa strada"—"follow ₄
this road"—must be interpreted to mean: "It's around here
somewhere, and if you follow this road, you should see
it." But do not think that just because you've understood
you are within minutes of locating the museum and can
start thinking about lunch. You have asked someone who
thinks you are on the right track, but it is time to follow
my grandfather's advice and ask someone else. If you still
don't find the museum, either it is in the other direction
or you are standing in front of it.

Another sign of unreliability is the phrase "mi pare"— ₅
"I think" or "it seems." A good general rule is to be
suspicious of anything starting with the words "mi pare"
because what follows will inevitably be too vague to be
trusted.

Don't waste time with people who respond to your ₆
question by asking *you* a question. This is a strange linguistic habit some Romans have. As a reply to a request for
information, some people respond by inquiring, "Is it
really around here?" or "Do you know if it's in this area?"
These people aren't being perfidious; they're buying time.
It's best to say "Grazie. Buona giornata," and move on.

It is important to remember that giving accurate direc- ₇
tions is much easier in Manhattan than in Mantua. Many

Italian cities are composed of a myriad of tiny streets, many of which are named after people no one has ever heard of. Moreover, the numbering systems change from place to place. In some cities, the numbers, instead of alternating, proceed up one side of the street and then down the other. Piazzas often have an official name and another by which they are popularly known. Often the best any native can do is give an approximation of where you want to go.

What Americans must avoid is a certain Anglo-Saxon 8
rigidity that manifests itself by taking words (especially words in foreign languages) too literally. For example, "laggiù in fondo" literally means "at the end of the street," but it hardly ever means that the building you are looking for is smack dab at the end of the street you are on. It may, in fact, mean that by walking straight on this street you will see what you are looking for. Or that by going straight *in the direction of* the end of the street you will see a sign directing you to your destination.

I have witnessed innocents abroad rush off happily in 9
the direction of a "laggiù in fondo," only to return minutes later more confused than ever. They didn't realize that just before the literal end of the street, they were supposed to make a turn that their informant never mentioned because he never expected to be taken quite so literally.

Gestures are another source of misunderstanding. In 10
this culture, gestures have the weight of words, a situation that can cause confusion. For example, there is often a confusing discrepancy between gestures and words, especially as regards the words "destra" ("right") and "sinistra" ("left").

Furthermore, Italians don't indicate directions by point- 11
ing with their index fingers. Straight ahead, for example, is rendered by a vertical slicing gesture with the open palm outstretched in front of the speaker. But if the person you have asked raises his palm over his head and wiggles it back and forth in the air, it means that you are in big trouble. His reassuring "si si's" may encourage you to continue in the same direction, but his gesture is saying

something entirely different. It means something like, "My God! You are nowhere near where you want to go," or "That street is way over on the other side of the city!" If the person should drop both palms to his sides, raise his eyebrows and exhale deeply, you're in the wrong city.

There is, of course, always the question of who to ask 12 for instructions. Police officers and taxi drivers are a good choice; newspaper and magazine vendors at sidewalk kiosks are even better. A general rule to follow is to put your trust in whoever answers by mentioning a specific place or landmark, such as, "It's behind Piazza Navona," or "It's next to St. John's Church." Be more than a little suspicious of replies such as, "Over there," or "Two or three streets in that direction."

When asking directions in Italy, an inquiry to one in- 13 dividual very soon erupts into a group effort, with everyone in earshot joining in to offer an opinion. It takes some skill to extract reliable information from the middle of a heated debate in dialect, but when such a debate erupts, I tend to put my faith in the person who seems to be arguing the *least* vehemently. A fact is a fact to this signora, and she sees no merit in wasting time or energy proving the existence of the moon. On you might wait out the debate until one participant offers to guide you to your destination to prove to herself and the others she knows what she is talking about.

I once saw a woman on a bus in Naples rescue a Scan- 14 dinavian tourist from a very loud discussion over the best stop for getting the funicular. Silently, and with mounting anger, the woman listened to the debate, which involved most of the passengers as well as the driver, until the bus arrived at what she knew was the right stop. Abruptly, she stood up, grabbed the Scandinavian by the arm and gently eased her off the bus, while her fellow passengers continued to discuss the issue.

None of this should discourage you from asking ques- 15 tions in your high school or Berlitz Italian. Italians have one of the healthiest attitudes toward their language of any Europeans. They do not expect you to speak their language fluently nor are they ecstatic if you mouth a few words correctly. Rarely do they waste time by making you submit to a grammar lesson in the middle of the street. When they do correct you, it is more of a conditioned response than an admonition.

Armed with this advice, as well as your dictionary and   16
a large-scale map, forge forward with a strong sense of adventure, a keen appreciation of the flexibility of words—and always with my grandfather's advice clearly in the back of your mind.

Comment

Writing for the travel section of *The New York Times*, Louis Inturrisi tells travelers to Italy what to expect when they ask directions in the street. Inturrisi shows that cultural differences play a role in everyday situations. In illustrating these differences, he gives us numerous insights into Italians and Italian culture, and into American habits and culture too. Inturrisi also shows that definition often depends on an unspoken contract between people. Asked to define a word, few of us give as much information as the dictionary provides; we usually begin our definition believing that those asking for information possess some knowledge about the word.

Quesitons for Study and Discussion

1. What mistaken assumptions do Americans hold in receiving directions from Italians? What assumptions do Italians hold in giving directions?
2. What do these differences reveal about the Italian character and Italian life?
3. What do these differences reveal about American character and habits?
4. How does Inturrisi organize his essay? Is he proceeding from less interesting to more interesting facts about Italians, or does he organize the essay in another way?

5. Does Inturrisi describe your own assumptions in asking directions in a strange city? Do you find that age, gender, or ethnic background affects how a person gives directions or receives them?

Vocabulary Study

Describe how each word is used within the sentence.

1. *opinionated* (paragraph 1)
2. *dumbfounded* (paragraph 2)
3. *linguistic, perfidious* (paragraph 5)
4. *myriad, piazza* (paragraph 6)
5. *rigidity* (paragraph 7)
6. *literally* (paragraph 8)
7. *gesture, discrepancy* (paragraph 9)
8. *landmark* (paragraph 11)
9. *dialect, vehemently, signora* (paragraph 12)
10. *fluently, admonition* (paragraph 14)
11. *flexibility* (paragraph 15)

Suggestions for Writing

1. Describe an experience in which confusion resulted after giving or receiving instructions. Then explain what attitudes or assumptions caused the confusion.
2. Characterize a professional class of people or an age group by how they give directions or behave in a social situation similar to the one presented by Inturrisi. In the course of your discussion, contrast this class with another, as Inturrisi does in comparing Italians with Americans.
3. Show how a lack of information about local customs can lead to confusion or misunderstanding between people. Be as specific as you can in illustrating the causes.

Sue Hubbell

FELLING TREES

Born in 1935 in Kalamazoo, Michigan, Sue Hubbell worked for
many years as a librarian in New Jersey and Rhode Island. Since
1973, she has lived in the Ozark Mountains of southern Missouri,
where she is a commercial beekeeper. She has written about her
experiences in Missouri in *A Country Life: Living the Questions*
(1986) and *A Book of Bees* (1988). In describing the process of
woodcutting, Hubbell tells us much about day-to-day country life
and the chores at which everyone must be competent.

1   I was out in the woods early in the morning cutting
firewood for the winter. I do that every day this time of
year. For an hour or two I cut wood, load it into the pickup
and carry it back to my cabin and stack it. It isn't such
a tiring job when I do a bit of it each day, before it gets
hot, and I like being out there at that hour, when the
woods are fresh and fragrant.

2   This morning I finished sawing up a tree from the
place where I had been cutting for the past week. In the
process I lost my screwrench, part screwdriver, part
wrench, that I use to make adjustments on my chain saw.
I shouldn't carry it in my pocket, but the chain had been
loose; I had tightened it and had not walked back to the
truck to put the wrench away. Scolding myself for being
so careless, I began looking for another tree to cut and
found a big one that had recently died.

3   I like to cut the dead trees from my woodlot, leaving
the ones still alive to flourish, but this one was bigger than
I feel comfortable about felling. I've been running a chain
saw and cutting my own firewood for six years now, but
I am still awed by the size and weight of a tree as it crashes
to the ground. I have to nerve myself to cut the really big
ones. I wanted this tree to fall onto a stretch of open
ground that was free of other trees and brush, so I cut
a wedge-shaped notch on that side of it. The theory is that
the tree, thus weakened, will fall slowly on the side of the

notch when the serious cut, slightly above the notch on the other side, is made. The trouble is that trees, particularly dead ones that may have rot on the inside, do not know the theory and may fall in an unexpected direction. That is the way accidents happen.

I was aware of that and was scared, besides, to be cutting down such a big tree; as a result, perhaps, I cut too timid a wedge. I started sawing through on the other side, keeping an eye on the treetop to detect the characteristic tremble of a tree about to fall. I did not have time to jam the plastic wedge in my back pocket into the cut to hold it open because the tree began to sway and started to fall in my direction. I killed the engine on the saw and jumped out of the way.   4

There was no danger, however. Directly in back of where I had been standing were a number of other trees, which was why I had wanted to have the dead one fall the other way, and as it started down, its top branches snagged. I had sawed completely through the tree, but now the butt end had trapped the saw against the stump. I had cut what is descriptively called a widow maker. If I had been cutting with someone else, we could have used the second saw to free mine and perhaps brought the tree down, but it is dangerous and I don't like to do it. I couldn't even free my saw by taking it apart, for I had lost my screwrench, so I drove back to the barn, gathered up the tools I needed, a socket wrench, chains and a portable winch known as a come-along.   5

The day was warming and I was sweating by the time I got back to the woods, but I was determined to repair the botch I had made. Using the socket wrench, I removed the bar and chain from the saw and set the saw body aside. The weight of the saw gone, I worked the bar and chain free from under the butt of the tree. Then I spat and drank ice water from my thermos and figured out how I was going to pull down the tree with chain and winch.   6

The come-along is a cheery, sensible tool for a woman. It has a big hook at one end and a hook connected to a steel cable at the other. The cable is wound around a   7 ratchet gear operated by a long handle to give leverage. It divides a heavy job into small, manageable bits that require no more than female strength, and I have used it many times to pull my pickup free from a mudhole. I decided that if I wound a chain around the butt of the widow maker and another chain around a nearby standing tree and connected the two with a come-along, I might be able to winch the felled tree to the ground. I attached the chains and come-along appropriately and began. Slowly, with each pump of the handle against the ratchet gear, the tree sank to the ground. The sun was high, the heat oppressive, and my sweatshirt was soaked with sweat, so I decided to leave the job of cutting up the tree to firewood lengths until tomorrow. I gathered up my tools and, in the process, found the screwrench almost hidden in leaf mold.

I am good friends with a woman who lives across the 8 hollow. She and her husband sell cordwood to the charcoal factory in town. Her husband cuts the logs because a chain saw, in the Ozarks, is regarded as a man's tool, and she helps him load and unload the logs. Even though the wood is going to be turned into charcoal, it is traditional to cut it to four-foot lengths. A four-foot oak log is heavy; a strong man can lift it, but a woman has to use all her strength to do her part. My friend returns from her mornings sick with exhaustion, her head throbbing. She and I talk sometimes about how it would be if women were the woodcutters: the length would be less than four feet. Having to do work beyond her strength makes my friend feel weak, ineffectual, dependent and cross.

My friend, and other Ozark women, often ask me 9 curiously about my chain saw. Most people out here heat with wood, and if families in the suburbs quarrel about taking out the garbage, here the source of squabbles is getting enough firewood cut early in the year so that it can season. Women usually help by carrying the cut wood to the truck, but it is the men who cut the wood, and since the women think they cannot cut it, they frequently worry and sometimes nag about it.

My female Ozark friends envy me having my firewood   10
supply under my own control, and they are interested
when I tell them that they have had the hardest part of
the job anyway, carrying the wood to the trucks. Cutting
the wood into lengths with the chain saw is not hard work,
although it does require some skill. So far, however, my
friends have not taken up my offer to come over so that
I can give them a lesson in using a chain saw. Forty years
ago chain saws were heavy and certainly beyond the
strength of a woman to use; today they are much improved and light. My saw is a small, light one, but with
its 16-inch bar it is big enough to cut any tree I want to fell.

I know that feeling of helplessness and irritation that   11
my friends have, for that is the way I used to be. Like
many women my age, I would stand back and let a man
change a flat tire. I could press a button on a washing
machine but not fix the machine if something failed. I felt
uneasy with tools other than a needle, a typewriter or
kitchen utensils.

When I began living here alone I had to learn how   12
to break down work into parcels that I could perform with
my strength and I had to learn to use tools that I had never
used and use them easily. Either that, or I would have
had to leave. It was the hardest schooling I've ever taken
but the most exhilarating. When there were Things in the
world too heavy to move where I wanted them to be and
too mysterious to be kept doing what I wanted them to
do, I was filled with dissatisfaction and petulance. Those
Things controlled me.

I prefer it the other way around.   13

Comment

The personal truth to which Hubbell builds her essay will have
no meaning for the reader without the extended example she
gives in her account of cutting firewood. To make her experiences clear to the reader who knows nothing about woodcutting, she combines several kinds of exposition: she defines

the "come-along," describes the process of cutting down a tree, analyzes why trees fall in unexpected directions, and compares her woodcutting with that of the woman who lives nearby. For the reader experienced in woodcutting, she might have chosen another order of ideas.

Questions for Study and Discussion

1. What is the idea or truth that Hubbell illustrates through the felling of trees? How do the details of the essay illustrate this idea?
2. How different would the effect of the essay be if Hubbell had stated her purpose and central idea at the beginning?
3. Were the essay directed to readers experienced in woodcutting, what might Hubbell have omitted and how might she have reorganized the essay?
4. What personal qualities emerge in the course of the essay— particularly in the description of the tree cuttings? Which of these qualities stand out most?
5. Is Hubbell arguing for a change in attitude toward women like herself, or is she merely contrasting her own life with that of her female neighbors?

Vocabulary Study

Be ready to discuss how the details of the essay or the dictionary help you understand the following terms:

1. *widow maker*
2. *come-along*
3. *screwrench*

Suggestions for Writing

1. Develop the central idea of Hubbell's essay through an extended example of your own. You might build to the idea through your example as Hubbell does or begin the essay with a statement of the idea.

2. Develop one of the following through examples drawn from personal experience:
    a. I have known people to stop and buy an apple on the corner and then walk away as if they had solved the whole unemployment problem.—Heywood Broun
    b. If you have to keep reminding yourself of a thing, perhaps it isn't so.—Christopher Morley
    c. There is no substitute for talent. Industry and all the virtues are of no avail.—Aldous Huxley

L. Rust Hills

HOW TO EAT AN ICE-CREAM CONE

L. Rust Hills was born in 1924 in Brooklyn, New York, and attended the United States Merchant Marine Academy and Wesleyan University. He was fiction editor of *Esquire* and *The Saturday Evening Post*, has taught writing, and is now a freelance writer. His books include *How to Do Things Right* (1972), *How to Retire at 41* (1973), and *How to Be Good* (1976).

Before you even get the cone, you have to do a lot of planning about it. We'll assume that you lost the argument in the car and that the family has decided to break the automobile journey and stop at an ice-cream stand for cones. Get things straight with them right from the start. Tell them that after they have their cones there will be an imaginary circle six feet away from the car and that no one—man, woman, or especially child—will be allowed to cross the line and reenter the car until his ice-cream cone has been entirely consumed and he has cleaned himself up. Emphasize: Automobiles and ice-cream cones don't mix. Explain: Melted ice cream, children, is a fluid that is eternally sticky. One drop of it on a car-door handle spreads to the seat covers, to trousers, to hands, and thence to the steering wheel, the gearshift, the rearview mirror, all the knobs of the dashboard—spreads *everywhere* and lasts *forever*, spreads from a nice old car like this, which might have to be abandoned because of stickiness, right into a nasty new car, in secret ways that even scientists don't understand. If necessary, even make a joke: ''The family that eats ice-cream cones together sticks together.'' Then let their mother explain the joke and tell them you don't mean half of what you say, and no, we won't be getting a new car.

Blessed are the children who always eat the same fla-   2 vor of ice cream or always know beforehand what kind they will want. Such good children should be quarantined from those who want to ''wait and see what flavors there are.'' It's a sad thing to observe a beautiful young child who has always been perfectly happy with a plain vanilla ice-cream cone being subverted by a young schoolmate who has been invited along for the weekend—a pleasant and polite visitor, but spoiled by permissive parents and scarred by an overactive imagination. This schoolmate has a flair for contingency planning: ''Well, I'll have banana if they have banana, but if they don't have banana then I'll have peach, if it's fresh peach, and if they don't have banana or fresh peach I'll see what else they have that's like that, like maybe fresh strawberry or something, and if they don't have that or anything like that that's good I'll just have chocolate marshmallow chip or chocolate rip- ple or something like that.'' Then—turning to one's own once simple and innocent child, now already corrupt and thinking fast—the schoolmate invites a similar rigmarole. ''What kind are *you* going to have?''

I'm a great believer in contingency planning, but none   3 of this is realistic. Few adults, and even fewer children, are able to make up their minds beforehand what kind of ice-cream cone they'll want. It would be nice if they could all be lined up in front of the man who is making up the cones and just snap smartly when their turn came, ''Strawberry, please,'' ''Vanilla, please,'' ''Chocolate, please.'' But of course it never happens like that. There is always a great discussion, a great jostling and craning of necks and leaning over the counter to see down into the tubs of ice cream, and much interpersonal consulta- tion—''What kind are *you* having?''—back and forth, as if that should make any difference. Until finally the first child's turn comes and he asks the man, "What kinds do you have?"

Now, this is the stupidest question in the world, be-   4
cause there is always a sign posted saying what kinds of ice cream they have. As I tell the children, that's what they put the sign up there for—so you won't have to ask what kinds of ice cream they have. The man gets sick of telling everybody all the different kinds of ice cream they have, so they put a sign up there that *says*. You're supposed to read it, not ask the man.

"All right, but the sign doesn't say strawberry."   5

"Well, that means they don't have strawberry."   6

"But there *is* strawberry, right there."   7

"That must be raspberry or something." (Look again   8
at the sign. Raspberry isn't there, either.)

When the child's turn actually comes, he says, "Do   9
you have strawberry?"

"Sure."   10

"What other kinds do you have?"   11

The trouble is, of course, that they put up that sign say-   12
ing what flavors they have, with little cardboard inserts to put in or take out flavors, way back when they first opened the store. But they never change the sign—or not often enough. They always have flavors that aren't on the list, and often they don't have flavors that *are* on the list. Children know this—whether innately or from earliest experience it would be hard to say. The ice-cream man knows it, too. Even grownups learn it eventually. There will always be chaos and confusion and mind-changing and general uproar when ice-cream cones are being ordered, and there has not been, is not, and will never be any way to avoid it.

Human beings are incorrigibly restless and dissatisfied,   13
always in search of new experiences and sensations, seldom content with the familiar. It is this, I think, that accounts for people wanting to have a taste of your cone, and wanting you to have a taste of theirs. "*Do* have a taste of this fresh peach—it's delicious," my wife used to say to me, very much (I suppose) the way Eve wanted Adam to taste her delicious apple. An insinuating look of

calculating curiosity would film my wife's eyes—the same look those beautiful, scary women in those depraved Italian films give a man they're interested in. "How's *yours?*" she would say. For this reason, I always order chocolate chip now. Down through the years, all those close enough to me to feel entitled to ask for a taste of my cone—namely, my wife and children—have learned what chocolate chip tastes like, so they have no legitimate reason to ask me for a taste. As for tasting other people's cones, never do it. The reasoning here is that if it tastes good, you'll wish you'd had it; if it tastes bad, you'll have had a taste of something that tastes bad; if it doesn't taste either good or bad, then you won't have missed anything. Of course no person in his right mind ever *would* want to taste anyone else's cone, but it is useful to have good, logical reasons for hating the thought of it.

Another important thing. Never let the man hand you   14
the ice-cream cones for the whole group. There is no sight more pathetic than some bumbling disorganized papa holding four ice-cream cones in two hands, with his money still in his pocket, when the man says, "Eighty cents." What does he do then? He can't hand the cones back to the man to hold while he fishes in his pocket for the money, for the man has just given them to *him*. He can start passing them out to the kids, but at least one of them will have gone back to the car to see how the dog is doing, or have been sent round in back by his mother to wash his hands or something. And even if papa does get them distributed, he's still going to be left with his own cone in one hand while he tries to get his money with the other. Meanwhile, of course, the man is very impatient, and the next group is asking him, "What flavors do you have?"

No, never let the man hand you the cones of others.   15
Make him hand them out to each kid in turn. That way, too, you won't get those disgusting blobs of butter pecan and black raspberry on your own chocolate chip. And insist that he tell you how much it all costs and settle with him *before* he hands you your own cone. Make sure everyone has got paper napkins and everything *before* he

hands you your own cone. Get *everything* straight before he hands you your own cone. Then, as he hands you your own cone, reach out and take it from him. Strange, magical, dangerous moment! It shares something of the mysterious, sick thrill that soldiers are said to feel on the eve of a great battle.

Now, consider for a moment just exactly what it is that you are about to be handed. It is a huge, irregular mass of ice cream, faintly domed at the top from the metal scoop, which has first produced it and then insecurely balanced it on the uneven top edge of a hollow inverted cone made out of the most brittle and fragile of materials. Clumps of ice cream hang over the side, very loosely attached to the main body. There is always much more ice cream than the cone could hold, even if the ice cream were tamped down into the cone, which of course it isn't. And the essence of ice cream is that it melts. It doesn't just stay there teetering in this irregular, top-heavy mass; it also melts. And it melts *fast*. And it doesn't just melt—it melts into a sticky fluid that *cannot* be wiped off. The only thing one person could hand to another that might possibly be more dangerous is a live hand grenade from which the pin had been pulled five seconds earlier. And of course if anybody offered you that, you could say, "Oh. Uh, well—no thanks." 16

Ice-cream men handle cones routinely, and are inured. They are like professionals who are used to handling sticks of TNT; their movements are quick and skillful. An ice-cream man will pass a cone to you casually, almost carelessly. Never accept a cone on this basis! Too many brittle sugar cones (the only good kind) are crushed or chipped, or their ice-cream tops knocked askew, by this casual sort of transfer from hand to hand. If the ice-cream man is attempting this kind of brusque transfer, keep your hands at your side, no matter what effort it may cost you to overcome the instinct by which everyone's hand goes out, almost automatically, whenever he is proffered something delicious and expected. Keep your hands at your side, and the ice-cream man will look up at you, startled, questioning. Lock his eyes with your own, and *then*, slowly, and above all deliberately, take the cone from him. 17

Grasp the cone with the right hand firmly but gently   18
between thumb and at least one but not more than three
fingers, two-thirds of the way up the cone. Then dart
swiftly away to an open area, away from the jostling crowd
at the stand. Now take up the classic ice-cream-cone-eating
stance: feet from one to two feet apart, body bent forward
from the waist at a twenty-five-degree angle, right elbow
well up, right forearm horizontal, at a level with your col-
larbone and about twelve inches from it. But don't start
eating yet! Check first to see what emergency repairs may
be necessary. Sometimes a sugar cone will be so crushed
or broken or cracked that all one can do is gulp at the thing
like a savage, getting what he can of it and letting the rest
drop to the ground, and then evacuating the area of
catastrophe as quickly as possible. Checking the cone for
possible trouble can be done in a second or two, if one
knows where to look and does it systematically. A trouble
spot some people overlook is the bottom tip of the cone.
This may have been broken off. Or the flap of the cone
material at the bottom, usually wrapped over itself in that
funny spiral construction, may be folded in a way that is
imperfect and leaves an opening. No need to say that
through this opening—in a matter of perhaps thirty or, at
most, ninety seconds—will begin to pour hundreds of
thousands of sticky molecules of melted ice cream. You
know in this case that you must instantly get the paper
napkin in your left hand under and around the bottom
of the cone to stem the forthcoming flow, or else be
doomed to eat the cone far too rapidly. It is a grim moment. No one wants to eat a cone under that kind of
pressure, but neither does anyone want to end up with
the bottom of the cone stuck to a messy napkin. There's
one other alternative—one that takes both skill and
courage: Forgoing any cradling action, grasp the cone more
firmly between thumb and forefinger and extend the other
fingers so that they are out of the way of the dripping from
the bottom, then increase the waist-bend angle from
twenty-five degrees to thirty-five degrees, and then eat the
cone, *allowing* it to drip out of the bottom onto the ground

in front of you! Experienced and thoughtful cone-eaters enjoy facing up to this kind of sudden challenge.

So far, we have been concentrating on cone problems, but of course there is the ice cream to worry about, too. In this area, immediate action is sometimes needed on three fronts at once. Frequently the ice cream will be mounted on the cone in a way that is perilously lopsided. This requires immediate corrective action to move it back into balance—a slight pressure downward with the teeth and lips to seat the ice cream more firmly in and on the cone, but not so hard, of course, as to break the cone. On other occasions, gobs of ice cream will be hanging loosely from the main body, about to fall to the ground (bad) or onto one's hand (far, far worse). This requires instant action, too; one must snap at the gobs like a frog in a swarm of flies. Sometimes, trickles of ice cream will already (already!) be running down the cone toward one's fingers, and one must quickly raise the cone, tilting one's face skyward, and lick with an upward motion that pushes the trickles away from the fingers and (as much as possible) into one's mouth. Every ice-cream cone is like every other ice-cream cone in that it potentially can present all of these problems, but each ice-cream cone is paradoxically unique in that it will present the problems in a different order of emergency and degree of severity. It is, thank God, a rare ice-cream cone that will present all three kinds of problems in exactly the same degree of emergency. With each cone, it is necessary to make an instantaneous judgment as to where the greatest danger is, and to *act!* A moment's delay, and the whole thing will be a mess before you've

even tasted it (*Fig. 1*). If it isn't possible to decide between any two of the three basic emergency problems (i.e., lopsided mount, dangling gobs, running trickles), allow yourself to make an arbitrary adjudication; assign a "heads" value to one and a "tails" value to the other, then flip a coin to decide which is to be tended to first. Don't, for heaven's

Fig. 1   sake, *actually* flip a coin—you'd have to dig

in your pockets for it, or else have it ready in your hand before you were handed the cone. There isn't remotely enough time for anything like that. Just decide *in your mind* which came up, heads or tails, and then try to remember as fast as you can which of the problems you had assigned to the winning side of the coin. Probably, though, there isn't time for any of this. Just do something, however arbitrary. Act! *Eat!*

In trying to make wise and correct decisions about the ice-cream cone in your hand, you should always keep the objectives in mind. The main objective, of course, is to get the cone under control. Secondarily, one will want to eat the cone calmly and with pleasure. Real pleasure lies not simply in eating the cone but in eating it *right*. Let us assume that you have darted to your open space and made your necessary emergency repairs. The cone is still dangerous—still, so to speak, "live." But you can now proceed with it in an orderly fashion. First, revolve the cone through the full three hundred and sixty degrees, snapping at the loose gobs of ice cream; turn the cone by moving the thumb away from you and the forefinger toward you, so the cone moves counterclockwise. Then, with the cone still "wound," which will require the wrist to be bent at the full right angle toward you, apply pressure with the mouth and tongue to accomplish overall realignment, straightening and settling the whole mess. Then, unwinding the cone back through the full three hundred and sixty degrees, remove any trickles of ice cream. From here on, some supplementary repairs may be necessary, but the cone is now defused.

At this point, you can risk a glance around you. How badly the others are doing with their cones! Now you can settle down to eating yours. This is done by eating the ice cream off the top. At each bite, you must press down cautiously, so that the ice cream settles farther and farther into the cone. Be very careful not to break the cone. Of course, you never take so much ice cream into your mouth at once that it hurts your teeth; for the same reason, you never let unmelted ice cream into the back of your

Fig. 2

mouth. If all these procedures are followed correctly, you should shortly arrive at the ideal—the way an ice-cream cone is always pictured but never actually is when it is handed to you. (*Fig. 2*). The ice cream should now form a small dome whose circumference exactly coincides with the large circumference of the cone itself—a small skullcap that fits exactly on top of a larger, inverted dunce cap. You have made order out of chaos; you are an artist. You have taken an unnatural, abhorrent, irregular, chaotic form, and from it you have sculpted an ordered, ideal shape that might be envied by Praxiteles or even Euclid.

Now at last you can begin to take little nibbles of the cone itself, being very careful not to crack it. Revolve the cone so that its rim remains smooth and level as you eat both ice cream and cone in the same ratio. Because of the geometrical nature of things, a constantly reduced inverted cone still remains a perfect inverted cone no matter how small it grows, just as a constantly reduced dome held within a cone retains *its* shape. Because you are constantly reshaping the dome of ice cream with your tongue and nibbling at the cone, it follows in logic—and in actual practice, if you are skillful and careful—that the cone will continue to look exactly the same, except for its size, as you eat it down, so that at the very end you will hold between your thumb and forefinger a tiny, idealized replica of an ice-cream cone, a thing perhaps one inch high. Then, while the others are licking their sticky fingers, preparatory to wiping them on their clothes, or going back to the ice-cream stand for more paper napkins to try to clean themselves up—*then* you can hold the miniature cone up for everyone to see, and pop it gently into your mouth.

22

Comment

Hills is writing about the joys of eating ice-cream cones, and he is writing humorously. The problems he describes are real ones, but these are part of the fun of eating ice-cream cones, and he knows that his readers will share this view. Though he gives instructions for each stage in the process, he also knows that his readers are probably familiar with all of the details. The many kinds of analysis—from comparison and contrast to process—can be used for many different purposes, as this delightful essay shows.

Questions for Study and Discussion

1. What in the description of the process depends on the reader's recognition of the problems? How does Hills remind the reader of these problems?
2. What explains the order of the steps in the process? Is Hills moving from the easier to the more difficult steps, or has he chosen another principle of order?
3. What is the overall tone of the essay? How do the drawings contribute to it?
4. Are the various statements about human nature to be taken seriously, though they are presented humorously?
5. The most effective humor develops out of genuine problems and observations—not out of invented ones. Is this true of the humor of this essay?
6. What impression do you get of the writer—his personality, his outlook on life, his sense of humor?

Vocabulary Study

Formal words will often seem humorous in an informal setting: "This schoolmate has a flair for *contingency* planning. . . ." Identify formal words of this sort in the essay, and explain the humor they provide.

Suggestions for Writing

1. Write a humorous description of a process similar to eating an ice-cream cone—perhaps wrapping a large gift, or eating an unfamiliar food for the first time. Let your details reveal something unusual and important about human beings.
2. Write a set of instructions for a job that involves a number of related processes, for example, changing a flat tire. Keep each of the processes distinct, and be careful to define important terms for the person who has never performed the process.

Richard Selzer

MY BROTHER SHAMAN

A former surgeon and teacher at the Yale School of Medicine, Richard Selzer has written numerous essays on medicine and the art of surgery. Selzer grew up in Troy, New York, the son of a doctor, who, impoverished by the Depression, consoled himself by writing a novel. "It is one of my lifelong regrets," Selzer writes in an essay about his father, "that the manuscript has not been preserved. Now that I too have been reduced to the anguish of writing fiction, it should be my holy scripture, my beacon, and my emblem. As it is, I am a writer unmoored, in search of a heritage, catching at stray ancestors." His fiction and essays are collected in *Rituals of Surgery* (1974), *Mortal Lessons: Notes on the Art of Surgery* (1976), *Confessions of a Knife* (1979), *Letters to a Young Surgeon* (1982), and *Taking the World in for Repairs* (1986). In his fiction and essays, Selzer describes the special qualities of mind and spirit needed by the doctor. In this essay on the doctor and the shaman, he discusses one of his ancestors in the profession of healing.

In the cult of the Bhagavati, as it has been practiced in southern India, there is a ritual in which two entranced shamans dressed in feathered costumes and massive headgear enter a circle of witnesses. All night long in the courtyard off a temple they lunge and thrust at each other, give shouts of defiance, make challenging gestures. It is all done to the sound of drums, conches and horns. Come daybreak, the goddess Kali "slays" the demon Darika, then plunges her hands into the very bowels of Darika, drinking of and smearing herself with blood. At last Kali withdraws from the field of battle having adorned herself with the intestines of the vanquished.

It is a far cry from the bloody trances of shamans to the bloody acts of surgery. Or is it? Take away from Kali and Darika the disciplinary beat of tautened hide and the moaning of flutes, and you have . . . an emergency intestinal resection. The technique is there, the bravado, the zeal. Only lacking in surgery is the ecstasy.   2

In both surgery and shamanism the business is done largely by the hands of the operator. The surgeon holds his scalpel, hemostat, forceps; the shaman, his amulet of bone, wood, metal. For each there is the hieratic honoring of ritual objects. The handling of these objects induces a feeling of tranquillity and power. One's mind is nudged from the path of self-awareness into the pathless glade of the imagination. The nun, too, knows this. She tells her beads, and her heart is enkindled. Surely it is true that the handling of instruments is conducive to the kind of possession or devotion that is the mark of all three—nun, surgeon, shaman. The surgeon and the shaman understand that one must honor, revere and entreat one's tools. Both do their handiwork with a controlled vehemence most dramatically seen in those offshoots of Buddhism wherein the shaman ties his fingers in "knots," giving them a strange distorted appearance. These priests have an uncanny flexibility of their finger joints, each of which has a special name. During these maneuvers the shaman is possessed by finger spirits. He invokes the good spirits and repels the evil ones. Such hand poses, or mudras, seen in Buddhist iconography, are used in trancelike rituals to call down the gods to possess the shaman. In like manner the surgeon restrains his knife even as he gives it rein. He, too, is the medium between man and God.   3

The shaman has his drum which is the river of sound through which he can descend to the Kingdom of Shadows   4 to retrieve the soul of his tribesfellow. The surgeon listens to the electronic beep of the cardiac monitor, the regulated respiration of anesthesia, and he is comforted or warned. Even the operating table has somewhat the shape and size of the pagan altars I saw in a tiny sixth-century baptistry in the Provençal village of Vénasque. Upon these slabs beasts and, in certain instances, humans were laid open to appease the gods. Should one of these ancient pagans undergo resurrection and be brought to a modern operating room with its blazing lamps and opulence of linen and gleaming gadgetry, where masked and gowned figures dip their hands in and out of the body of someone who has been plunged into magical sleep, what else would he think but that he has happened upon a ritual sacrifice?

Nor is the toilet of decoration less elaborate for surgeon 5 than for shaman. Take the Washing of the Hands: Behold the surgeon at his ablutions. His lavabo is a deep sink, often of white porcelain, with a central faucet controlled by the knee. The soap he uses is thick and red as iodine. It is held in a nozzled bottle on the wall. The surgeon depresses a pedal on the floor. Once, twice, three times and collects in his cupped palm a puddle of the soap. There it would sit, lifeless, if he did not add a little water from the faucet and begin to brush. Self-containment is part of the nature of soap. Now, all at once, suds break as air and water are incorporated. Here and there in the play of the bristles, bubbles, first one, then another and another, lift from the froth and achieve levitation. For a moment each globule sways in front of the surgeon's dazzled eyes, but only long enough to give him its blessing before winking out. Meanwhile, the stern brush travels back and forth through the slush of forearms, raising wakes of gauze, scratching the skin . . . Oh, not to hurt or abrade, but tenderly, as one scratches the ears of a dog. At last the surgeon thrusts his hands into the stream of water. A dusky foam darkens the porcelain and fades like smoke. A moment later the sink is calm and white. The surgeon too is calm. And purified.

The washing of the hands, then, is at once a rational 6 step in the achievement of sterile technique and a ritual act carried out under the glance of God by which one is made ready to behold, to perform. It is not wholly unlike the whirling of dervishes, or the to and fro rocking of the orthodox Jew at his prayers. The mask, cap, gown and gloves that the surgeon puts on prior to surgery echo, do they not, the phylacteries of this same Jew? Prophetic wisdom, if it will come at all, is most likely to come to one so sacredly trussed. By these simple acts of bathing and adorning, both surgeon and shaman are made receptacular.

Time was when, in order to become a shaman, one 7 had to undergo an initiatory death and resurrection. The aspirant had to be taken to the sky or the netherworld; often he would be dismembered by spirits, cooked in a pot and eaten by them. Only then could he be born again as a shaman. No such rite of passage goes into the making of a surgeon, it is true, but there is something about the process of surgical training that is reminiscent of the sacred ur-drama after all. The modern surgical intern must undergo a long and arduous novitiate during which the subjugation of the will and spirit to the craft is virtually complete. After a number of years of abasement and humiliation he or she is led to a room where no one else is permitted. There is the donning of special raiment, the washing of the hands and, at last, the performance of secret rites before the open ark of the body. In this, surgery remains a hieratic pantomime marked by exorcism, propitiation and invocation. God dwells in operating rooms as He does everywhere. More than once I have surmised a presence . . . something between hearing and feeling. . . .

In the selection of students to enter medical school, I 8 wonder whether the present weight given to academic excellence in organic chemistry is justified. At least as valid a selection would be based upon the presence of a bat-shaped mole on the inner aspect of the thigh of the aspirant, or a specific conjunction of the planets on his birthday. Neither seems more prophetic than the other in the matter of intuition, compassion and ingenuity which form the trinity of doctorhood.

The shaman's journey through disorder and illness to   9
health has parallels to the surgeon's journey into the body.
Both are like Jason setting out in the Argos, weathering
many storms to return at last with the Golden Fleece. Or
Galahad with the Holy Grail. The extirpated gallbladder,
then, becomes the talisman of the surgeon's journey, the
symbol of his hard-won manhood. What is different is that
the surgeon practices inherited rites, while the shaman is
susceptible to visions. Still, they both perform acts bent
upon making chaos into cosmos.

Saint John of the Cross alludes to the mystic as a soli-   10
tary bird who must seek the heights, admit of no companionship even with its own kind, stretch out its beak
into the air, and sing sweetly. I think of such a shaman
soaring, plummeting, riding ecstatic thermals to the stars,
tumbling head over heels, and at last descending among
the fog of dreams. If, as it seems, the mark of the shaman
was his ability to take flight, soaring to the sky or plummeting to the earth in search of his quarry, only the astronaut or the poet would now qualify.

Ever since Nietzsche delivered his stunning pronounce-   11
ment—"Dead are all the gods"—man has been forced to
assume the burden of heroism without divine assistance.
All the connections to the ancestral past have been
severed. It is our rashest act. For no good can come to
a race that refuses to acknowledge the living spirit of ancient kingdoms. Ritual has receded from the act of surgery.
Only the flavor of it is left, giving, if not to the performers,
then to the patients and to those forbidden to witness
these events, a shiver of mysticism. Few and far between
are the surgeons who consider what they do an encounter
with the unknown. When all is said and done, I am left
with the suspicion that we have gone too far in our ar-
rogant drift from the priestly forebears of surgery. It is
pleasing to imagine surgeons bending over their incisions
with love, infusing them with the impalpable. Only then
would the surgeon, like the shaman, turn himself into a
small god and re-create the world.

Comment

"The machine does not exist that can take the place of the divining physician," Selzer writes in another of his essays, "Textbook." "The physical examination affords the opportunity to touch your patient. It gives the patient the opportunity to be touched by you. In this exchange, messages are sent from one to the other that, if your examination is performed with honesty and humility, will cause the divining powers of the Augurs to be passed on to you—their last heir." The Augurs were the official soothsayers of ancient Rome, prophets or diviners who depended on intuitive powers. In this essay on the doctor and the shaman, Selzer compares the medical doctor and another of his ancestors who drew on special powers of mind and spirit to heal.

Questions for Study and Discussion

1. What details in the ritual described in paragraph 1 suggest to Selzer that the goddess Kali is performing an act of healing by slaying the demon Darika?

2. What similarities in the use of hands lead Selzer to the conclusion that the surgeon and the shaman act as a "medium between man and God"? What additional support does Selzer find for this conclusion in the washing of hands?

3. What other similarities between the surgeon and the shaman does Selzer discuss? Does he draw the same conclusion from these similarities, or does he draw other conclusions?

4. Does Selzer stress any differences between the surgeon and the shaman? Or is he concerned only with similarities?

5. What is Selzer's purpose in making comparisons between the surgeon and the shaman and between the surgeon, the nun, and the orthodox Jew?

6. What is the thesis of the essay and where does it appear? Does Selzer restate the thesis in the course of the essay?

7. Is the comparison developed point by point or in blocks— that is, the characteristics of the doctor presented first and then those of the shaman?

Vocabulary Study

1. Does the dictionary definition of *shaman* mention qualities that Selzer does not discuss? Does Selzer define the word formally, or instead assume that his readers know its meaning?
2. Be ready to define the following words:
   a. *resection* (paragraph 2)
   b. *hemostat, forceps, amulet* (paragraph 3)
   c. *cardiac monitor, baptistry* (paragraph 4)
   d. *ablutions, lavabo, levitation, abrade* (paragraph 5)
   e. *phylacteries, trussed* (paragraph 6)
   f. *netherworld, novitiate, exorcism, surmised* (paragraph 7)
   g. *extirpated* (paragraph 9)
   h. *thermals* (paragraph 10)
3. Selzer refers to the "hieratic honoring of ritual objects" (paragraph 3). What do the words *hieratic* and *ritual* mean? What is the "Buddhist iconography" that is referred to in the same paragraph?
4. Use a classical dictionary and other special dictionaries to explain the references to Jason and the Golden Fleece (paragraph 9), Saint John of the Cross (paragraph 10), and Friedrich Nietzsche (paragraph 11).

Suggestions for Writing

1. Selzer defines other qualities of the medical doctor and surgeon in various essays: *Mortal Lessons: Notes on the Art of Surgery, Confessions of a Knife,* and *Taking the World in for Repairs.* After reading an essay in one of these collections, discuss the insight it gives into Selzer's conception of the ideal doctor or surgeon.
2. Discuss significant similarities and differences between one of the following pairs. Use your comparison to develop a thesis:
   a. learning to swim and learning to drive
   b. the experienced and the inexperienced driver
   c. reading a newspaper and reading a novel
   d. listening to a recording and attending a concert
   e. high school and college friends

Noel Perrin

CLASS STRUGGLE IN THE WOODS

Noel Perrin graduated from Williams College in 1949 and later did graduate work at Duke and Cambridge universities. Since 1959, Perrin has taught English at Dartmouth College, in Hanover, New Hampshire, and has farmed in nearby Vermont. His numerous essays on Vermont life are collected in *First Person Rural: Essays of a Sometime Farmer* (1978) and later books. In the essay reprinted here from *Third Person Rural* (1983), Perrin compares two Vermont social classes and their diverse interests. Perrin reveals much about his own interests and background in the course of his discussion.

Americans are notoriously hard to divide along class   1
lines. With the exception of professors of sociology (who know exactly where in the upper middle class they fit) and a few billionaires—who hope they are upper-class, but have a horrible fear there may be a real aristocracy hiding somewhere in Boston or Philadelphia—most of us have only the vaguest idea what class we belong to.

American sports are notoriously even harder to classify   2
than most activities. I mean more than the obvious fact that rich and poor rub shoulders at baseball games, or that a carload of Cornell professors may turn up at a quite grubby boxing match, having driven four hours to get there. I mean that even where myth says there is a distinction, it won't stand up under examination. Myth says, for example, that people with yachts are upper-class and people with motorboats aren't. Myth is full of it. The board of directors of any large corporation is likely to contain some old poop who owns a yacht and another old poop who is commodore of a power squadron. Sometimes it's even the same old poop at different stages of his career. Similarly, one and the same lower-income family on the Maine coast is likely enough to own both a little motorboat and a little sailboat.

There is one exception to all this camaraderie. At least   3
there is in New England. The two winter sports of snowmobiling and cross-country skiing split along class lines

so sharply that if I were a sociologist engaged in classify-
ing some little town in Massachusetts or Vermont, I
wouldn't even bother to study residence patterns or sex-
ual habits. I'd just wait for winter. Then I'd hang around
in the woods and see who came humping by on skis and
who roared past on a snow machine. I could divide that
town in one day, provided snow conditions were good.

Why cross-country skiing and snowmobiling reflect   4
class lines so perfectly is not easy to figure out. Certainly
it is not a conscious act of group loyalty. No one says,
"Hm, I run the town dump, so I'd better get a snow
machine," or "Well, I *was* a Wellesley dropout; I need
some knickers and a pair of Finnish touring skis."

It is tempting to think it must have something to do   5
with instant gratification versus patience and discipline.
After all, what is supposed to characterize middle-class
behavior is the ability to defer pleasure. Give a lower-class
type a thousand dollars, and he blows it in three days, the
theory goes; whereas if you give a middle-class person the
thousand, he invests it at fourteen percent. Then six months
later he blows the interest. (Unless he's *really* committed
to bourgeois values, in which case he waits thirty-five years,
and then spends the interest on the interest.)

But that won't wash. It's true enough that you can   6
leap on a snowmobile as a total novice and vroom right
off, while the technique of cross-country takes some acquiring. But it's also true that the snowmobiler may be
a devoted pool player as well, and he devoted plenty of
time to learning *that*. Or he may have put in hundreds
or even thousands of hours practicing basketball shots,
punting technique, you name it, all in hopes of future
glory. Some other principle is at work.

Could it be the well-known theory of compensation?   7
This says that the poor, leading relatively powerless lives,
make up for it as much as they can by owning powerful
machines. The more menial your job, the greater your
desire to spend your spare time scaring the wits out of
people with your huge motorcycle. Or dominating the
woods with your snowmobile.

That won't wash, either. *All* classes in America like 8
powerful machinery. People with very unmenial jobs still
get excited about Mercedes-Benzes, and like to dominate
the fast lanes. The really rich go in for private jets. We
need a third principle.

I suspect, though I can't prove it, that the real reason 9
is that both snowmobiling and cross-country skiing started
as rural sports. And to the rural mind the key difference
is that one is a great deal more work than the other.

A countryman's life consists, basically, of an endless 10
amount of physical activity. You get up early in the morning in order to do the chores: feeding livestock, milking,
cleaning the barn, etc. As soon as chores are finished, you
go off to fix fence. As soon as that's done, you climb on
the tractor and start mowing rowen. Since it's just one of
the givens that you are going to be tired every night, you
never waste a movement if you can help it. It is for this
reason that summer people are sometimes amazed and even
scornful to see a native who is cutting wood throw his chain-
saw in a truck and drive three hundred yards back into the
woods where he is working. *They* would have walked,
carrying the saw, saving gas, observing the beauties of
nature. They are environmentalists; he's a clod. Actually,
he's just saving a little extra energy for splitting wood.

It is this Principle of Conservation of Energy, I think, 11
that originally determined who rode snowmobiles and who
put on the cross-countries. In the old days, rural people
simply didn't go out much in the winter—except to bring
in wood and do chores. They could have; they had surplus
time and energy both. The work of a farm is lightest in
the winter. But the principle is deeply ingrained, and their
instinctive preference was to hang around the house, being bored if necessary, rather than go out and do a lot
of hard slogging through the snow in pursuit of something
as ephemeral as mere pleasure. It is for the same reason
that Midwestern grain farmers, who are richer and don't
have chores, tend to go to Florida in the winter. Florida
is essentially the big house around which they hang, until it's time for spring planting.

Then snowmobiles came along. "Ski-doos" they were   12
first called in New England, after the original Canadian
make. Every person in the country perked up his or her
head. I stress "her" because ski-doos were especially appealing to rural wives. All spring, summer, and fall they
were used to working as hard in the house (and sometimes
the barn, too) as their husbands did out in the fields and
woods. With so much cooking to do, lots of them became
pretty hefty women.

Now suddenly here was a way to go effortlessly out in   13
the winter—and not only that, you're riding on the same
machine with your husband. A second honeymoon! The
two of you may revisit, traveling at high speed up the
mountainsides, places you once picnicked when you were
carefree courting youngsters. I know one elderly farm
couple in Vermont, avid snowmobilers, who particularly
like to visit his old work sites. Fifty years ago, they were
just married and didn't have a cent. It was in the depth
of the great depression. He would be out chopping cordwood for two dollars a cord. She would walk all the way
out to where he was, to bring him his dinner (which is
what country people eat for lunch) in a pail. Now they
whoosh out by snowmobile and recall old times.

But, of course, rural people are not the only ones who   14
live in the country. There are also large numbers of ur-
banites. There are the summer people, the young college
graduates who have joined the counter-culture and moved
here for good, the people with year-round second homes.
Their working lives have been very different—mostly
cooped up in offices. If they're tired at night, it's from too
much mental tension. Their bodies cry out for use. So their
principle has been that when you have free time, you try
to find a way to use up energy as rapidly as possible. (This
is the true and original cause of jogging.)

Consequently, they tend to see the countryside as a   15
sort of enormous gymnasium, just as Midwestern farmers
see Florida as an enormous living room. They naturally
opt for skis. And their Principle of Hard Play, like the
countryman's conservation of energy principle, applies

even when the original conditions don't. The young back-to-the-landers aren't cooped up in offices; they're out logging with horses, or spading up a two-acre garden. But come the first big snow, they wouldn't dream of going out on a machine. Childhood conditioning is too strong. They snap on their skis, load a little backpack with gorp, and go out to spend even more energy.

I have been in an especially good position to observe   16
all this, because I happen to be right in the middle. I am one of perhaps ten people in my part of Vermont who is both a snowmobiler and a cross-country skier. I really like both sports. This reflects a deep division in my whole life. Half the time I am a middle-class teacher at Dartmouth, and the other half I am a working-class farmer. I mow fields on contract to summer people, sell wood and stack it for the customers, know what it's like to be one of the help. ("That's not where I told you to stack it," the lady informs me in a cool, regal voice; "move the pile behind the garage.") I am so deeply into rurality that my own childhood conditioning has almost been overcome.

There's just enough left, though, so that I understand   17
very well why cross-country skiers despise snowmobilers. Sometimes when I'm out on skis I do myself. Yes, snow machines are noisy. Smelly, too—fouling the crisp winter air with their exhausts. Yes, it's annoying to spend two hours skiing to some remote and peaceful ridge, alone or with a silent friend, and to think you are utterly away from everything—and suddenly a herd of nine snowmobilers roars up right behind you, and thunders on over the ridge, all but throwing beer cans at you as they pass. Maybe damaging the young forest growth without either knowing or caring. And, yes, it can just about wreck a weekend if some neighbor's nine-year-old child spends most of the daylight hours on daddy's machine, going monotonously round and round one field, wasting gas, forever gunning the engine, doing something very close to profaning the Sabbath. In such moods I reflect quite gleefully that as fuel prices continue to rise, snow machines may just up and vanish. At least in New England, they are already in

decline. Ten years ago, there were 26,654 registered in Vermont. Five years ago, still building: there were 34,715. Now the number has shrunk to 22,107.

But when it's my own daughter out circling our own 18 back pasture, I feel quite differently. Then I admire the skill with which she takes sharp turns on a steep hillside, and the daring of her jumps. I love to see her shining eyes as she comes in from the kind of morning she wouldn't dream of spending on skis.

And when I go out myself, which is usually with a 19 few farmer friends and mechanics, there are two things I understand. One is the sheer pleasure of hurtling headlong across the landscape, and winding up in places one might otherwise never have reached in a lifetime. A clifftop two towns away, say, known to no one but the snowmobilers and an occasional hawk or owl. The damned skiers think we don't notice nature, because we're too busy steering our machines. What they don't realize is that we're usually going somewhere—a further place than *they're* likely to get—and when we reach it, we stop and dismount. Then we see everything. Especially the good views, since we go up a lot of hills. We know their landscape better than they do, as a rule. (A lot of skiers just shuffle around golf courses, anyway—jogging with flaps on their feet.)

The other thing I understand is just how infuriating the 20 middle class is, with its assumptions of moral superiority. They used to say we kept coal in our bathtubs. (If you have a stove right near the bathroom, it can be a handy place, too.) Then they criticized us for having big TV sets when we were poor, and buying expensive cars on time. They didn't stop to reflect that if we didn't buy on time, they wouldn't be *getting* fourteen percent on their money. They need our installment payments to run their economy.

And now they scorn us for our snow machines. 21 They're the ones who are aggressive, not us. If any of them are up here in the winter, they'll call the police in a minute if we go across a corner of "their" land. Even if, and perhaps especially if, it was land they bought from one of us about two years ago. They're the ones who pointedly avert their faces when we pass—do all but hold their noses. We're willing to share the outdoors with them, but they'd like to abolish us. (Though the ones that dare to venture off the golf courses and their little pre-arranged routes seem surprisingly often to take advantage of the trails we've packed down. Then they're outraged if one of us happens to come along our own trail that we made, while they're using it. They think they own that, too.)

I know what they say. They say we are perfectly wel-   22 come to be outdoors, but we should all learn to cross-country ski ourselves. Including Aunt Etty, who is sixty-eight, weighs 185, and has varicose veins. Maybe it would be better for Aunt Etty if she were only thirty-eight, weighed 125, and skied like an angel. But she's not an angel, she's a fat old lady who still works hard (she cleaned your house last week, skier), and this is the only way she'll ever be out here, and she loves it.

And you, you want to take her snow machine away,   23 because it spoils your image of rural New England. It offends your eardrums. But you're smart, skier. You don't say that. You say in a sincere voice that she'd really be far happier, and in much better health, if she did high-energy sports like you.

One time one of you told us to eat cake, and that ad-   24 vice was just about as useful.

Comment

Noel Perrin writes about winter sports in Vermont from a double point of view. As English professor and Vermont farmer, he belongs to both worlds—that of the middle-class skier and the working-class snowmobiler. He writes about the two groups with humor and insight, revealing American attitudes toward class. Although he discusses similarities between snowmobilers and cross-country skiers, his chief concern in the essay is with the differences. For these are central to his thesis. Perrin states his thesis early in the essay, but we do not understand it fully until he has completed his informal comparison.

Questions for Study and Discussion

1. Is Perrin writing a sociological analysis of Vermont winter sports? Or does he have another purpose in writing—perhaps to comment humorously on the character and life of Vermonters or on Americans in general?
2. What is Perrin's thesis and where does it appear? Does Perrin restate the thesis in the course of the essay?
3. How does Perrin develop his thesis through his informal comparison between snowmobilers and cross-country skiers?
4. Is the comparison a block comparison or a point-by-point one (p. 76)? Or does Perrin employ both methods of organization?
5. Why are Americans "notoriously hard to divide along class lines"? What class lines does Perrin distinguish?
6. Does Perrin identify himself with middle-class cross-country skiers rather than with working-class snowmobilers? Or does he identify with both classes?
7. What does the analysis reveal about Vermont life? Does Perrin consider Vermonters typical of Americans? How do you know?
8. Can you think of other sports that reveal class differences? If so, are work habits the explanation for sport preferences, as in snowmobiling and cross-country skiing?

Vocabulary Study

Give the general dictionary meaning of the following words. Then explain the specific meaning of the word or phrase as used in the paragraph:

1. *myth* (paragraph 2)
2. *camaraderie* (paragraph 3)
3. *novice* (paragraph 6)
4. *compensation, menial* (paragraph 7)
5. *Principle of Conservation of Energy, ingrained, ephemeral* (paragraph 11)
6. *counter-culture* (paragraph 14)

Suggestions for Writing

1. Explain why you enjoy one sport more than another. If you
    enjoy two sports equally, describe the pleasures you derive
    from each. In the course of your discussion, compare and
    contrast the sports—noting similarities and differences.
2. Discuss another sport played by Americans that may reveal
    class differences. Explain why it does or does not.
3. Perrin describes the attitudes toward work in Vermont. Dis-
    cuss whether these attitudes reflect your own or are the
    attitudes of people in your state or hometown.

Arthur L. Campa

ANGLO VS. CHICANO: WHY?

Arthur L. Campa was chairman of the Department of Modern
Languages at the University of Denver and the director of the
Center of Latin American Studies from 1946 to 1978. He served in
the U.S. Air Force and the Peace Corps. His several books on
Hispanic-American culture include *Treasure of the Sangre de Cristos*
and *Hispanic Culture in the Southwest*. Campa depends chiefly on
contrast to develop his exposition.

The cultural differences between Hispanic and Anglo-   1
American people have been dwelt upon by so many
writers that we should all be well informed about the
values of both. But audiences are usually of the same persuasion as the speakers, and those who consult published
works are for the most part specialists looking for affirma-
tion of what they believe. So, let us consider the same subject, exploring briefly some of the basic cultural differences
that cause conflict in the Southwest, where Hispanic and
Anglo-American cultures meet.

Cultural differences are implicit in the conceptual con-   2
tent of the languages of these two civilizations, and their
value systems stem from a long series of historical circumstances. Therefore, it may be well to consider some of

the English and Spanish cultural configurations before these Europeans set foot on American soil. English culture was basically insular, geographically and ideologically; was more integrated on the whole, except for some strong theological differences; and was particularly zealous of its racial purity. Spanish culture was peninsular, a geographical circumstance that made it a catchall of Mediterranean, central European and north African peoples. The composite nature of the population produced a marked regionalism that prevented close integration, except for religion, and led to a strong sense of individualism. These differences were reflected in the colonizing enterprise of the two cultures. The English isolated themselves from the Indians physically and culturally; the Spanish, who had strong notions about *pureza de sangre* [purity of blood] among the nobility, were not collectively averse to adding one more strain to their racial cocktail. Cortés led the way by siring the first *mestizo* in North America, and the rest of the conquistadores followed suit. The ultimate products of these two orientations meet today in the Southwest.

Anglo-American culture was absolutist at the onset;   3
that is, all the dominant values were considered identical for all, regardless of time and place. Such values as justice, charity, honesty were considered the superior social order for all men and were later embodied in the American Constitution. The Spaniard brought with him a relativistic viewpoint and saw fewer moral implications in man's actions. Values were looked upon as the result of social and economic conditions.

The motives that brought Spaniards and Englishmen to   4
America also differed. The former came on an enterprise of discovery, searching for a new route to India initially, and later for new lands to conquer, the fountain of youth, minerals, the Seven Cities of Cíbola and, in the case of the missionaries, new souls to win for the Kingdom of Heaven. The English came to escape religious persecution, and once having found a haven, they settled down to cultivate the soil and establish their homes. Since the Spaniards were not seeking a refuge or running away from

anything, they continued their explorations and circled the globe twenty-five years after the discovery of the New World.

This peripatetic tendency of the Spaniard may be ac-   5
counted for in part by the fact that he was the product of an equestrian culture. Men on foot do not venture far into the unknown. It was almost a century after the landing on Plymouth Rock that Governor Alexander Spotswood of Virginia crossed the Blue Ridge Mountains, and it was not until the nineteenth century that the Anglo-Americans began to move west of the Mississippi.

The Spaniard's equestrian role meant that he was not   6
close to the soil, as was the Anglo-American pioneer, who tilled the land and built the greatest agricultural industry in history. The Spaniard cultivated the land only when he had Indians available to do it for him. The uses to which the horse was put also varied. The Spanish horse was essentially a mount, while the more robust English horse was used in cultivating the soil. It is therefore not surprising that the viewpoints of these two cultures should differ when we consider that the pioneer is looking at the world at the level of his eyes while the *caballero* [horseman] is looking beyond and down at the rest of the world.

One of the most commonly quoted, and often mis-   7
interpreted, characteristics of Hispanic peoples is the deeply ingrained individualism in all walks of life. Hispanic individualism is a revolt against the incursion of collectivity, strongly asserted when it is felt that the ego is being fenced in. This attitude leads to a deficiency in those social qualities based on collective standards, an attitude that Hispanos do not consider negative because it manifests a measure of resistance to standardization in order to achieve a measure of individual freedom. Naturally, such an attitude has no *reglas fijas* [fixed rules].

Anglo-Americans who achieve a measure of success   8
and security through institutional guidance not only do not mind a few fixed rules but demand them. The lack of a concerted plan of action, whether in business or in politics, appears unreasonable to Anglo-Americans. They

have a sense of individualism, but they achieve it through action and self-determination. Spanish individualism is based on feeling, on something that is the result not of rules and collective standards but of a person's momentary, emotional reaction. And it is subject to change when the mood changes. In contrast to Spanish emotional individualism, the Anglo-American strives for objectivity when choosing a course of action or making a decision.

The Southwestern Hispanos voiced strong objections to the lack of courtesy of the Anglo-Americans when they first met them in the early days of the Santa Fe trade. The same accusation is leveled at the *Americanos* today in many quarters of the Hispanic world. Some of this results from their different conceptions of polite behavior. Here too one can say that the Spanish have no *reglas fijas* because for them courtesy is simply an expression of the way one person feels toward another. To some they extend the hand, to some they bow and for the more *intimos* there is the well-known *abrazo*. The concepts of "good or bad" or "right and wrong" in polite behavior are moral considerations of an absolutist culture.

Another cultural contrast appears in the way both cultures share part of their material substance with others. The pragmatic Anglo-American contributes regularly to such institutions as the Red Cross, the United Fund and a myriad of associations. He also establishes foundations and quite often leaves millions to such institutions. The Hispano prefers to give his contribution directly to the recipient so he can see the person he is helping.

A century of association has inevitably acculturated both Hispanos and Anglo-Americans to some extent, but there still persist a number of culture traits that neither group has relinquished altogether. Nothing is more disquieting to an Anglo-American who believes that time is money than the time perspective of Hispanos. They usually refer to this attitude as the *"mañana* psychology." Actually, it is more of a "today psychology," because Hispanos cultivate the present to the exclusion of the future; because the latter has not arrived yet, it is not a reality. They are reluctant to relinquish the present, so they hold on to it until it becomes the past. To an Hispano, nine is nine until it is ten, so when he arrives at nine-thirty, he jubilantly exclaims: *"¡Justo!"* [right on time]. This may be why the clock is slowed down to a walk in Spanish while in English it runs. In the United States, our future-oriented civilization plans our lives so far in advance that the present loses its meaning. January magazine issues are out in December; 1973 cars have been out since October; cemetery plots and even funeral arrangements are bought on the installment plan. To a person engrossed in living today the very idea of planning his funeral sounds like the tolling of the bells.

It is a natural corollary that a person who is present   12 oriented should be compensated by being good at improvising. An Anglo-American is told in advance to prepare for an "impromptu speech," but an Hispano usually can improvise a speech because *"Nosotros lo improvisamos todo"* [we improvise everything].

Another source of cultural conflict arises from the dif-   13 ference between *being* and *doing*. Even when trying to be individualistic, the Anglo-American achieves it by what he does. Today's young generation decided to be themselves, to get away from standardization, so they let their hair grow, wore ragged clothes and even went barefoot in order to be different from the Establishment. As a result they all ended up doing the same things and created another stereotype. The freedom enjoyed by the individuality of *being* makes it unnecessary for Hispanos to strive to be different.

In 1963 a team of psychologists from the University of   14 Guadalajara in Mexico and the University of Michigan compared 74 upper-middle-class students from each university. Individualism and personalism were found to be central values for the Mexican students. This was explained by saying that a Mexican's value as a person lies in his *being* rather than, as is the case of the Anglo-Americans, in concrete accomplishments. Efficiency and accomplishments are derived characteristics that do not affect worthiness in the Mexican, whereas in the American it is equated with success, a value of highest priority in the American culture. Hispanic people disassociate themselves from material things or from actions that may impugn a person's sense of being, but the Anglo-American shows great concern for material things and assumes responsibility for his actions. This is expressed in the language of each culture. In Spanish one says, *"Se me cayó la taza"* [the cup fell away from me] instead of "I dropped the cup."

In English, one speaks of money, cash and all related   15
transactions with frankness because material things of this high order do not trouble Anglo-Americans. In Spanish such materialistic concepts are circumvented by referring to cash as *efectivo* [effective] and when buying or selling as something *al contado* [counted out], and when without it by saying *No tengo fondos* [I have no funds]. This disassociation from material things is what produces *sobriedad* [sobriety] in the Spaniard according to Miguel de Unamuno, but in the Southwest the disassociation from materialism leads to *dejadez* [lassitude] and *desprendimiento* [disinterestedness]. A man may lose his life defending his honor but is unconcerned about the lack of material things. *Desprendimiento* causes a man to spend his last cent on a friend, which when added to lack of concern for the future may mean that tomorrow he will eat beans as a result of today's binge.

The implicit differences in words that appear to be   16
identical in meaning are astonishing. Versatile is a compliment in English and an insult in Spanish. An Hispano student who is told to apologize cannot do it, because the word doesn't exist in Spanish. *Apologia* means words in praise of a person. The Anglo-American either apologizes, which is a form of retraction abhorrent in Spanish, or compromises, another concept foreign to Hispanic culture. *Compromiso* means a date, not a compromise. In colonial Mexico City, two hidalgos once entered a narrow street from opposite sides, and when they could not go around, they sat in their coaches for three days until the viceroy ordered them to back out. All this because they could not work out a compromise.

It was that way then and to some extent now. Many of   17
today's conflicts in the Southwest have their roots in polar-
ized cultural differences, which need not be irreconcilable
when approached with mutual respect and understanding.

Comment

Campa states the subject of his essay in his opening paragraph—the "basic cultural differences that cause conflict in the
Southwest." And he states his thesis at the start of his second:
"Cultural differences are implicit in the conceptual content of
the languages of these two civilizations, and their value systems
stem from a long series of historical circumstances." Paragraphs
2 through 6 deal with the second part of this statement, identifying important Hispanic and Anglo-American values and historical circumstances. Paragraphs 7 through 17 explore related
values and connect these values to the conceptual content of
Hispanic and Anglo-American words and phrases.

Campa depends on formal transitions throughout, sometimes using the opening sentences of his paragraphs as signposts
to show the major turns in his analysis:

> A century of association has inevitably acculturated both His-
> panos and Anglo-Americans to some extent, but there still
> persist a number of culture traits that neither group has re-
> linquished altogether. (paragraph 11)

The topic sentence of the paragraph immediately follows:

> Nothing is more disquieting to an Anglo-American who be-
> lieves that time is money than the time perspective of
> Hispanos.

Both the transitional and the topic sentences here mark the contrasts Campa is developing. Campa gives emphasis to these
contrasts in the opening sentences of most of the paragraphs.

Questions for Study and Discussion

1. What topic does Campa begin his analysis with in paragraph
   2? What topic does he turn to in paragraph 3?

2. Campa turns in paragraph 4 to the first of several historical circumstances. Which circumstance does he begin with? How are the circumstances discussed in paragraphs 5 and 6 related to that of paragraph 4?
3. How is Hispanic individualism—introduced in paragraph 7 and explored by contrast in paragraph 8—suggested by the Hispanic equestrian role discussed in paragraph 6?
4. Paragraph 9, which illustrates the differences in Hispanic and Anglo-American individualism, introduces differences in the conceptual content of Spanish and English. What are these concepts?
5. What different values does Campa explore in paragraph 10? How are the different values discussed in paragraph 11 related to these? How does Campa illustrate the differences in these paragraphs? How does paragraph 12 develop the difference discussed in paragraph 11?
6. How do previous differences help to explain that discussed and illustrated in paragraphs 13 through 15?
7. What is the function of paragraphs 16 and 17?
8. Campa develops his essay chiefly by contrast. Which paragraphs open with transitional sentences that mark major turns in the analysis?
9. Are any of the values Campa discusses your own? Is your ethnic background chiefly responsible for them?

Vocabulary Study

1. Find synonyms for the following words. Be ready to discuss what the etymology of the word contributes to your understanding of its use in the paragraph:
   a. *conceptual, configurations, insular, peninsular, conquistador* (paragraph 2)
   b. *peripatetic, equestrian* (paragraph 5)
   c. *incursion* (paragraph 7)
   d. *pragmatic, myriad* (paragraph 10)
   e. *corollary, improvising, impromptu* (paragraph 12)
   f. *circumvented, lassitude, disinterestedness* (paragraph 15)
   g. *abhorrent* (paragraph 16)

2. What are the meanings of the words *absolutist* and *relativistic* in paragraphs 3 and 9? What dictionary meanings do these words not have in the essay?

Suggestions for Writing

1. Contrast values of your own with those of a friend, perhaps referring to some of the values identified by Campa. Then discuss the possible causes of these differences—upbringing, ethnic background, friends, school. Refer to ideas of Campa if these help explain the differences.
2. Campa states: "Even when trying to be individualistic, the Anglo-American achieves it by what he does." Discuss the extent to which this statement describes your way of being an individual. Compare or contrast your individualism with that of one or more friends. Use your analysis to verify or challenge Campa's analysis of American values.
3. Contrast the meaning you give particular words relating to money or success with the meaning given them by friends, parents, or teachers. Try to explain these different uses, referring to ideas of Campa if you find them useful.

Sydney J. Harris

CLIMBING THE MOUNTAIN OF SUCCESS

Sydney J. Harris (p. 77) here explores a popular idea by looking closely at its supporting analogy. As in his essay on the words *liberal, conservative,* and *radical,* Harris writes with the extreme concision and clarity required of a newspaper column, yet without a sacrifice of depth.

It has long struck me that the familiar metaphor of "climbing the ladder" for describing the ascent to success or fulfillment in any field is inappropriate and misleading. There are no ladders that lead to success, although there may be some escalators for those lucky enough to follow in a family's fortunes.

A ladder proceeds vertically, rung by rung, with each   2
rung evenly spaced, and with the whole apparatus lean-
ing against a relatively flat and even surface. A child can
climb a ladder as easily as an adult, and perhaps with a
surer footing.

Making the ascent in one's vocation or profession is far   3
less like ladder climbing than mountain climbing, and here
the analogy is a very real one. Going up a mountain requires a variety of skills, and includes a diversity of dangers, that are in no way involved in mounting a ladder.

Young people starting out should be told this, both to   4
dampen their expectations and to allay their disappointments. A mountain is rough and precipitous, with uncertain footing and a predictable number of falls and scrapes,
and sometimes one has to take the long way around to
reach the shortest distance.

One needs different tools and the knowledge and skill to   5
use them most effectively—as well as knowing when not to
employ them. Most of all, a peculiar combination of daring
and prudence is called for, which not all persons possess.

The art of rappelling is important, because sometimes   6
one has to go down a little in order to go up. And the
higher one gets, the greater the risk and the greater the
fall; there is much exhilaration—but little security and less
oxygen—in altitude. As many stars and standouts and
company presidents have found to their regret, it is often
harder to stay there than to get there.

Then, too, one must learn that there is no necessary   7
relationship between public success and private satisfaction. The top of the ladder is shaky unless the base is
firmly implanted and the whole structure is well defended
against the winds of envy and greed and duplicity and
the demands of one's own ego. The peak of the mountain is even more exposed to a chilling wind, as well as
to a pervasive sense of loneliness. Many may have admired
the ascent, but many more, eager to make the same
endeavor, are waiting at the foot of the slope to witness
an ignominious fall. It is easier to extend good will to those
who do not threaten our own sense of worth.

People who are not prepared for failure are not pre-   8
pared for success; if not for failure, at least for setbacks
and slides and frustrations, and the acceptance of the
deficits that so often accompany the assets. Ambition un-
tempered by realism will never see the missing rung it falls
through on that mythical ladder.

Comment

A special kind of comparison—analogy—is an important method
of exposition and, as Harris points out, a difficult method because of the precision required of the analogy. The writer who
uses analogy must be careful that the differences between the
two things being compared are unimportant and do not weaken
the point being made through significant similarities. Harris
begins his essay by criticizing a weak analogy—climbing the ladder of success. He then develops an analogy of his own—with
mountain climbing—developing each point of similarity and, at
the end of the essay, comparing the weak analogy with which
he began to his own.

Questions for Study and Discussion

1. Why is the analogy of climbing the ladder and trying to succeed in one's vocation or profession a weak one? Why does
   mountain climbing provide a stronger analogy?
2. What similarities between mountain climbing and trying to
   succeed does Harris discuss? Are these similarities of equal
   importance, or does Harris stress some more than others?
3. What is the thesis of the essay and where does it appear?
4. Why does Harris return at the end of the essay to the weak
   analogy criticized at the beginning?
5. Are there other similarities between mountain climbing and
   trying to succeed that Harris might have discussed? Are
   there differences that he might have noted? Do these differences weaken the analogy and therefore the thesis of the
   essay, in your opinion, or are they insignificant?

Vocabulary Study

Define each of the following words, and explain how each differs in meaning from the word immediately following it:

1. *metaphor* (paragraph 1), *simile*
2. *precipitous* (paragraph 4), *steep*
3. *prudence* (paragraph 5), *caution*
4. *rappelling* (paragraph 6), *ascending*
5. *duplicity* (paragraph 7), *cunning*
6. *deficits* (paragraph 8), *hazards*

Suggestions for Writing

Develop a topic of your own by analogy, noting similarities as well as differences between the things being compared. In the course of your discussion, explain why these differences do not weaken the analogy. Here are a few possible topics:

1. making an enduring friendship
2. losing a friend
3. winning an argument fairly
4. winning an argument unfairly
5. asking for a raise in salary and getting it

John Garvey

THINKING IN PACKAGES

John Garvey, a columnist for *Commonweal* for many years, attended Notre Dame University, and after college taught high school and worked as an editor. Garvey writes about contemporary religious and social issues in his column. "There are true and false things," he has said, "and choices which align you with or against the universe." His essay discusses how we think about these things and the dangers of thinking too narrowly.

There is a grave problem which faces those of us who care about ideas. (Notice how I have gathered us all together in a noble little bunch.) It is something I have been   1

paying attention to in a half-conscious way ever since I
first started arguing with people, but it has only recently
surfaced in all its silly array, probably because Ronald
Reagan was elected president. It has to do not so much
with ideas as with the way we relate to them. What I have
noticed at long last, after years of doing all the wrong
things, is embarrassing. It makes me think that everyone—
every anarchist, libertarian, conservative, radical, and
socialist—ought to take a vow of emotional poverty where
ideas are concerned.

We have an investment in our ideas which has noth-   2
ing to do with the particular worth of our ideas. Our ideas
are like clan totems or old school ties. We tend to think
that our ideas make us decent. If we have the right opinion about something, it means that we ourselves must be
basically good folks; and the other side of this is that those
who do not share our feelings on any particular subject
are indecent, even perverse. Our ideas become tokens
which we shove across the table at one another during
conversations to show who we are. They are signals to
people we often don't know very well, which we send
through the space between us to let them know what to
expect of us, and we are delighted when their response
is approving: it means they are our sort. If they bat our
tokens back at us with a cool stare or, more politely,
through careful disagreement, our first impulse is often
to assume that their motive for doing so must be base.

I believe, for example, that the arms race is suicidal and   3
that it is almost certainly bound to end in such destruction as the world has never seen. I am putting this as
mildly as I can. I also believe that to accept it as a tactical
necessity means assuming something which is morally in-
defensible: the military use of civilian populations, and the
willingness to hold them hostage to possible annihilation.
I have noticed that people who disagree with me assume
all sorts of things I not only have not said, but which I
definitely do not believe. They assume that I believe the
Soviet Union to be basically trustworthy and decent, not
at all bad politically; they assume that I do not object to

totalitarianism, and in fact have some sneaky attachment to it, and that I think of America as the world's greatest evil.

The problem is that people on my side of this life and   4
death question do the same sort of thing. Because I agree with them, I tend to forgive them more easily for the moves which, coming from the other side, properly infuriate me. One problem I have always had with *Dr. Strangelove,* much as I enjoyed it, was the sickly consolation it gave to liberals with all of its easy targets. The assumption was that those crazy hawks enjoyed destruction, that they had a romance going with Armageddon. They—our ideological opponents—couldn't honestly believe that unless we met and overtook the Soviets weapon for weapon, we would be faced with a situation in which we might really be forced to accept the domination of a group of people who believe that the Gulag is the proper answer to dissent. They must have a darker reason, something to do with their being anal sorts. They must have had a dreadful relationship with their fathers, or they must have been sexually confused. They couldn't have an honestly different view of the world, a different reading of the same facts.

I disagree with a view of the world which can envision   5
a situation in which our superior strength will force our enemies to back down; we wouldn't be cowed so easily, and it seems naive to suppose that they are that much unlike us. I not only disagree with that view. I think that if it does not kill me off, it will kill my children or grandchildren. Or it may keep them from being killed—at the expense of other people's children and grandchildren. Even if those who defend the arms race as a necessary evil were right in their predictions, I would have to oppose them.

But it is too easy, too self-satisfying, to assume that our   6
own motives in this argument are pure while our opponents are indecent. They are wrong, I think; but to think that they are simply base (or even complicatedly base) involves us in doing several false things. We assume

an ulterior motive, which handily keeps us from having to consider seriously the possibility that our opponents could be right. We assume that no other vision of the world could possibly have anything to recommend it, which keeps us from having to examine our own assumptions very closely. And we assume that our having the right idea, which is usually projected at people who already agree with us anyway, ought to gain us support, applause, and moral approval. We do this whether we are on the left or right. And by offering package deals we make it all easier for ourselves. A woman who knew that I opposed the war in Vietnam was shocked to learn that I opposed abortion, because in her package-deal way of thinking a person who opposed war must be in favor of abortion. The left is assumed by its enemies to be predictable, and so is the right. Both sides are right too often. Left and right *are* both pretty predictable, nearly tribal, and ideas and opinions are frequently waved around as signs of respectability within the tribe, as if language had nothing to do with exploring, or with moving towards a truth in a tentative way, or with being doubtful, or with taking a chance at the edge—which means being willing not only to be wrong, because the only thing at stake here is not whether an opinion falls into the true or false column, but also takes into account the possibility that your opponent is a human being as richly complicated and oddly formed as you are.

That does not make your opponent right. One must firmly believe that there are ideas beyond decent debate. Genocide and child molestation are closed issues, I think. It is wrong not to be passionate about the things we care for deeply. I feel as strongly about nuclear war as I do about abortion, and find it difficult to have much sympathy with defenders of capital punishment. If Matthew 25 is right and what is done to the least human being is done to Christ, then capital punishment, abortion, the notion of a war in which whole populations may be destroyed, and the idea that hunger is in some circumstances acceptable, are all under a terrible judgment. But to think of those whose disagreements with us are deep as indecent or base is to put ourselves under the same judgment. An idea must bear fruit; a Christian perception is meant to go out from itself. If we see it as a personal possession we are on the wrong track. As a possession it is something we have to get rid of.

The Quaker saint John Woolman opposed slaveholders   8 and the men who were about to make the Revolutionary War. He thought that their decisions were profoundly wrong, and he let them know that. His life was a lived disagreement—but he always assumed that he was talking to a human being, one loved by God. Even where we believe that there is no room for debate, we must have compassion—which means *suffering with*, which means understanding how a person could arrive at the place where he is—and we must realize that we share the disease of the heart which allows people to wound one another in the name of truth. Erasmus once wrote about one aspect of this universal problem: "There is great obscurity in many matters, and man suffers from this almost congenital disease, that he will not give in once a controversy is started, and after he is warmed up he regards as absolutely true that which he began to sponsor quite casually."

The point is not to become less committed, or to   9 assume that all ideas are of equal merit, but to be as clear as we can about our own motives, and to approach those who disagree with us the way Woolman did. We should not allow ourselves the luxury of thinking that our ideas have anything at all to do with our decency. We should realize that Matthew 25 applies to our judgments: the least of the brethren includes our opponents.

Comment

Garvey focuses his discussion on both the causes and effects of "thinking in packages." He begins with causes, as in these sentences of paragraph 2: "Our ideas are like clan totems or old school ties. We tend to think that our ideas make us decent." The transition to the effects occurs in paragraph 6: "but to think that they are simply base (or even complicatedly base) involves us in doing several false things." The concluding paragraphs present a solution to the problem. The basic organization, then, is a movement from problem to solution.

Garvey analyzes causes and effects informally, as we would in ordinary conversation. Indeed, that is how he addresses the reader—as a friend with whom he might on another occasion engage in argument. He talks to the reader as he would like to in an argument: casually, amiably, without heat, and without such a narrow focus on the issues that understanding or honest concession becomes impossible.

Questions for Study and Discussion

1. In what ways are "our ideas . . . like clan totems or old school ties"? How does Garvey develop these similes?
2. How does he illustrate the causes identified in paragraphs 4 through 6?
3. What are the effects—the "several false things"—that result from "thinking in packages"?
4. Garvey refers in paragraph 6 to the need of examining our assumptions closely. What is an assumption in thinking, and how does Garvey explain and illustrate the term?
5. If there are "ideas beyond decent debate," how can and should they be discussed with those who hold opposite opinions? How does the statement of Erasmus help Garvey to deal with this question? And what use does he make of Matthew 25?

Vocabulary Study

1. Explain the difference between the following words. The first word in each pair is Garvey's:
   a. *investment* (paragraph 2), *interest*
   b. *tactical* (paragraph 3), *diplomatic*
   c. *totalitarianism* (paragraph 3), *dictatorship*
   d. *hawks* (paragraph 4), *fanatics*

e. *ulterior* (paragraph 6), *deceitful*
f. *opponents* (paragraph 6), *enemies*
g. *genocide* (paragraph 7), *murder*
h. *obscurity* (paragraph 8), *misunderstanding*
i. *congenital* (paragraph 8), *inborn*

2. Be ready to distinguish between the following words in paragraph 1: *anarchist, libertarian, conservative, radical, socialist.*

Suggestions for Writing

1. Analyze an editorial in a newspaper or newsmagazine, or a letter to the editor, to determine whether the writer is "thinking in packages." In the course of your analysis, explain what Garvey means by this term and what his ideas on thinking are as a whole.

2. Develop one of the following statements from your own experience and point of view. If you disagree with the statement, explain why you do:
   a. "We have an investment in our ideas which has nothing to do with the particular worth of our ideas."
   b. "Our ideas are like clan totems or old school ties. We tend to think that our ideas make us decent."
   c. "And by offering package deals we make it all easier for ourselves."
   d. "It is wrong not to be passionate about the things we care for deeply. . . . But to think of those whose disagreements with us are deep as indecent or base is to put ourselves under the same judgment."

K. C. Cole

WOMEN AND PHYSICS

A former editor of *Saturday Review* and *Newsday*, K. C. Cole has written on science and on women today for various periodicals. In the preface to her collection of essays *Between the Lines*, Cole states, "But precisely what I find both so rich and so confusing about women's roles today is that so often what seem to be irreconcilable opposites are just two different aspects of the same thing—two different windows on the same rapidly changing world." She adds, "I think there's more to the many sides of today's woman than meets the eye—and more common ground on many 'women's issues' than most people think." Cole deals with the important issue of women and science in *Sympathetic Vibrations: Reflections on Physics as a Way of Life* (1984) and in this essay, first published in 1981.

I know few other women who do what I do. What I do 1
is write about science, mainly physics. And to do that, I spend a lot of time reading about science, talking to scientists and struggling to understand physics. In fact, most of the women (and men) I know think me quite queer for actually liking physics. "How can you write about that stuff?" they ask, always somewhat askance. "I could never understand that in a million years." Or more simply, "I hate science."

I didn't realize what an odd creature a woman inter- 2
ested in physics was until a few years ago when a science magazine sent me to Johns Hopkins University in Baltimore for a conference on an electrical phenomenon known as the Hall effect. We sat in a huge lecture hall and listened as physicists talked about things engineers didn't understand, and engineers talked about things physicists didn't understand. What *I* didn't understand was why, out of several hundred young students of physics and engineering in the room, less than a handful were women.

Some time later, I found myself at the California Insti- 3
tute of Technology reporting on the search for the origins
of the universe. I interviewed physicist after physicist, man
after man. I asked one young administrator why none of
the physicists were women. And he answered: "I don't
know, but I suppose it must be something innate. My
7-year-old daughter doesn't seem to be much interested
in science."

It was with that experience fresh in my mind that I at- 4
tended a conference in Cambridge, Massachusetts, on
science literacy, or rather the worrisome lack of it in this
country today. We three women—a science teacher, a
young chemist and myself—sat surrounded by a company
of august men. The chemist, I think, first tentatively raised
the issue of science illiteracy in women. It seemed like an
obvious point. After all, everyone had agreed over and
over again that scientific knowledge these days was a key
factor in economic power. But as soon as she made the
point, it became clear that we women had committed a
grievous social error. Our genders were suddenly showing; we had interrupted the serious talk with a subject unforgivably silly.

For the first time, I stopped being puzzled about why 5
there weren't any women in science and began to be
angry. Because if science is a search for answers to fundamental questions then it hardly seems frivolous to find out
why women are excluded. Never mind the economic consequences.

A lot of the reasons why women are excluded are 6
spelled out by the Massachusetts Institute of Technology
experimental physicist Vera Kistiakowsky in a recent article in *Physics Today* called "Women in Physics: Unnecessary, Injurious and Out of Place?" The title was taken
from a 19th-century essay written in opposition to the ap-
pointment of a female mathematician to a professorship
at the University of Stockholm. "As decidedly as two and
two make four," a woman in mathematics is a "monstros-
ity," concluded the writer of the essay.

Dr. Kistiakowsky went on to discuss the factors that   7
make women in science today, if not monstrosities, at least
oddities. Contrary to much popular opinion, one of those
is *not* an innate difference in the scientific ability of boys
and girls. But early conditioning does play a stubborn and
subtle role. A recent Nova program, "The Pinks and the
Blues," documented how girls and boys are treated differently from birth—the boys always encouraged in more
physical kinds of play, more active explorations of their
environments. Sheila Tobias, in her book, *Math Anxiety*,
showed how the games boys play help them to develop
an intuitive understanding of speed, motion and mass. The
main sorting out of the girls from the boys in science seems
to happen in junior high school. As a friend who teaches
in a science museum said, "By the time we get to elec-
tricity, the boys already have had some experience with
it. But it's unfamiliar to the girls." Science books draw
on boys' experiences. "The examples are all about throwing a baseball at such and such a speed," said my stepdaughter, who barely escaped being a science drop-out.

The most obvious reason there are not many more   8
women in science is that women are discriminated against
as a class, in promotions, salaries and hirings, a conclusion reached by a recent analysis by the National Academy
of Sciences.

Finally, said Dr. Kistiakowsky, women are simply made   9
to feel out of place in science. Her conclusion was supported
by a Ford Foundation study by Lynn H. Fox on the problems of women in mathematics. When students were asked
to choose among six reasons accounting for girls' lack of
interest in math, the girls rated this statement second: "Men
do not want girls in the mathematical occupations."

A friend of mine remembers winning a Bronxwide   10
mathematics competition in the second grade. Her friends
—both boys and girls—warned her that she shouldn't be
good at math: "You'll never find a boy who likes you."
My friend continued nevertheless to excel in math and
science, won many awards during her years at the Bronx

High School of Science, and then earned a full scholarship to Harvard. After one year of Harvard science, she decided to major in English.

When I asked her why, she mentioned what she called   11
the "macho mores" of science. "It would have been O.K. if I'd had someone to talk to," she said. "But the rules of comportment were such that you never admitted you didn't understand. I later realized that even the boys didn't get everything clearly right away. You had to stick with it until it had time to sink in. But for the boys, there was a payoff in suffering through the hard times, and a kind of punishment—a shame—if they didn't. For the girls it was O.K. not to get it, and the only payoff for sticking it out was that you'd be considered a freak."

Science is undeniably hard. Often, it can seem quite   12
boring. It is unfortunately too often presented as laws to be memorized instead of mysteries to be explored. It is too often kept a secret that science, like art, takes a well developed esthetic sense. Women aren't the only ones who say, "I hate science." That's why everyone who goes into science needs a little help from friends. For the past ten years, I have been getting more than a little help from a friend who is a physicist. But my stepdaughter—who earned the highest grades ever recorded in her California high school on the math Scholastic Aptitude Test—flunked calculus in her first year at Harvard. When my friend the physicist heard about it, he said, "Harvard should be ashamed of itself."

What he meant was that she needed that little extra   13
encouragement that makes all the difference. Instead, she got that little extra discouragement that makes all the difference. "In the first place, all the math teachers are men," she explained. "In the second place, when I met a boy I liked and told him I was taking chemistry, he immediately said: 'Oh, you're one of those science types.' In the third place, it's just a kind of social thing. The math clubs are full of boys and you don't feel comfortable joining."

In other words, she was made to feel unnecessary, and   14
out of place.

A few months ago, I accompanied a male colleague   15
from the science museum where I sometimes work to a
lunch of the history of science faculty at the University
of California. I was the only woman there, and my
presence for the most part was obviously and rudely ig-
nored. I was so surprised and hurt by this that I made
an extra effort to speak knowledgeably and well. At the
end of the lunch, one of the professors turned to me in
all seriousness and said: "Well, K. C., what do the women
think of Carl Sagan?" I replied that I had no idea what
"the women" thought about anything. But now I know
what I should have said: I should have told him that his
comment was unnecessary, injurious and out of place.

Comment

The issue that Cole explores—whether women lack ability in
science and mathematics—is related to a broader issue considered briefly in paragraphs 6 and 7. This is whether males and
females differ innately in scientific ability. Cole reviews some
recent evidence, then presents personal experiences that support the view that social conditioning plays a decisive role; she
wishes to show, mainly, that girls are discouraged from excel-
ling in science and mathematics. The evidence she presents is
not, and cannot be, conclusive; but it is strong enough to answer
the question she poses at the beginning of the essay—"why,
out of several hundred young students of physics and engineering in the room, less than a handful were women." Her question cannot yet be answered definitely, but the evidence she
assembles from various sources provides what she believes is
a highly probable answer.

Questions for Study and Discussion

1. How various is the evidence Cole presents for the conclusion
   she reaches? Where does she state that conclusion?

2. How many causes does she distinguish for the failure of many women to excel in science and mathematics?
3. Does Cole say that innate differences in scientific ability do not exist between males and females, or does she reach a limited or qualified conclusion?
4. What other kind of evidence might be presented in consideration of the issue of innate scientific ability? For what kind of audience would this evidence have to be presented? For what audience is Cole writing?
5. Does your personal experience support the idea that ability in science and mathematics depends on encouragement and social conditions? Or do you have reason to believe that such ability is inborn?
6. How persuasive do you find the evidence Cole presents in support of her ideas?

Vocabulary Study

Explain the specific use Cole makes of the italicized words:

1. "Our *genders* were suddenly showing; we had interrupted the serious talk with a subject unforgivably *silly*" (paragraph 4).
2. "Dr. Kistiakowsky went on to discuss the *factors* that make women in science today, if not *monstrosities*, at least *oddities*" (paragraph 7).
3. "When I asked her why, she mentioned what she called the *'macho mores'* of science" (paragraph 11).
4. "But the rules of *comportment* were such that you never admitted you didn't understand" (paragraph 11).

Suggestions for Writing

1. Discuss your own experiences in learning science and mathematics, giving attention to the conditioning and encouragement you received, and in general the reasons for your good or bad or just average performance in them. Use your discussion to reach a limited conclusion or opinion on the issue Cole discusses.

2. Discuss the extent to which your personal experience supports one of the following statements:
    a. "The games boys play help them to develop an intuitive understanding of speed, motion and mass."
    b. "The main sorting out of the girls from the boys in science seems to happen in junior high school."
    c. "But the rules of comportment were such that you never admitted you didn't understand."
    d. "Science is undeniably hard. Often, it can seem quite boring. It is unfortunately too often presented as laws to be memorized instead of mysteries to be explored."

Lewis Yablonsky

THE VIOLENT GANG

Lewis Yablonsky, professor of sociology at California State University in Northridge, has written much about juvenile crime. First published in 1960, his essay on a New York City killing shows how social and political conditions at a particular time influence social groups—specifically, youth gangs like the one that committed the crime. Yablonsky draws on a wide range of evidence in his analysis.

It is a truism that criminal organizations and criminal   1
activities tend to reflect social conditions. Just as surely as the Bowery gang mirrored aspects of the 1900's, the Capone mob aspects of the twenties, and the youth gangs of the depression elements of the thirties, so do the delinquent gangs that have developed since the 1940's in the United States reflect certain patterns of our own society.

The following quotations indicate the tone and ethos of   2
a representative gang of today, the so-called Egyptian Kings, whose members beat and stabbed to death a fifteen-year-old boy named Michael Farmer, who had been crippled by polio, was not known to the Kings before the killing, nor had he been acquainted with any members of the gang.

He couldn't run any way, 'cause we were all around him. So then I said, "You're a Jester," and he said "Yeah," and I punched him in the face. And then somebody hit him with a bat over the head. And then I kept punchin' him. Some of them were too scared to do anything. They were just standin' there, lookin'.

I was watchin' him. I didn't wanna hit him, at first. Then I kicked him twice. He was layin' on the ground, lookin' up at us. I kicked him on the jaw, or some place; then I kicked him in the stomach. That was the least I could do, was kick 'im.

I was aimin' to hit him, but I didn't get a chance to hit him. There was so many guys on him—I got scared when I saw the knife go into the guy, and I ran right there. After everybody ran, this guy stayed, and started hittin' him with a machete.

Somebody yelled out, "Grab him. He's a Jester." So then they grabbed him. Magician grabbed him, he turned around and stabbed him in the back, I was . . . I was stunned. I couldn't do nuthin'. And the Magician—he went like that and he pulled . . . he had a switch blade and he said, "You're gonna hit him with the bat or I'll stab you." So I just hit him lightly with the bat.

Magician stabbed him and the guy he . . . like hunched over. He's standin' up and I knock him down. Then he was down on the ground, everybody was kickin' him, stompin' him, punchin' him, stabbin' him so he tried to get back up and I knock him down again. Then the guy stabbed him in the back with a bread knife.

The attitudes toward homicide and violence that emerge from these statements led to eleven gang killings last summer and can be expected to produce an even greater number from now on.

One important difference between the gangs of the past and those that now operate on our city streets is the prevalence of the psychopathic element in the latter. The violent gangs of the twenties contained psychopaths, but they were used to further the profitmaking goal of the gang, and were themselves paid for their violence. Here, for example, is how Abe "Kid Twist" Reles—who informed on Murder, Inc., and confessed to having committed over eighteen murders himself—described the activities of the Crime Trust to a writer in the *Nation:*

> The Crime Trust, Reles insists, never commits murders out of passion, excitement, jealousy, personal revenge, or any of the usual motives which prompt private unorganized murders. It kills impersonally and solely for business considerations. No gangster may kill on his own initiative; every murder must be ordered by the leaders at the top, and it must serve the welfare of the organization. . . . Any member of the mob who would dare kill on his own initiative or for his own profit would be executed. . . . The Crime Trust insists that murder must be a business matter organized by the chiefs in conference and carried out in a disciplined way.

Frederic Thrasher's famous analysis of Chicago gangs   4
in the mid-twenties describes another group that bears only a limited resemblance to the violent gangs of today. Thrasher's gangs

> broke into box cars and "robbed" bacon and other merchandise. They cut out wire cables to sell as junk. They broke open telephone boxes. They took autos for joy-riding. They purloined several quarts of whiskey from a brewery to drink in their shack.

Nor do the gangs of the thirties and early forties de-   5
scribed by W. F. Whyte in *Street Corner Society* bear much resemblance to the violent gang of today. The difference becomes strikingly evident when we compare the following comments by two Egyptian Kings with those of Doc, the leader of Whyte's Norton Street gang.

> I just went like that, and I stabbed him with the bread knife. You know I was drunk so I stabbed him. *[Laughs]* He was screamin' like a dog. He was screamin' there. And then I took the knife out and told the other guys to run. . . .

> The guy that stabbed him in the back with the bread knife, he told me that when he took the knife out o' his back, he said, "Thank you."

Now Doc, leader of the Norton Street gang:

> Nutsy was a cocky kid before I beat him up. . . . After that, he seemed to lose his pride. I would talk to him and try to

get him to buck up. . . . I walloped every kid in my gang
at some time. We had one Sicilian kid on my street. When
I walloped him, he told his father and the father came out
looking for me. I hid up on a roof, and Nutsy told me when
the father had gone. When I saw the kid next, I walloped him
again—for telling his father on me. . . . But I wasn't such a
tough kid, Bill. I was always sorry after I walloped him.

Doc's comments about beating up Nutsy—"I would   6
talk to him and try to buck him up"—or about fighting
the other kids—"I was always sorry after I walloped
them"—are in sharp contrast to the post-assault comments
of the Egyptian Kings. Here is how one of the Kings who
stabbed Farmer replied to my questions about his part in
the homicide. The interview took place in a reformatory.

> KING: "I stab him with the butcher—I mean the bread-knife
> and then I took it out."
>
> QUESTION: "What were you thinking about at the time, right
> then?"
>
> KING: "What was I thinking? [Laughs] I was thinking whether
> to do it again."
>
> QUESTION: "Are you sorry about what happened?"
>
> KING: "Am I sorry? Are you nuts; of course, I'm sorry. You
> think I like being locked up?"

The element of friendship and camaraderie—one might
almost call it cooperativeness—that was central to the Norton Street gang and others like it during the depression
is entirely absent from the violent gang of today. To be
sure, "candy store" or corner hang-out groups similar to
those described by Whyte still exist, but it is not such
groups who are responsible for the killings and assaults
that have caused so much concern in our major cities in
recent years.

Today's violent gang is, above all, characterized by   7
flux. It lacks all the features of an organized group, having neither a definite number of members, nor specific
membership roles, nor a consensus of expected norms, nor
a leader who supplies directive for action. It is a moblike
collectivity which forms around violence in a spontaneous

fashion, moving into action—often on the spur of an evening's boredom—in search of "kicks." Violence ranks extremely high in the loose scheme of values on which such
gangs are based. To some boys it acts as a kind of existen-
tial validation, proving (since they are not sure) that they
are alive. Others, clinging to membership in this marginal
and amorphous organization, employ violence to demonstrate they are "somebody." But most members of the
gang use violence to acquire prestige or to raise their
"rep."

> I didn't want to be like . . . you know, different from the
> other guys. Like they hit him, I hit him. In other words, I
> didn't want to show myself as a punk. You know, ya always
> talkin', "Oh, man, when I catch a guy, I'll beat him up," and
> all of that, you know. And after you go out and you catch
> a guy, and you don't do nothin' they say, "Oh, man, he can't
> belong to no gang, because he ain't gonna do nothin'."

> Momentarily I started to thinking about it inside: I have
> my mind made up I'm not going to be in no gang. Then I
> go on inside. Something comes up, den here come all my
> friends coming to me. Like I said before, I'm intelligent and
> so forth. They be coming to me—then they talk to me about
> what they gonna do. Like, "Man, we'll go out here and kill
> this cat." I say, "Yeah." They kept on talkin'. I said, "Man,
> I just gotta go with you." Myself, I don't want to go, but when
> they start talkin' about what they gonna do, I say, "So, he
> isn't gonna take over my rep. I ain't gonna let him be known
> more than me." And I go ahead just for selfishness.

> If I would of got the knife, I would have stabbed him. That
> would have gave me more of a build-up. People would have
> respected me for what I've done and things like that. They
> would say, "There goes a cold killer."

> It makes you feel like a big shot. You know some guys
> think they're big shots and all that. They think, like you
> know, they got the power to do everything they feel like
> doing. They say, like, "I wanna stab a guy," and then the
> other guy says, "Oh, I wouldn't dare to do that." You know,
> he thinks I'm acting like a big shot. That's the way he feels.
> He probably thinks in his mind, "Oh, he probably won't do
> that." Then, when we go to fight, you know, he finds out
> what I do.

The structure of the violent gang can be analyzed into   8
three different levels. At the center, on the first level, are
the leaders, who—contrary to the popular idea that they
could become "captains of industry if only their energies
were redirected"—are the most psychologically disturbed
of all the members. These youths (who are usually between eighteen and twenty-five years old) need the gang
more than anyone else, and it is they who provide it with
whatever cohesive force it has. In a gang of some thirty
boys there may be five or six such leaders who desperately
rely on the gang to build and maintain a "rep," and they
are always working to keep the gang together and in action. They enlist new members (by force), plot, and talk
gang warfare most of their waking hours.

At the second level, there are youths who claim affilia-   9
tion to the gang but only participate in it sporadically. For
example, one of the Egyptian Kings told me that if his
father had not given him a "bad time" and kicked him
out of the house the night of the homicide, he would not
have gone to the corner and become involved in the
Michael Farmer killing. The gang was for this boy, on that
night, a vehicle for acting out aggressions related to
another area of his life. Such a "temporal" gang need,
however, is a common phenomenon.

At the third level are boys who occasionally join in   10
with gang activity but seldom identify themselves as
members of the gang at any other time. One boy, for instance, went along with the Egyptian Kings and participated in the Farmer killing, as he put it, "for old time's
sake." He never really "belonged" to the gang: he just
happened to be around that night and had nothing else
to do.

The "size" of violent gangs is often impossible to de-   11
termine. If a leader feels particularly hemmed in at a given
moment, he will say—and believe—that his gang is very
large. But when he is feeling more secure, he will include
in his account of the gang's size only those members he
actually knows personally. In the course of a one-hour interview, for example, a gang leader variously estimated the

size, affiliations, and territory of his gang as follows: membership jumped from one hundred to four thousand, affiliation from five brother gangs or alliances to sixty, and territorial control from about ten square blocks to jurisdiction over the boroughs of New York City, New Jersey, and part of Philadelphia. To be sure, gangs will often contact one another to discuss alliances, and during the streetcorner "negotiations," the leaders will brag of their ability to mobilize vast forces in case of a fight. On a rare occasion, these forces will actually be produced, but they generally appear quite spontaneously—the youths who participate in such alliances have very little understanding of what they are doing.

The meaning of gang membership also changes according to a boy's needs of the moment. A youth will belong one day and quit the next without necessarily telling any other member. To ask certain gang boys from day to day whether they are Dragons or Kings is comparable to asking them, "How do you feel today?" So, too, with the question of role. Some boys say that the gang is organized for protection and that one role of a gang member is to fight—how, when, whom, and for what reason he is to fight are seldom clear, and answers vary from member to member. One gang boy may define himself more specifically as a protector of the younger boys in the neighborhood. Another will define his role in the gang by the statement, "We are going to get all those guys who call us Spics." Still others say their participation in the gang was forced upon them against their will.

Despite these differences, however, all gang members believe that through their participation they will acquire prestige and status; and it is quite clear, furthermore, that the vagueness which surrounds various aspects of gang life and organization only enables the gang to stimulate such expectations and, in some respects, actually helps it to fulfill them. Similarly, if qualifications for membership were more exact, then most gang members would not be able to participate, for they lack the ability to assume the responsibilities of more structured organizations.

The background out of which the violent gang has   14
emerged is fairly easy to sketch. In contemporary American
society, youth is constantly bombarded by images—from
the media, schools, and parents—of a life of ownership
and consumption, but for the great majority of young people in this country, and especially for those from depressed
social and economic backgrounds, the means of acquiring
such objectives are slim. Yet something more definite than
class position or the inadequate relation between means
and ends disturbs young people. It is the very fact of their
youth which places them at an immediate disadvantage;
objects and goals that adults take for granted are, for them,
clearly unattainable. As a consequence, many young people step beyond the accepted social boundaries in an attempt to find through deviant means a dramatic short-cut
to an immediate feeling of success.[1]

Drugs and alcohol are two possible short cuts; another   15
characteristic deviant path is the search for thrills or
"kicks." The violent gang, especially because it is both
flexibly organized and amenable to the distortions of fantasy, is an obvious vehicle for acting out the desire for
ownership and status. In the gang, a youth can be "president" and control vast domains, while the members can
reinforce one another's fantasies of power—"Don't call my
bluff and I won't call yours." In the gang, it is only
necessary to talk big and support the talk with some
violent action in order to become a "success," the
possessor of power and status: "We would talk a lot and
like that, but I never thought it would be like this. Me
here in jail. It was just like fun and kidding around and
acting big."

The choice of violence as a means toward achieving   16
"social" success seems to be the result in part of the past
two decades of war as well as the international unrest that
filters down to the gang boy and gives him the same

---

[1]This statement is a gross oversimplification of conceptual developments of Emile
Durkheim, Robert Merton, and others, who have examined the means-goal
dislocation.

feelings of uneasiness that the average citizen experiences. At this level of analysis, direct casual relations are by *no means* precise; yet a number of connections do seem apparent.

A considerable amount of explicit data indicates that recent wars and current international machinations serve as models for gang warfare. For example, one form of gang battle is called a "Jap": "a quick stomp where a group of guys go into an enemy's territory, beat up some of their guys and get out fast. The thing is not to get caught." "Drafting" members is another common gang practice. The boys themselves freely use such terms as "drafting," "allies" (brother gangs), "war counselor," "peace treaty," etc., and they often refer, both directly and indirectly, to more complex patterns of conflict and structure. Here is one Egyptian King talking about a territorial dispute: [17]

> You have a certain piece of land, so another club wants to take over your land, in order to have more space, and so forth. They'll fight you for it. If you win, you got your land; if you don't win, then they get your land. The person that loses is gonna get up another group, to help out, and then it starts all over again. Fight for the land again.

Here is another discussing gang organization:

> First, there's the president. He got the whole gang; then there comes the vice president, he's second in command; then there's the war counselor, war lord, whatever you're gonna call it—that's the one that starts the fights; then there's the prime minister—you know, he goes along with the war counselor to see when they're gonna fight, where they're gonna fight. And after that, just club members.

Murder, Inc., Thrasher's gangs, and Whyte's Norton Street gang did not have the "divisions," "war lords," and "allies" typical of the contemporary violent gang.

In addition to this international model, it is important to note that many weapons now used by gangs were brought to this country by veterans of recent wars. Where in former years, gang wars were more likely to be fought [1] with sticks, stones, and fists, today abandoned World War II weapons such as machetes (one was used in the Michael Farmer killing) and Lugers consistently turn up. The returning soldiers also brought back stories of violence to accompany the weapons. War and violence dominated not only the front pages of the press, but everyday family discussion, and often it was a father, an uncle, or an older brother whose violent exploits were extolled.

Another aspect of international events which gang youths may have absorbed, and which they certainly now emulate, is the authoritarian-dictatorial concept of leadership. Earlier gangs sometimes utilized democratic processes in appointing leaders. But, today, in the violent gang, the leader is usually supreme and gang members tend to follow him slavishly. In recent years, in fact, there have been many abortive attempts—several on the Upper West Side of New York City—to pattern gangs specifically upon the model of Hitler and the Nazi party.

What finally confronts the youth of today is the possibility of total destruction by atomic power—everyone is aware of this on some level of consciousness—and the possibility of induction into the army at a point when he might be establishing himself in the labor force. In short, the recent history of international violence, the consequences of the past war, and the chance of total annihilation, establish a framework which may not only stimulate the formation of gangs but in some respects may determine its mode of behavior—in other words, its violence.

But such background factors, however much they create an atmosphere that gives implicit social approval to the use of violence, cannot actually explain how violence functions for the gang boy. As I have already indicated, gang youths feel extremely helpless in their relations to the "outside" world. The gang boy considers himself incapable of functioning in any group other than the gang, and is afraid to attempt anything beyond the minimal demands of gang life. One interesting indication of this is the way gang boys respond to flattery. They invariably become flustered and confused if they are complimented, for the suggestion that they are capable of more constructive activity upsets their conviction of being unfit for the hazards of a life outside the protective circle of the gang.

Given this low self-estimate, the gang boy has carved 22 out a world and a system of values which entail only the kind of demands he can easily meet. Inverting society's norms to suit himself and the limits of his partly imagined and partly real potential, he has made lying, assault, theft, and unprovoked violence—and especially violence—the major activities of his life.

The very fact that it is *senseless* rather than premedi- 23 tated violence which is more highly prized by the gang, tells us a great deal about the role violence plays for the gang boy. He is looking for a quick, almost magical way of achieving power and prestige, and in a single act of unpremeditated intensity he at once establishes a sense of his own existence and impresses this existence on others. No special ability is required—not even a plan— and the anxiety attendant upon executing a premeditated (or "rational") act of violence is minimized in the ideal of a swift, sudden, and "meaningless" outbreak. (To some extent, the public's reaction to this violence, a reaction, most obviously of horror, also expresses a sort of covert aggrandizement—and this the gang boy instinctively understands.)

Thus the violent gang provides an alternative world for 24 the disturbed young who are ill-equipped for success in a society which in any case blocks their upward mobility. The irony is that this world with its nightmare inversion of the official values of our society is nevertheless constructed out of elements that are implicitly (or unconsciously) approved—especially in the mass media—and that its purpose is to help the gang boy achieve the major value of respectable society: success. "I'm not going to let anybody be better than me and steal my 'rep' . . . when I go to a gang fight, I punch, stomp, and stab harder than anyone."

Comment

Division is an important method of exposition in Yablonsky's essay. First Yablonsky classifies gangs of the past and gangs of the present, then defines their purpose and structure. Second, he divides gangs of the present—the violent street gangs— according to their "levels." This division is, in fact, a more detailed analysis of the structure of the gang, for Yablonsky's earlier discussion of that structure is concerned only with its general features. The three levels reveal the various motives of the gang members. Reflecting the values of the fifties, the violent gang shows how people are directed by forces beyond their control. Yablonsky's concern over the death of Michael Farmer is in part a concern over wanton acts by boys who did not know their victim or themselves. He returns to this point at the end. His essay shows how an episode (the murder of Michael Farmer) can be used to say much about a society—its values, its structure, the motives of acts that seem "senseless."

Questions for Study and Discussion

1. How does Yablonsky explain the difference between gangs of the past and the violent gang of the fifties?
2. By what other principles might the violent gang be divided? To what use could these divisions be put in another essay?
3. Yablonsky states: "In contemporary American society, youth is constantly bombarded by images—from the media, schools, and parents," and he identifies those images and their effect. Yablonsky was writing in 1960. Do you believe youth in the early nineties is bombarded by the same images? Are the effects of images the same today?
4. What does Yablonsky mean in paragraph 14 by "the inadequate relation between means and ends"? How does the context of the statement help to explain it?
5. The phrase "society's norms" (paragraph 22) refers to the values or standards by which people live. How does Yablonsky show that not all of these "norms" are admitted or recognized by the people who live by them?

6. What is Yablonsky's thesis and where is it first stated? How does he restate it in the course of the essay?
7. Yablonsky cites the Second World War and the atomic bomb as causes of certain attitudes and behavior in youth of the fifties. Do you believe war and fear of destruction are a major cause of juvenile crime today, as reported in recent periodicals? Do you believe the pressures to conform are as strong today as they were in the fifties?
8. What kinds of evidence does Yablonsky present for his thesis?

Vocabulary Study

Complete the following sentences, using the italicized word according to one of its dictionary meanings:

1. It is a *truism* of life that
2. One *aspect* of the energy crisis is
3. There was no *consensus*
4. The *phenomenon* of flying saucer reports
5. The teacher was *amenable* to
6. She could distinguish between *fantasy* and
7. They could not *emulate*
8. The contract *entails*
9. There was a *covert* recognition

Suggestions for Writing

1. Analyze the attitudes and organization of a group you belong to. Use your analysis to develop a thesis, relating perhaps to how people behave in groups.
2. Support or argue against one of Yablonsky's conclusions, drawing on your own experiences and observations.
3. Investigate recent accounts of juvenile gang warfare. Then discuss the extent to which these accounts support Yablonsky's interpretation of juvenile criminal behavior.

Robert Coles

SETTLING IN

Robert Coles is Professor of Psychiatry and Medical Humanities at
Harvard University. A psychiatrist concerned with children, he has
served on various boards, commissions, and foundations devoted
to the education and welfare of children. Coles has written a
series of books on American children under the general title
Children of Crisis, the first of these appearing in 1967; the second
and third volumes—*Migrants, Sharecroppers, Mountaineers* and *The
South Goes North*—were awarded the Pulitzer Prize in 1973. With
Jane Hallowell Coles, he wrote another series under the general
title *Women of Crisis*. Coles is also the author of books on
American Eskimos; children of migrant farm workers; the moral,
spiritual, and political life of children; and the fiction and poetry
of some American and English writers. The essay reprinted here is
taken from *The South Goes North*, a study of Southern rural people
living in Northern cities.

Automobiles are hardly anything new to America's   1
youth. Up the remotest hollows one can find them, often
enough broken down and abandoned. But they are used,
too—and in the course of my work with young Ap-
palachian men I have often wondered what we would
have talked about had there not been an automobile to
mention, then discuss at some length, then go over and
look at, and finally drive in. I suppose before there were
cars, men talked about horses. When one first begins to
spend time in Kentucky or West Virginia the roads seem
thoroughly dangerous. If one is like me, possessed of and
sometimes victimized by a particular vocabulary, thoughts
begin to assert themselves: am I crazy or suicidal to be
on these roads with these drivers, or are *they* all crazy or
suicidal—or "aggressive" or "antisocial"? The roads are
narrow and winding and at times tortuous beyond all
others in the nation. Asphalt can without warning turn
into sand or mud. And the drivers: they seem so casual
and vigorous; they move along as though lanes and lanes
of road were on either side of them, and no cars were in
sight for miles ahead—even when only a few inches

separate them from the steepest of hills, or a curve approaches around which totally unseen, a car or huge coal truck may be coming in the opposite direction. Yet throughout the years of my work in Appalachia, I have never seen an accident—which is not to say accidents don't occur, but simply to suggest that my fearfulness must have had something to do with the limitations of my own experience: as a driver I took for granted certain road conditions, consequently I was made nervous when I found them lacking.

By the same token a youth from, say, Leslie County, 2 Kentucky, can find superhighways and most especially city traffic puzzling if not terrifying. All that space and all those cars and all those traffic lights and traffic signs! So many distractions: horns blowing, stores with things in the window and pictures of wine and women! And the turnoffs, the constant intersections, the warnings which insist this highway has now become something else, or is about to join with yet another road—all of that is confusing, as are those constant reminders that one is so-and-so miles from such-and-such a town or city, not to mention from some state line. Then, there are the restaurants and gas stations: how can they all stay open? How can there be so many people eager to use such places? How can there be so many people at all?

For Larry Walker, age seventeen and a half, who is 3 originally from a creek near Thousand-Sticks, Leslie County, Kentucky, but now lives in Dayton, Ohio, those questions are not openly asked. They are very much on his mind, though; and after a beer or two they come to expression. Larry has been in Dayton for five years, but he is not *from* Dayton. His little brother and sister may have the notion at times that they are from Ohio, that Dayton is their home, that their future is to be found in a growing city, but not Larry: "I'm from Leslie County, and I'll always say that's where my home is. When I turn eighteen I'll probably go into the Army. I hurt my arm once, broke it, but I don't think they will hold that against me. They'd be fools to; I'd make a good soldier, I believe.

I've always dreamed I might one day go into the service and maybe stay there for a while. If you stay in twenty years, you can retire, and you have a good pension, and then you can go back to Leslie County and there's no ache over money. We only left the county because we had to leave. My father's brother left first, my Uncle Jim. He got a job here in a factory, and he came back with all those green bills in his hand and told my father he had to come up to Ohio, too; so here we are. My mother says it's like in the stories you see on television: people go away for a while, but then they come home, and they're glad. She means they go on vacation. Like my dad says: it's a vacation having a job and money; you don't have to stand around all the time and worry if you're going to survive the winter.

"If I had my choice, I'd go into the Navy. I know it's   4
strange, because I've never seen the ocean, only a lake or two in Kentucky. But I saw a movie once about the Navy when I was real little, maybe seven, I'd say. I've wanted ever since to join the Navy. The Navy people might decide I'm no good, being from the mountains. I'd probably get seasick. I'm going to wait to be drafted; I'll have a chance to go back to Leslie County then and take my physical. The government will pay for my travel home, I believe. The Army can tell me where they want me to go, and I'll be glad to serve my country—even if it means Vietnam. There's too many people these days who don't salute the flag the way they should. This is the greatest country in the world, and if there's going to be a great country, there has to be a great Army.

"Until we moved to Ohio I never realized how *big* the   5
country is, and how you can go from one place to another, and it all changes. I knew we had these cities, these big cities, but like I tell my friends when we go back home and I can talk with them: seeing is believing. If I'd stayed there and seen pictures of Dayton on the television, I wouldn't know much, not compared to what I know now. I mean, you have to drive in a city to know it. You can't believe it's like it is until you try to drive from one place

to another, one street to another; then you find out. The guys back home, kids I grew up with, they say a road is a road, and that's all there is to it. I tell them they don't know what they're talking about. I have my car, and I've got to keep my foot on the brake more than on the gas— that's what it means to live in the city. Living in the city for a guy like me is learning to brake the car all the time, and wearing the clutch out, and using gas like it's water that's come down the mountain and is waiting to be picked up in buckets and poured into the tank. Living in the city means you have to turn your head every other minute you're driving and keep your eye out for almost anything—when all you want to do is push that gas pedal to the floor and take off.

"I love my car. She's a beauty. She's a Chevy, the best   6 car there is. The motor is good. The tires are good. I think there's no use driving a car if you can't have good tires. Have you ever had a flat on a city street? That's no fun. I'd rather have to fix a flat right in the middle of a curve up one of those hills; there I could hear the car coming and flag it down. Here in Dayton no one pays any attention to the next guy driving, and it is so noisy you can't hear your own voice speaking. They tell me it's even worse in Cleveland. I can get around here, though; now I can. And if my car goes bad, I can take it off the road and fix it myself. I've learned everything I can about car engines. I like new cars and I like old cars. Don't you love the old Thunderbirds? They were some car—1955 or 1956, I believe. I was only a baby then. When I was a little older and just beginning to go to school I remember a big shot, someone from Hazard, coming up to the little schoolhouse we had; and it was a Thunderbird he drove. I think they were talking about closing down the school and sending us someplace else. I think a mine company bought the hill nearby, and they were going to tear it up for coal. I recall telling my friend Carl—he was my best friend—that I hoped one day I could drive a car like that, a Thunderbird; then I'd have everything I wanted. I still don't have a Thunderbird, but now I don't think I'd buy one even if

I had a huge bankroll on me. I'd buy a Mustang or a Cougar, maybe. But for a beginner like me, this old Chevy is a good car to have.

"I've taken the motor apart three times. I painted the   7
car myself. I know how. I know how to spray the right way. If I go into the Army, I hope I can be near some of those jeeps and trucks. I wouldn't mind driving them; I hear they're something to drive all right! I'd rather work on the motors, though; that way I could learn more about the different kinds and how they all work. If I could only get a job back home working in a garage or a gas station! But it's not easy to do. I don't know anyone who owns a gas station, and if I did he'd want to use his own son, I'm sure. Jobs are scarce back home. That's why we drove here, and that's why my car is going to spend most of its life in Ohio. The poor car will suffer plenty on that account, but that's just how it works out. I'll be driving— and stopping and starting and stopping and starting—and I can hear the motor saying: stop it, and get me out of here, fast. So, I just talk back to it. I say: motor, take it easy and just keep going, because there's not a thing in the world you or I can do anyway, except keep going. Then I baby her a bit; I go easy on the brakes and try not to shift more times than I have to—and the old motor seems happier.

"I get nervous when I'm in a crowd of cars; that's   8
when I guess I keep shifting the gears back and forth, and it's not good to do. But how are you supposed to live with all those other cars? I never knew there were so many real, live, honest-to-goodness people in America until we came up here. To this day I can hardly believe it. In school they taught us that it was New York City that was most crowded, and next Chicago. But I asked the teacher if it could get much more crowded than Dayton, Ohio, when the factories were letting out, and she said no, she was sure it couldn't, because there are hundreds and hundreds of cars all over the road, and they're coming in and turning off and switching from one lane to the other, and the horns are going, and you get the meanest looks, and

all you're trying to do is mind your own business and not get yourself in a giant of a wreck.

"I've had two accidents. If I'd have been driving only ⁹ in Kentucky I'm sure I wouldn't have any accidents to my name. They weren't big accidents, just small ones, a fender each time. I fixed them myself, did the straightening and sanding and painting. I knew how to do that from watching my dad. He learned as a boy himself. He'd hit the car into a tree going up or down the creek sometimes. Mostly he's a good driver, though. He never had an accident in Leslie County, but he's had one up here, and that makes three in the family—two for me and one for him. It's different, driving in Kentucky. There aren't all the other cars. There aren't a lot of signs every mile or so, confusing you, always confusing you. They'll drive me to wearing glasses, those signs will, I do believe. And I don't mean to say anything against the people up here, but I think it's friendlier back in Leslie County, and it comes out on the road, because at home people will be more helpful to each other.

"I'll drive out away from Dayton sometimes. I'm not ¹⁰ going anyplace special. I'm not going to see someone. I just want to give my Chevy a rest from the city. I want to give her a good time. I want to take her on a road and let her roll along, and not stop and start. I don't want to have to clutch her and shift her and brake her and idle her and get her so tired and hot she's ready to explode or go dead on me. Out in the country I can bring her up to sixty or seventy pretty fast. She holds the road good. She's no new racing car. She's no big new car. She's light and six years old. But she's got pep in her, a lot of life in her. I hope I'll be like her when I'm that old. A car is like a dog, you know. Each year is six or seven. I figure my car is getting on to forty-five, and that's old.

"My dad says it is not old, forty-five, but to me that's ¹¹ a long way off. I can't picture what it's like to be twenty-five, never mind forty or forty-five. You must begin to feel real tired. I get tired myself. I'll be in the stockroom, handling all those crates, from eight in the morning to five in the afternoon. When I punch my card, and it says five minutes after five, I ask myself where the day has gone to, and my muscles answer that they can tell me, they surely can. Then I come home and have my supper, and I go and drive around. I rest that way. I'm sitting in my car, and I have a good, soft blanket on the seat, and that rests my back. I have some friends I take for a ride—a few of the guys I know up here. And I have two girls I take out. I switch to one, then I switch to the other; they're both from Ohio, born here, and I don't know if I want to get serious with a girl who isn't from Kentucky. I don't have to marry a girl from Leslie County, but Kentucky is my home state, and I want to be going back there someday, so I don't see why I should get myself married to a girl who has other ideas in her head, you know. I've heard them talk, the girls from around here. A lot of them are spoiled. They want everything. They *expect* everything.

"I went to school until last year, until I was sixteen. I   12 didn't graduate from high school, but I went there, and you get taught a lot. My friends back home, a lot of them never bothered going beyond sixth or seventh grade. They said: what's the reason to? I can see how they think that way. I wish I'd gone and finished high school. It's just that I had this chance for a job, and I couldn't turn a good job down. The job means money for all of us, and I save some for a new car. In school that's all the girls wanted, a guy with a new car; they didn't care much what the guy himself was like. I always thought it showed something about the girls, the way they looked at you for your car and not yourself. I don't believe a girl in Leslie County would be like that, though my mother and dad say they would, because it's only natural. I guess a girl is going to like a car, just like a toy, and that's why they ask you right away: what are you driving?

"They want to know your *plans*, the girls do. I tell   13 them I don't have any. I tell them I may one day get into my car and drive and drive and fill the tank and empty it, until the road ends, and I'm somewhere, but I don't know where. Then, wherever it is I stop, I'll settle down.

I'll get settled in, settled into a house, and there'll be a garage for my Chevy, and another garage in case I decide to get a second car, and I'll work in a job—I don't know what kind. The girl will be waiting for me to mention her. They don't know how much they tell about what's on their mind by the way they look. I try to keep myself from laughing, and I keep talking—but I never mention getting married. They always ask me why I may get myself a second car, and I tell them it's nice to give one car a rest and use the other, and then switch back again. You can get attached to a car. You have driven it so long and worked on it all that time, so it's yours, and you don't want to lose what's yours. The nice thing about living in Dayton is you stand a chance of making money, all the money you need. Then you can treat your car right!''

He thinks about it more than he talks about it, the   14
money Dayton, Ohio, permits him to make, the money he cannot make in Leslie County, Kentucky. With each year he is more and more a city dweller, an owner of property, a worker—hence, less likely to return for very long to his home in the mountains, unless things should drastically change there, which is highly unlikely. He is no longer a child, yet not quite a grown-up. Almost half his childhood has been spent in Ohio, but with each month the balance changes, and he feels increasingly ''settled in.'' He often uses that term ''settled in,'' uses it as he did just above, in connection with what I suppose can be called a daydream or a fantasy—or an utterly exact way of describing what is on his mind and what he at least presently intends to do. He cannot really go back home, he knows that, yet he is not very happy living in even a medium-sized city like Dayton. He dreams of the West, the open and endless West, perhaps in the way his ancestors dreamed of what stretched ahead as they left the eastern seaboard. But he may actually spend the rest of his life in Ohio.

As one talks with him it becomes quite apparent that   15
he finds a life without automobiles inconceivable, and a life without a decent home and a garage and suitable

clothes and enough food also impossible to contemplate. He very much enjoys buying himself a sporty new jacket, unworn by someone else, not handed down to him to be used for a while and then in turn handed over to a brother or a cousin. And he likes to do other things that in sum reassure him how well he is coming along, how able he is to take care of himself, put away a little cash, and feel like what he calls "a going business." His father always had wished he could raise the money to have just that, a gas station or a garage, "a going business," he also puts it when he reminisces. The son now has those same dreams, but of course knows that if his business is going to grow, or even survive, Dayton will have to be the address and not some very small town in Leslie County.

So, step by step, innocently but decisively, the young 16 man thinks things and dreams things and says things and decides things that commit him more and more to the life of a northern city, or maybe a far western one—and commit him, perhaps, to a girl who does not come from home, from the mountain country of eastern Kentucky. He does not say out and out what I have just written. How many of us at seventeen (maybe at any age) want to say exactly what we will be doing, come five or ten years? But we do at all times have certain assumptions, silent but influential, and during his five or so years in the city Larry Walker has become a different youth than he would be had he not been brought to Ohio as a child by his parents. He especially notices those various differences when he goes back home on a visit, and when he returns to Dayton he is most likely to talk about such matters. He is most likely to observe what he does in the day, and contrast all of his activities with those of his friends he knew as a small child. He is most likely to notice the way he dresses and the way others who live near Thousand-Sticks, Kentucky, dress. And yes, he is most likely to look at those girls he once knew and had crushes on and fought with and felt close to, and then think of the girls he met when he went to school in Dayton, three or four of whom he has courted in an offhand fashion, then forsaken, then gone back to, then again withdrawn from.

What distinguishes those girls from the girls in Ken-   17
tucky, what distinguishes him from the boys in Kentucky,
is something he finds hard to find words for, yet very
much wants to clarify in his mind—hence the effort of
language: "It's my home, my folks' home, Leslie County
is. When I go back there I feel like I'm back where I
belong. I can sit back and enjoy myself with the best people the Lord ever made. But after a few days I don't mind
it too much if I have to leave. I begin to hear myself saying: it's near time to go, Larry, it's near time. There will
even be a time when I start having a talk with myself. I
say I'm ready to leave. Then I say why on earth are you
actually looking forward to going, when you know full
well how you'll soon be complaining about Dayton?

"I guess that the more you live in a place, the more it   18
grows on you. I don't mean to say I like living here in
the city rather than up in the hills, but a man has to earn
a living, like my dad says. And if I'm going to get married and have kids, I can't see being so down and out,
the way a lot of people in Kentucky are. I don't want my
son to see me just sitting on a porch and carving wood
and maybe picking on my guitar. My dad said he'd never
have stayed alive, if he had kept on spending his days
like that. He came up here, instead, and he was lucky to
get a job for himself and hold on to it, and I've been lucky
to get a job for myself and hold on to it—and that's why
I don't think either of us can go back to Leslie County
for more than a few days. There's no work, compared to
the work you get here.

"But I do admit work isn't the only thing good up   19
here. I talk a lot about my job, because I'm grateful to have
it, and the money is good; it's sweet, real sweet, that
money. I like Dayton, though. There are the movies, all
of them; I've never seen the number of movie houses we
have here in all of Kentucky I've been through, not just
Leslie County. There are restaurants, good ones. You can
live it up here. You can take a girl out on the town. You
can have a good supper, any kind you want, then go to

a movie, almost any kind you want. You can go bowling and you can go play pool and you can hear a good singer in a club and have a few drinks. It's not bad living in a city. There's a lot you miss, but there's a lot you have, too. I guess it's a matter of what your philosophy is, and where you can get the money.

''I'm not sure I could bring a girl up here from Ken- 20 tucky, though. It might be real hard on someone to live here—a person who hasn't grown into the place, like I have. I think the kids I grew up with, they'd have a hard time coming up here now. The reason I don't mind a lot of things, and like living here, at times, anyway, is that I was brought up here when I was much younger. I wasn't a baby. I was over twelve. I was growing fast. I was outgrowing everything, I can recall my mother saying. But I was still a kid, and I wasn't set in my ways. I'm getting set now; my dad says so, and he's right. I might want to get married soon, except that I may go into the service in a few months. Sometimes I think I'd be smarter to come back to Dayton after two years in the Army, rather than make a career of it, go regular. I'll have to wait and see.

''If I meet a real nice, pretty girl from here in Dayton, 21 I might just marry her, if she'd have me. I once asked my favorite girl in Leslie County, Sylvia is her name, if she'd think of coming back with me, just for a week or so. I told her she could stay with us, and she knows my folks. She's distant kin to us, I believe. No, she said; she didn't want to leave the county. I asked her why. She said she didn't have anything against me or my folks, no sir; she'd love to stay with us, she said, and for longer than a week, she said. But to go all the way up to Dayton, out of the county and out of the state, that was too much for her, she said. She gave me a long look, right into my eyes, and I could see she really wanted me to propose marriage to her then and there, but I believe she knew, like I did, that I had to go back up North, and there wasn't any two ways about it. I said to her: Sylvia, just come and give it a try; come and travel through Kentucky and cross the

river, the Ohio River, and look at Cincinnati, and then go
up into the state of Ohio and get to know Dayton a little.
But she kept on shaking her head. She didn't answer me.
She just turned her head to the left and to the right, and
I knew what she was telling me. Maybe the reason she
couldn't speak her thoughts out loud was that she really
did want to go with me, and she couldn't bear hearing
herself say she wouldn't.

"I came home and told my folks what I'd said to   22
Sylvia and what her answer had been. I never mentioned
the word *marriage*, or anything like that, but my mother
said she thought that since we all are settling in, me included, and we're not going to leave Dayton for a long
time, then I might have better luck if I chose a girl from
Dayton, provided she's a good girl, for my wife than
someone like Sylvia from back home. I was mad as I've
ever been. I told my mother she was talking out of her
head, because I wasn't thinking of getting married now,
and when I did think of marriage, that would be the time
I would go home to Kentucky and by God I'd stay there
until I found a wife, and if my wife wanted to stay there
and never leave, I'd stay that long myself and be glad to
do it. Then my mother told me to cool myself down, and
she said the way I was talking, she was sure I wasn't going to get married in a long, long time, not if I meant every
word I'd said to her. Well, I had to smile then. I saw what
she meant."

He not only saw what his mother meant; he knew it in   23
his bones, her message. He is glad in so many ways to
be in Dayton, bothersome as its traffic is, hard as his car
finds the going, crowded and anonymous and noisy as
the city, any city, can always be. He is glad that he is not
living in a cabin up a hollow or creek. He is glad he does
not live in a small town whose "unemployment problem"
is severe and chronic and to a youth like him discouraging beyond the power of words to convey. Still, he does
straddle two worlds, does go back and forth, feel divided
loyalties, dream of one place while he lives in another.

At seventeen nostalgia can be as powerful and summoning as at any other age, but at seventeen the meaning of a job and money is no less influential. What an observer like me has to watch very closely is the temptation to take a young man like Larry Walker too seriously *at any one moment in his life*. One day he can sound utterly convinced that he will soon, very soon, be a mountaineer again—a real one, not a distant, would-be one. The next time we talk, all of that seems not gone or buried or forgotten or "repressed" or denied or contradicted, but gently and tactfully put aside.

It is in such moments of "adjustment" to Dayton that 24 a youth like Larry feels most alert, most challenged, most sure of himself—and most at loose ends. What indeed will he do and where—now that he has ("sort of") decided that his destiny is to be found in Ohio's industrial cities, or perhaps in Illinois, or (who knows?) California, to which the Army might one day order him? And will he, therefore, slowly lose contact with Leslie County? Will he less and less think of those hills and valleys, those waterfalls and high trees and soaring birds, those clever animals and those dumb animals, those innocent but ever so swift and elusive fish? Will his car lose forever the feel of a narrow mountain road, with the sharp rises and the sudden falls, with the exciting twists and turns and curves? Will traveling by car become a bore, a nuisance, a tedious necessity? Will he one day say good-bye to that Chevy and good-bye to the notion that motors are wonderful, demanding, endlessly stimulating puzzles—objects of interest, exploration, and passion? Will he instead find his woman, his wife; find his job that lasts and lasts; find his nice, comfortable home, near others, near dozens and dozens of others? And for his two cars will he have no proud old two-door Chevy, no Mustang or Cougar, but a station wagon and perhaps a brand new Chevy four-door sedan? At seventeen one often doesn't *ask* such questions; instead, one does things—and so Larry's actions gradually will supply the answers to those questions.

Comment

Coles might have summarized his interview with the young man from an economically depressed Kentucky mountain community to give one example of the process of adjustment to Northern urban life. Coles chooses instead to let us hear Larry Walker talk about his life in Dayton, Ohio, and his much different life in Leslie County, Kentucky. Verbatim testimony helps us discover the conflict in attitudes and values that a witness like Larry is experiencing. Larry is typical for Coles of many young Southerners who do not want to lose contact with the rural world they grew up in; Coles might therefore have stated his conflict in the abstract language of the sociologist or social psychologist. But Larry is an individual and his conflict is a personal one. Coles does not want us to forget that although people belong to classes, they are also individuals.

Questions for Study and Discussion

1. What is the personal conflict that Larry is experiencing? How does Larry express that conflict?
2. What point does Coles make through Larry about southern people who live in northern cities? Why does he title his essay "Settling In"?
3. What personal qualities emerge in Larry's account of his life? What most distinguishes him as a person?
4. Is Larry's love of his Chevy typical only of the American teenager's love of cars? Or does Coles want us to see something more than this general attitude?
5. Is Sylvia typical for Coles of young Southern women? Or does she represent one set of attitudes only?

Suggestions for Writing

1. Describe the experience of living in two different worlds— perhaps a small town and a large city. Then discuss an important change in attitude or values, or a conflict in attitudes, that resulted from this experience. Use your discussion to develop a thesis.

2. Coles says the following about Larry Walker and people generally:

> How many of us at seventeen (maybe at any age) want to say exactly what we will be doing, come five or ten years? But we do at all times have certain assumptions, silent but influential, and during his five or so years in the city Larry Walker has become a different youth than he would be had he not been brought to Ohio as a child by his parents. (paragraph 16)

Discuss one or two assumptions that shape your own attitudes and life at the present time. Discuss the possible origin of these assumptions. In the course of your discussion, compare them with the assumptions of Larry or Sylvia.

William Safire

LIBERAL AND CONSERVATIVE

William Safire began his career in journalism as a reporter for the *New York Herald Tribune*. A senior speechwriter for President Richard M. Nixon from 1968 to 1972, he describes his White House experience in *Before the Fall: An Inside View of the Pre-Watergate White House*. A political columnist for the *New York Times* since 1973, Safire was awarded the Pulitzer Prize for Commentary in 1978. He is also a novelist and the author of several books on English words and phrases. His short essays on the words *liberal* and *conservative* are from *Safire's Political Dictionary*, a book showing that the "new, old, and constantly changing language of politics is a lexicon of conflict and drama, of ridicule and reproach, of pleading and persuasion." Sydney J. Harris discusses the meaning of *liberal* and *conservative* in his philosophical essay on page 77.

LIBERAL currently one who believes in more govern- 1
ment action to meet individual needs; originally one who resisted government encroachment on individual liberties.

In the original sense the word described those of the 2
emerging middle classes in France and Great Britain who

wanted to throw off the rules the dominant aristocracy had made to cement its own control.

During the 1920s the meaning changed to describe those who believed a certain amount of governmental action was necessary to protect the people's "real" freedoms as opposed to their purely legal—and not necessarily existent—freedoms. 3

This philosophical about-face led former New York Governor Thomas Dewey to say, after using the original definition, "Two hundred years later, the transmutation of the word, as the alchemist would say, has become one of the wonders of our time." 4

In U.S. politics the word was used by George Washington to indicate a person of generosity or broad-mindedness, as he expressed distaste for those who would deprive Catholics and Jews of their rights. 5

The word became part of the American vocabulary in its earlier meaning during a rump convention of Republicans dissatisfied with the presidency of Ulysses S. Grant, at Cincinnati in 1872. German-born Carl Schurz, who chaired the convention, used the word often. So did the leading journalist-thinker of the rebellion, Edwin L. Godkin of *The Nation*, who began his career in England. The short-lived party born of the convention was called "The Liberal Republican" party. 6

In its present usage, the word acquired significance during the presidency of Franklin D. Roosevelt, who defined it this way during the campaign for his first term": Say that civilization is a tree which, as it grows, continually produces rot and dead wood. The radical says: 'Cut it down.' The conservative says: 'Don't touch it.' The liberal compromises: 'Let's prune, so that we lose neither the old trunk nor the new branches.'" 7

Liberalism takes criticism from both right and left, leading to various terms of opprobrium. Herbert Hoover in a magazine article referred to "fuzzy-minded totalitarian liberals who believe that their creeping collectivism can be adopted without destroying personal liberty and representative government." 8

To its opponents, liberalism and liberals seem to call   9
out for qualifying adjectives expressing contempt. Barry
Goldwater, trying to combat the popularity of President
Johnson with businessmen, told a U.S. Chamber of Com-
merce conference, "If you think President Johnson is going to give you any better attention than you have got,
you're very, very mistaken. If he's a conservative," said
the senator, "I'm a screaming liberal."

Sometimes even liberals cannot avoid the temptation   10
to assault the term. Adlai Stevenson, quoting an uncertain source, once described a liberal as "one who has both
feet firmly planted in the air." And columnist Heywood
Broun, who came to consider himself a radical, wrote: "A
liberal is a man who leaves a room when a fight begins,"
a definition adopted by militant Saul Alinsky.

The word has fallen on hard times. In the 1976 presi-   11
dential primaries, Representative Morris Udall told columnist David Broder: "When a word takes on connotations
you don't like, it's time to change the label." Henceforth,
Udall said—though he would think of himself as a liberal—
he would use the word "progressive" instead because the
word "liberal" was "associated with abortion, drugs, bus-
ing and big-spending wasteful government."

Liberals are variously described as limousine, double-   12
domed, screaming, knee jerk, professional, bleeding heart.

CONSERVATIVE a defender of the status quo who,   13
when change becomes necessary in tested institutions or
practices, prefers that it come slowly, and in moderation.

In modern U.S. politics, as in the past, "conservative"   14
is a term of opprobrium to some, and veneration to others.
Edmund Burke, the early defender and articulator of the
conservative philosophy, argued that the only way to preserve political stability was by carefully controlling change
and seeking a slow, careful integration of new forces into
venerable institutions. In his *Reflections on the Revolution
in France*, he wrote: "It is with infinite caution that any
man ought to venture upon pulling down an edifice which
has answered in any tolerable degree for ages the common

purposes of society, or on building it up again without having models and patterns of approved utility before his eyes." Abraham Lincoln called it "adherence to the old and tried, against the new and untried."

The philosophy has had some famous detractors as 15 well. Disraeli, who was to become a Tory Prime Minister, wrote in his sprightly novel *Coningsby:* "Conservatism discards Prescription, shrinks from Principle, disavows Progress; having rejected all respect for antiquity, it offers no redress for the present, and makes no preparation for the future." Lord Bryce was of two minds about it in *The American Commonwealth:* "This conservative spirit, jealously watchful even in small matters, sometimes prevents reforms, but it assures the people an easy mind, and a trust in their future which they feel to be not only a present satisfaction but a reservoir of strength."

The political origin of the word can be traced to the 16 *Sénat Conservateur* in the 1795 French Constitution, and was used in its present English sense by British statesman, later Prime Minister, George Canning in 1820. J. Wilson Croker, in the *Quarterly Review* of January 1830, made the concrete proposal: "We have always been conscientiously attached to what is called the Tory, and which might with more propriety be called the Conservative party." It was soon applied in America to the Whigs, amid some derision: *"The Pennsylvania Reporter,"* wrote the *Ohio Statesman* in 1837, "speaking of a probable change in the name of the opposition, from Whig to 'Conservative,' says the best cognomen they could adopt would be the 'Fast and Loose' party."

Today the more rigid conservative generally opposes 17 virtually all governmental regulation of the economy. He favors local and state action over federal action, and emphasizes fiscal responsibility, most notably in the form of balanced budgets. William Allen White, the Kansas editor, described this type of conservative when he wrote of Charles Evans Hughes as "a businessman's candidate, hovering around the status quo like a sick kitten around a hot brick."

But there exists a less doctrinaire conservative who [18] admits the need for government action in some fields and for steady change in many areas. Instead of fighting a rear-guard action, he seeks to achieve such change within the framework of existing institutions, occasionally changing the institutions when they show need of it.

Comment

Safire states in the introduction to the first edition (1968) that his dictionary records "words and phrases that have misled millions, blackened reputations, held out false hopes, over-simplified ideas to appeal to the lowest common denominator, shouted down inquiry, and replaced searching debate with stereotypes that trigger approval or hatred." His dictionary also shows "how the choice of a word or metaphor can reveal sensitivity and genius, crystallize a mood and turn it to action; some political language captures the essence of an abstraction and makes it understandable to millions." The words *liberal* and *conservative* have some of these effects, Safire shows.

Questions for Study and Discussion

1. How do the historical and political backgrounds of *liberal* and *conservative* help you to understand their contemporary meanings?
2. What is gained by knowing the various meanings, past and present, of terms like *liberal* and *conservative*?
3. Is Safire writing to suggest how we should use these words, or is he merely describing their past and present meanings?
4. How does Safire's purpose in writing differ from Sydney J. Harris's, in his discussion of *liberal, conservative,* and *radical* (page 77)?

Vocabulary Study

The *Oxford English Dictionary* (or *New English Dictionary*) and *Dictionary of American English*, and other historical dictionaries trace the history and use of words like *liberal* and *conservative*. Unabridged dictionaries of contemporary usage like *Webster's Third New International Dictionary* and *The Random House Dictionary of the English Language*, and abridged dictionaries like *Webster's Ninth New Collegiate Dictionary* and *Webster's New World Dictionary of the English Language* give current meanings but also cite obsolete and rare uses of words. Special dictionaries and reference works like the *Dictionary of American Biography* and *Encyclopedia of American History*, as well as special studies of British and American history, give additional information and background. Examine a historical, an unabridged, and an abridged dictionary in the reference section of your library to determine the differences in the information they provide about *liberal, conservative,* or *radical.*

Suggestion for Writing

Use historical dictionaries and other sources to write a history of one of the followng words. Give enough details about the word to distinguish it from similar ones, and discuss the special qualities or effects associated with it. Include information about its etymology:

1. *anarchism*
2. *appeasement*
3. *apartheid*
4. *nihilism*
5. *toryism*

Robert Ramirez

THE WOOLEN SARAPE

Robert Ramirez was born in Edinburg, Texas, in 1950. He graduated from Pan American College, where he later taught freshman composition. He also taught elementary school and has worked as a photographer, a reporter, and an announcer for a television news department in Texas. His essay on the barrio illustrates a special kind of definition.

The train, its metal wheels squealing as they spin along the silvery tracks, rolls slower now. Through the gaps between the cars blinks a streetlamp, and this pulsing light on a barrio streetcorner beats slower, like a weary heartbeat, until the train shudders to a halt, the light goes out, and the barrio is deep asleep.

Throughout Aztlán (the Nahuatl term meaning ''land to the north''), trains grumble along the edges of a sleeping people. From Lower California, through the blistering Southwest, down the Rio Grande to the muddy Gulf, the darkness and mystery of dreams engulf communities fenced off by railroads, canals, and expressways. Paradoxical communities, isolated from the rest of the town by concrete columned monuments of progress, and yet stranded in the past. They are surrounded by change. It eludes their reach, in their own backyards, and the people, unable and unwilling to see the future, or even touch the present, perpetuate the past.

Leaning from the expressway or jolting across the tracks, one enters a different physical world permeated by a different attitude. The physical dimensions are impressive. It is a large section of town which extends for fifteen blocks north and south along the tracks, and then advances eastward, thinning into nothingness beyond the city limits. Within the invisible (yet sensible) walls of the barrio, are many, many people living in too few houses. The homes, however, are much more numerous than on the outside.

Members of the barrio describe the entire area as their ₄
home. It is a home, but it is more than this. The barrio is
a refuge from the harshness and the coldness of the Anglo
world. It is a forced refuge. The leprous people are isolated
from the rest of the community and contained in their section of town. The stoical pariahs of the barrio accept their
fate, and from the angry seeds of rejection grow the flowers
of closeness between outcasts, not the thorns of bitterness
and the mad desire to flee. There is no want to escape, for
the feeling of the barrio is known only to its inhabitants,
and the material needs of life can also be found here.

The *tortillería*¹ fires up its machinery three times a day, ₅
producing steaming, round, flat slices of barrio bread. In
the winter, the warmth of the tortilla factory is a wool *sarape*²
in the chilly morning hours, but in the summer, it
unbearably toasts every noontime customer.

The *panadería*³ sends its sweet messenger aroma down ₆
the dimly lit street, announcing the arrival of fresh, hot
sugary *pan dulce.*⁴

The small corner grocery serves the meal-to-meal needs ₇
of customers, and the owner, a part of the neighborhood,
willingly gives credit to people unable to pay cash for
foodstuffs.

The barbershop is a living room with hydraulic chairs, ₈
radio, and television, where old friends meet and speak
of life as their salted hair falls aimlessly about them.

The pool hall is a junior level country club where ₉
'*chucos*,⁵ strangers in their own land, get together to shoot
pool and rap, while veterans, unaware of the cracking,
popping balls on the green felt, complacently play dominos
beneath rudely hung *Playboy* foldouts.

The *cantina*⁶ is the night spot of the barrio. It is the ₁₀
country club and the den where the rites of puberty are

¹*tortillería:* tortilla bake shop
²*sarape:* blanket or shawl
³*panadería:* bakery
⁴*pan dulce:* sweet bread or roll
⁵'*chucos: pachuco,* or Mexican (derogatory term)
⁶*cantina:* tavern or saloon

enacted. Here the young become men. It is in the taverns that a young dude shows his *machismo*[7] through the quantity of beer he can hold, the stories of *rucas*[8] he has had, and his willingness and ability to defend his image against hardened and scarred old lions.

No, there is no frantic wish to flee. It would be absurd to leave the familiar and nervously step into the strange and cold Anglo community when the needs of the Chicano can be met in the barrio. 11

The barrio is closeness. From the family living unit, familial relationships stretch out to immediate neighbors, down the block, around the corner, and to all parts of the barrio. The feeling of family, a rare and treasurable sentiment, pervades and accounts for the inability of the people to leave. The barrio is this attitude manifested on the countenances of the people, on the faces of their homes, and in the gaiety of their gardens. 12

The color-splashed homes arrest your eyes, arouse your curiosity, and make you wonder what life scenes are being played out in them. The flimsy, brightly colored, wood-frame houses ignore no neon-brilliant color. Houses trimmed in orange, chartreuse, lime-green, yellow, and mixtures of these and other hues beckon the beholder to reflect on the peculiarity of each home. Passing through this land is refreshing like Brubeck, not narcoticizing like revolting rows of similar houses, which neither offend nor please. 13

In the evenings, the porches and front yards are occupied with men calmly talking over the noise of children playing baseball in the unpaved extension of the living room, while the women cook supper or gossip with female neighbors as they water the *jardines*.[9] The gardens mutely echo the expressive verses of the colorful houses. The denseness of multicolored plants and trees gives the house 14

---

[7]*machismo:* manhood
[8]*rucas:* girls
[9]*jardines:* gardens

the appearance of an oasis or a tropical island hideaway, sheltered from the rest of the world.

Fences are common in the barrio, but they are fences   15 and not the walls of the Anglo community. On the western side of town, the high wooden fences between houses are thick, impenetrable walls, built to keep the neighbors at bay. In the barrio, the fences may be rusty, wire contraptions or thick green shrubs. In either case you can see through them and feel no sense of intrusion when you cross them.

Many lower income families of the barrio manage to   16 maintain a comfortable standard of living through the communal action of family members who contribute their wages to the head of the family. Economic need creates interdependence and closeness. Small barefooted boys sell papers on cool, dark Sunday mornings, deny themselves pleasantries, and give their earnings to *mamá*. The older the child, the greater the responsibility to help the head of the household provide for the rest of the family.

There are those, too, who for a number of reasons   17 have not achieved a relative sense of financial security. Perhaps it results from too many children too soon, but it is the homes of these people and their situation that numbs rather than charms. Their houses, aged and bent, oozing children, are fissures in the horn of plenty. Their wooden homes may have brick-pattern asbestos tile on the outer walls, but the tile is not convincing.

Unable to pay city taxes or incapable in influencing the   18 city to live up to its duty to serve all the citizens, the poorer barrio families remain trapped in the nineteenth century and survive as best they can. The backyards have well-worn paths to the outhouses, which sit near the alley. Running water is considered a luxury in some parts of the barrio. Decent drainage is usually unknown, and when it rains, the water stands for days, an incubator of health hazards and an avoidable nuisance. Streets, costly to pave, remain rough, rocky trails. Tires do not last long, and the constant rattling and shaking grind away a car's life and spread dust through screen windows.

The houses and their *jardines*, the jollity of the people   19
in an adverse world, the brightly feathered alarm clock
pecking away at supper and cautiously eyeing the children
playing nearby, produce a mystifying sensation at finding
the noble savage alive in the twentieth century. It is easy
to look at the positive qualities of life in the barrio, and
look at them with a distantly envious feeling. One wishes
to experience the feelings of the barrio and not the hardships. Remembering the illness, the hunger, the feeling
of time running out on you, the walls, both real and imagined, reflecting on living in the past, one finds his envy
becoming more elusive, until it has vanished altogether.

Back now beyond the tracks, the train creaks and   20
groans, the cars jostle each other down the track, and
as the light begins its pulsing, the barrio, with all its
meanings, greets a new dawn with yawns and restless
stretchings.

Comment

Robert Ramirez defines the barrio denotatively and connotatively
(page 88) through his details of barrio life. In doing so, he
defines not only a place but a culture: the quality of life that
distinguishes the barrio from other cultural worlds in the United
States. So detailed a description might have become disunified;
instead, Ramirez achieves unity in his description by letting us
see the barrio as a stranger would. Once he establishes his point
of view, with the reference to the train that approaches the barrio, he does not stray from it. Each part of the scene Ramirez
describes is dealt with fully before he turns to another. The concluding paragraph reminds us that the barrio is a world set apart
physically and emotionally from the world outside.

Questions for Study and Discussion

1. What statements and details show that Ramirez is writing to
   an audience unfamiliar with the barrio?

2. What qualities do the people of the barrio share? Does Ramirez show qualities or attitudes that mark them as individuals—as separate people living in the same neighborhood?
3. How does he introduce these qualities without disturbing his focus on the physical qualities of the barrio?
4. In what order are those physical qualities presented? Once the physical point of view is established, how does Ramirez remind us of it as the essay progresses?
5. What details of barrio life do you recognize in your own neighborhood, town, or city? In general, what similarities and differences are there between the barrio and your world?

Vocabulary Study

Write sentences of your own, using the following words to reveal their dictionary meanings: *paradoxical, permeated, stoical, pariahs, mutely, adverse.*

Suggestions for Writing

1. Discuss how the title of the essay contributes to the overall tone and point of view. Then analyze the order of ideas and development of the thesis.
2. Describe the prevailing culture, or variety of cultures, in a neighborhood or community you know well. Include the extent to which people of the neighborhod share a common language, perhaps a slang that protects them from the world outside. Give particular attention to their feelings and attitudes toward that outside world.

Nathan Irvin Huggins

AFRO-AMERICANIZATION

Nathan Irvin Huggins, professor of history at Harvard University, has written widely on slavery and the Afro-American experience. His books include *Voices from the Harlem Renaissance* (1971), *Slave and Citizen: The Life of Frederick Douglass* (1980), and *Black Odyssey* (1977), from which this section has been taken. Huggins traveled and did research in Senegal, Ghana, Nigeria, and other African countries to gather material for this book on slavery. Huggins tells us that the American slave owner communicated with his slaves in a pidgin dialect, a tongue consisting of English and African words and a simplified grammar that became the "good" and "sensible" dialect spoken on the Southern plantation. In their contribution to this dialect, transplanted Afro-Americans made important contributions to American English.

Afro-Americanization began in the first forced con-   1
tacts with strangers—other blacks of peculiar aspect and habit, white men from beyond the seas. It began in the frantic and hysterical efforts to explain oneself, to say who one was, where one belonged, to plead to be returned— all to men who seemed not to hear. Nothing more immediately showed the world to be upside down than that one's words bounced back, unattended, and those of others seemed a cacophony, a gibberish. At its worst, meaning was reduced to gestures of hands, arms, and head, to grunts and explosive sounds, and to physical force.

Except for those so shocked as to be dumb to all   2
meaning, a human will to communicate would span the chasm. The ears detected familiar sounds, perhaps strange inflections, among Africans from other parts, and minds stretched to understand and be understood. The process of Afro-Americanization obliterated, in due course, age-old barriers that had existed among Africans. Bridges of language were the first efforts to link them into one people.

Communication was also necessary as a tool of trade. 3
European traders and their African partners had to find
words and signs—a code—which would allow their business with one another to advance with minimal misunderstanding. So language on both sides—African and European—reduced itself to bare simplicity, free of subtleties
and complexities. There developed languages of European
and African vocabulary and simplified syntax. Such blends,
based on African with Portuguese, French, and English,
became the *linguae francae* of the Atlantic basin.

The pidgin languages that served the traders also al- 4
lowed the captives to understand and be understood. The
slave traders, and later the slave owners, preferred to mix
the Africans, avoiding concentrating any one people together. This strategy rested on the desire to play on traditional hostilities and language differences so as to prevent
conspiracies and uprisings. Yet, this mixture of tongues itself
encouraged the invention of new languages. African languages within language families were not so dissimilar that
those who would put forth effort could not be understood.
Out of the mix and flux of peoples, various pidgins were
born.

Children, despite the shock of rupture, found it easy to 5
mouth new sounds for old meanings. Adults, on the other
hand, would know how a thing was supposed to be said,
and they would never feel new words approximated what
they meant to say. They would always be uneasy that they
were not being understood or that they had missed something said to them.

White men who wanted Africans to labor had to under- 6
stand them and be understood. It might appear to the slave
buyer, as he picked among newly arrived Africans, that they
talked a ''gibberish,'' and he might hope to have someone
familiar with African languages to communicate for him.
But his success as a master of African slaves would depend
on his sharing a common language. He had to learn and
contribute further to a workable pidgin dialect.

Circumstances and personality determined how the 7
African fared. For some, the heart had been forever closed

by tragedy, and the mind and spirit would never open to accept the new reality; the tongue would never untie itself in crude and alien sounds. Most, living among others like themselves, used the convenience of language to draw them together. There were a few whose company was mainly whites, whose language picked up more of the cadences and sounds of Ireland or England. Others would find themselves among Indians, learning and teaching words. Occasionally, there would be one like Phyllis Wheatley, brought from Africa at the age of nine, petted in a New England household, educated on the standard Greek and Latin classics, who would write poetry in the language of Alexander Pope. She was to be the second American woman, after Anne Bradstreet, to publish a book of poems in the English language.

Most African immigrants were to find their lives   8
among others like themselves, with few whites about. Since they spoke most often to one another, there was little need to measure their words against an English spoken by whites. As generations passed and children native to America grew up, their language was to be an expansion and development of that used on the plantations. It would be their native tongue—thought in and spoken in as a natural thing—not artificial and strained as it had been with their mothers and fathers. It was familiar to them, just as it would have become familiar to whites with whom they spoke. Thus, their masters, now also a native American generation, could describe them as "country born" and speaking a "good" or "sensible" English, even though it was no less the language of black men and women on plantations.

English settlers made little effort to teach Africans   9
English and made none to learn African languages; but each people had to find a halfway point. As they both became more skillful at it, the whites would come to consider the blacks more "sensible."

White men and women also became more "sensible"   10
as time went on. Their tongues became accustomed to "goober," "tote," "gumbo," "banjo," "cooter,"

"chigger," "yam," "okra," "juke," and other such words from Africa. They picked up word patterns and tonalities as well. Through the generations following the first "country born" of both races, black and white children grew up together, playing the same games, using the same words. It would take a sensitive ear to distinguish native white from native black language. Many foreign visitors who came to the South in the nineteenth century remarked that English in the South had much to do with black influence.

Africa persisted in the language in subtle ways. Africans had often named their children according to the days of the week. There were day names for both boys and girls. Quashee or Quasheba, Cudjo or Juba, Cuba, Abba, Cuffee or Phibbi, all were to echo through two centuries, although sometimes in distorted form. English ears heard these sounds differently. So they were to be written in the plantation journals as Squash or Sheba, Joe, Abby, Cuff or Phoebe. White men might think that Juba was a dance and not Monday, that Cuba was an island and not Wednesday. They might think of the name Jack when they heard the name Quack. They might smile at what they heard as poor elocution, changing the name to sound right to their own ears. But black mothers and fathers continued to understand that the name stood for a given day or a season. In time, as Africa and England blended into America, black children would be given names like Monday, Friday, or Saturday, Winter or Summer.

Down into the nineteenth century, African names would survive. Ledgers of the slave merchant Dr. Louis de Saussure, dated 1864, list slaves named Rinah, Summer, Saturday, Kezia, Molsey, Sopha, Cinda, Tyra, Winter, Nelpey, and Sukey. Some were Anglicized versions of what had once been African; others were pure continuations of African names.

Language is a way of bringing peoples together, and it did bring diverse African words into the English-, French-, or Spanish-based Creoles. But language is also a way of maintaining social distance among people, and it did that too in the new American tongues. Europeans and Africans had always made distinctions among themselves by how one used words. The higher orders marked themselves off from the lower by accent, tone, diction, and vocabulary. So, too, in America, Negro speech and white speech became marks of social disparity. Those blacks who mastered the white man's language were, in so doing, placing themselves socially at a remove from those blacks who did not. How a black person would come to speak American English would depend on more than opportunity, intelligence, and facility. There needed to be a choice to emulate white people, the ability to slip from one style of speech into another when the occasion warranted, and the willingness to bear the ridicule of fellow blacks who might think him a mimic and sycophant.

White people, however, were anxious to keep their 14 language to themselves. They wanted it as an emblem of the social superiority they felt to blacks and the lower orders. They wanted to talk to one another, among blacks, and not have their meaning understood. They wanted language to serve in limited ways to communicate between themselves and slaves, but they also wanted it to remain enigmatic. Language to them was a mark of civilization as well as a tool of communication, and they needed the sense of security a monopoly on good speech and literacy gave them. Furthermore, they knew that language transported ideas, and ideas could be weapons against established order. So, rather than finding a prideful, missionizing achievement in the acculturation of Afro-Americans into English, the Anglo-Americans were protective and jealous. Above all, as far as it was possible, slaves were to be kept ignorant of the written word.

Blacks, too, had their secret codes, the most obvious 15 and universal being drum sounds. Significantly, the earliest slave laws made the use of drums a criminal act for slaves. The need for secrecy would encourage blacks to hold on to African elements as long as they could. They also worked to speak in symbol, parable, and metaphor. They masked meaning by stories and song. White prohibitions against reading gave an almost cabalistic weight to the written word (the Bible); there was something magical in translating marks on a page into meaning, in making the book "talk." Some learned to read as an underground thing, secret and forbidden.

Like all oppressed people, black Americans learned   16
that in talking to whites, language could be a shield. Whites presumed that blacks knew little, and whites often showed the strain in trying to make themselves understood. It was easy enough to hide behind the barrier of language, to feign ignorance or incomprehension. To fall suddenly dumb before the white master's words was an instinctive evasion, a first line of defense.

An American language and style emerged out of the   17
blendings of peoples—European, African, and Indian. Not merely did new words come into English, but cadences, rhythms, and inflections were affected. Characteristic ways the body moved in gesturing, the head was held, the eyes were cast, were formed from a relationship where two language codes were assumed, where one people was presumed servile and deferential, the other authoritative and masterful.

Aside from the human interaction, America itself called   18
for invention, for expression beyond conventional language. The frontier wilderness, the rawness of the coupling of people and nature, the collisions of people with one another outside legal and social systems of control, the unspeakable grandeur of the country, all called forth a lexicon befitting the experience. When white men and black men exploded onto the frontiers or onto the riverboats and barges of the Ohio and Mississippi, they wanted to blow themselves up to the size of the country. The stories they told became incredible, challenging a reality that itself was beyond belief. And their words grew with strange inventions: absquatulate, slantendicular, cahoot, catawampus, spyficated, flabbergasted, tarnacious, bodacious, rampagious, concussence, supernatiousness, rumsquattle. Genteel Easterners would call such language

gibberish and their inventors savages, but it was merely that America and Europe and Africa were building a language to fit the country.

Comment

"Within that tyranny, looking beyond the acts of defiance, rebellion, and escape," Huggins writes in his introduction to *Black Odyssey*, "we will find a quality of courage still unsung. It is in the triumph of the human spirit over unmitigated power. It raised no banners. It gained no vengeance. It was only the pervasive and persistent will among Afro-Americans to hold together through deep trauma and adversity." The struggle to hold together, Huggins shows, occurred in a world that spoke a different language and refused to acknowledge the human identity of a people who seemed to speak no comprehensible tongue. Slave owners needed, however, to communicate with their slaves, a need that shaped attitudes toward and treatment of the slave. In exploring these attitudes and treatment, Huggins gives us insight into the nature and the role of language in human society.

Questions for Study and Discussion

1. What does Huggins mean by "Afro-Americanization"? Under what circumstances did Afro-Americanization occur?
2. How did the need to communicate affect both owner and slave?
3. Does Huggins suggest that, once enslaved, all Africans lost their original language and culture?
4. What point is Huggins making about the development of American language and culture?

Vocabulary Study

Explain the use Huggins makes of the following words and phrases:

1. *cacophony, gibberish* (paragraph 1)
2. *subtleties* (paragraph 3)

3. *pidgin languages* (paragraph 4)
4. *dialect* (paragraph 6)
5. *cadences* (paragraph 7)
6. *elocution* (paragraph 11)
7. *Creoles, social disparity, facility, emulate, mimic, sycophant* (paragraph 13)
8. *enigmatic, literacy, acculturation* (paragraph 14)
9. *symbol, parable, metaphor* (paragraph 15)
10. *instinctive evasion* (paragraph 16)
11. *lexicon* (paragraph 18)

Suggestions for Writing

1. Discuss a misconception about a class of people that you once held and later corrected. Explain how the misconception arose and what experiences led to its correction.
2. Huggins shows that differences in language and culture can be bridged, yet personal attitudes and social forces prevent this bridging from occurring. Illustrate this point from your own personal experience and observation.
3. Discuss social attitudes that divide people of different color, religion, or culture, and illustrate how these divisions are sometimes overcome.

Robert J. Samuelson

COMPUTER COMMUNITIES

Robert J. Samuelson writes a column on economics for *Newsweek*. He frequently writes about federal economic policy and its effects. His column on computer communities deals with changes in marketing and consumption that have led to a "massive paradox." Samuelson explores the implications of these changes for the American consumer and marketer.

This holiday season is also the high season for catalogs. I'm sitting with 30 of them, offering everything from teddy bears to electronic scrabble games. They all arrived at our house in recent months. My wife tells me we get about 100 a year. This bothered me. Were we such lavish consumers to attract every selling organization in America? I checked it out. We're about average. There are roughly 10 billion catalogs mailed out annually, which is more than 50 for every American over 18, and the number has more than doubled since 1978.

Historian Daniel Boorstin's apt phrase—consumption   2 communities—describes people connected by what they buy, not where they live. The modern analogue is computer communities. We are, in part, defined by the computer lists we're on: the lists for catalogs, magazines, credit cards, alumni associations, unions and trade groups. They are windows to our pocketbooks, and almost all can be rented. Bob Castle, a major list broker, offers 40,000 lists. His biggest has 165 million Americans by age and address, but for a client selling an executive jet, "I once rented a list of 40 oil sheiks living in America."

Our language overflows with marketing jargon: 3 "niches," "segments" and "clusters." We're coded according to age, income, education, reading habits and spending patterns, even if these things are inferred from the census tract where we live. Lists are run against each other to produce new lists with more information. Suitably grouped, we're fair game for catalogs, charitable solicitations, political appeals and advertising fliers. We're peddled mutual funds, insurance policies and vacations. In 1985, third-class—alias "junk"—mail totaled 52 billion pieces; it's growing four times faster than other mail.

This direct-mail boom is said to cater to working   4 women. Shopping time is scarce. Nearly 60 percent of people who order by mail or phone are women. This pop theory, though true, is much overrated. Computers have been the dominant agent of change by making it cheaper to analyze and address Americans by groups. Direct mail's rise, for example, does not parallel the gradual increase of working women. The explosive growth was triggered in 1979 by cuts in bulk-mail rates, based on computerized presorting of letters to individual postal routes. Some third-class mail rates are now lower than in 1978.

The computers are trying to straddle a huge schism in 5
national culture. Americans exalt individuality, but our economic success rests on a mass market that stresses com-
monality. By creating huge new groups—big enough to
produce economies of scale, but small enough to seem
personal—the computers seek to skirt this conflict. Magazines and television audiences are dissected by the same
computerized scanning to determine which are best for
cameras and which for beer. All advertisers want the right
niche, which sounds like a cozy group. The mass market
is supposed to be dead, but, of course, any niche worth
selling has hundreds of thousands, usually millions, of
customers.

This hypocrisy—marketers trying to make us feel 6
select, when we're not—offends some. Columnist Richard
Cohen of the *Washington Post* recently unleashed this splendid tirade against the direct-mail avalanche: "Every day,
I come home to open a newly arrived stack of lies. . . .
The Book-of-the-Month Club tells me, in the manner of
the Marines, that it is seeking 'a few people in
Washington,' when, of course, it will take anyone it can
get. . . . I get letters in which my name [is] misspelled
each and every time: 'Yes, Rojhard Cohen, the whales are
in danger.''

Well Rojhard, it's an old story. The early mail-order 7
houses—Montgomery Ward (1872) and Sears (1888)—succeeded in part by cultivating a personal bond with their
customers. Confidence was essential, notes historian Boorstin, "to induce farmers to buy goods sight unseen from
a distant warehouse." Many customers wrote personal letters that were answered. "I suppose you wondered why
we haven't ordered anything from you since the fall," one
letter to Ward's founder said. "Well, the cow kicked my
arm and broke it and besides my wife was sick, and there
was the doctor bill."

The pretense of exclusivity doesn't fool most of us. We 8
tolerate or enjoy the obvious deceptions of advertising,
including direct mail. For all the excesses, we secretly
appreciate the attention. Even throwing the stuff away
unopened provides a perverse satisfaction that someone

wants our business. A friend of mine peruses catalogs while pedaling an exercise bike. She is surely treated to the constant surprises of the commercial imagination. A place in Maine will send you a telephone shaped like a piano (you dial on the keyboard) for $59, and then there's the $39 Snore Stopper from California:

"A snoring sleeper can cause a loving bedmate to en- 9 dure many a sleepless night. . . . The static electrical pulse which Snore Stopper emits, each time you snore, is very light—and it goes on for only 5/100 of a second. . . . [B]ut it will stop even the heaviest sleeper from snoring"

But the result of all this computerized marketing—the 10 obsession with niche building—is a massive paradox. The point of splintering consumers into finer subdivisions is to give vent to individual differences and choices. In fact, our high-tech marketing simply fosters new, more variegated styles of conformity. What the marketers call niches and segments, you and I call friends. People don't compare themselves with strangers. They look at their peers: people like themselves. Most of us—along with our friends —are being bombarded by the same appeals for the same specialized products.

There's a shortening of the half-lives of fads and fash- 11 ions. Nothing remains novel very long, because the tools of mass marketing accelerate the introduction of new products aimed at particular groups: whether Yuppies, prosperous retirees or skiing buffs. Our marketers pander to the rhetoric of individuality, but in our new computer communities, differences are still hard to detect. The more refined customer markets become, the faster the spread of new products. The ultimate irony of computerized merchandising is that it's made being a snob a more exhausting and exacting exercise than ever.

Comment

In his discussion of Americans as consumers, Samuelson depends chiefly on classification and division (page 94) to develop his thesis. He first shows how advertisers put consumers into a broad class, defined by Daniel Boorstin as "consumption communities." Samuelson then divides this class in various ways, and draws a number of conclusions about consumer attitudes and marketing technology. Comparison and causal analysis also play an important part in describing this technology. Samuelson uses his analysis to say something important about advertising and marketing today.

Questions for Study and Discussion

1. Into what groups do mail advertisers divide consumers?
2. Why do advertisers seek to create "huge new groups" of consumers? Why must these groups not be too big?
3. What point is Samuelson making in his comparison of consumption communities and computer communities (paragraph 2)? Where else does he use comparison, and what point does he make through this comparison?
4. What is the "massive paradox" that results from computerized marketing? What point is Samuelson making through discussion of this paradox? What is the "ultimate irony" of computerized marketing?
5. Samuelson is writing to increase our understanding of mail advertising. Does he have another purpose in writing—for example, to encourage readers of his *Newsweek* column to change their buying habits?

Vocabulary Study

Give the dictionary meaning of the following words. Then explain how Samuelson uses the word in the paragraph:

1. *analogue* (paragraph 2)
2. *inferred* (paragraph 3)
3. *schism, dissected, niche* (paragraph 5)
4. *exclusivity, perverse* (paragraph 8)
5. *paradox* (paragraph 10)
6. *irony* (paragraph 11)

Suggestions for Writing

1. Samuelson states: "The pretense of exclusivity doesn't fool most of us. We tolerate or enjoy the obvious deceptions of advertising, including direct mail. For all the excesses, we secretly appreciate the attention." Discuss the extent to which this statement describes your attitude toward mail advertising.
2. Discuss the extent to which the advertising of a particular product—for example, automobiles—illustrates one of the following statements in paragraph 11:
   a. "There's a shortening of the half-lives of fads and fashions."
   b. "Nothing remains novel very long, because the tools of mass marketing accelerate the introduction of new products aimed at particular groups. . . ."
   c. "Our marketers pander to the rhetoric of individuality, but in our new computer communities, differences are still hard to detect."

Paul Lancaster

EXHALE! . . . INHALE! . . . EXHALE! . . .

Paul Lancaster was reporter and feature editor for the *Wall Street Journal* for sixteen years. He has also written a number of articles on popular history for *American Heritage,* in which the following essay on exercise appeared. His biography of an early newspaper reporter is scheduled for publication in 1992. The American "cult of health," H. L. Mencken wrote in 1931, led in his time to "the striated muscle fetish." The American interest in exercise, Lancaster shows in his essay, has a long and fascinating history, marked by "periodic changes" in attitude and practice.

All you joggers out there dodging garbage trucks at dawn, listen to this: "I am fully convinced that exercise is bosh. . . . Find ways to exert yourself and you find ways to harm yourself. . . . Do not stand when you can sit; or sit when you can lie down; or just lie down when you can nap. Do not run if you can walk. . . . To have a strong heart it is essential to give up all unnecessary exercise." 1

In a day when sixty-year-olds train for marathons,   2
middle-aged cyclists rack up the miles on their ten-speeds,
and tennis players of all shapes and sizes crowd the courts,
the advice sounds strange. But it was written little more
than a generation ago by Dr. Peter Steincrohn, a reputable
physician. His view was shared widely at the time. For
anyone beyond the flush of youth, strenuous exercise was
thought to carry the risk of heart strain. Now most physicians hold the precise opposite to be true: *failure* to engage
regularly in vigorous exercise is believed to increase the
risk of heart disease.

This about-face is only one of the periodic changes in   3
direction that have occurred since Americans in large
numbers began to concern themselves with exercise for
the sake of health. That doesn't seem to have happened
until sometime toward the end of the nineteenth century.
There had always been a few, of course, who kept playing games—cricket, rounders, and, later, baseball—after
school days were over. The well-to-do took up golf and
tennis in the last decades of the century. Young Theodore
Roosevelt, an awkward but enthusiastic tennis player,
battled through ninety-one games one day in 1882.

Cycling had its devotees beginning with the introduc-   4
tion of the high-wheeler in the 1870's, and there were also
some early advocates of rigorous physical training routines.
German immigrants of the mid-1800's transplanted the
Turners, athletic societies devoted to gymnastics on rings,
bars, and vaulting horses. In the 1870's some colleges
started formal physical education classes where students
tossed medicine balls and performed drills designed to improve posture. Even in the years just before his death at
the age of eighty-three in 1878, William Cullen Bryant rose
early to heft dumbbells for an hour and then strode the
three miles from his house in lower Manhattan to the *New
York Evening Post*. There, scorning the newfangled elevator,
he ran up ten flights of stairs to his office, where he sometimes stopped at the door to seize the lintel and raise and
lower himself by his arms several times.

But for most people of that era the physical demands 5
of ordinary life were quite enough, and the notion that
they should seek out extra work for their muscles would
have seemed bizarre. That was particularly true for the
great majority of Americans who still lived in rural areas—
almost 75 per cent in 1870—and for whom heavy farm
labor from dawn to dusk was often the rule. But it also
held true for many city dwellers. They drew water, chop-
ped wood, walked to work and church. Understandably,
technological advances that saved human effort—elevators,
streetcars, telephones, running water—were seen as un-
diluted blessings.

Attitudes toward exercise were changing as 1890 ap- 6
proached, however. Urbanization was steadily reducing
the proportion of Americans who had to spend their days
wrestling plows and pitching hay. "Americans went indoors to serve machines, stand behind counters, or sit at
desks," observes one historian. When a handful of self-
proclaimed "experts" on physical fitness began spreading
the message that the "nineteenth-century method of living" was making the nation soft, they found a receptive
audience, and their numbers proliferated. "Professors" of
physical culture opened gymnasiums where businessmen
paid to swing Indian clubs and "in-hale! . . . ex-hale!"
to the cadence of instructors. Doctors, who were often
scornful of the physical culturists muscling into what they
considered their purview, offered their own regimens.
Books and magazine articles poured forth promoting one
new system of exercise after another and exhorting readers
to shape up in tones so stirring that it is almost impossible to dip into their musty pages today without instinctively squaring the shoulders and taking a deep breath.

If a man feels he is getting soft, the most obvious 7
solution is to acquire a handsome pair of biceps, and the
early exercise manuals stressed straightforward muscle
building. One was entitled *How to Get Strong*. Another demanded: "Why be weakly?" The goal was more modest
than the exaggerated musculature of today's body-building

cultists; one set of arm exercises was designed to produce arms "which look well either in rowing or exercising costume, that is, with nothing on them, or which set off a well-cut coat to great advantage." But the authors themselves were nevertheless pretty impressive specimens who were not at all reticent about their own physical accomplishments—one, for example, invited two-hundred-pounders to don heavy boots and take a running jump onto his abdomen—and the clear implication was that readers could achieve similar physiques if only they would pay attention.

The recommended exercise was demanding, often calling for the use of weights and other strengthening equipment. In the nineties many bedrooms were graced by A. G. Spalding & Bros. Victor No. 5 Machine, a contraption of pulleys and weights that attached to the wall. In the same decade, J. R. Judd, a professor of physical culture with a luxuriant handlebar mustache, published *Always Strong and Happy*, a course that required a whole array of equipment manufactured by Judd, including dumbbells weighing up to forty pounds, a racklike affair called the Extensor, and his Columbia Parlor General Exercising and Rowing Machine. After punishing himself with this paraphernalia, the victim was instructed to plunge into a cold bath, which was the standard conclusion for most of the exercise programs.

The best known of the early body builders was Bernarr Macfadden. In 1898, when he was a sleek-muscled, narcissistic thirty-year-old, Macfadden published a five-cent pamphlet called *Physical Culture*. It evolved into a monthly magazine with a circulation of half a million and helped make Macfadden a cult figure among health faddists. Macfadden, who in time built a publishing enterprise that also included such magazines as *True Story* and *True Romance* and a sleazy newspaper known formally as the *New York Evening Graphic* but informally as the *Pornographic*, presented a body-building scheme, using a contrivance of pulleys and cords, in a book in 1900. Sprinkled among nude or near-nude photographs of Macfadden posing on a pedestal or on a leopard skin were stern admonitions: "Clear your system of accumulated corruption from inactivity, and live! . . . If you are weak, there is absolutely no excuse for your continuing so."

Macfadden's methods worked for him. He lived to the 10 age of eighty-seven, and he celebrated his seventy-fifth birthday by standing on his head during an interview and his eighty-third by making a parachute jump into the Hudson River. But in the eyes of many, muscle building had a couple of serious disadvantages. One was that it entailed considerable effort. The other was that no matter how hard they heaved and strained, when most men stood before a mirror—Macfadden recommended exercising there—they were never going to see a Greek god.

So another crop of experts came to the rescue with the 11 good news that large muscles were out of date. They were contemptuous of the muscle builders. "The ordinary gymnasium 'professor' knows no more about the principles of bodily development than he does about ancient Coptic," scoffed a physician named Latson in 1910. Another doctor, writing in *Harper's*, warned that muscle building was positively dangerous to the health. Backing came from a 1910 editorial in the *New York Times* deploring the emphasis on "brute strength" in physical education. "The cultivation of huge muscles belonged to the hunting, grazing, peasant, and warrior stages of civilization," said the *Times*.

To replace arduous muscle building, the doctors and 12 others proposed less taxing calisthenics. There were variations in the systems; one school held, for example, that touching the toes without bending the knees was beneficial, while a rival camp insisted that if God had intended man to do that, He would not have provided knee joints. But for the most part the movements were similar—stretch, twist, turn, bend. They were the sort of mild exercises a lot of people dutifully performed a few decades ago upon arising, sometimes under the guidance of an instructor on the radio or on a record—and, indeed, that some people still do. Such calisthenics can ease muscular kinks, but more fundamental benefits seem to have been ruled out by competition among the originators of the systems to see who could come up with the easiest program. The ideal appeared to be exercise that required no effort, and some of the systems came close.

Dr. Latson, the critic of the physical culture professors, 13 asserted that a great advantage of his own gentle twists and turns was that "they require practically no effort of body or mind." In 1907 Sanford Bennett, an elderly eccentric from San Francisco, published *Exercising in Bed*. The book is exactly what the title indicates, a manual of exercises that can be done in bed, alone, without even throwing off the covers. "I believe that muscles develop . . . more rapidly under these comfortable conditions than in the cold, bracing air usually advocated for physical exercise," explained Bennett.

The experts also vied to see who could devise the 14 shortest exercise routines. Bernarr Macfadden had advocated working out as much as an hour a day, but in 1905 J. P. Müller, a Dane, began promoting *My System—* "15 Minutes' Work a Day for Health's Sake"—in America. Within a few years, however, competitors offered systems even less time-consuming, and so in 1924 Müller issued a revised version of his book called *The Daily Five Minutes*. Then somebody undercut this with a sure-fire four-minute program.

The most popular exercises in the 1920's were Walter 15 Camp's Daily Dozen. Camp, a robust former Yale football star and the inventor of the All-American team, said he got the inspiration for his system by watching lions stretch at the Bronx Zoo. He gave the movements in his ten-minute routine alliterative names—hands, hips, head; grind, grate, grasp; crawl, curl, crouch; wave, weave, wing. "The essential thing is to go slowly," he advised. A casual test shows that the Daily Dozen will not raise a drop of sweat on a desk-bound forty-seven-year-old writer. The exercises approximate what a moderately serious jogger might do to loosen up before starting *real* exercise.

Considering the modest investment of effort, the bene-   16
fits claimed for such exercises were truly remarkable.
Constipation and dyspepsia, which seem to have afflicted
people back then more than they do now, would vanish.
So would sluggish livers, following a few repetitions of
the "liver squeezer," a widely prescribed exercise that involved lying on the back and drawing the knees up to the
chin. This was said to wring out the liver like a sponge.
Preoccupation with fat was frowned on. "A prejudice
against fat amounting to an abhorrence ought to be condemned," wrote a Boston physician, Samuel Delano, in
1918. But if you did want to lose weight, it was no problem provided you conscientiously practiced the deep
breathing that was part of most systems. "Deep, purpose-
ful breathing in the open air prevents the accumulation
of fat, as it acts like a pair of active bellows on a furnace
fire," said William J. Cromie, an instructor of physical
education at the University of Pennsylvania.

Now and then a voice from the past expresses ideas   17
about exercise not too far removed from present theories.
As far back as 1890, a physical culturist named Edwin
Checkley came out in favor of running, although he added
sadly: "When I run for a few streets on a city thorough-
fare, the populace look after me as if I were a 'freak,' or
as if I were making off with something not belonging to
me. . . ." Perhaps that explains why another pioneer jogger, Theodore Roosevelt, sometimes did his running at
night while President, going out from the White House
and trotting around the Washington Monument. Among
medical men, Dudley A. Sargent, who directed physical
education at Harvard from 1879 to 1919, sounded much
like physicians today. Sustained, vigorous exertion that
stimulates the heart and lungs strengthens the vital systems, he preached.

But where those of middle age or older were con-   18
cerned, Sargent and the other exercise specialists who
agreed with him generally cautioned against really strenuous workouts of the sort their theories seemed to require,

such as long runs. Some of the authorities said that "gentle" running was safe, but they really meant "gentle." C. Ward Crampton of New York, one of the first physicians to sound the alarm over the mounting number of heart attacks among Americans, insisted that the focus of exercise should be to strengthen the heart and that running was well suited for this purpose. But, he said in 1924, sixty-four steps "is sufficient for anyone." That's a couple of laps around the living room.

At the time, even that would have been considered 19 overdoing it in some circles. It was commonly believed that everyone was endowed with a fixed, limited supply of "vitality" and that strenuous exercise could lead to premature exhaustion of the supply, followed by invalidism or early death. A 1931 article on exercise in *Hygeia*, a health magazine published for laymen by the American Medical Association, commented: "It seems that the more prodigiously we give of our vitality the sooner we exhaust it."

To buttress their case, exponents of this theory seized 20 on every instance of an athlete dying young. Such deaths were not rare in those days; athletes, like nonathletes, could be struck down in their prime by infectious diseases since conquered by antibiotics. But the foes of strenuous exercise claimed in such cases that the athletes had squandered their vitality, weakening their hearts and their defenses against disease. Arthur A. McGovern, the proprietor of a gym in New York, kept a scrapbook of obituaries of athletes who had died by the age of forty, presumably to show clients who might be tempted to push themselves too hard.

McGovern and most of his fellow experts just about 21 ruled out vigorous exercise of any type for anyone over forty. It went without saying that running was foolhardy, and the list of potentially perilous activities usually included bicycling, rowing, squash, handball, and tennis— even doubles. Warning of the dire fate in store for "those disciples of strenuosity," Dr. Delano of Boston offered fairly typical advice. "The heart and breathing are not to be unduly juggled," he asserted. Beware of the bicycle, which has produced "many a damaged heart and circulation." Tennis is risky because "in the volleying much *qui vive* and much holding of breath is necessary. It does the heart up easily—especially in the case of the nervous temperament." The only sport Delano wholeheartedly approved was golf. As for calisthenics, the doctor propounded his own thirty-four-movement system in *How Shall I Take Exercise and Set-Up?* Judging from the illustrations, for which the rather modestly muscled doctor himself posed somewhat sheepishly ("Let not the eye fall at once on the quantity of muscle. . . . For muscle by itself we have, as the reader must know, but scant respect"), the exercises consisted mainly of assorted grimaces.

If exercise was fraught with peril for men, it was even more so for women. Fielding Yost, who dispensed advice on exercise besides coaching football at the University of Michigan, said women should quit tennis at thirty-five. The idea of exercises to strengthen female muscles was absurd on its face. As Dr. Delano put it: "Femininity was plainly created not to have much muscle." The permissible exercises for the ladies in their middy tops and bloomers were mild in the extreme, with a trim waist and a "graceful carriage" the primary goals. An article by a woman doctor in the *Ladies' Home Journal* in 1907 reflected the tone that prevailed for decades. It recommended the exercise of touching the toes ("Austrian officers, who are noted for their tapering waists, make a special point of its use"). It also said that "healthy girls"—but apparently not adult women—could hazard stationary running in the bathroom, provided they started with no more than twenty-five steps and lay down for at least five minutes immediately after. [22]

Clearly, even healthy girls couldn't tolerate much strain. Arthur McGovern, the gym proprietor, frowned on all strenuous competitive games for girls "as the element of excitement very easily leads to exertion injurious to the feminine physique." In a 1915 issue of the *Delineator*, Dr. B. Wallace Hamilton told the harrowing tale of fifteen-year-old Emily. She went off to boarding school, where [23] she became nervous and jumpy from playing too much basketball. Hamilton prescribed a transfer to a school where the staff appreciated the frailty of young women, and a switch to golf and croquet.

If the theory that each person has a fixed stock of 24 vitality is accepted as valid, then the logical conclusion must be that the wisest course is no exercise at all, and that is precisely the direction in which things moved. Whereas the electric horses that became popular in the early twenties demanded at least modest effort from the user, the abdominal massage machines that came into wide use a few years later required no exertion whatever. These machines, which whipped a broad belt back and forth on the user's stomach, supposedly stimulated the internal organs and dissolved fat, but by 1930 the American Medical Association, not always the most enlightened voice on the subject of exercise, felt compelled to state that they not only did no good but had caused some grievous injuries.

In 1925 a grim article entitled "Too Much Exercise" 25 appeared in the *Saturday Evening Post*. Citing "overwhelming evidence that a great many Americans, of middle age or beyond, are exercising too much," it warned that any man over forty "who persists in putting unnecessary strains on his heart is fixing to make the acquaintance of the undertaker." The article ridiculed calisthenics and went on to question the safety of golf, which was just about the only sport left to doddering forty-year-olds by then. The stress and exertion of golf were vastly underrated, readers were told, and the nation's courses were more or less littered with the corpses of players who had collapsed from the strain.

The ultimate stand against exercise was taken by Peter 26 Steincrohn, the doctor who dismissed all such activity as "bosh." In 1942 Steincrohn, a prolific writer on health topics, published a book that bore the alluring title *You Don't Have to Exercise* and the subtitle *"Rest Begins at Forty."* It sounds like satire now, but it was dead serious.

In fact, when the book came out, it was quoted approvingly by Dr. Morris Fishbein, editor of the *Journal of the American Medical Association*.

Steincrohn's thesis was that the heart needed rest, not   27
exercise, to stay healthy. Therefore, on reaching middle age it was best to avoid all exertion beyond that necessary for conducting the business of life. "Don't lift a finger unnecessarily after forty" was Steincrohn's motto. "Bending over to tie and untie your shoes; bringing the fork to your mouth; the rubdown after a shower; laughing; talking and reading—all these furnish your daily exercise requirements." Steincrohn, then in his forties, made clear that he had managed to shake the exercise habit completely, but for those who insisted on continuing to play a bit of golf, he advised dawdling on the course and taking a break for a smoke and a drink between nines. As for old codgers of fifty who persisted in playing tennis, he had nothing but reproach—"infantile exhibitionism."

Steincrohn reiterated his antiexercise arguments, only   28
slightly hedged, in a 1968 book, but by then even he conceded that the tide of medical opinion had turned against him. A major force behind that change was Paul Dudley White, the cardiologist. In the 1930's White had become convinced that exercise to the point of pleasant fatigue— long bicycle rides were his favorite form—benefited the heart. When he came into the public eye after being summoned to treat President Dwight Eisenhower following his heart attack in 1955, White made use of his new prominence to promote the cause of exercise through speeches, articles, and interviews. Dr. White, who died in 1973 at the age of eighty-seven, was a dogged exerciser himself, pedaling his bicycle thirty miles a day even in his later years.

In the sixties and seventies White was joined in his   29
crusade by many other physicians and medical researchers. Their central message was that the most valuable exercise for general health was activity that forced the respiratory and circulatory systems to work hard for prolonged

periods. Far from draining the organism of vitality, such exercise was said to increase the efficiency of the heart and to expand its capability. The exercise needed to achieve this effect involves considerable effort; there is no such thing as effortless exercise. A typical program might call, for example, for jogging as long as an hour several times a week, or perhaps for sustained stints of cycling or swimming. Most Americans still don't exercise much, of course, and many are still overweight, but, as the jogging craze in particular illustrates, millions have heeded the message. And their ranks include many well along in years. "Age is not a major obstacle to fitness," insists Dr. Kenneth H. Cooper. As the developer of the widely followed "aerobics" system, Cooper is more responsible than anyone else for starting Americans jogging.

It is conceivable that the new experts are wrong. But 30 the assumption has to be that the march of medical science is generally onward and upward and that the exercise advocates know what they're talking about. Moreover, they are beginning to gather some statistical evidence that backs them up. A report issued in 1977 on a study of seventeen thousand men who enrolled at Harvard between 1916 and 1950 concluded that those who habitually exercised intensively suffered markedly fewer heart attacks than those who didn't. Similar reports are not yet available on women, and indeed one recent medical study of top women athletes such as Olympics trainees revealed the curious fact that a prolonged program of heavy exercise temporarily makes some women stop menstruating. There seems to be every reason to think, however, that the beneficial results of regular, energetic exercise are not confined to males.

Then, too, there is the subjective evidence of those 31 who have found that they don't have to put aside games at forty and who derive deep satisfaction from the discovery that stamina can even grow with age. We are learning that we are not as delicate as was once thought and that we do not need to coddle ourselves, slow our step, and consign the tennis racket to the back of the closet shelf just because we are no longer young. In short, we are developing a whole new attitude toward growing old. And we can only feel sorry for all those who in the past were made to feel old before their time by the misguided fitness "experts" and the sedentary doctors.

Comment

In selecting evidence, the historian seeks evidence that represents typical attitudes and practices. In presenting this evidence, the historian must convince the reader that the evidence presented is representative. Paul Lancaster seeks to convince us through a series of examples and judicious quotations—focusing on prominent people who shaped public attitudes, describing popular exercise equipment, and quoting statements that highlight contrasting views of exercise. He also interprets his evidence and places it in its historical context. Woven into a single narrative, his evidence reveals a pattern or cycle of attitudes, "periodic changes in direction." Because these changes extend into our own time, Lancaster can appeal to our own experience and observation and use his exposition to give us a reminder. For even though his essay is expository in tracing the recent history of exercise, it also has an argumentative edge.

Questions for Study and Discussion

1. What point is Lancaster making in quoting Dr. Peter Steincrohn's statements about exercise?
2. What "periodic changes in direction" does Lancaster trace? Does he make an explicit or implicit point about these changes?
3. What does Bernarr Macfadden's personal history and career as a journalist tell us about the history of exercise in America?
4. How did the attitude toward female exercise differ from that of male exercise? Does the evidence presented suggest that attitudes toward female exercise changed less?

5. How does Lancaster reveal his own attitude toward exercise in the course of the essay? What direct or implied comment on or recommendation about exercise does he make?

Vocabulary Study

1. Lancaster reminds us that words often had a special meaning in the past. Use the *Oxford English Dictionary* and other dictionaries to discover the original meaning of *calisthenics* and find out whether the word is used in the same sense today.
2. Explain the following words and phrases:
   a. *flush of youth* (paragraph 2)
   b. *lintel* (paragraph 4)
   c. *purview* (paragraph 6)
   d. *physique* (paragraph 7)
   e. *paraphernalia* (paragraph 8)
   f. *alliterative* (paragraph 15)
   g. *buttress* (paragraph 20)
   h. qui vive, *sheepishly, grimace* (paragraph 21)
   i. *bloomers, tapering* (paragraph 23)
   j. *prolific* (paragraph 26)
   k. *exhibitionism* (paragraph 27)
   l. *aerobics* (paragraph 29)
   m. *coddle, sedentary* (paragraph 31)

Suggestions for Writing

1. Use current articles and advertisements in a variety of sources —newspapers, health and sports magazines, consumer newsletters and magazines, medical journals—to compare attitudes toward male and female exercise today. Distinguish between attitudes based on medical research and those based on social attitudes and popular conceptions of health. Develop a thesis based on your evidence. Document your sources, following instructions in your college handbook.
2. Use the same sources to determine current attitudes toward exercise by people over 70. Distinguish between the same attitudes cited above. Limit your conclusions, and document your sources.

PART 4

Strategies for Arguing and Persuading

7

The frame of neighborly knowledge, which contained both an allowance for weakness and an unwillingness to allow for real ambition, is gone and nothing has taken its place.

— Margaret Mead
Rhoda Metraux

PART 4

Strategies for Arguing
and Persuading

Argument, or proof, is different from exposition, but the two usually occur together in essays. Most arguments require the explanation or illustration that exposition provides, and many explanations seem to be proving an idea.

Arguments seek to establish the truth or falseness, or the degree of probability, of a statement. They often have different purposes and use different kinds of evidence. A lawyer in a court trial may argue the innocence of his client on the basis of eyewitness testimony and supporting circumstantial evidence. A scientist may argue on the basis of repeated experiments that heredity plays a role in some kinds of cancer. A newspaper editorial may argue for equal educational opportunity for the handicapped through an appeal to constitutional precedents.

Arguments are classified as either *inductive* or *deductive* on the basis of the kind of evidence used to prove the conclusion. In the examples above, the lawyer and scientist are developing inductive arguments that reason from observation, personal experience, and experiment; the editorialist is developing a deductive argument that reasons from established truths or principles. Many writers use both kinds of reasoning to prove various ideas that together form the essay.

An essay that contains argument usually does more than prove or demonstrate the truth of a statement. In developing the argument, the writer usually is trying to change the thinking of people on an issue or is trying to encourage them to take some kind of action. The purpose of the argument in these instances is persuasive. The argument employs strategies intended to capture the reader's or listener's attention and assent to the argument. But not all persuasive writing uses formal argument. Political cartoons are persuasive without being argumentative, for example. So are many satirical essays and poems. In this part of the book, we will discuss argument and persuasion separately, though some of the essays in the two sections illustrate both.

✦

Inductive Argument

When we reason from personal experience, observation, experiments, facts and statistics, and other empirical evidence, we are reasoning inductively. We would be doing so if we predicted that it will rain on the upcoming Fourth of July because it has rained on previous Fourths in the past ten years. A scientist would do so in predicting that vaccines will be effective in fighting new viral diseases because of the success of vaccines in combatting polio, smallpox, and measles. In the essay that follows, Edwin H. Peeples, Jr., uses various kinds of evidence—personal experience, social work, medical observation, testimony, statistical studies—to reach a conclusion concerning hunger and malnutrition in America.

Inductive arguments make predictions about the future on the basis of past and present experience or experimentation. Because it is based on experience, and experience changes, the prediction or conclusion of an inductive argument can only be probable, and it cannot go beyond the particular evidence presented. The probability increases that it will rain this Fourth of July if it did in fact rain on every Fourth of July in the last forty years. But the fact that it has rained does not guarantee that it will do so again; nor can we use the history of the Fourth to predict what will happen on other holidays. The success in treating viral disease suggests that vaccines may be effective in fighting new viral diseases; however, it does not prove that vaccination is the only effective method, or that it will be effective with newly discovered bacterial and other nonviral diseases.

The writer of an inductive argument must decide how much evidence is needed to draw a well-founded conclusion—to make the "inductive leap." There is, of course, no end to the amount of evidence that can be presented for a conclusion such as Peeples reaches in his essay (p. 297):

There are those who argue that we do not have enough
hard data on the human consumption of pet foods. Must we
wait for incontrovertible data before we seriously seek to solve
the problems of hunger and malnutrition in America? I submit that we have data enough.

As Peeples suggests in this statement, the researcher must make
the decision at some point in conducting an investigation that
enough evidence has been found to warrant a conclusion. The
conclusion, however, must be properly limited or qualified: the
writer or researcher must tell us how broad a conclusion can
be drawn from the evidence available. The phrase "inductive
leap" sometimes means that the writer has drawn a conclusion
too soon, on the basis of incomplete evidence.

Probably few writers are satisfied that they have found all
the evidence needed to make the argument convincing to everyone. Like Peeples, they find it necessary to draw a conclusion
from a limited amount of evidence because a current situation
is growing critical and must be exposed at once:

Isn't it sufficient to know that one American child or a single
elderly person in this bountiful land is reduced to eating the
forage of animals or exposed to unknown toxic levels of mercury, lead or salmonella to know that something very extraordinary must be done?

Peeples admits that his personal experience imposes a limit on
his conclusions; he is careful to state this limitation. If writers
have wide and expert experience in their subject, as Peeples has,
their experience alone may be sufficient to give weight to the
conclusion. But the greater the variety of evidence provided for
the conclusion, the greater the weight it may possess.

Causal analysis—reasoning about causes and effects—is
another kind of inductive argument: identifying causes that produce an event is the same as drawing a conclusion from
particulars of experience. In his explanation of "computer communities," Robert J. Samuelson (p. 272) reasons about causes
in arguing that computerized marketing has led to "niche
building," or persuading consumers that they are special or
"select," and with unexpected results:

The point of splintering consumers into finer subdivisions is
to give vent to individual differences and choices. In fact, our

high-tech marketing simply fosters new, more variegated styles of conformity. What the marketers call niches and segments, you and I call friends. People don't compare themselves with strangers. They look at their peers: people like themselves. Most of us—along with our friends—are being bombarded by the same appeals for the same specialized products.
—"Computer Communities"

Though advertisers appeal to the "rhetoric of individuality" in aiming at a particular group or segment of consumers, individual differences turn out to matter little. Samuelson is appealing to our experience with mass marketing to argue this point. In the course of his essay, he gives examples of mass marketing that illustrate these effects. His causal analysis is inductive in drawing upon these particulars of experience.

The word *cause* has different meanings (see p. 81). Sometimes the word refers to the immediate event that produces an effect—failure of an engine part that leads to a car crash, a drought that leads to widespread starvation. Sometimes the word refers to one or more events that led to the engine failure or to the drought. The immediate cause of the event may be of less concern to us than the remote cause: we want to know why the engine failed or what changing weather patterns or atmospheric pollution, or both, led to the drought.

We sometimes use the word *condition* to refer to cause. We may speak of a condition necessary for an event to occur: wheat cannot grow without water. Water is a necessary condition, but water is not a sufficient condition; water alone is not enough to produce a strong crop. Other conditions must be present— fertile soil, proper cultivation, sunlight, to name a few. We would know the sufficient condition if we knew all the conditions that must be present to ensure a strong crop. It is difficult, however, to claim to know all conditions; knowledge of why things happens is seldom complete. The word *condition* is thus used to avoid this implication. Statements about causes and effects need to be qualified carefully.

An *analogy* is a point-by-point comparison used for illustration (see p. 212) or to prove a thesis. An argument from analogy is inductive because, like causal analysis, it makes an appeal to experience. For example, you might argue that a candidate for the presidency should be elected on the basis of resemblances to an admired former president. Your analogy covers a range of similarities in character traits, policies, and governmental acts. In an effective argument from analogy, the points of similarity must be pertinent to the issue—here, the qualifications for the presidency. It would be immaterial to the argument if the candidate were shorter in height than the former president. Important differences would weaken the analogy: it would be a material difference if the candidate had no previous governmental experience. If the similarities noted are genuine and if no significant differences weaken the analogy, it can be argued that the candidate probably would make a good president.

Notice the qualification *probably*. The analogy does not allow us to say with certainty that the candidate will make a good president. Inductive arguments are probable only. As in causal analysis, we can never be certain that we have discovered all the facts—that an exception may not exist to the conclusion drawn from the evidence. In inductive arguments, the major problem is not to claim more in the conclusion than the evidence warrants. The conclusion must be limited properly.

Edward H. Peeples, Jr.

. . . MEANWHILE, HUMANS EAT PET FOOD

Edward H. Peeples, Jr., is associate professor of preventive medicine at Virginia Commonwealth University. Born in 1935 in Richmond, Virginia, Peeples attended Richmond Professional Institute, the University of Pennsylvania, and the University of Kentucky, where he received his Ph.D. in 1972. In the 1960s, he gained knowledge of urban poverty as a social worker in Richmond and South Philadelphia. He has been a leader of the Richmond Human Rights Coalition and Council on Human Relations and has long been concerned with the nutritional problems and medical care of poor people.

The first time I witnessed people eating pet foods was 1 among neighbors and acquaintances during my youth in the South. At that time it was not uncommon or startling to me to see dog-food patties sizzling in a pan on the top of a stove or kerosene space heater in a dilapidated house with no running water, no refrigerator, no heat, no toilet and the unrelenting stench of decaying insects. I simply thought of it as the unfortunate but unavoidable consequence of being poor in the South.

The second time occurred in Cleveland in the summer of 1953. Like many other Southerners, I came to seek my fortune in one of those pot-at-the-end-of-the-rainbow factories along Euclid Avenue. Turned away from one prospective job after another ("We don't hire hillbillies," employers said), I saw my nest egg of $30 dwindle to nothing. As my funds diminished and my hunger grew, I turned to pilfering food and small amounts of cash. With the money, I surreptitiously purchased, fried and ate canned dog and cat food as my principal ration for several weeks.

I was, of course, humiliated to be eating something that, in my experience, only "trash" consumed. A merciless pride in self-sufficiency kept me from seeking out public welfare or asking my friends or family for help. In fact, I carefully guarded the secret from everyone, because I feared being judged a failure. Except for the humiliation I experienced, eating canned pet food did not at the time seem to be particularly unpleasant. The dog food tasted pretty much like mealy hamburger, while the cat food was similar to canned fish that I was able to improve with mayonnaise, mustard or catsup.

The next time I ate dog food was in 1956 while struggling through a summer session in college without income for food. Again, I was ashamed to admit it, fearing that people would feel sorry for me or that others who had even less than I would feel compelled to sacrifice for my comfort. I never again had to eat pet food. Later, while working as a hospital corpsman at the Great Lakes Illinois Naval Training Center in the late 1950's I had the opportunity to ask new recruits about their home life and nutrition practices. While I was not yet a disciplined scientist, I was able to estimate that about 5 to 8 percent of the thousands of young men who came to Great Lakes annually consumed pet foods and other materials not commonly thought to be safe or desirable for humans. Among these substances were baking soda, baking powder, laundry starch, tobacco, snuff, clay, dirt, sand and various wild plants.

My later experience as a public assistance caseworker in Richmond, a street-based community worker in South Philadelphia, and my subsequent travels and studies as a medical sociologist throughout the South, turned up instances of people eating pet food because they saw it as cheaper than other protein products. Through the years, similar cases found in the Ozarks, on Indian reservations and in various cities across the nation have also been brought to my attention.

While there do exist scattered scientific reports and commentary on the hazards and problems associated with eating such things as laundry starch and clay, there is little solid epidemiological evidence that shows a specific percentage of American households consume pet food. My experience and research, however, suggest that human consumption of pet food is widespread in the United States. My estimate, one I believe to be conservative, is that pet foods constitute a significant part of the diet of at least 225,000 American households, affecting some one million persons. Who knows how many more millions supplement their diet with pet-food products? One thing that we can assume is that current economic conditions are increasing the practice and that it most seriously affects the unemployed, poor people, and our older citizens.

There are those who argue that we do not have enough hard data on the human consumption of pet foods. Must we wait for incontrovertible data before we seriously seek to solve the problems of hunger and malnutrition in America? I submit that we have data enough. Isn't it sufficient to know that one American child or a single elderly person in this bountiful land is reduced to eating the forage of animals or exposed to unknown toxic levels of mercury, lead or salmonella to know that something very extraordinary must be done?

Questions for Study and Discussion

1. Why do people eat pet food, according to Peeples?
2. What is his purpose in writing, and where does he state it? What makes the essay inductive?
3. To what audience is he writing, and how do you know? Were he writing to public health officials only, would he approach the subject in a different way, or present different evidence?
4. How does Peeples qualify his conclusion that people who eat pet food are affected by it seriously—that is, how does he indicate the degree of probability that this is so?
5. Has Peeples persuaded you that the situation he describes is serious and that something must be done about it? If not, what other evidence would persuade you?

Vocabulary Study

1. Complete the following to show the meaning of the italicized words:
   a. His *disciplined* way of living was shown by
   b. A *conservative* action is one that
   c. An *incontrovertible* proof can never
   d. The *bountiful* harvest
2. Identify the denotative and connotative meanings of the following:
   a. *sizzling, dilapidated, stench* (paragraph 1)
   b. *pilfering, surreptitious* (paragraph 2)
   c. *"trash"* (paragraph 3)
   d. *cheaper* (paragraph 5)
   e. *extraordinary, forage* (paragraph 7)

Suggestions for Writing

1. Write an essay that builds to a thesis through a series of observations and experiences. Qualify your thesis by stating the limitations of your experience and knowledge of the subject.

2. Discuss an experience that resulted when you found yourself short of or without money. Discuss what you did and what you learned about yourself and perhaps about other people.
3. Discuss how your ideas about people changed through experiences in a world different from that you grew up in. Use this experience to persuade a particular audience to change their thinking about these people.

Richard Moran

MORE CRIME AND LESS PUNISHMENT

Richard Moran teaches criminology at Mount Holyoke College, and he has published a number of articles on crime in America. He is the author of *Knowing Right from Wrong: The Insanity Defense of Daniel McNaughten* (1981). His essay on the problems created by the high crime rate is inductive because his evidence draws upon particulars of experience. Moran makes a number of inferences from available statistical evidence. He also depends upon illustrative analogy—a point by point comparison used to explain an idea—(p. 212) to clarify his argument.

If you are looking for an explanation of why we don't get tough with criminals, you need only look at the numbers. Each year almost a third of the households in America are victimized by violence or theft. This amounts to more than 41 million crimes, many more than we have the capacity to punish. There are also too many criminals. The best estimates suggest that 36 million to 40 million people or 16 to 18 percent of the U.S. population have arrest records for nontraffic offenses. We already have 2.4 million people under some form of correctional supervision, 412,000 of them locked away in a prison cell. We don't have room for any more!

The painful fact is that the more crime there is the less we are able to punish it. This is why the certainty and severity of punishment must go down when the crime rate goes up. Countries like Saudi Arabia can afford to mete out harsh punishments precisely because they have so little crime. But can we afford to cut off the hands of those who committed more than 35 million property crimes each year? Can we send them to prison? Can we execute more than 22,000 murderers?

We need to think about the relationship between pun-   3
ishment and crime in a new way. A decade of sophisticated research has failed to provide clear and convincing
evidence that the threat of punishment influences the rate
of most major crimes committed. We assume that punishment deters crime, but it just might be the other way
around. It just might be that crime deters punishment: that
there is so much crime that it simply cannot be punished.

This is the situation we find ourselves in today. Just as   4
the decline in the number of high-school graduates has
made it easier to gain admission to the college of one's
choice, the gradual increase in the criminal population has
made it more difficult to get into prison. While elite colleges and universities have held the line on standards of
admissions, some of the most "exclusive" prisons now
require about five prior felony convictions before an inmate is accepted into their correctional program. Our current crop of prisoners is an elite group, on the whole much
more serious offenders than those who inhabited Alcatraz
during its heyday.

Given the reality of the numbers it makes little sense to   5
blame the police, judges or correctional personnel for being soft on criminals. There is not much else they can do.
The police can't find most criminals and those they find
are difficult and costly to convict. Those convicted can't
all be sent to prison. The social fact is that we cannot afford to do nothing about crime. The practical reality is that
there is very little the police, courts or prisons can do about
the crime problem. The criminal-justice system must then
become as powerless as a parent who has charge of hundreds of teenage children and who is nonetheless expected
to answer the TV message: "It's 10 o'clock! Do you know
where your children are?"

A few statistics from the Justice Department's recent   6
"Report to the Nation on Crime and Justice" illustrate my
point. Of every 100 felonies committed in America, only

33 are actually reported to the police. Of the 33 reported, about 6 are cleared by arrest. Of the six arrested, only three are prosecuted and convicted. The others are rejected or dismissed due to evidence or witness problems or diverted into a treatment program. Of the three convicted, only one is sent to prison. The other two are placed on probation or some form of supervision. Of the select few sent to prison, more than half receive a maximum sentence of five years. The average inmate, however, graduates into a community-based program in about two years. Most prisoners gain early release not because parole boards are soft on crime, but because it is much cheaper to supervise a criminal in the community. And, of course, prison officials must make room for the new entering class of recruits sent almost daily from the courts.

We could, of course, get tough with the people we already have in prison and keep them locked up for longer periods of time. Yet when measured against the probable reduction in crime, prolonged incarceration is not worth the financial burden it imposes on state and local governments who pay the bulk of criminal-justice costs. Besides, those states that have tried to gain voter approval for bonds to build new prisons often discover that the public is unwilling to pay for prison construction. 7

And if it were willing to pay, prolonged incarceration may not be effective in reducing crime. In 1981, 124,000 convicts were released from prison. If we had kept them in jail for an additional year, how much crime would have been prevented? While it is not possible to know the true amount of crime committed by people released from prison in any given year, we do know the extent to which those under parole are reconfined for major crime convictions. This number is a surprisingly low 6 percent (after three years it rises to only 11 percent). Even if released prisoners commit an average of two crimes each, this would amount to only 15,000 crimes prevented: a drop in the bucket when measured against the 41 million crimes committed annually. 8

More time spent in prison is also more expensive. The best estimates are that it costs an average of $13,000 to 9 keep a person in prison for one year. If we had a place to keep the 124,000 released prisoners, it would have cost us $1.6 billion to prevent 15,000 crimes. This works out to more than $100,000 per crime prevented. But there is more. With the average cost of prison construction running around $50,000 per bed, it would cost more than $6 billion to build the necessary cells. The first-year operating cost would be $150,000 per crime prevented, worth it if the victim were you or me, but much too expensive to be feasible as a national policy.

Faced with the reality of the numbers, I will not be so foolish as to suggest a solution to the crime problem. My contribution to the public debate begins and ends with this simple observation: getting tough with criminals is not the answer.

¹⁰

Comment

Statistical arguments that are worth considering include the following tests. The group sampled must be sufficiently broad and varied; that is, enough people must be interviewed to support a significant conclusion. A conclusion bearing on the whole population will be weak if the sample is based on two or three people or drawn from a single segment. The sample must not be based on unusual circumstances, and all pertinent facts and circumstances must be taken into account in interpreting the evidence. Furthermore, the conclusion must be warranted by the evidence; that is, the evidence must be pertinent to the conclusion, and the conclusion must not go beyond the limits of the evidence. Moran does not base his argument on the incidence of crime in a few densely populated areas with high unemployment—special circumstances that would call his conclusion into question; his statistical evidence covers the whole United States. Moran further draws a limited conclusion from his evidence: we must learn to think about crime in a new way. Finally, he qualifies his argument by noting the limitation of his evidence: he tells us that his estimate of crime in America is approximate, not exact, and he is not using this evidence to speculate about crime worldwide.

Questions for Study and Discussion

1. Why does Moran not propose a solution to the problems he discusses? Why does he consider his analysis useful even though he does not propose a solution?
2. Why can Moran not provide exact statistical information on the rate of crime in America? Why can he provide exact information on the reimprisonment of paroled criminals?
3. Does Moran say or imply that he would favor harsh punishments, including capital punishment, if it were practical to administer them? Or is he only pointing out a fact?
4. What kind of evidence does Moran present for his conclusion that public thinking about punishment is inconsistent? Why does Moran emphasize this inconsistency?
5. What use does Moran make of illustrative analogy?

Vocabulary Study

State the differences in meaning of the words in each group. Then explain why Moran uses the first of the words in the paragraph cited:

1. *severity* (paragraph 2), intensity, harshness
2. *sophisticated* (paragraph 3), intense, serious
3. *deters* (paragraph 3), forbids, stops
4. *felonies* (paragraph 6), crimes, misdemeanors
5. *incarceration* (paragraph 7), punishment, penalty

Suggestions for Writing

1. Analyze advertisements for similar products—for example, cosmetics and toothpaste—to discover what evidence each of the advertisers presents for statements about the product. Use your analysis to draw a conclusion about the particular advertising of these products. Limit your conclusion carefully.
2. Your college library contains reference books and government documents that report crime statistics for particular cities and regions of the United States. Locate statistical

reports on crime in two large American cities—Miami and Los Angeles, for example—and compare the information given about the crimes named. Use your comparison to draw a conclusion about the nature of crime in these cities.

Page Smith

HUMAN TIME AND THE COLLEGE STUDENT

Page Smith is Professor Emeritus of American History at the University of California, Santa Cruz. His books include *John Adams* (1962)—which received the Bancroft Award in American History— *Daughters of the Promised Land: Women in American History* (1970), *Thomas Jefferson: A Revealing Biography* (1976), and *Shaping the Nation* (1980). First published in 1957, his essay on college examinations may be compared with Edward Rivera's account of a sociology exam (p. 46).

The tension in the large room is almost palpable. The   1
air is tainted with the odor of sweat. The faces of the men
and women are drawn and taut. Their bodies are twisted
in postures of agonized thought, of supplication, of despair. The scene is not that of a torture chamber but of
a roomful of students taking a final examination.

Surely a professor's most disheartening experience is   2
to patrol the classroom during the final examination for
his course. If he has tried to make the course a vital one,
if he has tried to catch the students up in an adventure
of learning that has contained some joy and play as well
as high seriousness, he cannot but feel downhearted as
he watches their strained faces, observes their exhaustion
and anxiety. This is certainly a dismal end to an at least
theoretically enlivening experience. Only convention can
make it tolerable to the professor and his students. We
are bound to ask ouselves, it seems to me, how well the
aims of a particular course or of education in general are
served by this ordeal. Its avowed purpose is to make sure
that the student has accomplished something measurable

in mastering a certain body of material, that he has increased his efficiency or his knowledge. We assure ourselves that the final examination accomplishes this, but we have ample testimony that it does not. I suspect that most of us have little conviction that six years or six months after the completion of this or that course, its graduates could pass even a vastly simplified examination on its content. What we might call the "retention quotient" is, in most courses, very low indeed. There is much to suggest that because the final examination presents both a frightening hurdle and an obvious terminus, it actually inhibits retention of the course content. Students at least believe so and often speak cynically of final examinations as a kind of intellectual purge by which the mind is evacuated of all the material that has been stored in it during the course.

It should be obvious that the typical examination is not 3 the proper means to ensure the student's carrying away from the work of a semester an important residue of information or knowledge. It does give us, however, a conviction that we are discriminating, that we are forcing the student to comply with certain standards, that we have transferred, even if on a temporary basis, certain information to our passive auditors. What is perhaps most important of all, we have provided a means by which the student's advance toward his ultimate goal—a degree—can be measured. Using it we are able to assign a "mark" which presumably measures the student's accomplishment. And this mark is an integral part of our educational process.

While the final examination is only the concluding trial 4 of the average course, we might take it as a symbol of much that is wrong with our instructional methods on the college level. The fact is that our colleges are, to a considerable degree, neither subject-oriented nor student-oriented but mark-oriented. They are set up, on the undergraduate level, to facilitate the awarding and the recording of marks. Individual courses of instruction are almost invariably organized with an eye on marking procedures. In large courses where the instructor is assisted by graduate students who read and grade the papers, it is especially important to devise examinations that require essentially factual answers. These answers may be in the form of multiple choices, in which case they are often graded by a machine, or they may be in the form of an essay. The essay-type question is an improvement over the true-false or multiple-choice examination since it requires that the student be more or less literate. But in practice this type of examination must still place its emphasis on the factual in order to make possible a uniform system of grading by one or more "readers."

However much, in courses of this kind, the professor   5 may affirm his desire to have the students "think for themselves," the students cannot in fact do so. Ideal answers in these mass-administered and mass-graded tests have to be devised and marks awarded on the basis of the number of essential points included in each answer. Such courses, moreover, are usually taught in conjunction with a textbook, and here the student's impulse, not unnaturally, is to memorize the text at the expense of a thoughtful, critical review of the lecture material. The large lecture courses which use a textbook and in which the grading is done by "readers" or "assistants" are self-defeating. The complex, unfamiliar, and elusive ideas given in lectures cannot compete successfully, in most instances, with the neatly assembled data in the textbook. The student is further discouraged in any speculation by the consciousness that he may have missed or misunderstood the precise point the lecturer was trying to make and may thus render it up in mutilated or unrecognizable form.

Let us assume that the student accepts the invitation to   6 "think for himself." In most cases his thoughts will be confused and banal, a mish-mash of rather unformed ideas that he has picked up in high-school civics courses, at home, from random reading, from movies and television. They will not be worth much in terms of a mark. How is the professor, or his surrogate, the reader, to react? Does he give the student an A for effort, thus encouraging him in the idea that he is a thinker of considerable power and originality? Or does he admonish him gently and give him a C, thus confirming the student's suspicions that the professor never meant what he said anyway?

Again the mark is the culprit. The fact is that the mark   7
should be used only as an incentive, as a corrective, as a stimulus. A first-rate student often needs to be most severely marked for sloppy thinking, for intellectual short cuts, for the facile use of academic clichés. As a Cambridge tutor expressed it to me, "The teacher should be free, if the character of the student suggests it is the best course, to tear up his paper before him, denounce his work as careless and inaccurate, berate him soundly, and send him off to do the work of which he is capable." Perhaps the student who suffers most under our marking system is the outstanding individual who, in any comparison with his fellows, must be given an A and thus cannot be treated with the rigor that would eventually make the most of his superior capacities.

Since all marks are carefully recorded, added up,   8
weighed and assessed, and stand unalterable upon the student's record, they cannot be used with any real freedom or flexibility. Most of us are reluctant to give a mark that will perhaps count against a scholarship, a job, or a cherished academic plum.

I suspect that largely as a result of the grading system   9
a majority of the students regard the professor as, in a sense, the enemy. That is to say, the professor represents an unknown quantity that has the potentiality of damaging the student. As professor he is in a position of almost unlimited power. To counter this the student has a kind of cunning which he has acquired as a by-product of the educational process. He is conditioned to play the game according to the rules. He knows that if, like the psychologist's pigeon, he pecks the right button, he will get a kernel of corn. He has, therefore, very little to gain and much to lose by taking liberties with the system. The prevailing educational conventions combine to make him cagey. He knows that his teachers are at least partly human and that however remote most of them may seem

from his real life and interests, they have their crotchets, their small vanities, and their prejudices. At the beginning of a class the student is alert to penetrate these and to discern in what way they can be made to work to his advantage. He knows that despite a pretense of professional objectivity, the instructor has a fairly well-developed set of biases, and the student welcomes evidences of these because they are guideposts to him. Correspondingly, the absence of discernible prejudices is unsettling for the student—it means another anxiety-producing unknown element in the equation that should yield up the desired mark.

The only way that the professor can overcome the student's habit of calculation, which is generally fatal to the learning process, is by lessening some of his apprehensions. The student's attitude is indeed ambivalent, and this is the professor's opportunity. In addition to their feelings of anxiety and hostility, many students genuinely wish to be touched and affected by the professor. The student has had, in his learning experience, a few teachers who have done this and he knows that, while it is unlikely, it can happen. But the professor, in his efforts to create this kind of *rapport*, is at a disadvantage. He is inviting a confidence that he cannot honor. The student may in fact be drawn from his shell and inspired to venture some independent judgment, but the assessment of this hesitant enterprise will not be made by the man who has solicited it but, in many instances, by a third party, the reader.   10

Even if it were possible to set up a grading procedure by which efforts at original and independent thinking would be encouraged and rewarded, there would still be little incentive for the bright student to make the effort. Being examination-oriented and acutely mark-conscious, he knows that there is always an element of chance in examinations and he has a strong impulse to keep this to a minimum.   11

He realizes that it is often not so much what he knows as how much mileage he can get out of the information that he has committed to memory. The means of testing   12

now used in most colleges and universities often fall short
of measuring the excellence or the capacity of the student.
For the most part they record his ability to memorize and
record a certain rather narrow range of information, and
here technique is of great importance. If, by the painstak-
ing accumulation of facts and approved theories and their
careful regurgitation, the student can get the desired mark,
he is borrowing trouble to attempt something more ambitious.

The teacher is, of course, as much the victim of our   13
testing conventions as the student is. Examinations play
an important part in his conception of himself as teacher
and scholar. Not infrequently he comes to view them as
weapons in a contest between himself and his students.
Unexpected and unorthodox questions affirm his
"toughness" and give a comforting spread in marks. Even
in the most straightforward examination, some conscientious students will have failed to prepare certain questions
adequately since all the significant material in a given
course can seldom be mastered with complete thorough-
ness and an element of chance inevitably enters in. Difficult and obscure questions will scatter the field even further, reducing the number of A's and B's and giving the
professor the reassuring feeling that he is a stern marker
who is upholding "standards."

It might be said that the whole matter of "distribution"   14
and grading on the "curve" is one of the most patent
fallacies in the marking system. It seems to be based on
the assumption that the student population in any particular course should be spread out with a certain percentage
of A's, B's, and C's, and so on, but this assumption, which
is treated by many professors with the sanctity of a kind
of natural law of education, will not bear close scrutiny.
It is certainly conceivable that rigorous and demanding
courses can be given to large numbers of students in which
no "proper" distribution occurs. When this happens,
however, the professor involved often feels under compulsion to revamp his testing techniques to produce a
result more in accord with accepted practice lest his

colleagues suspect that he is "soft" or perhaps trying to win students by relaxed standards—a kind of academic scab who is willing to accept less than the prevailing scale.

What I have to say about the inadequacies of the mark-   15
ing system applies most directly to freshman and sopho-more "survey" courses taken by large numbers of students who, it is hoped, will thereby get a nodding acquaintance with, say, Western Civilization, or Art in World History, or Patterns of Social Development. My strictures apply with somewhat less force to the more advanced courses, but even here, especially in the larger institutions, readers are in evidence, and the more onerous features of the grading system are only slightly ameliorated.

In the first place, by the time they are upperclassmen,   16
the majority of students are thoroughly conditioned to the corruption of marks, and it is correspondingly difficult to break through to the individual, to lure him into any free and uninhibited expression of feeling or opinion. As an advanced student he has found his level—A, B, or C. He knows what kind of effort is required to maintain it in the average course, provided again that the student-intelligence service is functioning effectively.

The student accepts the system because it can be fig-   17
ured out, anticipated, and made, in general, to yield the desired token. The professor often values it for its very impersonality, or "objectivity." Every student, if he is known, presents the teacher with a unique problem. Is the middle-aged schoolteacher from Louisiana, seeking a salary increase by the accumulation of additional course credits, to be judged by the same standards as the brilliant and precocious high school student, or the man with two children who works twenty or thirty hours a week, or the boy who works on a night shift in a railroad yard to help put a younger brother through school, or the housewife who wishes to secure a primary-school teaching creden-tial? Perhaps it can be argued that these are extreme cases, but our existing canons of grading dictate that we treat all individuals the same way.

Now this is not quite as bad if we are giving an essen- 18
tially professional education to a homogeneous student
body with a common cultural background, but if this is
no longer our basic task, the only alternative is to attempt
to assess each student individually. Of course, such a suggestion alarms the bureaucrats since it involves difficult
and dangerous decisions on the part of the professor and
smacks of the "progressive" ideas that most of us view
with suspicion when we observe them in operation on the
secondary-school level. But it might be answered that the
failure of the secondary schools is not so much caused by
trying to meet the needs of the individual student as it
is by watering down and destroying the content of the
traditional curriculum in the name of "adjustment" or of
"practical" education. If the liberal arts curriculum is maintained and strengthened as the heart of higher education,
the effort to adopt a more flexible and more personal approach to the student can only be salutary in its effects.
Both the mediocre and the outstanding student will profit
from such a change in emphasis, and standards, instead
of being lowered, will be raised, since the student who
is in a one-to-one relationship to his teacher will more often
have his best efforts evoked.

The answer to such proposals will, of course, be that 19
the present ratio of professors to students is not great
enough to permit attention to the needs and capacities of
individual students. I believe that there is much that can
be done within the existing framework of most college and
university curriculums without submerging the professor,
but it is probably true that some institutional reforms are
needed to reduce the rigidity of the present system. In any
event, a necessary first step toward breaking the tyranny
of the marking and examination system is the frank admission that these are at best necessary evils that have
about them no savor of salvation, but rather, by their own
interior logic, work toward the increasing formalization of
higher education. Perhaps an uprising against the existing
practices should begin with the destruction of the I.B.M.

machines and the dispersion of those who tend them, followed by the rout of the academic bureaucrats.

Such a revolt would open the way for the establish- [20] ment of more human and more flexible procedures. One hesitates to say what these procedures should be. Perhaps it is enough, at this stage, to insist that time spans must be created for the student that will relieve him of the continual anxiety of recurrent tests and examinations. The fragmentation of the student's learning experience seriously inhibits his intellectual growth and his personal development. Information can be dispensed on a unit basis, but formation and reformation require unbroken increments of time. In our present curriculum all marks, all assignments, all chapters are of equal significance because, as weighed by a mark, all weigh the same. The trivial takes equal rank with the important and the student's power of discrimination is soon lost.

A renewed dialogue, the creation of generous time [21] spans, the bold and unabashed reenactment of the historic drama of the self confronting the cosmos, these are the directions American higher education must take if it is not to degenerate into a fact mill or a colossal trade school.

Comment

Page Smith draws upon his experience as a university professor to describe the educational establishment of 1957. In doing so, he assumes that the classrooms and methods of examination in his own university are typical of those in others. Readers of the essay must therefore test Smith's analysis by comparison with their own university experience. His characterization of students is based upon observation, and here too Smith generalizes about how the marking system affects students. He notes exceptions but suggests that much of his characterization fits all students. The system prevailing in 1957 was dismal enough to injure everyone involved in it, and Smith insists upon this fact strongly.

Questions for Study and Discussion

1. How does Smith suggest what his own experience has been, without giving a detailed account of his teaching career?
2. Why does the marking system discourage independent thought and creativity? Does Smith suggest that other features of university education also discourage students?
3. How would Smith define ideal learning? What are the necessary conditions—the conditions that must be present—if this learning is to take place?
4. Who does Smith blame for the marking system? Or does he blame no one?
5. Does Smith propose abolishing marks or grades? Or can they serve a useful purpose?
6. To what extent does Smith accurately describe the marking system and general attitudes toward learning that prevail in your school? Does your experience suggest that the situation has changed in any way since 1957?
7. Do you agree with Smith's proposals for reform? Would the abolition of grades make you a better student?

Vocabulary Study

Explain the following words and phrases:

1. *palpable, supplication* (paragraph 1)
2. *retention quotient, terminus* (paragraph 2)
3. *residue, integral* (paragraph 3)
4. *oriented, facilitate* (paragraph 4)
5. *speculation* (paragraph 5)
6. *academic clichés* (paragraph 7)
7. *crotchets, prejudices, biases* (paragraph 9)
8. *apprehensions, rapport* (paragraph 10)
9. *regurgitation* (paragraph 12)
10. *academic scab* (paragraph 14)
11. *ameliorated, onerous* (paragraph 15)
12. *uninhibited* (paragraph 16)
13. *canons* (paragraph 17)
14. *bureaucrats, curriculum, mediocre* (paragraph 18)

15. *formalization, dispersion* (paragraph 19)
16. *fragmentation* (paragraph 20)
17. *unabashed, cosmos* (paragraph 21)

Suggestions for Writing

1. Discuss your own conception of the ideal classroom or ideal relationship between student and teacher. Draw on your personal experience in explaining this conception.
2. Discuss the extent to which one of the following statements by Smith reflects your own experience in high school or college. Use your discussion to evaluate one of Smith's proposals for reform of education:
    a. "What we might call the 'retention quotient' is, in most courses, very low indeed."
    b. "There is much to suggest that because the final examination presents both a frightening hurdle and an obvious terminus, it actually inhibits retention of the course content."
    c. "I suspect that largely as a result of the grading system a majority of the students regard the professor as, in a sense, the enemy."
    d. "The only way that the professor can overcome the student's habit of calculation, which is generally fatal to the learning process, is by lessening some of his apprehensions."
    e. "The means of testing now used in most colleges and universities often fall short of measuring the excellence or the capacity of the student."
    f. "The student accepts the system because it can be figured out, anticipated, and made, in general, to yield the desired token."

Wendell Berry

GETTING ALONG WITH NATURE

Wendell Berry taught English at the University of Kentucky from 1964 to 1977. He has written about his native Kentucky in numerous poems, novels, and essays. *Collected Poems* was published in 1985; his novels include *Nathan Coulter* (1960) and *The Memory of Old Jack* (1974); his essays appear in *The Long-Legged House* (1969) and other collections. Berry has long been associated with the environmental movement and its effort to preserve wilderness areas throughout the United States. His many essays on nature reveal what the critic Edward Abbey describes as "a certain nobility of spirit and sentiment" in Berry's writings—a "sanctity" springing "from his deliberate choice of an old and fundamental way of life, his apparently firm-rooted attachment to his original and right place on earth."

The defenders of nature and wilderness—like their enemies the defenders of the industrial economy—sometimes sound as if the natural and the human were two separate estates, radically different and radically divided. The defenders of nature and wilderness sometimes seem to feel that they must oppose any human encroachment whatsoever, just as the industrialists often apparently feel that they must make the human encroachment absolute or, as they say, "complete the conquest of nature." But there is danger in this opposition, and it can be best dealt with by realizing that these pure and separate categories are pure ideas and do not otherwise exist.

Pure nature, anyhow, is not good for humans to live in, and humans do not want to live in it—or not for very long. Any exposure to the elements that lasts more than a few hours will remind us of the desirability of the basic human amenities: clothing, shelter, cooked food, the company of kinfolk and friends—perhaps even of hot baths and music and books.

It is equally true that a condition that is *purely* human is not good for people to live in, and people do not want to live for very long in it. Obviously, the more artificial a human environment becomes, the more the word "natural" becomes a term of value. It can be argued, indeed, that the conservation movement, as we know it today, is largely a product of the industrial revolution. The people who want clean air, clear streams, and wild forests, prairies, and deserts are the people who no longer have them.

People cannot live apart from nature; that is the first 4 principle of the conservationists. And yet, people cannot live in nature without changing it. But this is true of *all* creatures; they depend upon nature, and they change it. What we call nature is, in a sense, the sum of the changes made by all the various creatures and natural forces in their intricate actions and influences upon each other and upon their places. Because of the woodpeckers, nature is different from what it would be without them. It is different also because of the borers and ants that live in tree trunks, and because of the bacteria that live in the soil under the trees. The making of these differences is the making of the world.

Some of the changes made by wild creatures we would 5 call beneficent: beavers are famous for making ponds that turn into fertile meadows; trees and prairie grasses build soil. But sometimes, too, we would call natural changes destructive. According to early witnesses, for instance, large areas around Kentucky salt licks were severely trampled and eroded by the great herds of hoofed animals that gathered there. The buffalo "streets" through hilly country were so hollowed out by hoof-wear and erosion that they remain visible almost two centuries after the disappearance of the buffalo. And so it can hardly be expected that humans would not change nature. Humans, like all other creatures, must make a difference; otherwise, they cannot live. But unlike other creatures, humans must make a choice as to the kind and scale of the difference they make. If they choose to make too small a difference, they diminish their humanity. If they choose to make too great a difference, they diminish nature, and narrow their subsequent choices; ultimately, they diminish or destroy themselves. Nature, then, is not only our source but also our limit and measure. Or, as the poet Edmund Spenser put it almost four hundred years ago, Nature, who is the "greatest goddesse," acts as a sort of earthly lieutenant of God, and Spenser represents her as both a mother and judge. Her jurisdiction is over the relations between the creatures; she deals "Right to all . . . indifferently," for she is "the equall mother" of all "And knittest each to each, as brother unto brother." Thus, in Spenser, the natural principles of fecundity and order are pointedly linked with the principle of justice, which we may be a little surprised to see that he attributes also to nature. And yet in his insistence on an "indifferent" natural justice, resting on the "brotherhood" of *all* creatures, not just of humans, Spenser would now be said to be on sound ecological footing.

In nature we know that wild creatures sometimes exhaust their vital sources and suffer the natural remedy: drastic population reductions. If lynxes eat too many snowshoe rabbits—which they are said to do repeatedly—then the lynxes starve down to the carrying capacity of their habitat. It is the carrying capacity of the lynx's habitat, not the carrying capacity of the lynx's stomach, that determines the prosperity of lynxes. Similarly, if humans use up too much soil—which they have often done and are doing—they they will starve down to the carrying capacity of *their* habitat. This is nature's "indifferent" justice. As Spenser saw in the sixteenth century, and as we must learn to see now, there is no appeal from this justice. In the hereafter, the Lord may forgive our wrongs against nature, but on earth, so far as we know, He does not overturn her decisions. 6

One of the differences between humans and lynxes is that humans can see that the principle of balance operates between lynxes and snowshoe rabbits, as between humans and topsoil; another difference, we hope, is that humans have the sense to act on their understanding. We can see, too, that a stable balance is preferable to a balance that tilts back and forth like a seesaw, dumping a surplus 7 of creatures alternately from either end. To say this is to renew the question of whether or not the human relationship with nature is necessarily an adversary relationship, and it is to suggest that the answer is not simple.

But in dealing with this question and in trying to do justice to the presumed complexity of the answer, we are up against an American convention of simple opposition to nature that is deeply established both in our minds and in our ways. We have opposed the primeval forests of the East and the primeval prairies and deserts of the West, we have opposed man-eating beasts and crop-eating insects, sheep-eating coyotes and chicken-eating hawks. In our lawns and gardens and fields, we oppose what we call weeds. And yet more and more of us are beginning to see that this opposition is ultimately destructive even of ourselves, that it does not explain many things that need explaining—in short, that it is untrue. 8

If our proper relation to nature is not opposition, then what is it? This question becomes complicated and difficult for us because none of us, as I have said, wants to live in a "pure" primeval forest or in a "pure" primeval prairie; we do not want to be eaten by grizzly bears; if we are gardeners, we have a legitimate quarrel with weeds; if, in Kentucky, we are trying to improve our pastures, we are likely to be enemies of the nodding thistle. But, do what we will, we remain under the spell of the primeval forests and prairies that we have cut down and broken; we turn repeatedly and with love to the thought of them and to their surviving remnants. We find ourselves attracted to the grizzly bears, too, and know that they and other great, dangerous animals remain alive in our imaginations as they have been all through human time. Though we cut down the nodding thistles, we acknowledge their beauty and are glad to think that there must be some place where they belong. (They may, in fact, not always be out of place in pastures; if, as seems evident, overgrazing makes an ideal seedbed for these plants, then we must understand them as part of nature's strategy to protect the ground against abuse by animals.) Even the 9 ugliest garden weeds earn affection from us when we consider how faithfully they perform an indispensable duty in covering the bare ground and in building humus. The weeds, too, are involved in the business of fertility.

We know, then, that the conflict between the human 10 and the natural estates really exists and that it is to some extent necessary. But we are learning, or relearning, something else, too, that frightens us: namely, that this conflict often occurs at the expense of *both* estates. It is not only possible but altogether probable that by diminishing nature we diminish ourselves, and vice versa.

The conflict comes to light most suggestively, perhaps, 11 when advocates for the two sides throw themselves into absolute conflict where no absolute difference can exist. An example of this is the battle between defenders of coyotes and defenders of sheep, in which the coyote-defenders may find it easy to forget that the sheep ranchers are human beings with some authentic complaints against coyotes, and the sheep-defenders find it easy to sound as if they advocate the total eradication of both coyotes and conservationists. Such conflicts—like the old one between hawk-defenders and chicken-defenders—tend to occur between people who use nature indirectly and people who use it directly. It is a dangerous mistake, I think, for either side to pursue such a quarrel on the assumption that victory would be a desirable result.

The fact is that people need both coyotes and sheep, 12 need a world in which both kinds of life are possible. Outside the heat of conflict, conservationists probably know that a sheep is one of the best devices for making coarse foliage humanly edible and that wool is ecologically better than the synthetic fibers, just as most shepherds will be aware that wild nature is of value to them and not lacking in interest and pleasure.

The usefulness of coyotes is, of course, much harder to 13 define than the usefulness of sheep. Coyote fur is not a likely substitute for wool, and, except as a last resort, most people don't want to eat coyotes. The difficulty lies in the difference between what is ours and what is nature's:

What is ours is ours because it is directly useful. Coyotes are useful *indirectly*, as part of the health of nature, from which we and our sheep alike must live and take our health. The fact, moreover, may be that sheep and coyotes need each other, at least in the sense that neither would prosper in a place totally unfit for the other.

This sort of conflict, then, does not suggest the pos-   14
sibility of victory so much as it suggests the possibility of a compromise—some kind of peace, even an alliance, between the domestic and the wild. We know that such an alliance is necessary. Most conservationists now take for granted that humans thrive best in ecological health and that the test or sign of this health is the survival of a diversity of wild creatures. We know, too, that we cannot imagine ourselves apart from those necessary survivals of our own wildness that we call our instincts. And we know that we cannot have a healthy agriculture apart from the teeming wilderness in the topsoil, in which worms, bacteria, and other wild creatures are carrying on the fundamental work of decomposition, humus making, water storage, and drainage. "In wildness is the preservation of the world," as Thoreau said, may be a spiritual truth, but it is also a practical fact.

On the other hand, we must not fail to consider the   15
opposite proposition—that, so long at least as humans are in the world, in human culture is the preservation of wildness—which is equally, and more demandingly, true. If wildness is to survive, then *we* must preserve it. We must preserve it by public act, by law, by institutionalizing wildernesses in some places. But such preservation is probably not enough. I have heard Wes Jackson of the Land Institute say, rightly I think, that if we cannot preserve our farmland, we cannot preserve the wilderness. That said, it becomes obvious that if we cannot preserve our cities, we cannot preserve the wilderness. This can be demonstrated practically by saying that the same attitudes that destroy wildness in the topsoil will finally destroy it everywhere; or by saying that if *everyone* has to go to a

designated public wilderness for the necessary contact with wildness, then our parks will be no more natural than our cities.

But I am trying to say something more fundamental   16 than that. What I am aiming at—because a lot of evidence seems to point this way—is the probability that nature and human culture, wildness and domesticity, are not opposed but are interdependent. Authentic experience of either will reveal the need of one for the other. In fact, examples from both past and present prove that a human economy and wildness can exist together not only in compatibility but to their mutual benefit.

One of the best examples I have come upon recently is   17 the story of two Sonora Desert oases in Gary Nabhan's book, *The Desert Smells Like Rain*. The first of these oases, A'al Waipia, in Arizona, is dying because the park service, intending to preserve the natural integrity of the place as a bird sanctuary for tourists, removed the Papago Indians who had lived and farmed there. The place was naturally purer after the Indians were gone, but the oasis also began to shrink as the irrigation ditches silted up. As Mr. Nabhan puts it, "an odd thing is happening to their 'natural' bird sanctuary. They are losing the heterogeneity of the habitat, and with it, the birds. The old trees are dying. . . . These riparian trees are essential for the breeding habitat of certain birds. Summer annual seed plants are conspicuously absent. . . . Without the soil disturbance associated with plowing and flood irrigation, these natural foods for birds and rodents no longer germinate."

The other oasis, Ki:towak, in old Mexico, still thrives   18 because a Papago village is still there, still farming. The village's oldest man, Luis Nolia, is the caretaker of the oasis, cleaning the springs and ditches, farming, planting trees: "Luis . . . blesses the oasis," Mr. Nabhan says, "for his work keeps it healthy." An ornithologist who accompanied Mr. Nabhan found twice as many species of birds at the farmed oasis as he found at the bird sanctuary, a fact that Mr. Nabhan's Papago friend, Remedio, explained in this way: "That's because those birds, they come where the people are. When the people live and work in a place, and plant their seeds and water their trees, the birds go live with them. They like those places, there's plenty to eat and that's when we are friends to them."

Another example, from my own experience, is sugges- [19] tive in a somewhat different way. At the end of July 1981, while I was using a team of horses to mow a small triangular hillside pasture that is bordered on two sides by trees, I was suddenly aware of wings close below me. It was a young red-tailed hawk, who flew up into a walnut tree. I mowed on to the turn and stopped the team. The hawk then glided to the ground not twenty feet away. I got off the mower, stood and watched, even spoke, and the hawk showed no fear. I could see every feather distinctly, claw and beak and eye, the creamy down of the breast. Only when I took a step toward him, separating myself from the team and mower, did he fly. While I mowed three or four rounds, he stayed near, perched in trees or standing erect and watch- ful on the ground. Once, when I stopped to watch him, he was clearly watching me, stooping to see under the leaves that screened me from him. Again, when I could not find him, I stooped, saying to myself, "This is what he did to look at me," and as I did so I saw him looking at me.

Why had he come? To catch mice? Had he seen me [20] scare one out of the grass? Or was it curiosity?

A human, of course, cannot speak with authority of [21] the motives of hawks. I am aware of the possibility of ex- plaining the episode merely by the hawk's youth and in- experience. And yet it does not happen often or depen- dably that one is approached so closely by a hawk of any age. I feel safe in making a couple of assumptions. The first is that the hawk came because of the conjunction of the small pasture and its wooded borders, of open hunting ground and the security of trees. This is the phenomenon of edge or margin that we know to be one of the power- ful attractions of a diversified landscape, both to wildlife and to humans. The human eye itself seems drawn to such margins, hungering for the difference made in the countryside by a hedgy fencerow, a stream, or a grove of trees. And we know that these margins are biologically rich, the meeting of two kinds of habitat. But another difference also is important here: the difference between a large pasture and a small one, or, to use Wes Jackson's terms, the difference between a field and a patch. The pasture I was mowing was a patch—small, intimate, nowhere distant from its edges.

My second assumption is that the hawk was emboldened to come so near because, though he obviously recognized me as a man, I was there with the team of horses, with whom he familiarly and confidently shared the world. 22

I am saying, in other words, that this little visit between the hawk and me happened because the kind and scale of my farm, my way of farming, and my technology *allowed* it to happen. If I had been driving a tractor in a hundred-acre cornfield, it would not have happened. 23

In some circles I would certainly be asked if one can or should be serious about such an encounter, if it has any value. And though I cannot produce any hard evidence, I would unhesitatingly answer yes. Such encounters involve another margin—the one between domesticity and wildness—that attracts us irresistibly; they are among the best rewards of outdoor work and among the reasons for loving to farm. When the scale of farming grows so great and obtrusive as to forbid them, the *life* of farming is impoverished. 24

But perhaps we do find hard evidence of a sort when we consider that *all* of us—the hawk, the horses, and I— were there for our benefit and, to some extent, for our *mutual* benefit: The horses live from the pasture and maintain it with their work, grazing, and manure; the team and I together furnish hunting ground to the hawk; the hawk serves us by controlling the fieldmouse population. 25

These meetings of the human and the natural estates, the domestic and the wild, occur invisibly, of course, in any well-farmed field. The wilderness of a healthy soil, too complex for human comprehension, can yet be husbanded, 26 can benefit from human care, and can deliver incalculable benefits in return. Mutuality of interest and reward is a possibility that can reach to any city backyard, garden, and park, but in any place under human dominance—which is, now, virtually everyplace—it is a possibility that is *both* natural and cultural. If humans want wildness to be possible, then they have to make it possible. If balance is the ruling principle and a stable balance the goal, then, for humans, attaining this goal requires a consciously chosen and deliberately made partnership with nature.

In other words, we can be true to nature only by being   27 true to human nature—to our animal nature as well as to cultural patterns and restraints that keep us from acting like animals. When humans act like animals, they become the most dangerous of animals to themselves and other humans, and this is because of another critical difference between humans and animals: Whereas animals are usually restrained by the limits of physical appetites, humans have mental appetites that can be far more gross and capacious than physical ones. Only humans squander and hoard, murder and pillage because of notions.

The work by which good human and natural possibili-   28 ties are preserved is complex and difficult, and it probably cannot be accomplished by raw intelligence and information. It requires knowledge, skills, and restraints, some of which must come from our past. In the hurry of technological progress, we have replaced some tools and methods that worked with some that do not work. But we also need culture-borne instructions about who or what humans are and how and on what assumptions they should act. The Chain of Being, for instance—which gave humans a place between animals and angels in the order of Creation—is an old idea that has not been replaced by any adequate new one. It was simply rejected, and the lack of it leaves us without a definition.

Lacking that ancient definition, or any such definition,   29 we do not know at what point to restrain or deny ourselves. We do not know how ambitious to be, what or how much we may safely desire, when or where to stop. I knew a barber once who refused to give a discount to a bald client, explaining that his artistry consisted, not in the cutting off, but in the knowing when to stop. He spoke, I think, as a true artist and a true human. The lack of such knowledge is extremely dangerous in and to an individual. But ignorance of when to stop is a modern epidemic; it is the basis of "industrial progress" and "economic growth." The most obvious practical result of this ignorance is a critical disproportion of scale between the scale of human enterprises and their sources in nature.

The scale of the energy industry, for example, is too big, as is the scale of the transportation industry. The scale of agriculture, from a technological or economic point of view, is too big, but from a demographic point of view, the scale is too small. When there are enough people on the land to use it but not enough to husband it, then the wildness of the soil that we call fertility begins to diminish, and the soil itself begins to flee from us in water and wind.

If the human economy is to be fitted into the natural economy in such a way that both may thrive, the human economy must be built to proper scale. It is possible to talk at great length about the difference between proper and improper scale. It may be enough to say here that that difference is *suggested* by the difference between amplified and unamplified music in the countryside, or the difference between the sound of a motorboat and the sound of oarlocks. A proper human sound, we may say, is one that allows other sounds to be heard. A properly scaled human economy or technology allows a diversity of other creatures to thrive.

"The proper scale," a friend wrote to me, "confers freedom and simplicity . . . and doubtless leads to long life and health." I think that it also confers joy. The renewal of our partnership with nature, the rejoining of our works to their proper places in the natural order, reshaped to their proper scale, implies the reenjoyment both of nature and of human domesticity. Though our task will be difficult, we will greatly mistake its nature if we

30

31

32

see it as grim, or if we suppose that it must always be necessary to suffer at work in order to enjoy ourselves in places specializing in "recreation."

Once we grant the possibility of a proper human scale, we see that we have made a radical change of assumptions and values. We realize that we are less interested in technological "breakthroughs" than in technological elegance. Of a new tool or method we will no longer ask: Is it fast? Is it powerful? Is it a labor saver? How many workers will it replace? We will ask instead: Can we (and our children) afford it? Is it fitting to our real needs? Is it becoming to us? Is it unhealthy or ugly? And though we may keep a certain interest in innovation and in what we may become, we will renew our interest in what we have been, realizing that conservationists must necessarily conserve *both* inheritances, the natural and the cultural. 33

To argue the necessity of wildness to, and in, the human economy is by no means to argue against the necessity of wilderness. The survival of wilderness—of places that we do not change, where we allow the existence even of creatures we perceive as dangerous—is necessary. Our sanity probably requires it. Whether we go to those places or not, we need to know that they exist. And I would argue that we do not need just the great public wildernesses, but millions of small private or semiprivate ones. Every farm should have one; wildernesses can occupy corners of factory grounds and city lots—places where nature is given a free hand, where no human work is done, where people go only as guests. These places function, I think, whether we intend them to or not, as sacred groves—places we respect and leave alone, not because we understand well what goes on there, but because we do not. 34

We go to wilderness places to be restored, to be instructed in the natural economies of fertility and healing, to admire what we cannot make. Sometimes, as we find to our surprise, we go to be chastened or corrected. And we go in order to return with renewed knowledge by which to judge the health of our human economy and our 35 dwelling places. As we return from our visits to the wilderness, it is sometimes possible to imagine a series of fitting and decent transitions from wild nature to the human community and its supports: from forest to woodlot to the "two-story agriculture" of tree crops and pasture to orchard to meadow to grainfield to garden to household to neighborhood to village to city—so that even when we reached the city we would not be entirely beyond the influence of the nature of that place.

What I have been implying is that I think there is a bad reason to go to the wilderness. We must not go there to escape the ugliness and the dangers of the present human economy. We must not let ourselves feel that to go there is to escape. In the first place, such an escape is now illusory. In the second place, if, even as conservationists, we see the human and the natural economies as necessarily opposite or opposed, we subscribe to the very opposition that threatens to destroy them both. The wild and the domestic now often seem isolated values, estranged from one another. And yet these are not exclusive polarities like good and evil. There can be continuity between them, and there must be. 36

What we find, if we weight the balance too much in favor of the domestic, is that we involve ourselves in dangers both personal and public. Not the least of these dangers is dependence on distant sources of money and materials. Farmers are in deep trouble now because they have become too dependent on corporations and banks. They have been using methods and species that enforce this dependence. But such a dependence is not safe, either for farmers or for agriculture. It is not safe for urban consumers. Ultimately, as we are beginning to see, it is not safe for banks and corporations—which, though they have evidently not thought so, are dependent upon farmers. Our farms are endangered because—like the interstate highways or modern hospitals or modern universites—they cannot be inexpensively used. To be usable at all they require great expense. 37

When the human estate becomes so precarious, our   38
only recourse is to move it back toward the estate of
nature. We undoubtedly need better plant and animal
species than nature provided us. But we are beginning to
see that they can be too much better—too dependent on
us and on "the economy," too expensive. In farm animals,
for instance, we want good commercial quality, but we
can see that the ability to produce meat or milk can actually be a threat to the farmer and to the animal if not
accompanied by qualities we would call natural: thriftiness,
hardiness, physical vigor, resistance to disease and para-
sites, ability to breed and give birth without assistance,
strong mothering instincts. These natural qualities decrease
care, work, and worry; they also decrease the costs of production. They save feed and time; they make diseases and
cures exceptional rather than routine.

We need crop and forage species of high productive   39
ability also, but we do not need species that will not produce at all without expensive fertilizers and chemicals.
Contrary to the premise of agribusiness advertisements and
of most expert advice, farmers do not thrive by production or by "skimming" a large "cash flow." They cannot
solve their problems merely by increasing production or
income. They thrive, like all other creatures, according to
the difference between their income and their expenses.

One of the strangest characteristics of the industrial   40
economy is the ability to increase production again and again
without ever noticing—or without acknowledging—the *costs*
of production. That one Holstein cow should produce 50,000
pounds of milk in a year may appear to be marvelous—a
miracle of modern science. But what if her productivity is
dependent upon the consumption of a huge amount of grain
(about a bushel a day), and therefore upon the availability
of cheap petroleum? What if she is too valuable (and too
delicate) to be allowed outdoors in the rain? What if the proliferation of her kind will again drastically reduce the
number of dairy farms and farmers? Or, to use a more obvious example, can we afford a bushel of grain at a cost of
five to twenty bushels of topsoil lost to erosion?

"It is good to have Nature working for you," said   41
Henry Besuden, the dean of American Southdown
breeders. "She works for a minimum wage." That is true.
She works at times for almost nothing, requiring only that
we respect her work and give her a chance, as when she
maintains—indeed, improves—the fertility and productivity
of a pasture by the natural succession of clover and grass
or when she improves a clay soil for us by means of the
roots of a grass sod. She works for us by preserving health
or wholeness, which for all our ingenuity we cannot make.
If we fail to respect her health, she deals out her justice
by withdrawing her protection against disease—which we
can make, and do.

To make this continuity between the natural and the   42
human, we have only two sources of instruction: nature
herself and our cultural tradition. If we listen only to the
apologists for the industrial economy, who respect neither
nature nor culture, we get the idea that it is somehow our
goodness that makes us so destructive: The air is unfit to
breathe, the water is unfit to drink, the soil is washing
away, the cities are violent and the countryside neglected,
all because we are intelligent, enterprising, industrious,
and generous, concerned only to feed the hungry and to
"make a better future for our children." Respect for nature
causes us to doubt this, and our cultural tradition confirms
and illuminates our doubt: No good thing is destroyed by
goodness; good things are destroyed by wickedness. We
may identify that insight as Biblical, but it is taken for
granted by both the Greek and the Biblical lineages of our
culture, from Homer and Moses to William Blake. Since
the start of the industrial revolution, there have been voices
urging that this inheritance may be safely replaced by intelligence, information, energy, and money. No idea, I believe, could be more dangerous.

Comment

Berry uses particulars of experience to state probable truths, on the basis of which he argues a thesis. Berry begins his discussion by citing the mistaken view of nature shared by conservationists and industrialists; he wants to correct this view and find a basis for reconciliation between opposing views. Because so much misunderstanding on the issue of conservation exists, he needs to correct mistaken assumptions before arguing the basis for reconciliation. In the concluding paragraphs, Berry suggests measures that conservationists and their opponents can take to satisfy what he has shown to be mutual needs.

Questions for Study and Discussion

1. What evidence does Berry present in paragraphs 1–9 for the statement that "our proper relation to nature is not opposition"? If this relation is not an opposition, in what sense is there a "conflict" between sheep and coyotes and other animals, and between human beings and nature in general?

2. What is the difference between the direct and indirect use of nature (paragraph 11), and how does Berry illustrate these different uses? How does this distinction advance his discussion?

3. In what way does human culture preserve nature (paragraph 15)? In what way do the "same attitudes that destroy wildness in the topsoil . . . finally destroy it everywhere"?

4. Berry builds up to his thesis, a statement of the basis for reconciliation between conservationists and industrialists, in paragraph 16. What is the basis of reconciliation? How do the examples given in paragraphs 17–25 illustrate and support Berry's thesis?

5. What point is Berry making about human nature and animal nature in paragraph 27? How does this point advance his argument?

6. How can conservationists and industrialists fit the "human economy" into the "natural economy" and in this way meet the needs of nature and human beings? How does Berry develop this point in paragraphs 34 and 35?

7. What dangers does Berry explore in paragraphs 36–40? How does this discussion further develop his thesis?
8. How does Berry remind the reader of the conflicting claims of conservationists and industrialists in paragraphs 41 and 42, and also restate his thesis?

Vocabulary Study

1. How do the details of paragraph 21 explain what Berry means by "the phenomenon of edge or margin"?
2. What does he mean in paragraph 24 by the margin between "domesticity and wildness"?
3. Explain the following words and phrases:
   a. *encroachment* (paragraph 1)
   b. *human amenities* (paragraph 2)
   c. *ecological* (paragraph 5)
   d. *habitat* (paragraph 6)
   e. *primeval, humus* (paragraph 9)
   f. *domesticity* (paragraph 16)
   g. *silted* (paragraph 17)
   h. *conjunction* (paragraph 21)
   i. *notions* (paragraph 27)
   j. *illusory, polarities* (paragraph 36)
   k. *precarious* (paragraph 38)

Suggestions for Writing

1. Write a summary or précis of Berry's essay, paraphrasing (in your own words) his chief ideas. A précis usually omits examples and supporting details, but you may wish to include any that you consider essential to the argument.
2. Look up the phrase "Chain of Being" (or "Great Chain of Being") in an encyclopedia or other reference book, noting its origin and implications. Then write a short essay on how Berry's essay illustrates the idea.
3. Discuss a statement in Berry's essay with which you strongly agree or disagree and explain why you do. Base your essay on personal experiences and observation, perhaps your own encounter with "pure nature" or with a wild animal.

Deductive Argument

Deductive arguments draw inferences or conclusions from statements that the author of the argument believes to be true. In the essay that follows, "The Confessions of a Miseducated Man," Norman Cousins presents his basic argument as follows:

> In order to be at home anywhere in the world I had to forget the things I had been taught to remember. It turned out that my ability to get along with other peoples depended not so much upon my comprehension of the uniqueness of their way of life as upon my comprehension of the things we had in common.

Cousins restates this argument in subsequent paragraphs:

> Only a few years ago an education in differences fulfilled a specific if limited need. That was at a time when we thought of other places and peoples largely out of curiosity or in terms of exotic vacations. It was the mark of a rounded man to be well traveled and to know about the fabulous variations of human culture and behavior. But it wasn't the type of knowledge you had to live by and build on.
>
> Then overnight came the great compression. Far-flung areas which had been secure in their remoteness suddenly became jammed together in a single arena. And all at once a new type of education became necessary, an education in liberation from tribalism. . . .

Cousins summarizes his argument in the following statement:

> The old emphasis upon superficial differences had to give way to education for mutuality and for citizenship in the human community.

We may restate Cousins's argument informally:

Since getting along with other people depends on understanding what we have in common, an education that teaches only the differences between people doesn't prepare us to live in a world that has become a single arena.

This argument may be restated in positive terms and arranged as a formal argument or *syllogism:*

[*Major premise*] An education that prepares us to live in a world that has become a single arena is an adequate one.

[*Minor premise*] An education that teaches what we have in common with other people prepares us to live in a world that has become a single arena.

[*Conclusion*] Such an education is an adequate one.

Such an argument is called deductive because it makes an inference from statements assumed to be true—beliefs held as "self-evident" or axiomatic or truths established by experience, observation, or experimentation. A deductive argument says that *if* the premises of the formal argument are true, the conclusion or inference properly drawn from these statements must also be true. These statements or premises are the evidence for the conclusion. We know that Cousins holds the first two statements to be true because he says so in introducing his basic argument:

As I write this, I have the feeling that my words fail to give vitality to the idea they seek to express. Indeed, the idea itself is a truism which all peoples readily acknowledge even if they do not act on it.

Writers of arguments know that people will disagree with their premises—with the beliefs, assumptions, or truisms on which they base the argument. For this reason they may defend one or both of the premises by illustrating or explaining them. Cousins does so in describing the contents of the new education. Even if the premises are defended, the argument is deductive as long as the premises themselves provide the evidence for the conclusion. Inferences are drawn from the premises and not from factual evidence like personal experience, observation, or statistical studies—the evidence of inductive arguments (see p. 294).

In arguing, we often omit one of the premises or the conclusion. We do so because we consider the omitted premise or conclusion obvious. Shortened arguments of this sort are called *enthymemes*. Here are some examples:

> Since an education that teaches what we have in common prepares us to live in a world that has become a single arena, such an education is adequate. [Major premise omitted: *An adequate education prepares us to live in a world that has become a single arena.*]

> Since an adequate education prepares us to live in a world that has become a single arena, an education that teaches what we have in common with other people is an adequate one. [Minor premise omitted: *An education that teaches what we have in common with others prepares us to live in a world that has become a single arena.*]

> An adequate education prepares us to live in a world that has become a single arena, and an education that teaches what we have in common with other people prepares us to live in such a world. [Conclusion implied: *Such an education is adequate.*]

These examples are typical of arguments we hear everyday—arguments that require us to supply one of the premises or even the conclusion. In other words, we need to consider implied as well as explicit statements in testing the validity of an argument and weighing its soundness.

A deductive argument is considered *sound* if its premises are true and the process of reasoning is proper or *valid*. If the process of reasoning is faulty or invalid or the premises are untrue—if the premises are "glittering generalities" or statements that cannot be defended or do not cover all instances—the argument is considered unsound. Cousins' argument would be judged unsound if an opponent could disprove his assertion that teaching what people have in common is necessary to live in a changing world.

Here is a valid argument:

> Successful farmers are hard-working people.
> My parents are successful farmers.
> My parents are hard-working people.

What is true of all successful farmers must be true of anyone who belongs to the same class. But note this much different argument:

Successful farmers are hard-working people.
My parents are hard-working people.
My parents are successful farmers.

This argument is invalid because neither premise claims that all hard-working people are successful farmers. Some may be farmers, and some may not be. Deductive arguments take many forms and the tests of validity are therefore complex—the subject of formal logic. Common sense often can detect an error in invalid arguments, but many deceptive arguments require a knowledge of these formal tests. Here are two simple ones:

First, no conclusion can be drawn from two negative premises. If one of the premises is negative, so must be the conclusion. The following informal argument is invalid because it draws a conclusion when none is possible:

Since no sick people are happy people, and none of us are sick people, we must be happy people.

Second, the terms of the argument must not shift in meaning:

Since sick people are not happy people, and bigots are sick people, bigots are not happy people.

The phrase *sick people* ordinarily refers to the physically ill. If the word *sick* in the minor premise refers to mental aberration, then the term has shifted in meaning in this argument. Bigots may very well be unhappy people, but not for the reason stated.

Norman Cousins

CONFESSIONS OF A MISEDUCATED MAN

Norman Cousins edited the *Saturday Review* from 1940 to 1971, and again from 1971 to 1973. During these years he wrote editorially on a wide range of topics relating to national and international issues. *Present Tense* (1967) contains editorials Cousins wrote between 1940 and 1966; the editorial reprinted here appeared on May 10, 1952. Cousins's other books include *In God We Trust: The Religious Beliefs of the Founding Fathers* (1958), *Doctor Schweitzer of Lambaréné* (1960), *The Celebration of Life* (1975), and *The Human Option* (1981). *Anatomy of an Illness* (1979) describes how he overcame a serious illness. Among his numerous awards are the Benjamin Franklin citation for magazine journalism in 1956, the Eleanor Roosevelt Peace award in 1963, and the United National Peace medal in 1971. Cousins died in 1991.

These notes are in the nature of a confession. It is the [1]
confession of a miseducated man.

I have become most aware of my lack of a proper edu- [2]
cation whenever I have had the chance to put it to the
test. The test is a simple one: am I prepared to live in and
comprehend a world in which there are 3 billion people?
Not the world as it was in 1850 or 1900, for which my
education might have been adequate, but the world today.
And the best place to apply that test is outside the
country—especially Asia or Africa.

Not that my education was a complete failure. It pre- [3]
pared me superbly for a bird's-eye view of the world. It
taught me how to recognize easily and instantly the things
that differentiate one place or one people from another.
Geography had instructed me in differences of terrain,
resources, and productivity. Comparative culture had instructed me in the differences of background and group
interests. Anthropology had instructed me in the differences of facial bone structure, skin pigmentation, and
general physical aspect. In short, my education protected
me against surprise. I was not surprised at the fact that
some people lived in mud huts and others in bamboo
cottages on stilts; or that some used peat for fuel and
others dung; or that some enjoyed music with a five-note
scale and others with twelve; or that some people were
vegetarian by religion and others by preference.

In those respects my education had been more than [4]
adequate. But what my education failed to do was to teach
me that the principal significance of such differences was
that they were largely without significance. The differences
were all but obliterated by the similarities. My education
had by-passed the similarities. It had failed to grasp and
define the fact that beyond the differences are realities
scarcely comprehended because of their shattering simplicity. And the simplest reality of all was that the human
community was one—greater than any of its parts, greater
than the separateness imposed by the nations, greater than
the divergent faiths and allegiances or the depth and color
of varying cultures. This larger unity was the most impor-

tant central fact of our time—something on which people could build at a time when hope seemed misty, almost unreal.

As I write this, I have the feeling that my words fail to 5 give vitality to the idea they seek to express. Indeed, the idea itself is a truism which all peoples readily acknowledge even if they do not act on it. Let me put it differently, then. In order to be at home anywhere in the world I had to forget the things I had been taught to remember. It turned out that my ability to get along with other peoples depended not so much upon my comprehension of the uniqueness of their way of life as upon my comprehension of the things we had in common. It was important to respect these differences, certainly, but to stop there was like clearing the ground without any idea of what was to be built on it. When you got through comparing notes, you discovered that you were both talking about the same neighborhood, i.e., this planet, and the conditions that made it congenial or hostile to human habitation.

Only a few years ago an education in differences ful- 6 filled a specific if limited need. That was at a time when we thought of other places and peoples largely out of curiosity or in terms of exotic vacations. It was the mark of a rounded man to be well traveled and to know about the fabulous variations of human culture and behavior. But it wasn't the type of knowledge you had to live by and build on.

Then overnight came the great compression. Far-flung 7 areas which had been secure in their remoteness suddenly became jammed together in a single arena. And all at once a new type of education became necessary, an education in liberation from tribalism. For tribalism had persisted from earliest times, though it had taken refined forms. The new education had to teach man the most difficult lesson of all: to look at someone anywhere in the world and be able to recognize the image of himself. It had to be an education in self-recognition. The old emphasis upon superficial differences had to give way to education for mutuality and for citizenship in the human community.

In such an education we begin with the fact that the 8
universe itself does not hold life cheaply. Life is a rare
occurrence among the millions of galaxies and solar systems that occupy space. And in this particular solar system
life occurs on only one planet. And on that one planet life
takes millions of forms. Of all these countless forms of life,
only one, the human species, possesses certain faculties
in combination that give it supreme advantages over all
the others. Among those faculties or gifts is a creative intelligence that enables man to reflect and anticipate, to en-
compass past experience, and also to visualize future
needs. There are endless other wondrous faculties the
mechanisms of which are not yet within the understanding of their beneficiaries—the faculties of hope, conscience,
appreciation of beauty, kinship, love, faith.

Viewed in planetary perspective, what counts is not 9
that the thoughts of men lead them in different directions
but that all men possess the capacity to think; not that
they pursue different faiths but that they are capable of
spiritual belief; not that they write and read different books
but that they are capable of creating print and communicating in it across time and space; not that they enjoy different art and music but that something in them
enables them to respond deeply to forms and colors and
ordered vibrations of sounds.

These basic lessons, then, would seek to provide a 10
proper respect for man in the universe. Next in order
would be instruction in the unity of man's needs. However
friendly the universe may be to man, it has left the conditions of human existence precariously balanced. All men
need oxygen, water, land, warmth, food. Remove any one
of these and the unity of human needs is attacked and
man with it. The next lesson would concern the human
situation itself—how to use self-understanding in the cause
of human welfare; how to control the engines created by
man that threaten to alter the precarious balance on which
life depends; how to create a peaceful society of the whole.

With such an education, it is possible that some nation 11
or people may come forward not only with vital under-

standing but with the vital inspiration that men need no less than food. Leadership on this higher level does not require mountains of gold or thundering propaganda. It is concerned with human destiny; human destiny is the issue; people will respond.

Questions

1. Is Cousins saying that an adequate education presents only what people have in common? Or does an adequate education also include the differences between people?
2. Cousins states that "what counts" is the capacity for "spiritual belief" and not the pursuit of different beliefs or faiths. Is he saying that differences in belief or faith are superficial and of no consequence or value?
3. What special view of people does a "planetary perspective" provide of human life? What conclusions does Cousins draw from this view?
4. Why does an adequate education "begin with the fact that the universe itself does not hold life cheaply"? Why should education not begin with the qualities people have in common?
5. Do you agree with Cousins that a person who is aware only of differences between people and cultures is miseducated? What is the basis of your agreement or disagreement with Cousins?

Vocabulary Study

1. Give synonyms for the following words:
   a. *comprehend* (paragraph 2)
   b. *terrain, productivity* (paragraph 3)
   c. *obliterated, allegiances* (paragraph 4)
   d. *mutuality* (paragraph 7)
   e. *mechanisms* (paragraph 8)
   f. *perspective* (paragraph 9)
   g. *precarious* (paragraph 10)
   h. *propaganda* (paragraph 11)

2. What does the word *tribalism* mean in paragraph 7, and how do you know?
3. Cousins concludes with the statement that "human destiny is the issue." What does he mean by *destiny?*

Suggestions for Writing

1. Discuss one or more ways in which you find your education lacking. Explain why it is lacking—what you should have been taught and what the cost of your miseducation has been.
2. State the qualities that you believe mark the educated person. Then explain why you hold these beliefs. Illustrate these qualities from personal experience or observation.
3. State why you agree or disagree with one of Cousins's statements. Then defend your reasons for agreeing or disagreeing by drawing on personal experience and observation.

Timothy S. Healy, S. J.

IN DEFENSE OF DISORDER

Timothy S. Healy, for many years president of Georgetown University in Washington, D.C., in now director of the New York Public Library. A specialist in the poetry of John Donne, Rev. Healy previously taught English at Fordham University, and he also has served as vice chancellor for academic affairs at the City University of New York and on federal government commissions on education. His essay on interruption of unpopular university speakers explores this specific issue and then moves on to the broader question of why universities exist.

Over the past weeks, the nation's colleges have taken 1
a beating because of loudmouths who shouted down invited speakers. Eldridge Cleaver at Wisconsin, Ambassador Jeane Kirkpatrick at Berkeley and Sheik Ahmad Zaki Yamani at Kansas were the speakers, and the noise raised in their defense is only slightly less deafening than the

shouts that drowned their speeches. No one in the academy approved or condoned the shouting: the clearest defense of the university as an open forum has come from university people themselves through the national associations that represent presidents, faculty members and students.

Whether or not they are aware of it, our critics misread our vulnerability to disruption. They seem to think that universities are orderly places, and if they aren't, presidents and trustees ought to make them so, even by force. Force is, however, our last and least resource, and order in the universities has seldom been more than skindeep. We order our planning, our upkeep, our payroll and the lawns. But where our most serious work is done, messiness, not to say a kind of anarchy, is part of our nature. 2

Look first at our teaching. Our job is to put students in touch with beauty or thought and then watch what happens. A young mind seeing for the first time into Virgil, Plato or Burke undergoes an intellectual chain reaction that is uncontrollable. Great works and young minds are "fire and powder which as they kiss consume." 3

There is an anarchy in the being of our students. The chaos of living in a 20-year-old body translates into the 20-year-old's steady probing at authority. Most students at one time or another tangle with it, not because they want it removed, but because they want to see whether it will stand still long enough for them to measure themselves against it. 4

At times, the faculty, like parents, cry out in Shakespearean eloquence: 5

> Let me not live . . . to be the snuff
> Of younger spirits, whose apprehensive senses
> All but new things disdain; whose judgments are
> Mere fathers of their garments; whose constancies
> Expire before their fashions.

But faculty, too, are caught up in our disorderly process. A good class crackles with intensity. The professor knows the long reach of his ideas and the challenge they put not only to his students but to himself. He is also aware of how hard he must crowd and pull to make student growth go as far as it can. The wrestle of mind on mind fills both, and neither faculty member nor student has much time for the dull business of keeping the world, even the world of the university, in good trim. To learn and to teach are beautiful things, but at their intense best, like laughter or pain, they distort.

The faculty knows also the messiness of research. Every scholar who finds himself treading ground no one has trod before feels as though he has been spun off his native planet into a solitary and chaotic orbit of speculation, hypothesis and doubt. Anarchy and loneliness go together. Scholarship in which facts stay in line or ideas in order is either vulgarization or echo.   6

Our critics take as given the basic tidiness of government, industry and the press, but authority within a university is tentative and dispersed. No one is completely in charge, and no one should be. Academic decisions are made by faculties. Students want a large say in the conduct of their lives on campus. Presidents and deans distribute the seven goods of the university (people, space, money, books, equipment, location and reputation) but are bigger fools than they look if they confuse the ground they walk with the windy heights where the young learn and grow.   7

That growth touches all of us. The faculty offer their experience and knowledge and the students their imagination and energy. The shock between them remakes all our worlds, including our democracy. Alfred North Whitehead's vision of the university as the smithy where a people's ideas and forms are rethought and recast in "the imaginative acquisition of knowledge" is still true. That vision doesn't work where premises or conclusions go untried or where a false neatness is forcibly laid on.   8

Because we are open in our process and open in our places, we are deliberately vulnerable to ill-aimed force, which can at times attack our own freedom. The very   9 being of a university makes it easy to disrupt, and our centuries have taught us that we are weakly defended by policemen. A university's great gift is the grant of room for young and old to speculate, to dream, to rear great buildings of ideas. A second gift is an absolution from consequence should those ideas crash down about our ears. Unless the young learn firsthand how supple and strengthening our freedoms are, they will never learn to defend them. Imposed order is a poor teacher for any free people.

Our strong defense, on halcyon as on stormy days, is   10
a discipline as old as man's mind. The worst of our errors are academic and intellectual and we can, given time, correct them. Correction comes not by crowd control, but by reason, by the slow, wearing rub of mind on mind. We live in a glass house that beckons the booby's stone, and none of the numerical barbed wire at the gates of admission can keep out boobies. All of us deal with disrupters, but we try to civilize them, or at least hold them at bay in the strong toils of talk, thought, persuasion. All of us know the acrid shame of failure whenever we must resort to force. We also know that authority alone can never lead a student out of "the prison of his days."

If America's colleges are to be roundly condemned be-   11
cause they feel the best way to handle disruption is to educate disrupters, then something of value to all of us will be lost. Our faculties have at least one large body of allies: the parents of their students. Parents know how hard it is for the young to grow without error, indeed how impossible. They understand why colleges react so often with ambiguous patience. We who teach distrust force because we take parentage of the mind seriously, because like parents we still at heart love our own.

Comment

Healy's argument is a deductive one. In paragraph 5 he states his conception of the ideal class and the ideal professor: "A good class crackles with intensity. The professor knows the long reach of his ideas and the challenge they put not only to his students but to himself." From this belief and others concerning the purpose and nature of education and the nature of twenty-year-old college students, he makes deductions and uses these to explain the behavior of students who disrupt speakers at college campuses. Healy supports his deductive argument with observations drawn from his experience as a university president; he states that college administrations, trustees, and faculty cannot make universities tidy and well-behaved. He concludes with an appeal to the experience of the reader.

Questions for Study and Discussion

1. What does Healy tell us in paragraphs 3 through 5 about the purpose and nature of education and the nature of college students? How does he develop his ideas about education in paragraphs 8 and 9?
2. What conclusions does he draw about campus life and, in particular, disruption of speakers from these ideas?
3. Why do college administrators, trustees, and faculty not have the power to control college life? Is Healy saying that anarchy is desirable or necessary? Is he saying that administrators and faculty should not discourage disruption of speakers?
4. What appeal to experience does he make to conclude the essay?

Vocabulary Study

1. What meanings of *order* does Healy explore in paragraphs 2 and 9? What is the meaning of *discipline* in paragraph 10? What kind of order does he believe is possible and desirable on a college campus?
2. In what sense of the word is there "anarchy" in twenty-year-old college students?
3. What images and ideas do the words *wrestle* (paragraph 5), *smithy* (paragraph 8), and *rub* (paragraph 10) convey? How are these metaphors related in idea?

4. What meanings do the words *parent* and *parentage* have in
    paragraph 11?

Suggestions for Writing

Write an essay stating your views on one of the following issues.
In the course of your essay, state and answer objections to your
position:

1. Disrupting speakers on college campuses
2. Appointing students to serve as college trustees
3. Requiring college students to study a foreign language
4. Requiring all students to read some of the classic writings
    of Western and non-Western cultures

Margaret Mead and Rhoda Metraux

NEIGHBORS VS. NEIGHBORHOODS

Margaret Mead (1901–1978), one of America's most distinguished
anthropologists, was a curator of ethnology at the Museum of
Natural History in New York City from 1926 to 1969. She also
taught at Columbia and other universities, and participated in the
work of numerous United States and United Nations agencies. She
traveled widely and wrote about many cultures, including her
own, in such widely read books as *Growing Up in New Guinea*
(1930), *And Keep Your Powder Dry* (1942), and *Male and Female*
(1949).

Rhoda Metraux was educated at Vassar, Yale, and Columbia, and
has done field work in anthropology in many countries including
Haiti, Mexico, Argentina, and New Guinea. She has been on the
staff of various government agencies and a research associate at
the Museum of Natural History. She and Margaret Mead worked
together for many years, collaborating in the writing of *The Study
of Culture at a Distance* (1953) and *Themes in French Culture* (1954).

Most Americans still carry them, like a well-loved pic-   1
ture in a frame, the idea of small-town life—as a way they
themselves once lived, or wish they had lived, or hope one

day to live. White houses on green lawns set not too far apart, lights in windows at which shades are not pulled down, safety for one's children wherever they wander, everyone known by name and reputation. These are the values remembered by families living in city houses that stand, one just like the other, in bleak and deteriorated or jerry-built rows; in anonymous apartments; and in the vast, unbounded suburbs where the lawns must be kept green but everyone is a stranger. Older people complain and younger people wonder about the disappearance of this neighborly friendliness and trust. In modern American life each family has become, or is fast becoming, a small, self-contained unit in a world of strangers.

One reason that small-town neighborliness has almost vanished is that time and again those who grew up with it found it too confining. "No, son, I wouldn't plan to be a pilot. You Atkinsons always had weak eyes." "You want to be an actress? Now, Mary, take a little advice from someone who knew you *before* you were born." However well meant, remarks like these could clip the wings of one's ambitions. A world in which the neighbors, which included most of the town, knew one's every act was restricting, limiting, confining. Each child grew up carrying the known and expected characteristics of his grandparents, his parents, his brothers and sisters, and even the marks of his own small failures as a little child. True, the neighbors often were kind, dependable people. But it was good to get away from them, to make a new life where no one knew you and where your aspirations were not treated as pretensions.

Yet, in the new life something is acutely felt to be missing. The frame of neighborly knowledge, which contained both an allowance for weakness and an unwillingness to allow for real ambition, is gone and nothing has taken its place. We have left behind (and may well lament) the familiarity and reassurance of the small, intimate neighborhood, but we have not realized the possibilities inherent in a larger, more complicated setting. In fact, in many instances we have retreated into a way of life even more limiting than the one we left.

In today's housing projects and in suburban develop- 4
ments, conformity—outward adjustment to the opinions
and tastes of other people—has been substituted for the
old closeness, longed for but also feared. People come to
the neighborhood as strangers, from widely different backgrounds and influences. After they arrive, they try to
become like the others in the community and hope that
the others will be like them. But the difficulty is that making oneself look like other people, and even act like them,
is quite different from sharing something with them.

In city neighborhoods and some suburban communi- 5
ties, people have a tendency to keep to themselves—often
they know their neighbors only to nod to and keep self-
protectively at arm's length—especially if they feel that certain elements of the neighborhood are "bad." Subtly,
neighbors are associated with difficulties and times of
trouble. They lend you things you have run out of unexpectedly, like butter, or extra things like party glasses and
chairs. They keep one child when another is sick. They
bring food at a time of death. But these contacts are limited
and intermittent, and when things go well there is little
give-and-take even with "good" neighbors.

So we are seldom fully aware of our neighbors as peo- 6
ple. In fact, many of us today care far less about our neighbors than we do about our neighbor*hoods*. In speaking of
"good" neighborhoods or "bad" neighborhoods, we often
are not thinking about the neighbors as people at all—
witty or dull, happy or sad, kind or indifferent—but as
accessories to the neighborhood and their effect on our
class position.

In this context, neighbors who spoil the neighborhood 7
are people who put the wrong decorations in their windows, drive the wrong cars, neglect their lawns or come
from the wrong racial or religious groups; the wrong
neighbors are people whom other people—one's rich or
more successful relatives and friends—might see and
criticize. The right kind of neighbors are just the opposite;
they are people who pull you up rather than drag you
down just by living on the same street.

Either way, this is thinking of people as things. If the 8
car stands in front of the house by the neat lawn and no
one bangs in and out of the door and the right kind of
tree stands in the picture window at Christmas, those who
are in search of the "right" neighborhood will be content.
When their friends come to visit, they won't mention
neighbors at all—just what a pleasant *neighborhood* it is.
If, on the other hand, the street is deteriorating, the family
will deplore having to live there in the same breath with
which they explain the advantages of their own house:
"The children can walk to school. It's near Jim's work.
We've put so much into fixing it up. But we don't really
belong here." All the other people on the block are excluded. So by our particularly American form of social
class—in which a class position can be invaded, diluted
and lost, in which people are judged not by what they
are but by how they dress, where they live and what kinds
of cars they drive—the human element that comes through
the sheer sharing of the vicissitudes of everyday life is
crowded out. People are treated as things, as objects by
which one hauls oneself up or is pushed down.

These attitudes need to be re-examined. We have the 9
opportunity to use our new-found freedom, away from
the small, familiar worlds that were safe and secure but
often stultifying, to develop and diversify our lives. We
are not doing this if we regard the neighbors as extensions
of ourselves, or as people to be "used" or kept at arm's
length, or merely as attractive or unattractive accessories
to the community. The child who grows up with such attitudes grows up with a sad lack of what he will need as
an American, as a person, as a dweller on this planet. He
is robbed of one important dimension of living in the
modern world—learning a mutual give-and-take with people of widely different tastes and backgrounds. Just as
relatives are, one hopes, people one loves (but may not
like) and friends are people one really likes and may come
to love, so neighbors can be people whom we may like,
or even come to love, or be indifferent to, or not like at

all. But we can, at least, come to see them—and ourselves—for what we are as *people*—highly individual people in a very large world.

Comment

Though they focus on neighborhoods and neighborliness,
Margaret Mead and Rhoda Metraux deal with aspects of small-
town life and city life. Mead and Metraux write from their experience of American small towns and cities. But the idea of
neighborliness is not the outcome of factual evidence; Mead and
Metraux do not arrive at it inductively. They present it rather
as a given truth:

> We have the opportunity to use our new-found freedom, away
> from the small, familiar worlds that were safe and secure but
> often stultifying, to develop and diversify our lives. We are not
> doing this if we regard the neighbors as extensions of ourselves,
> or as people to be "used" or kept at arm's length, or merely
> as attractive or unattractive accessories to the community.

Mead and Metraux state this truth several times in the course
of the essay. The statement is an extended definition that shapes
the whole discussion of neighborliness.

Questions for Study and Discussion

1. Where do Mead and Metraux first state their belief that people are not things? Where do they restate it?
2. What inferences do they make from the truth that people
   are not things?
3. Is the statement that people are not things the thesis of the
   essay? If not, what is the thesis? Where does it appear?
4. What explanation and factual support do Mead and Metraux
   give for their statement that "we are seldom fully aware
   of our neighbors as people" and that many people care
   more about their neighborhoods than about their neighbors? Why is their reasoning in paragraph 6 inductive
   rather than deductive?

5. Do you agree that city life encourages the attitude that people are things? If you agree, what evidence can you cite that city life has this effect? If you disagree, what evidence shows that it does not?

Vocabulary Study

Explain what the etymology of the following words and phases contributes to your understanding of the following:

1. *jerry-built, neighborly* (paragraph 1)
2. *aspirations, pretensions* (paragraph 2)
3. *intermittent* (paragraph 5)
4. *diluted, vicissitudes* (paragraph 8)
5. *stultifying, dimension* (paragraph 9)

Suggestions for Writing

1. Describe experiences you have had with neighbors in your town or city. Then discuss whether the ideas on neighbors and neighborliness of Mead and Metraux account for these experiences.
2. State whether you agree or disagree with one of the following statements, and explain why you do:
   a. "In modern American life each family has become, or is fast becoming, a small, self-contained unit in a world of strangers."
   b. "In today's housing projects and in suburban developments, conformity—outward adjustment to the opinions and tastes of other people—has been substituted for the old closeness, longed for, but also feared."
   c. "In speaking of 'good' neighborhoods or 'bad' neighborhoods, we often are not thinking about the neighbors as people at all. . . ."

Ellen Goodman

WHOSE LIFE IS IT ANYWAY?

Ellen Goodman wrote for *Newsweek* and the *Detroit Free Press* before joining the staff of the *Boston Globe* in 1967 as feature writer and columnist. In 1980 Goodman received the Pulitzer Prize for Commentary. Her columns on a wide range of social and political issues are collected in several books, including *At Large* (1981) and *Keeping in Touch* (1985). In her essay on the Elizabeth Bouvia case, Goodman reasons from truths she holds about the issue she characterizes as the right to die with the help of doctors. In Brian Clark's play and the later film, *Whose Life Is It Anyway?*, a hospitalized quadriplegic is successful in his legal fight to end efforts by his doctor and the hospital staff to maintain his life.

For a time, life has been imitating art in Riverside, California. The courtroom case of a twenty-six-year-old quadriplegic, Elizabeth Bouvia, is every bit as dramatic as the script of the movie, *Whose Life Is It Anyway?*

In September 1983, Bouvia admitted herself to the psychiatric ward of Riverside General Hospital with one goal in mind: to starve to death under their roof. She wanted doctors to give her only the medical attention needed to ease pain.

Unlike the character in the movie, Bouvia had been paralyzed since birth with cerebral palsy. Her grit was well-recorded in daily life and academic degrees. But after a failed marriage, failed attempts at pregnancy, and deepening depression over her future, her only determination was to die: "I choose no longer to be dependent on others."

Hers is a case that pushes just about all the buttons on our finely engineered ethical panel. The right-to-life and the right-to-die buttons. The one that labels suicide as rational act and the one that labels suicide as a crazy act. The one that opposes medical intervention against a patient's will and the one that supports medical intervention to save lives.

It presents us with the dilemma that we've been edging up to slowly, case after case. Ever since Karen Ann

Quinlan, we've debated whether a hospital could, should, keep someone "alive" after brain death. Today we discuss the ethics of "heroic" care for the terminally ill as well.

Slowly, we have also asserted certain rights to medical care. In 1973, in the case of a woman named Roe, the courts determined that a pregnant woman seeking an abortion had the right to privacy. Recently, in the case of a baby named Doe, the courts determined that parents could deny life-prolonging surgery to a severely handicapped infant. On our own we can refuse therapy, even maintenance therapy like dialysis, and willfully shorten our lives.

Meanwhile suicide, at least among the elderly or ill, has gained a certain odd legitimacy. In March 1983, the writer Arthur Koestler, ill with leukemia, committed suicide and his healthy wife, Cynthia, joined him. She was described as "devoted." A Florida couple in their eighties carefully killed themselves as a "solution to the problems of aging." The sheriff commented on how "thoughtful" they were.

In this atmosphere, Elizabeth Bouvia's request to be allowed to starve with painkillers and without force feeding seems almost routine. After all, if the parents of Baby Doe have the right to deny treatment, then doesn't the patient herself have the right to refuse it? If Roe has the right to "control her own body," then doesn't Bouvia? Isn't suicide a civil right?

The reality is that the Bouvia case has pushed over the established ethical line. We are now entering into a moral arena where words like "rights" begin to lose their meaning.

"I'm not asking for anybody to kill me," this woman has said. "I'm asking that the natural process of death take over." But refusing food is no more a natural process of death than falling is when you jump off a bridge.

What makes this case different from other "right-to-die" cases is that, however miserable she regards her life, Bouvia is not suffering a fatal disability. What makes it different is that she is not just proposing suicide; she is asking for the help of doctors. Indeed, Bouvia checked

into a ward that specializes in preventing suicide. There
are, as Freud said, no accidents.

The California Superior Court judge made a proper   12
distinction last week when he ruled that, yes, Bouvia had
the right to kill herself—it is her life, anyway—but not
"with the assistance of society." If she did not continue
to accept nourishment, the judge would allow the hospital
to force-feed her. Now, as I write this in December 1983,
the young woman has refused sufficient liquid protein to
sustain her ninety-five-pound body.

No matter how uncomfortable the idea, I think it is   13
appropriate, even imperative, for the hospital to forcibly
feed its despairing patient. Psychiatric wards are not suicide centers where people come for help in terminating
their despair.

Deep down, I'm afraid it is too easy for society to   14
"understand" the unhappiness of a quadriplegic instead
of alleviating it. It's too easy for us to begin to regard
suicides of the sick or the aged as "thoughtful" solutions.

If we support Elizabeth Bouvia's civil-rights stand, then   15
sooner or later we would passively watch a woman step
off a ledge and a man swallow sleeping pills. As we stood
there, bystanders, would we then remind each other not
to interfere? The "right to die" can easily become an excuse for our own unwillingness to reach out and help.

Comment

People sometimes agree about an ethical principle but disagree
about its definition or its application to a particular situation.
Those arguing about abortion usually agree that taking human
life is wrong but many disagree over the definition of *human
life*. The point at issue in these arguments is whether a fetus
is a human being. Goodman focuses on the issue of whether
a person has a right to ask others to assist in the act of suicide.
Suicide is not the issue for her. Others may disagree with Goodman, arguing that suicide is the issue, not how it takes place.
Goodman bases her argument on truths that she states in

explaining why she agrees with the judicial decision to forcibly feed Elizabeth Bouvia. Goodman also asks us to consider the implications of allowing Bouvia to die in the way she requested:

> If we support Elizabeth Bouvia's civil-rights stand, then sooner or later we would passively watch a woman step off a ledge and a man swallow sleeping pills. As we stood there, bystanders, would we then remind each other not to interfere?

Questions for Study and Discussion

1. What is "the dilemma that we've been edging up to slowly, case after case"? What is the "established ethical line" that the Bouvia case had made us cross?
2. Does Goodman say that suicide is a right, or does she not state her belief about suicide? Does Goodman say or imply that she agrees with the decisions in the Roe and the Baby Doe cases? Or does she state only that the courts have acknowledged certain rights?
3. What beliefs or truths lead Goodman to concur with the judicial ruling in the Bouvia case? Where in the essay does Goodman state these truths?
4. Why does Goodman note that Elizabeth Bouvia entered a ward specializing in suicide prevention?
5. Do you believe that the judicial ruling was correct? Do you agree with Goodman's reasoning in concurring with the judge? What beliefs guide your reasoning on the issue?

Vocabulary Study

1. What is the difference between a quadriplegic and a paraplegic?
2. Why does Goodman refer to the Bouvia case as a "dilemma"?
3. Goodman states that "suicide, at least among the elderly or ill, has gained a certain odd legitimacy." Does the word *legitimacy* mean *approval*?
4. Goodman quotes the Florida sheriff's comment that the elderly couple who committed suicide were "thoughtful" people, and she returns to this word in paragraph 14. Why is this word significant to her?

Suggestions for Writing

1. Argue your own views on the Bouvia case. State the beliefs
    that guide your thinking on the issue, and explain why you
    hold them.
2. State what beliefs guide your thinking on one of the follow-
    ing issues or another of concern to you. Then discuss the
    origin of these beliefs—for example, in your religion, school-
    ing, or upbringing:
    a. private ownership of handguns
    b. establishing the drinking age at 21
    c. drafting young men and women for military service
    d. exempting young women from military service
    e. making voting compulsory

George F. Will

BEARBAITING AND BOXING

George F. Will taught politics at Michigan State University and
other universities, and later observed the workings of government
as a congressional aide. Since 1972, he has given his full time to
journalism, first as editor of the *National Review*, and later as a
columnist for the *Washington Post* and *Newsweek*, and as
commentator for the American Broadcasting Company. In 1977,
Will received the Pulitzer Prize for Commentary. His columns have
been collected in a number of books, including *The Pursuit of
Virtue, and Other Tory Notions* (1982), *The Morning After* (1986), and
Political Essays (1990); his book *Statecraft as Soulcraft: What
Government Does* (1983) is a theoretical study of government. His
essay on boxing that follows and his essay on New York City in
the following section illustrate the range of Will's interests and
concerns.

For 150 years people have been savoring Macaulay's   1
judgment that the Puritans hated bearbaiting not because
it gave pain to the bear but because it gave pleasure to
the spectators. However, there are moments, and this is
one, for blurting out the truth: The Puritans were right. The
pain to the bear was not a matter of moral indifference,

but the pleasure of the spectators was sufficient reason for abolishing that entertainment.

Now another boxer has been beaten to death. The brain injury he suffered was worse than the injury the loser in a boxing match is supposed to suffer. It is hard to calibrate such things—how hard an opponent's brain should be banged against the inside of his cranium—in the heat of battle.

From time immemorial, in immemorial ways, men have been fighting for the entertainment of other men. Perhaps in a serene, temperate society boxing would be banned along with other blood sports—if, in such a society, the question would even arise. But a step toward the extinction of boxing is understanding why that is desirable. One reason is the physical injury done to young men. But a sufficient reason is the quality of the pleasure boxing often gives to spectators.

There is no denying that boxing, like other, better sports, can exemplify excellence. Boxing demands bravery and, when done well, is beautiful in the way that any exercise of finely honed physical talents is. Furthermore, many sports are dangerous. But boxing is the sport that has as its object the infliction of pain and injury. Its crowning achievement is the infliction of serious trauma on the brain. The euphemism for boxing is "the art of self-defense." No. A rose is a rose is a rose, and a user fee is a revenue enhancer is a tax increase, and boxing is aggression.

It is probably that there will be a rising rate of spinal cord injuries and deaths in football. The force of defensive players (a function of weight and speed) is increasing even faster than the force of ball carriers and receivers. As a coach once said, football is not a contact sport—dancing is a contact sport—football is a collision sport. The human body, especially the knee and spine, is not suited to that. But football can be made safer by equipment improvements and rules changes such as those proscribing certain kinds of blocks. Boxing is fundamentally impervious to reform.

It will be said that if two consenting adults want to 6
batter each other for the amusement of paying adults, the
essential niceties have been satisfied, "consent" being
almost the only nicety of a liberal society. But from Plato
on, political philosophers have taken entertainments
seriously, and have believed the law should, too. They
have because a society is judged by the kind of citizens
it produces, and some entertainments are coarsening.
Good government and the good life depend on good
values and passions, and some entertainments are inimical
to these.

Such an argument cuts no ice in a society where the 7
decayed public philosophy teaches that the pursuit of happiness is a right sovereign over all other considerations;
that "happiness" and "pleasure" are synonyms, and that
there is no hierarchy of values against which to measure
particular appetites. Besides, some persons will say, with
reason, that a society in which the entertainment menu
includes topless lady mud wrestlers is a society past worry-
ing about.

Some sports besides boxing attract persons who want 8
their unworthy passions stirred, including a lust for blood.
I remember Memorial Day in the Middle West in the 1950s,
when all roads led to the Indianapolis Speedway, where
too many fans went to drink Falstaff beer and hope for
a crash. But boxing is in a class by itself.

Richard Hoffer of the *Los Angeles Times* remembers 9
the death of Johnny Owen, a young 118-pound bantam-
weight who died before he had fulfilled his modest ambition of buying a hardware store back home in Wales. Hoffer remembers that "Owen was put in a coma by a single
punch, carried out of the Olympic (arena) under a hail of
beer cups, some of which were filled with urine."

The law can not prudently move far in advance of 10
mass taste, so boxing can not be outlawed. But in a world
in which many barbarities are unavoidable, perhaps it is
not too much to hope that some of the optional sorts will
be outgrown.

Comment

The statement on bearbaiting by the nineteenth-century English historian Thomas B. Macaulay on Oliver Cromwell and the English Puritans, who ruled from 1649 to 1660, is often quoted in the course of ridiculing puritanical views. Will defends the Puritan ethical view as "sufficient reason" for discouraging boxing. He shows that boxing resembles football and automobile racing in different ways, but he focuses on boxing because he considers the sport to be "in a class by itself." His argument is based on what he considers obvious truths about the ideal society. Recognizing that probably few boxing fans would agree with him, he supports his argument with factual evidence. His argument is a deductive one, however, because he makes inferences directly from these truths.

Questions for Study and Discussion

1. What is Will's definition of the ideal society, and where does he present it?
2. What inference does Will draw from this definition about the entertainments of a society?
3. Why does American society fall short of that ideal? What factual evidence does Will present to support this judgment?
4. How does boxing resemble football and automobile racing? Why does Will believe boxing is "in a class by itself"?
5. In paragraph 10, Will states an obvious truth and draws an inference from it. What is that truth and what is the inference?

Vocabulary Study

1. Find information on bear-baiting in a sports dictionary or other reference book. To what extent did bear-baiting in the seventeenth century and other times resemble the sports criticized by Will?
2. Give synonyms for the following:
    a. *calibrate* (paragraph 2)
    b. *temperate* (paragraph 3)

c. *honed, trauma, euphemism* (paragraph 4)
d. *proscribing, impervious* (paragraph 5)
e. *niceties, inimical* (paragraph 6)
f. *sovereign, hierarchy* (paragraph 7)
g. *prudently* (paragraph 10)

Suggestions for Writing

1. State whether or not you agree with Will on the issue of boxing. Explain your reasons for your agreement or disagreement.
2. Use the resources of your library to write a research paper on one of the following topics. Limit the topic to a particular period—perhaps a decade in which a large number of fatalities or accidents occurred—or to an aspect on which you find sufficient information to support a significant thesis. Your research paper might be an informative one that provides facts needed to understand an existing situation. Or your paper might be persuasive: you might use your findings to argue for or against a proposal or an existing policy:
    a. professional boxing fatalities and the public response
    b. injuries in stock car and other automobile races and the public response
    c. injuries in college and professional football
    d. gunshot deaths in the United States and Great Britain
    e. drug-related crime in two American cities
    f. the risks of nuclear power
    g. chemical warfare since 1913
    h. causes of homelessness in America in the 1980s
    i. the increasing cost of hospitalization in the 1990s
    j. standards of welfare eligibility in two American cities

Strategies of Persuasion

Most arguments are directed to a particular audience and organized in light of that audience's knowledge and beliefs; in other words, most arguments are meant to be *persuasive*. We have seen that inductive arguments build particulars of experience and similar kinds of evidence to generalizations or conclusions; deductive arguments, on the other hand, proceed from premises and build to conclusions. But the order of ideas may sometimes be changed to fit particular audiences. Thus the conclusion of the argument may be stated at the beginning, as a way of focusing attention on the point of most concern. Or the essay may start with the least controversial statement (or premise), proceed to the more controversial, and end with the most controversial. The order of ideas does not affect the strength or soundness of the argument itself.

The persuasiveness of the inductive argument depends on the strength of the facts presented. George F. Will, in the inductive argument that follows, immerses his audience in the facts of a notorious episode—one that raises important questions about the situation of poor people in our cities. Will does not ask these questions directly: instead he gives a full account of what happened to a young Harlem mother—stressing those details that dramatize the weakness of welfare systems.

The questions Will raises—in particular, what is a city's responsibility for the lives of the poor—might have been discussed theoretically, as in a sociology textbook. Will does discuss the issue theoretically toward the end of the essay, but he has no panacea to offer, though he grants that cities must provide "a floor of support" of some kind. It is the intractable problem, for which no solution now exists, that he focuses on in his extended example. The example is indispensable to our understanding—especially so if we believe it is easy to assign blame in crimes of the poor, or that easy solutions are available.

Yet Will does something more: in dramatizing the episode, he allows the reader to imagine the situation of the young woman. This appeal to imagination is his most important persuasive device.

The writer has available numerous strategies of persuasion. Will's essay illustrates dramatization, one of the most important. The satirist uses other means to persuade the audience to change its thinking on an issue or to take action. The satirist usually depends on ridicule and sometimes tries to awaken the conscience of the audience by appealing to shame and guilt. But appeals to conscience may take other forms; for example, writers also appeal to our common humanity. The essays in this section illustrate some of these many appeals.

George F. Will

ON HER OWN IN THE CITY

In his essay on a young woman's tragedy, George F. Will builds his argument to a general statement about the ability of society to care for the poor. The argument is thus different from Will's essay on boxing and other sports in America. In discussing the matter of poverty, Will might have used any one of the thousand daily tragedies that occur in American cities. The fate of the young woman described in the essay raises questions that the reader cannot ignore. For details on Will see page 357.

When police, responding to her call, arrived at her East 1 Harlem tenement, she was hysterical: "The dog ate my baby." The baby girl had been four days old, twelve hours "home" from the hospital. Home was two rooms and a kitchen on the sixth floor, furnished with a rug, a folding chair, and nothing else, no bed, no crib.

"Is the baby dead?" asked an officer. "Yes," the 2 mother said, "I saw the baby's insides." Her dog, a German shepherd, had not been fed for five days. She explained: ''I left the baby on the floor with the dog to protect it.'' She had bought the dog in July for protection from human menaces.

She is twenty-four. She went to New York three years 3 ago from a small Ohio community. She wanted to be on her own. She got that wish.

She was employed intermittently, until the fifth month 4 of her pregnancy, which she says was the result of a rape she did not report to the police. She wanted the baby. She bought child-care books, and had seven prenatal checkups at Bellevue Hospital. Although she rarely called home or asked for money, she called when the baby was born. Her mother mailed twenty-five dollars for a crib. It arrived too late.

When labor began she fed the dog with the last food in 5 the apartment and went alone to the hospital. The baby was born on Wednesday. When she left Bellevue Sunday evening, the hospital office holding her welfare payment was closed. With six dollars in her pocket and a baby in her arms, she took a cab home. The meter said four dollars and the driver demanded a dollar tip. When she asked his assistance in getting upstairs, he drove off.

The hospital had given her enough formula for three 6 feedings for the baby. Rather than spend her remaining dollar that night on food for herself and the dog, she saved it for the bus ride back to Bellevue to get her welfare money. Having slept with the baby on a doubled-up rug, she left the baby and the dog at 7 A.M. It was 53 degrees, too cold she thought to take the baby. She had no warm baby clothes and she thought the hospital had said the baby was ailing. She got back at 8:30 A.M. Then she called the police.

Today the forces of law and order and succor are strug- 7 gling to assign ''blame'' in order to escape it. Her attorney and Bellevue are arguing about how she was released, or expelled, on Sunday evening. Welfare officials are contending with charges that they are somehow culpable for her failure to receive a crib before giving birth, and for her living conditions. (She was receiving payment of $270 a month; her rent was $120.) She has been arraigned on a charge of negligent homicide, but no one seems anxious to prosecute. Late in New York's U.S. Senate primary, Daniel P. Moynihan, talking like a senator prematurely, said that this case dramatizes weaknesses of the welfare system, and indicated that it also dramatizes the need for him in Washington. Perhaps.

But because cities are collections of strangers, they are, inevitably, bad places to be poor. Not that there are good places, but cities, being kingdoms of the strong, are especially hellish for the poor. Cities have their indispensable purposes, and their charms, not the least of which is that you can be alone in a crowd. But that kind of living alone is an acquired taste, and not for the weak or unfortunate. They are apt to learn that no city's institutions can provide protective supports like those of an extended family or real community. No metropolis can provide a floor of support solid enough to prevent the bewildered—like the woman from Ohio—from falling through the cracks.

Through those cracks you get an occasional glimpse of what George Eliot meant: "If we had a keen vision and feeling of all ordinary human life, it would be like hearing the grass grow and the squirrel's heartbeat, and we should die of that roar which lies on the other side of silence."

Questions for Study and Discussion

1. What details of the episode show why it is difficult to assign blame for the death of the child?
2. Is Will suggesting that everyone involved in the death was to blame—the mother, the hospital and welfare officials, the city as a whole—or is he saying that blame is difficult or impossible to define in this case?
3. What is the point of George Eliot's statement, and what is gained by concluding the essay with it? Would the statement be as effective if it introduced the essay?
4. How persuasive do you find the example? Do you have a solution for the plight of the woman? Are there other solutions Will might have presented?

Vocabulary Study

Give the meaning of the following words, in the context of the sentence in which each appears:

1. *intermittently* (paragraph 4)
2. *succor, arraigned, negligent homicide* (paragraph 7)
3. *apt, extended, metropolis* (paragraph 8)

Suggestions for Writing

1. Will states in paragraph 8: "They are apt to learn that no city's institutions can provide protective supports like those of an extended family or real community." Discuss what the details of the essay tell us about an "extended family" or "real community" by implication.
2. Discuss what you believe a city can and should do for a person like the woman Will describes. You may wish to discuss what responsibility a city has for the lives of poor people in general. State your reasons for the views that you hold.
3. Will states earlier in paragraph 8: "But because cities are collections of strangers, they are, inevitably, bad places to be poor." And he adds in the same paragraph: "Cities have their indispensable purposes, and their charms, not the least of which is that you can be alone in a crowd." Develop one of these ideas from your own experience or observation, or compare his views with those of Robert Coles (p. 239) or Margaret Mead and Rhoda Metraux (p. 347).

E. B. White

THE DECLINE OF SPORT

(A Preposterous Parable)

E. B. White, the distinguished essayist, humorist, and editor, was born in Mount Vernon, New York, in 1899. He was long associated with *The New Yorker* as a writer and editor and also wrote for *Harper's Magazine* and other publications. His books include *Charlotte's Web* (1952) and *Stuart Little* (1945), both for children, and *One Man's Meat* (1943), *The Second Tree from the Corner* (1954), and *The Points of My Compass* (1962), collections of his essays. White died in 1985.

In the third decade of the supersonic age, sport grip- 1
ped the nation in an ever-tightening grip. The horse tracks, the ballparks, the fight rings, the gridirons, all drew crowds in steadily increasing numbers. Every time a game was played, an attendance record was broken. Usually some other sort of record was broken, too—such as the record for the number of consecutive doubles hit by left-handed batters in a Series game, or some such thing as that. Records fell like ripe apples on a windy day. Customs and manners changed, and the five-day business week was reduced to four days, then to three, to give everyone a better chance to memorize the scores.

Not only did sport proliferate but the demands it made 2
on the spectator became greater. Nobody was content to take in one event at a time, and thanks to the magic of radio and television nobody had to. A Yale alumnus, class of 1962, returning to the Bowl with 197,000 others to see the Yale-Cornell football game would take along his pocket radio and pick up the Yankee Stadium, so that while his eye might be following a fumble on the Cornell twenty-two-yard line, his ear would be following a man going down to second in the top of the fifth, seventy miles away. High in the blue sky above the Bowl, skywriters would be at work writing the scores of other major and minor

sporting contests, weaving an interminable record of victory and defeat, and using the new high-visibility pink news-smoke perfected by Pepsi-Cola engineers. And in the frames of the giant video sets, just behind the goalposts, this same alumnus could watch Dejected win the Futurity before a record-breaking crowd of 349,872 at Belmont, each of whom was tuned to the Yale Bowl and following the World Series game in the video and searching the sky for further news of events either under way or just completed. The effect of this vast cyclorama of sport was to divide the spectator's attention, over-subtilize his appreciation, and deaden his passion. As the fourth supersonic decade was ushered in, the picture changed and sport began to wane.

A good many factors contributed to the decline of   3
sport. Substitutions in football had increased to such an extent that there were very few fans in the United States capable of holding the players in mind during play. Each play that was called saw two entirely new elevens lined up, and the players whose names and faces you had familiarized yourself with in the first period were seldom seen or heard of again. The spectacle became as diffuse as the main concourse in Grand Central at the commuting hour.

Express motor highways leading to the parks and   4
stadia had become so wide, so unobstructed, so devoid of all life except automobiles and trees that sport fans had got into the habit of travelling enormous distances to attend events. The normal driving speed had been stepped up to ninety-five miles an hour, and the distance between cars had been decreased to fifteen feet. This put an extraordinary strain on the sport lover's nervous system, and he arrived home from a Saturday game, after a road trip of three hundred and fifty miles, glassy-eyed, dazed, and spent. He hadn't really had any relaxation and he had failed to see Czlika (who had gone in for Trusky) take the pass from Bkeeo (who had gone in for Bjallo) in the third period, because at that moment a youngster named Lavagetto had been put in to pinch-hit for Art Gurlack in the

bottom of the ninth with the tying run on second, and the skywriter who was attempting to write "Princeton O— Lafayete 43" had banked the wrong way, muffed the "3," and distracted everyone's attention from the fact that Lavagetto had been whiffed.

Cheering, of course, lost its stimulating effect on play-   5 ers, because cheers were no longer associated necessarily with the immediate scene but might as easily apply to something that was happening somewhere else. This was enough to infuriate even the steadiest performer. A football star, hearing the stands break into a roar before the ball was snapped, would realize that their minds were not on him, and would become dispirited and grumpy. Two or three of the big coaches worried so about this that they considered equipping all players with tiny ear sets, so that they, too, could keep abreast of other sporting events while playing, but the idea was abandoned as impractical, and the coaches put it aside in tickler files, to bring up again later.

I think the event that marked the turning point in sport   6 and started it downhill was the Midwest's classic Dust Bowl game of 1975, when Eastern Reserve's great right end, Ed Pistachio, was shot by a spectator. This man, the one who did the shooting, was seated well down in the stands near the forty-yard line on a bleak October afternoon and was so saturated with sport and with the disappointments of sport that he had clearly become deranged. With a minute and fifteen seconds to play and the score tied, the Eastern Reserve quarterback had whipped a long pass over Army's heads into Pistachio's waiting arms. There was no other player anywhere near him, and all Pistachio had to do was catch the ball and run it across the line. He dropped it. At exactly this moment, the spectator—a man named Homer T. Parkinson, of 35 Edgemere Drive, Toledo, O.—suffered at least three other major disappointments in the realm of sport. His horse, Hiccough, on which he had a five-hundred-dollar bet, fell while getting away from the starting gate at Pimlico and broke its leg (clearly visible in the video); his favorite shortstop,

Lucky Frimstitch, struck out and let three men die on base in the final game of the Series (to which Parkinson was tuned); and the Governor Dummer soccer team, on which Parkinson's youngest son played goalie, lost to Kent, 4–3, as recorded in the sky overhead. Before anyone could stop him, he drew a gun and drilled Pistachio, before 954,000 persons, the largest crowd that had ever attended a football game and the second-largest crowd that had ever assembled for any sporting even in any month except July.

This tragedy, by itself, wouldn't have caused sport to 7 decline, I suppose, but it set in motion a chain of other tragedies, the cumulative effect of which was terrific. Almost as soon as the shot was fired, the news flash was picked up by one of the skywriters directly above the field. He glanced down to see whether he could spot the trouble below, and in doing so failed to see another skywriter approaching. The two planes collided and fell, wings locked, leaving a confusing trail of smoke, which some observers tried to interpret as a late sports score. The planes struck in the middle of the nearby east-bound coast-to-coast Sunlight Parkway, and a motorist driving a convertible coupé stopped so short, to avoid hitting them, that he was bumped from behind. The pileup of cars that ensued involved 1,482 vehicles, a record for eastbound parkways. A total of more than three thousand persons lost their lives in the highway accident, including the two pilots, and when panic broke out in the stadium, it cost another 872 in dead and injured. News of the disaster spread quickly to other sport arenas, and started other panics among the crowds trying to get to the exits, where they could buy a paper and study a list of the dead. All in all the afternoon of sport cost 20,003 lives, a record. And nobody had much to show for it, except one small Midwestern boy who hung around the smoking wrecks of the planes, captured some aero news-smoke in a milk bottle, and took it home as a souvenir.

From that day on, sport waned. Through long, non- 8 competitive Saturday afternoons, the stadia slumbered. Even the parkways fell into disuse as motorists rediscovered the charms of old, twisty roads that led through main streets and past barnyards, with their mild congestions and pleasant smells.

Comment

Satire is an important kind of persuasive writing. An essay may be entirely satirical, as in E. B. White's satire on the American obsession with sports, or it may be satirical in part. The chief means of persuasion in satire is ridicule: the satirist makes fun of attitudes or behavior or holds them up to shame. The targets of social satire are foolish attitudes or behavior—social snobbery, pretentious talk, sloppy eating, and the like. Though amusing and sometimes even disgusting, these have no very serious consequences for the individual or for society. The targets of ethcial satire are vicious attitudes and behavior—for example, racial or religious prejudice, dishonesty, hypocrisy—that do have serious consequences. Social satire is always humorous; ethical satire may be humorous, as in many political cartoons like *Doonesbury*, but it is more often bitter or angry. Many satires like Twain's *Huckleberry Finn* contain both types of satire.

Some satirists are direct in their satire—their statements are angry and biting in their criticism. Others like E. B. White, James Thurber, and Art Buchwald depend on humorous understatement or exaggeration. These are forms of irony. An ironic statement generally implies more through inflection of voice or phrasing than the words actually say; sarcasm is a bitter kind of irony. You are being ironic when you smile or wink while saying something supposedly serious; your smile or wink may express humor or sarcasm.

Questions for Study and Discussion

1. What attitudes or habits is White satirizing in the America of late 1947, when this essay first appeared? Are the targets of the satire limited to attitudes and habits relating to sport, or does White have also in mind general attitudes and habits?

2. Is the satire social or ethical? Is White satirizing merely foolish or, instead, vicious attitudes or behavior?
3. To what extent does White depend on exaggeration or over-statement? Does he also use understatement?
4. Names like "Dejected" can be satirical as well as humorous. Do you find other humorous names in the essay, and are they used satirically?
5. White refers to the "high-visibility pink news-smoke perfected by Pepsi-Cola engineers." Why does he refer to "Pepsi-Cola" rather than to "U.S. Steel" or "Dow Chemical"?
6. Do you think the essay describes attitudes toward sport and the behavior of sports fans in the eighties? Do you find the satire persuasive?

Vocabulary Study

1. What is a "parable"? What does the subtitle "A Preposterous Parable" show about White's intention?
2. Write a paraphrase of paragraph 2 or paragraph 6—a sentence-for-sentence rendering in your own words. Be sure to find substitutes for *proliferate, interminable,* and *oversubtilize* (paragraph 2), or *deranged, whipped,* and *drilled* (paragraph 6). Try to retain the tone of White's original paragraph.

Suggestions for Writing

1. Identify the targets of White's satire and explain how you discover them in the course of reading.
2. Discuss the extent to which White's predictions in 1947 have come true. Cite contemporary events and attitudes that support the predictions or that show White to be mistaken.
3. Write a satirical essay of your own on a contemporary social or political issue. You may not discover the best strategy or tone until you have written several paragraphs. Revise your draft to make the strategy and tone consistent throughout.

Charles Osgood

"REAL" MEN AND WOMEN

Charles Osgood was born in New York City in 1933 and graduated from Fordham University in 1954. He worked in radio as a reporter and program director before joining CBS News in 1972. He is seen frequently on the CBS Evening News and other news programs. His essay on man and woman has the concision and sharp focus that we expect of journalism; Osgood combines these qualities with depth and force.

Helene, a young friend of mine, has been assigned a   1
theme in English composition class. She can take her choice: "What is a *real* man?" or, if she wishes, "What is a *real* woman?" Seems the instructor has some strong ideas on these subjects. Helene says she doesn't know which choice to make. "I could go the women's-lib route," she says, "but I don't think he'd like that. I started in on that one once in a class, and it didn't go over too well." So, what is a real man and what is a real woman?

"As opposed to what?" I asked.   2

"I don't know, as opposed to unreal men and women,   3
I suppose. Got any ideas?"

Yes, it just so happens I do. Let's start with the as-   4
sumption that reality is that which is, as opposed to that which somebody would like, or something that is imagined or idealized. Let's assume that all human beings who are alive, therefore, are real human beings, who can be divided into two categories: real men and real women. A man who exists is a real man. His reality is in no way lessened by his race, his nationality, political affiliation, financial status, religious persuasion, or personal proclivities. All men are real men. All women are real women.

The first thing you do if you want to destroy some-   5
body is to rob him of his humanity. If you can persuade yourself that someone is a gook and therefore not a real person, you can kill him rather more easily, burn down his home, separate him from his family. If you can

persuade yourself that someone is not really a person but a spade, a Wasp, a kike, a wop, a mick, a fag, a dike, and therefore not a real man or woman, you can more easily hate or hurt him.

People who go around making rules, setting standards 6 that other people are supposed to meet in order to qualify as real, are real pains in the neck—and worse, they are real threats to the rest of us. They use their own definitions of real and unreal to filter out unpleasant facts. To them, things like crime, drugs, decay, pollution, slums, et cetera, are not the real America. In the same way, they can look at a man and say he is not a real man because he doesn't give a hang about pro football and would rather chase butterflies than a golf ball; or they can look at a woman and say she is not a real woman because she drives a cab or would rather change the world than change diapers.

To say that someone is not a real man or woman is 7 to say that they are something less than, and therefore not entitled to the same consideration as, real people. Therefore, Helene, contained within the questions "What is a real man?" and "What is a real woman?" are the seeds of discrimination and of murders, big and little. Each of us has his own reality, and nobody has the right to limit or qualify that—not even English composition instructors.

Comment

Charles Osgood give us a minimum denotative definition of a "real" man and woman (p. 88), then explores connotations that some—not all—people make to these words. The dictionary does occasionally give us connotations that are widely held or even inherent in a word—objective connotations, as in the definition of *coward*. But these are usually conventional connotations, not personal or subjective ones such as Osgood writes about. In giving a minimum definition of man and woman, Osgood is using exposition for a persuasive purpose: he wants to change the way people think about men and women. He is attacking a common stereotype.

Questions for Study and Discussion

1. How does Osgood identify the audience he wants most to reach?
2. What minimum denotative definition of a "real" man or woman does he give? How does he defend this definition?
3. What other stereotypes does he attack? What do they have in common with the stereotypes of men and women?
4. What meanings does the word "real" gather as the essay builds to the concluding sentence?
5. Do you agree that "masculine" and "feminine" are not descriptive of interests and behavior—that men and women cannot be typed in this way? If not, on what do you base your disagreement?

Vocabulary Study

1. The items in the following synonym group share certain meanings with each other, but each word also has its own meanings. Use your dictionary to distinguish the two kinds of meanings. The first word in each group is used by Osgood:
   a. *idealized* (paragraph 4), romanticized
   b. *exists* (paragraph 4), lives
   c. *proclivities* (paragraph 4), preferences
   d. *discrimination* (paragraph 7), prejudice, bias
2. How many of the derogatory words given in paragraph 5 are defined in your college dictionary? What does the etymology of those given tell you about the current meaning of the word, if one is given?
3. The following words are mainly connotative in their meanings. Write definitions for two of them, distinguishing their objective from their subjective connotations—that is, the general associations that everyone makes from the special associations some people make: *cute, cool, flip, crazy, silly, flaky.*

Suggestions for Writing

Use one of the following statements as the basis for an essay of your own. You may wish to agree with the statement and illustrate it from your own experience. Or you may wish to disagree with it, providing counterexamples or ideas:

1. "People who go around making rules, setting standards that other people are supposed to meet in order to qualify as real, are real pains in the neck—and worse, they are real threats to the rest of us."
2. "They use their own definitions of real and unreal to filter out unpleasant facts."
3. "The first thing you do if you want to destroy somebody is to rob him of his humanity."
4. "Each of us has his own reality, and nobody has the right to limit or qualify that—not even English composition instructors."

Harvey and Nancy Kincaid

A LETTER ON STRIP MINING

Harvey and Nancy Kincaid lived with their seven children in Fayetteville, West Virginia, near Buffalo Creek at the time they wrote the following letter. On February 26, 1972, a dam consisting of slag from the mines and owned by a local coal company burst. The ensuing flood killed 125 people and injured many thousands; most of the victims were coal miners and members of their families. In 1971 Mrs. Kincaid had spoken about strip mining to the Congress Against Strip Mining, in Washington, D.C. Her letter was read before the West Virginia State Legislature and it helped to pass the Anti-Strip-Mining Bill. Mrs. Kincaid told an interviewer, "It used to be that the kids could keep fish, catfish, and minnows in the creeks. Now you can see the rocks in the creek where the acid has run off the mountains, off the limestone rocks. The rocks in the creek are reddish-looking, like they're rusted. There's nothing living in the creek now."

Gentlemen:

I don't believe there could be anyone that would like   1
to see the strip mines stopped any more than my husband
and myself. It just seems impossible that something like
this could happen to us twice in the past three and one
half years of time. We have been married for thirteen
years and worked real hard at having a nice home that
was ours and paid for, with a nice size lot of one acre.
Over the thirteen years, we remodeled this house a little
at a time and paid for it as we worked and did the work
mostly ourselves. The house was located about a quarter
of a mile off the road up Glenco Hollow at Kincaid, Fayette
County, West Virginia, where it used to be a nice, clean
neighborhood.

Then the strippers came four years ago with their big   2
machinery and TNT. I know that these men need jobs and
need to make a living like everyone else, but I believe there
could be a better way of getting the coal out of these
mountains. Have you ever been on a mountaintop and
looked down and seen about five different strips on one
mountain in one hollow?

My husband owns a Scout Jeep and he can get to the   3
top of the strip mines with the Scout. I would like to invite
you to come and visit us sometime and go for a ride with
us. It would make you sick to see the way the mountains
are destroyed.

First they send in the loggers to strip all the good tim-   4
ber out and then they come with their bulldozers. If their
engineers make a mistake in locating the coal they just
keep cutting away until they locate the seam of coal. When
the rains come and there isn't anything to stop the drainage, the mountains slide, and the spoil banks fall down
to the next spoil bank and so on until the whole mountain
slides. There is a small creek in the hollow and when the
spring rains come, its banks won't hold the water.

So where does it go?—into people's yards, into their   5
wells, under and into their houses. You have rocks, coal,
and a little bit of everything in your yards. When the

strippers came they started behind our house in the fall sometime before November. There was a hollow behind our house and we asked them not to bank the spoil the way they did, because we knew what would happen when the spring rains came. My father-in-law lived beside us and the property all ran together in a nice green lawn— four acres.

But the rains came in the spring and the spoil bank 6 broke and the water and debris came into our property every time it rained. It would only take a few minutes of rain and this is what we had for three years.

Then the damage comes to your house because of so 7 much dampness. The doors won't close, the foundation sinks and cracks the walls in the house, your tile comes up off your floors, your walls mold, even your clothes in our closets. Then your children stay sick with bronchial trouble, then our daughter takes pneumonia—X-rays are taken, primary T.B. shows up on the X-ray. This is in July of two years ago. About for a year this child laid sick at home. In the meantime we have already filed suit with a lawyer in Oak Hill when the water started coming in on us, but nothing happens. For three years we fight them for our property—$10,000. The lawyer settles out of court for $4,500. By the time his fee comes out and everything else we have to pay, we have under $3,000 to start over with.

So what do we have to do? Doctor's orders, move out 8 for child's sake and health. We sell for a little of nothing— not for cash, but for rent payments, take the $3,000 and buy a lot on the main highway four miles up the road toward Oak Hill.

The $3,000 goes for the lot, digging of a well and a 9 down payment on a new house. Here we are in debt for thirty years on a new home built and complete by the first of September. We moved the first part of September and was in this house *one month* and what happens? The same strip company comes up the road and puts a blast off and damages the new house—$1,400 worth. When they put one blast off that will crack the walls in your house, the foundation cracked the carport floor straight across in two places, pull a cement stoop away from the house and pull the grout out of the ceramic tile in the bathroom. This is what they can get by with.

How do they live in their $100,000 homes and have a clear mind, I'll never know. To think of the poor people who have worked hard all their lives and can't start over like we did. They have to stay in these hollows and be scared to death every time it rains. I know by experience the many nights I have stayed up and listened to the water pouring off the mountains and the rocks tumbling off the hills.

I remember one time when the strippers put a blast off up the hollow couple years ago and broke into one of the old mines that had been sealed off for 30 years. They put their blast off and left for the evening. Around seven o'clock that evening it started. We happened to look up the hollow, and thick mud—as thick as pudding—was coming down the main road in the hollow and made itself to the creek and stopped the creek up until the creek couldn't even flow.

The water was turned up into the fields where my husband keeps horses and cattle. I called the boss and told him what was happening and the danger we were in and what did he say? "There isn't anything I can do tonight. I'll be down tomorrow." I called the agriculture and they told us, whatever we did, not to go to bed that night because of the water backed up in those mines for miles.

This is just some of the things that happen around a strip mine neighborhood. But they can get by with it, unless they are stopped. Even if they are stopped it will take years for the trees and grass—what little bit they put on them—to grow enough to keep the water back and stop the slides.

Mr. and Mrs. Harvey Kincaid

Comment

The Swiss writer Henri Frédéric Amiel wrote in his journal: "Truth is the secret of eloquence and of virtue, the basis of moral authority." The Kincaid's great letter is an example of eloquence achieved through simple words that state facts plainly and exactly. Instead of reviewing the rights and wrongs of strip mining, Mr. and Mrs. Kincaid describe what happened to them and the land—in enough detail for the reader to imagine the life of people in the hollow. At the end of the letter they state the issue simply and without elaboration: "But they can get by with it, unless they are stopped."

Questions for Study and Discussion

1. The Kincaids state how their life was changed by strip mining. How do they show that their experiences were typical of people in the area?
2. Is the damage caused by strip mining the result of neglect or carelessness, or is it inherent in the process itself—given the details of the letter? Are the Kincaids mainly concerned with this question?
3. What is the central issue for them? Are they arguing against strip mining on moral grounds? Or are they concerned only with the practical consequences? What assumptions about the rights of individuals underlie their argument?
4. Are the Kincaids addressing a general or specific audience? How do you know?
5. What is the tone of the letter, and what in the letter creates it? What do the various questions asked in the letter contribute?

Vocabulary Study

Explain how the letter helps you understand the following words and phrases: *hollow, strips, spoil banks, grout, pudding.*

Suggestions for Writing

1. Write a letter protesting an activity that has changed your life in some way. Let the details of the change carry the weight of your protest.
2. Use the *New York Times Index; Social Sciences Index,* and other periodical indexes to find articles that state contrasting opinions on strip mining or a recent environmental or political issue. Analyze the assumptions and reasoning of each writer, noting similarities and differences. Then state which of the writers makes the stronger case, and why you think the writer does.

Roger Rosenblatt

THE MAN IN THE WATER

Born in 1940 in New York City, Roger Rosenblatt attended New York University and Harvard, where he later taught English. From 1973 to 1975, he was Director of Education for the National Endowment for the Humanities, and from 1975 to 1978 was the literary editor of *New Republic.* He is at present Editor at Large of *Life* magazine, and he is often heard on the NPR *McNeil-Lehrer Report.* Rosenblatt has published essays in numerous periodicals, and is the author of *Black Fiction* (1974). His essay on an airplane crash in Washington, D.C., in the winter of 1982, shows his gift for stating in simple language important truths about contemporary events.

As disasters go, this one was terrible, but not unique 1 certainly not among the worst on the roster of U.S. air crashes. There was the unusual element of the bridge, of course, and the fact that the plane clipped it at a moment of high traffic, one routine thus intersecting another and disrupting both. Then, too, there was the location of the event. Washington, the city of form and regulations, turned chaotic, deregulated, by a blast of real winter and a single slap of metal on metal. The jets from Washington National Airport that normally swoop around the presidential monuments like famished gulls are, for the moment, emblemized by the one that fell; so there is that detail. And there was the aesthetic clash as well—blue-and-green Air Florida, the name a flying garden, sunk down among gray chunks in a black river. All that was worth noticing, to be sure. Still, there was nothing very special in any of it, except death, which, while always special, does not necessarily bring millions to tears or to attention. Why, then, the shock here?

Perhaps because the nation saw in this disaster something more than a mechanical failure. Perhaps because people saw in it no failure at all, but rather something successful about their makeup. Here, after all were two forms of nature in collision: the elements and human character. Last Wednesday, the elements, indifferent as ever, brought down Flight 90. And on that same afternoon, human nature—groping and flailing in mysteries of its own—rose to the occasion.

Of the four acknowledged heroes of the event, three are able to account for their behavior. Donald Usher and Eugene Windsor, a park police helicopter team, risked their lives every time they dipped the skids into the water to pick up survivors. On television, side by side in bright blue jumpsuits, they described their courage as all in the line of duty. Lenny Skutnik, a 28-year-old employee of the Congressional Budget Office, said: "It's something I never thought I would do"—referring to his jumping into the water to drag an injured woman to shore. Skutnik added that "somebody had to go in the water," delivering every hero's line that is no less admirable for its repetitions. In fact, nobody had to go into the water. That somebody actually did so is part of the reason this particular tragedy sticks in the mind.

But the person most responsible for the emotional impact of the disaster is the one known at first simply as "the man in the water." (Balding, probably in his 50s, an extravagant mustache.) He was seen clinging with five other survivors to the tail section of the airplane. This man was described by Usher and Windsor as appearing alert and in control. Every time they lowered a lifeline and flotation ring to him, he passed it on to another of the passengers. "In a mass casualty, you'll find people like him," said Windsor. "But I've never seen one with that commitment." When the helicopter came back for him, the man had gone under. His selflessness was one reason the story held national attention; his anonymity another. The fact that he went unidentified invested him with a universal character. For a while he was Everyman, and thus proof (as if one needed it) that no man is ordinary.

Still, he could never have imagined such a capacity in   5 himself. Only minutes before his character was tested, he was sitting in the ordinary plane among the ordinary passengers, dutifully listening to the stewardess telling him to fasten his seat belt and saying something about the "no smoking sign." So our man relaxed with the others, some of whom would owe their lives to him. Perhaps he started to read, or to doze, or to regret some harsh remark made in the office that morning. Then suddenly he knew that the trip would not be ordinary. Like every other person on that flight, he was desperate to live, which makes his final act so stunning.

For at some moment in the water he must have rea-   6 lized that he would not live if he continued to hand over the rope and ring to others. He *had* to know it, no matter how gradual the effect of the cold. In his judgment he had no choice. When the helicopter took off with what was to be the last survivor, he watched everything in the world move away from him, and he deliberately let it happen.

Yet there was something else about our man that kept   7 our thoughts on him, and which keeps our thoughts on him still. He was *there*, in the essential, classic circumstance. Man in nature. The man in the water. For its part, nature cared nothing about the five passengers. Our man, on the other hand, cared totally. So the timeless battle commenced in the Potomac. For as long as that man could last, they went at each other, nature and man; the one making no distinctions of good and evil, acting on no principles, offering no lifelines; the other acting wholly on distinctions, principles and, one supposes, on faith.

Since it was he who lost the fight, we ought to come again to the conclusion that people are powerless in the world. In reality, we believe the reverse, and it takes the act of the man in the water to remind us of our true feelings in this matter. It is not to say that everyone would have acted as he did, or as Usher, Windsor and Skutnik. Yet whatever moved these men to challenge death on behalf of their fellows is not peculiar to them. Everyone feels the possibility in himself. That is the abiding wonder of the story. That is why we would not let go of it. If the man in the water gave a lifeline to the people gasping for survival, he was likewise giving a lifeline to those who observed him. 8

The odd thing is that we do not even really believe that the man in the water lost his fight. "Everything in Nature contains all the powers of Nature," said Emerson. Exactly. So the man in the water had his own natural powers. He could not make ice storms, or freeze the water until it froze the blood. But he could hand life over to a stranger, and that is a power of nature too. The man in the water pitted himself against an implacable, impersonal enemy; he fought it with charity; and he held it to a standoff. He was the best we can do. 9

Comment

The Air Florida crash described occurred in Washington, D.C., on January 14, 1982, during the evening rush hour at a crowded bridge over the Potomac River. The event received wide coverage because of these circumstances and extraordinary acts of heroism performed. Rosenblatt is doing more than describing these events: he wishes to persuade readers of an important truth. To do so, he must persuade them that the acts of the man in the water were indeed heroic, and much of his discussion toward the end of the essay is given to this point. Notice how appropriate the simple, direct style is to the subject and ideas of the essay. Rosenblatt presents the facts without overdramatizing them through colorful language. All the same, his simplicity of language is eloquent enough to bring the essay to a fitting emotional pitch:

> So the man in the water had his own natural powers. He could not make ice storms, or freeze the water until it froze the blood. But he could hand life over to a stranger, and that is a power of nature too.

Questions for Study and Discussion

1. Rosenblatt does not give us all the facts of the crash. What facts does he present, and what aspects does he emphasize?
2. Is Rosenblatt writing only to those readers familiar with the circumstances of the crash, or is he also providing information for those unfamiliar with what happened?
3. Rosenblatt builds from the details of the crash to reflections about it. In what order are these details presented? Is Rosenblatt describing the events in the order they occurred?
4. How does he explain the heroism of the man in the water, the helicopter police, and Larry Skutnik?
5. Rosenblatt builds to his thesis, instead of stating it toward the beginning of the essay. What is his thesis, and what is gained by building to it? Do you agree with it?

Vocabulary Study

1. How does the context of the final sentence in paragraph 4 help us to understand the reference to Everyman?
2. In what sense is Rosenblatt using the word *classic* in paragraph 7?
3. Does the word *power* have more than one meaning in paragraph 9?

Suggestions for Writing

1. Explain the following sentence in light of the whole essay: "If the man in the water gave a lifeline to the people gasping for survival, he was likewise giving a lifeline to those who observed him."
2. Explain the statement of Emerson, "Everything in Nature contains all the powers of Nature," in light of the final paragraph. Then illustrate it from your own experience.
3. First state the conception of heroism Rosenblatt presents in the essay. Then discuss the extent to which this conception fits an act of heroism you have observed, or accords with your idea of what makes a person heroic.
4. Discuss a recent event that taught you an important truth about people or life. Describe the event for readers unfamiliar with it, and build to your thesis as Rosenblatt does.

Controversy

Much of our persuasive writing is directed to specific issues of the day and usually to specific audiences—perhaps a person or group with whom we disagree. The controversy or question at issue usually defines the specific matters to be addressed. In the debate over the federal deficit in the fall of 1990, the Administration and Congress agreed that reduction of the enormous federal deficit is essential. How to reduce it required discussion of a number of controversial issues, including an increase in excise taxes, reduction of the capital gains tax, and an increase in taxes for people of high income. Vigorous national debate and numerous proposals from those in government as well as the general public assured that these issues would be discussed.

But what should be the chief focus or point at issue in the debate was a major topic of discussion. For some the point to be debated was increase in taxes; for others, a decrease in government spending. Much of the debate centered on the point at issue—on what was to be argued and negotiated. The debate in the fall of 1990 resembles that of our own arguments with friends on particular issues. We may agree that measures must be taken to reduce crime or protect the environment, but we may not agree on what measures deserve discussion.

Participants in debates usually find it necessary to define the central point at issue, and in addition the terms to be used in the argument (defining human life is a central issue in the debate over abortion). In the course of debate, assumptions need to be identified and defended. The appeal to experience and other kinds of evidence may also be controversial. Experimental and statistical evidence considered reliable by one participant may be considered unreliable by another, as in the debate over the effects of smoking. Indeed, debate often centers on the relevance of a particular kind of evidence.

In writing a persuasive essay, you will want to anticipate the view of opponents on the matters just discussed. You will need to defend the point at issue as you see it, as well as the kind of evidence you intend to present (you may need to argue that statistical evidence of public attitudes has bearing on the issue—or has no bearing). If you know that agreement exists on the point of issue or relevant evidence, you may decide to devote most of your essay to the issue itself. In writing a persuasive essay, as in writing other kinds of papers, making an estimate of your audience is essential.

Meg Greenfield

IN DEFENSE OF ANIMALS

Meg Greenfield graduated from Smith College in 1952, and afterward studied as a Fulbright scholar at Cambridge University in England, again at Smith College, and at Georgetown University. Her career as a journalist began with *The Reporter* magazine; her association with the *Washington Post* began in 1968, and since 1979 she has been editor of the editorial page. Greenfield also writes a regular column in *Newsweek*, in which the following essay on the use of animals in experiments appeared on April 17, 1989.

I might as well come right out with it: contrary to some of my most cherished prejudices, the animal-rights people have begun to get to me. I think that in some part of what they say they are right.

I never thought it would come to this. As distinct from the old-style animal rescue, protection and shelter organizations, the more aggressive newcomers, with their "liberation" of laboratory animals and periodic championship of the claims of animal well-being over human well-being when a choice must be made, have earned a reputation in the world I live in as fanatics and just plain kooks. And even with my own recently (relatively) raised consciousness, there remains a good deal in both their critique and their prescription for the virtuous life that I reject, being not just a practicing carnivore, a wearer of shoe leather and so forth, but also a supporter of certain indisputably agonizing procedures visited upon innocent animals in the furtherance of human welfare, especially experiments undertaken to improve human health.

So, viewed from the pure position, I am probably only 3 marginally better than the worst of my kind, if that: I don't buy the complete "speciesist" analysis or even the fundamental language of animal "rights" and continue to find a large part of what is done in the name of that cause harmful and extreme. But I also think, patronizing as it must sound, that the zealots are required early on in any movement if it is to succeed in altering the sensibility of the leaden masses, such as me. Eventually they get your attention. And eventually you at least feel obliged to weigh their arguments and think about whether there may not be something there.

It is true that this end has often been achieved—as in 4 my case—by means of vivid, cringe-inducing photographs, not by an appeal to reason or values so much as by an assault on squeamishness. From the famous 1970s photo of the newly skinned baby seal to the videos of animals being raised in the most dark, miserable, stunting environment as they are readied for their life's sole fulfillment as frozen patties and cutlets, these sights have had their effect. But we live in a world where the animal protein we eat comes discreetly prebutchered and prepacked so the original beast and his slaughtering are remote from our consideration, just as our furs come on coat hangers in salons, not on their original proprietors; and I see nothing wrong with our having to contemplate the often unsettling reality of how we came by the animal products we make use of. Then we can choose what we want to do.

The objection to our being confronted with these dra- 5 matic, disturbing pictures is first that they tend to provoke a misplaced, uncritical and highly emotional concern for animal life at the direct expense of a more suitable concern for human suffering. What goes into the animals' account, the reasoning goes, necessarily comes out of ours.

But I think it is possible to remain stalwart in your view that the human claim comes first and in your acceptance of the use of animals for human betterment and *still* to believe that there are some human interests that should not take precedence. For we have become far too self-indulgent, hardened, careless and cruel in the pain we routinely inflict upon these creatures for the most frivolous, unworthy purposes. And I also think that the more justifiable purposes, such as medical research, are shamelessly used as cover for other activities that are wanton.

For instance, not all of the painful and crippling experi-   6
mentation that is undertaken in the lab is being conducted for the sake of medical knowledge or other purposes related to basic human well-being and health. Much of it is being conducted for the sake of superrefinements in the cosmetic and other frill industries, the noble goal being to contrive yet another fragrance or hair tint or commercially competitive variation on all the daft, fizzy, multicolored "personal care" products for the medicine cabinet and dressing table, a firmer-holding hair spray, that sort of thing. In other words, the conscripted, immobilized rabbits and other terrified creatures, who have been locked in boxes from the neck down, only their heads on view, are being sprayed in the eyes with different burning, stinging substances for the sake of adding to our already obscene store of luxuries and utterly superfluous vanity items.

Oddly, we tend to be very sentimental about animals   7
in their idealized, fictional form, and largely indifferent to them in realms where our lives actually touch. From time immemorial, humans have romantically attributed to animals their own sensibilities—from Balaam's Biblical ass who providently could speak and who got his owner out of harm's way right down to Lassie and the other Hollywood pups who would invariably tip off the good guys that the bad guys were up to something. So we simulate phony cross-species kinship, pretty well drown in the cuteness of it all—Mickey and Minnie and Porky—and ignore, if we don't actually countenance, the brutish things done in the name of Almighty Hair Spray.

This strikes me as decadent. My problem is that it also causes me to reach a position that is, on its face philo- sophically vulnerable, if not absurd—the muddled, mid- dling, inconsistent place where finally you are saying it's all right to kill them for some purposes, but not to hurt them gratuitously in doing it or to make them suffer hor- ribly for one's own trivial whims.

I would feel more humiliated to have fetched up on this exposed rock, if I didn't suspect I had so much com- pany. When you see pictures of people laboriously trying to clean the Exxon gunk off of sea otters even knowing that they will only be able to help out a very few, you see this same outlook in action. And I think it *can* be defended. For to me the biggest cop-out is the one that says that if you don't buy the whole absolutist, extreme position it is pointless and even hypocritical to concern yourself with lesser mercies and ameliorations. The pres- sure of the animal-protection groups has already had some impact in improving the way various creatures are treated by researchers, trainers and food producers. There is much more in this vein to be done. We are talking about reject- ing wanton, pointless cruelty here. The position may be philosophically absurd, but the outcome is the right one.

Comment

Meg Greenfield devotes several paragraphs to defining the point at issue for her in the debate over animal rights. In doing so, she explains how she reached her position and states her view of the animal rights movement and its rhetoric or means of per- suasion. Greenfield might have devoted most of her defense to the experiments that concern her; instead she devotes most of her essay to the animal rights movements because the move- ment and its rhetoric present Greenfield (and possibly her readers) with a dilemma. Greenfield builds up to this dilemma in the concluding paragraphs, stating it and then discussing how to resolve it. Among the ways of resolving a dilemma, the most common are "seizing the horns" (the sharply opposed, exclusive alternatives) and "going between the horns." In "seizing the horns," the debater shows that one of the alternatives is false as stated; in "going between the horns," the debater shows that a better alternative exists to those presented. Greenfield uses one of these techniques to resolve her dilemma. (A less common but effective technique is to present a counterdilemma.)

Questions for Study and Discussion

1. What prompted Greenfield to consider the argument in favor of animal rights? What attitudes and practices originally led her to be indifferent or skeptical?
2. What in the argument and rhetoric of the animal rights movement does Greenfield reject? What has she come to accept, and why?
3. In paragraph 8 Greenfield states the dilemma that she faced in thinking about animal rights. What is that dilemma, and how do paragraphs 2–7 explain how she came to face it? How does Greenfield resolve the dilemma?
4. What audience is Greenfield addressing in the essay? Is she talking directly to the animal rights movement, to its opponents, or to both? Or is she addressing readers who have been indifferent to the issue, or skeptical of arguments for and against animal rights?

Vocabulary Study

Explain the following words and phrases:

1. *critique, prescription, carnivore* (paragraph 2)
2. *zealots* (paragraph 3)
3. *squeamishness, proprietors* (paragraph 4)
4. *stalwart, wanton* (paragraph 5)
5. *simulate, cross-species kinship* (paragraph 7)
6. *muddled, middling, gratuitously* (paragraph 8)
7. *cop-out, absolutist, ameliorations* (paragraph 9)

Suggestion for Writing

Using the *Essay Index, Readers' Guide to Periodical Literature, Social Sciences Index*, and other indexes and reference guides, locate an article that argues against animal research. Write an essay comparing the article with Greenfield's essay, giving attention to the following:

1. Statement and defense of the point at issue
2. Nature of the arguments opposing animal research
3. Persuasive devices used by each writer
4. Introduction of opposing arguments and response to them

Ron Karpati

A SCIENTIST: "I AM THE ENEMY"

A practicing physician, Ron Karpati writes about animal research from the point of view of a pediatrician concerned with immunological research. Karpati calls attention to the benefits of research to children, but he is also concerned with benefits to people of all ages. His essay on animal research appeared in *Newsweek* on December 18, 1989.

I am the enemy! One of those vilified, inhumane physician-scientists involved in animal research. How strange, for I have never thought of myself as an evil person. I became a pediatrician because of my love for children and my desire to keep them healthy. During medical school and residency, however, I saw many children die of leukemia, prematurity and traumatic injury—circumstances against which medicine has made tremendous progress, but still has far to go. More important, I also saw children, alive and healthy, thanks to advances in medical science such as infant respirators, potent antibiotics, new surgical techniques and the entire field of organ transplantation. My desire to tip the scales in favor of the healthy, happy children drew me to medical research.

My accusers claim that I inflict torture on animals for   2
the sole purpose of career advancement. My experiments
supposedly have no relevance to medicine and are easily
replaced by computer simulation. Meanwhile, an apathetic
public barely watches, convinced that the issue has no
significance, and publicity-conscious politicians increasingly
give way to the demands of the activists.

We in medical reserach have also been unconscionably   3
apathetic. We have allowed the most extreme animal-rights
protesters to seize the initiative and frame the issue as one
of "animal fraud." We have been complacent in our belief
that a knowledgeable public would sense the importance
of animal research to the public health. Perhaps we have
been mistaken in not responding to the emotional tone
of the argument created by those sad posters of animals
by waving equally sad posters of children dying of
leukemia or cystic fibrosis.

Much is made of the pain inflicted on these animals   4
in the name of medical science. The animal-rights activists
contend that this is evidence of our malevolent and sadistic
nature. A more reasonable argument, however, can be
advanced in our defense. Life is often cruel, both to animals and human beings. Teenagers get thrown from the
back of a pickup truck and suffer severe head injuries. Tod-
dlers, barely able to walk, find themselves at the bottom
of a swimming pool while a parent checks the mail. Physicians hoping to alleviate the pain and suffering these
tragedies cause have but three choices: create an animal
model of the injury or disease and use that model to
understand the process and test new therapies; experiment
on human beings—some experiments will succeed, most
will fail—or finally, leave medical knowledge static, hoping that accidental discoveries will lead us to the advances.

Some animal-rights activists would suggest a fourth   5
choice, claiming that computer models can simulate animal
experiments, thus making the actual experiments unnecessary. Computers can simulate, reasonably well, the effects
of well-understood principles on complex systems, as in
the application of the laws of physics to airplane and

automobile design. However, when the principles themselves are in question, as is the case with the complex
biological systems under study, computer modeling alone
is of little value.

One of the terrifying effects of the effort to restrict the 6
use of animals in medical research is that the impact will
not be felt for years and decades: drugs that might have
been discovered will not be; surgical techniques that might
have been developed will not be; and fundamental biological processes that might have been understood will
remain mysteries. There is the danger that politically ex-
pedient solutions will be found to placate a vocal minority, while the consequences of those decisions will not be
apparent until long after the decisions are made and the
decision makers forgotten.

Fortunately, most of us enjoy good health, and the 7
trauma of watching one's child die has become a rare experience. Yet our good fortune should not make us unap-
preciative of the health we enjoy or the advances that make
it possible. Vaccines, antibiotics, insulin and drugs to treat
heart disease, hypertension and stroke are all based on
animal research. Most complex surgical procedures, such
as coronary-artery bypass and organ transplantation, are
initially developed in animals. Presently undergoing animal
studies are techniques to insert genes in humans in order
to replace the defective ones found to be the cause of so
much disease. These studies will effectively end if animal
research is severely restricted.

In America today, death has become an event isolated 8
from our daily existence—out of the sight and thoughts
of most of us. As a doctor who has watched many children
die, and their parents grieve, I am particularly angered by
people capable of so much compassion for a dog or a cat,
but with seemingly so little for a dying human being.
These people seem so insulated from the reality of human
life and death and what it means.

Make no mistake, however: I am not advocating the 9
needlessly cruel treatment of animals. To the extent that
the animal-rights movement has made us more aware of

the needs of these animals, and made us search harder for suitable alternatives, they have made a significant contribution. But if the more radical members of this movement are successful in limiting further research, their efforts will bring about a tragedy that will cost many lives. The real question is whether an apathetic majority can be aroused to protect its future against a vocal, but misdirected, minority.

Comment

Like Meg Greenfield, Ron Karpati devotes a major part of his essay to defining the point at issue in the debate over animal research. And like Greenfield, he is also concerned with finding points of agreement with his opponents, for he knows that working out a solution depends on finding a common ground. To persuade his audience, Karpati draws on his own experience as a physician and researcher. This rational appeal is one of the three that the Greek philosopher Aristotle identified in persuasive discourse. The other two are the appeal to emotion and the ethical appeal that invites the reader to recognize that the speaker or writer is a person of good character and is arguing for good motives. The appeals that Karpati makes to the reader seek to make his essay persuasive.

Questions for Study and Discussion

1. How does Karpati define the point at issue in the debate over animal rights? Where does he restate it in the course of the essay?
2. What arguments in opposition to animal research does Karpati reject? How does he answer these opponents? How varied is the evidence he presents in support of animal research?
3. In what order does he introduce opposing arguments and his responses to them?

4. Where does Karpati state his main point or thesis? How does he give it emphasis?
5. What appeals does he make in seeking to persuade his readers?

Vocabulary Study

Explain the following words and phrases:

1. *vilified, leukemia, prematurity, traumatic injury* (paragraph 1)
2. *apathetic, computer simulation* (paragraph 2)
3. *cystic fibrosis* (paragraph 3)
4. *malevolent, sadistic, alleviate* (paragraph 4)
5. *placate* (paragraph 6)
6. *coronary-artery bypass* (paragraph 7)
7. *radical* (paragraph 9)

Suggestions for Writing

1. Extend your investigation of the debate over animal research (p. 388) by finding and analyzing additional articles pro and con. On the basis of this limited investigation, discuss points of agreement on which the issue might be conciliated or resolved. Take note also of differences that make conciliation and resolution difficult.
2. State your own views on animal research, explaining why you hold them, and responding to the arguments of Greenfield or Karpati or both.

James C. Puffer

N.C.A.A. PLAN IS DETERRENT

A member of the Division of Family Medicine at U.C.L.A. Medical Center, Dr. James C. Puffer is head physician of the U.S. Summer Olympic Team and chairperson of the National Collegiate Athletic Association (N.C.A.A.) Competitive Safeguards Committee. His argument in favor of collegiate drug testing is based on his experience with safety and health in intercollegiate athletic programs.

The untimely deaths of Len Bias and Don Rogers two   1
years ago focused our attention on the tragic role that substance abuse plays in the lives of performing athletes. The tremendous pressures placed upon them to perform to expectations that are often unrealistic have created circumstances in which athletes frequently turn to drug use either to escape from these pressures or to enhance performance. In fact, the widespread use of performance-enhancing drugs has perhaps become the single most important threat to the integrity of amateur and professional sport.

The use of drugs to enhance performance is not a   2
recent phenomenon. The writings of Homer documented ingestion of mushrooms by Greek athletes in the third century B.C. during the ancient Olympic Games. In the 19th century there were reports of widespread use of caffeine, alcohol, nitroglycerin, ethyl ether and opium by European athletes.

However, it was not until the death of Kurt Enemar   3
Jensen, a Danish cyclist, at the 1960 Summer Olympic Games in Rome that considerable attention was focused on this mounting problem. Jensen and two of his teammates had taken amphetamines in an attempt to improve their performance in the 100-kilometer team cycling trials and this helped contribute to Jensen's death. These events motivated the International Olympic Committee to begin

to question the integrity of games in which athletes were using artifical substances in an effort to enhance performance.

The rest is well known. The International Olympic   4 Committee instituted drug testing in the 1968 Olympics in both Grenoble and Mexico City and has tested for drugs since that time. For a time, drug testing remained a phenomenon that was predominantly limited to international events such as the Olympic Games and world championships. However, in the past several years drug testing has become widespread and is used by both the National Collegiate Athletic Association and numerous member institutions in an attempt to stem the increasing use of drugs by athletes.

The N.C.A.A. has just reported that 1.3 percent of the   5 1,589 athletes who were tested at championship events last fall tested positive for banned substances. This was a slight increase over the 1 percent of the 3,360 who tested positive in the 1986–87 academic year. Given the seemingly small number of positive tests, why would any organization or institution wish to invest the tremendous amount of financial and human resources necessary to conduct an exemplary drug testing program? In order to understand the reasoning, it is essential to understand the notion that drug testing is an adjunctive tool that is used to deter drug use. The low number of positive samples speaks to the positive effect that testing has had.

Is drug testing indeed a deterrent to drug use? It   6 would appear that it is. Reports from certified laboratories at which drug testing is performed indicate that when testing is voluntary and nonpunitive, as many as 50 percent of the samples may be positive. The institution of mandatory drug testing at N.C.A.A. championship events two years ago has had a profound effect on significantly reducing the use of injectable anabolic steroids by college athletes. This is based on the fact that a recent N.C.A.A. survey indicated that approximately 8 percent of college athletes admitted to using steroids. The performance of athletes in certain weight events in last year's N.C.A.A. track and field championships were far below those from the previous year, further testimony that drug testing can have a dramatic effect on the final results.

Many argue that while testing is an effective deterrent in the use of certain types of drugs, it nevertheless violates the personal rights of individual athletes as well as presumes guilt. It is important to note that six court cases have been brought against either the N.C.A.A. or its member institutions in the past year and a half in an attempt to resolve this issue. The cases have yet to resolve the issue satisfactorily.   7

While the preliminary results from one hearing would indicate that, in fact, drug testing may violate some of the personal rights of athletes in the state of California, others have determined that drug testing may not be an unreasonable condition of participation in intercollegiate athletics. If one appreciates the notion that drug testing is, in fact, a deterrent to drug use, and its sole purpose is to prevent athletes from using banned substances altogether, one can certainly dismiss the notion of presumptive guilt; it is the explicit intent of drug testing programs to find no positive samples if indeed the program is successful.   8

Finally, some comment must be made about the attitudes of the athletes who undergo drug testing. Numerous surveys on college campuses that conduct their own testing programs have shown that the overwhelming majority of athletes favor drug testing. They think that it guarantees the opportunity to participate in a drug-free environment and provides a valuable crutch that allows them to say no to drugs. This fact has been repeatedly demonstrated by the decreasing use of drugs by college athletes as documented by drug testing at these institutions since the inception of their programs.   9

Even though testing is far from totally eradicating drug use by college athletes, when used in conjunction with a sound drug education program, it serves as the best   10 method for deterring drug use. Until better means become available, drug testing remains our best option in guaranteeing the safety and well-being of athletes who participate in sport.

Comment

Essays that debate an issue often use an organization that originated in the legal orations of the ancient Greeks. This kind of persuasive essay usually contains the following:

1. An *introduction* that states the topic of the paper and seeks to generate interest in the proposal at issue;
2. The *background* or essential facts of the case, called the *narrative*;
3. A statement of the *thesis*, often following the narrative;
4. Arguments in support of the thesis, called the *confirmation*;
5. *Refutation* of opposing arguments; and
6. A *conclusion* that may restate the thesis, summarize the supporting arguments and evidence, and ask the audience to accept the argument.

Some writers combine supporting arguments with the refutation, making a case for the proposal in the course of answering objections to it.

James C. Puffer's argument in support of drug testing does the latter. Puffer introduces his main topic—the threat of performance-enhancing drugs—by reminding us of recent drug-related deaths of prominent collegiate athletes and the death of a bicyclist at the Olympic Games in Rome in 1960. This background leads into a statement of the central thesis (paragraph 5). Following a brief defense of his thesis (paragraph 6), Puffer turns to his main argument in support of drug testing—deterrence (paragraph 7). In the remaining paragraphs, Puffer makes his case for drug testing in the course of answering objections to the procedure. He concludes with a restatement of his thesis. This type of organization presents the argument in an economical and effective way.

Questions for Study and Discussion

1. How does Puffer establish the importance of the subject in his opening paragraphs?

2. What is his thesis, and how does Puffer defend it following its introduction in paragraph 5? What does he gain by defending drug testing in the course of answering objections to it?

3. What are the objections to drug testing, and how does Puffer answer them? What kind of evidence does he present in this refutation?

4. Why does Puffer conclude with the opinons of college athletes? Is he concluding with the strongest evidence in favor of drug testing? If a majority of college athletes opposed drug testing, would Puffer consider his argument to be weakened or refuted?

5. To what audience is Puffer addressing his argument? Is he writing to a special audience—specifically, those opposed to drug testing? Or is he writing to a general audience—to people who hold various opinions on drug testing or none? How do you know?

Vocabulary Study

Explain the following words and phrases:

1. *performance-enhancing* (paragraph 1)
2. *ingestion, amphetamines* (paragraph 3)
3. *adjunctive tool* (paragraph 5)
4. *anabolic steroids* (paragraph 6)
5. *presumptive guilt* (paragraph 8)

Suggestions for Writing

1. Write a persuasive essay on a current issue, using the form of argument outlined above. Address those people who hold opinions opposite to yours. You may wish to combine the arguments supporting your thesis with your refutation of opposing arguments, or you may wish to separate them. Make your thesis prominent by stating it in key places in the essay, as Puffer does.

2. Rewrite your persuasive essay, addressing it to a general audience—to people who hold various opinions on the issue. Present your supporting arguments and your refutation of opponents in an order best able to convince your audience.

Allen L. Sack

RANDOM TESTS ABUSE DIGNITY

Allen L. Sack, chairman of the Honors program at the University of New Haven, writes in opposition to the N.C.A.A. policy, defended by James C. Puffer in his essay on drug testing. Puffer's and Sack's essays appeared together in *The New York Times* on May 29, 1988.

Nothing better illustrates the low regard that the National Collegiate Athletic Association has often had for the rights of student-athletes than its random drug-testing policy. There are a number of alternatives for addressing the problem of substance abuse. Unfortunately, the N.C.A.A. chooses an approach that protects the public-relations image of its member institutions but shows little or no concern for the dignity and privacy of the vast majority of hard-working young athletes who are drug-free.

Random drug-testing treats all athletes like suspected criminals when there is no probable cause for doing so, and it expects them to surrender rights docilely that are the cornerstone of American democracy. Most disturbing is the fact that this policy was approved without even the slightest consultation with the athletes themselves.

The actual procedure for gathering urine samples from randomly selected athletes is precisely spelled out in N.C.A.A. documents. Immediately following participation in a championship event, student-athletes are selected for drug-testing, and are instructed to report to a urine-collection station within one hour. At the collection station, what the N.C.A.A. calls a "urine validator" monitors the furnishing of the specimen.

Judge Conrad L. Rushing of the Superior Court of 4 California describes the process graphically. "Under the N.C.A.A. program last year, Jennifer Hill was accompanied to a doorless bathroom stall by the monitor, who stood a few feet away and watched while Hill removed her shorts and undergarments . . . and urinated into a beaker."

Why should an athlete who has exhibited no behavior 5 that would give rise to suspicion of illegal activity have to submit to this sort of humiliation, inconvenience, and violation of privacy? Why should athletes who only an hour before may have participated in the greatest athletic event of their careers have to agree to be herded like cattle into a urine-collection station and to be treated like common criminals?

One way to justify the extreme diminution of Fourth 6 Amendment rights implicit in a search without probable cause is to argue that random drug testing of college athletes is crucial to public safety. Few people oppose the kinds of general searches that are carried out at airports while passengers are preparing to board planes. The fact that it is impossible to tell from the outside whether a person is carrying a weapon and the fact that weapons carried illegally onto a plane could take the lives of hundreds of passengers seem like fairly strong justifications for performing searches without reasonable suspicion of a particular individual. In a similar vein, there may be compelling reasons for performing random drug tests on airline pilots and nuclear power operators.

The case for testing college athletes without probable 7 cause seems far less compelling. It is difficult to argue that athletes hold positions of responsibility analogous to those of pilots or air-traffic controllers. There is little doubt that athletes serve as role models for millions of young people. But no one can seriously believe that isolated instances of drug use by college athletes have been a major cause of the rampant substance abuse that plagues this nation.

Tragic incidents such as the death of Len Bias of Maryland of a drug overdose can have a devastating effect on a university's public image, but a concern with preventing bad publicity does not justify an assault on the Bill of Rights. Subjecting all athletes to random testing when other less intrusive methods for fighting substance abuse exist seems like the kind of policy the framers of the United States Constitution would have opposed.

It is not my intention here to cover the many complex 8 constitutional issues surrounding random drug testing. My argument is simple. The vast, vast majority of college athletes are good, decent, dedicated and drug-free. If the N.C.A.A. had respected these athletes as students and as sensitive human beings, random drug testing would have been instituted only as a last resort, and even then, only after encouraging athletes to consider the constitutional issues involved.

Efforts to fight substance abuse in college sports must 9 be concerned with more than keeping athletes drug-free in the short-term. The goal should be to help athletes understand the role that drugs play in our society and to prepare them to fight drug abuse throughout their lives. The N.C.A.A. should take the hundreds of thousands of dollars that are going into random drug testing and undertake a massive program in drug education. Drug education should be an integral part of every athletic department curriculum, and should consist of far more than a couple of talks by prominent athletes.

Drug education should extend to coaches and others 10 who work closely with athletes. Coaches should be taught the symptoms of substance abuse so that they can refer athletes for counseling and treatment. They should also be able (in conjunction with a team physician and the athletic director) to insist that an athlete submit to a drug test if there is some observance of suspicious activity. Athletes who abuse drugs should be subject to strict disciplinary action. Repeat offenders should lose athletic eligibility.

Drug education and drug testing based on probable 11 cause will probably not be as effective in deterring short-term substance abuse as having random drug-testing programs at every university in the country. It should be noted however that a democratic society has to be concerned with more than deterrence. There is no doubt in my mind that certain types of crime could be substantially reduced if the police could ignore large segments of the Constitution. The case of Nazi Germany offers considerable proof that searching people's property and their persons without probable cause can be an effective deterrent. But the price that is exacted is a wholesale assault on human dignity and personal freedom. Such measures have little place in a democracy, and they clearly cannot be justified in college sport.

Comment

Sack summarizes his argument against random drug testing and presents the background of the issue (paragraphs 1–5); then states arguments in support of the N.C.A.A. policy and refutes them (paragraphs 6–7). In his concluding paragraphs, he restates his thesis, makes recommendations, and presents a final argument in opposition to the policy. Sack points out that, in a brief argument on the issue, he cannot explore all of the complex issues related to drug testing. But he can establish the point at issue in drug testing and argue that point as fully as space permits.

Questions for Study and Discussion

1. Sack states his general topic in his opening sentence—the "low regard" for students revealed in the N.C.A.A. policy; then summarizes the faults of the policy. What are these faults, and in what order does Sack present them in paragraphs 1 and 2?

2. Sack argues that the N.C.A.A. humiliates the student athlete and gives an example of such humiliation in paragraph 4. If an alternate procedure that did not humiliate the student could be established, would Sack be less opposed to random drug testing?

3. What analogy in support of the N.C.A.A. policy does Sack criticize?
4. What additional evidence does Sack present for his thesis in his concluding paragraph? Why does he save this evidence for the end of the essay?
5. Is Sack addressing a special audience or a general one (see p. 402)? How do you know?
6. Do you agree in whole or in part with Sack on random drug testing? Or do you disagree completely? Have you other reasons for supporting or opposing the N.C.A.A. policy?

Suggestions for Writing

1. In an essay on the issue of drug testing, state your own opinion, citing observations you have made, personal beliefs, your reasons for agreeing or disagreeing with Puffer and Sack. You might introduce the ideas of Puffer and Sack in your opening paragraphs, as part of your background or narrative. Or you might save mention of Puffer and Sack until your statement of your position and your refutation of opposing views.
2. Compare the kind of arguments present in the essays of Puffer and Sack on drug testing. Note any similarities or differences in the evidence they present. Does either writer argue from fundamental beliefs or assumptions from which they draw direct conclusions and perhaps illustrate these? Does either argue from well-founded opinion or judgments based on particulars of experience, analogy, causes and effects—inductive evidence that leads to a probable conclusion?

PART 5

Effective Sentences and Diction

> Doris's hat tumbles off. She does not realize it is gone, which is not surprising, since hats are as foreign to these girls as bustles or U.S. army fatiques would be.
>
> — Frank Deford

The sentences we speak and write derive from sentences we hear and read from day to day. The same is true of the words we use. We adopt new words and new turns of phrase and ways of giving ideas emphasis usually without realizing we have done so. And usually the change is slight, for habits of speech and writing are established early and are not easy to change. Adopting new words is, however, easier for us than adopting new sentence patterns.

How conscious we are of language depends on the formality of the speaking or writing situation. Each of us has an informal and a formal way of speaking—each appropriate to different occasions, each expressive and useful. We make adjustments in our spoken language usually without realizing we are doing so. Writing calls for more deliberate choice, particularly in tightening sentences that derive from our informal speech.

The following is a transcription of spoken English:

> In the minor leagues we spent a lot of hours riding in buses, and they were so hot and you didn't have too many stops to eat. You ate poorly because you had bad meal money. We got $1.50 a day. But you were young. When I was with a class B league, I got a long distance call. My wife went to the hospital in labor. It was the first baby. I had to get home. The ticket was forty-some dollars. We didn't have it between us—the manager, everybody. I got there a day late.   —Studs Terkel, *Working*

These informal sentences are expressive despite the loose organization and the looseness of the first sentence and the fragmented sound of the short sentences that follow. Informal writing usually follows the same loose patterns of speech and uses familiar phrases, colloquial words, and contracted words:

> The excitement of the rodeo comes not so much from the competition between the cowboys themselves as from the competition between man and animal. The fans, of course, are partisans; they root for their own species. The crowd always cheers when a cowboy wins even if they've never heard of the chap. But the animals must be good, or the contest will be no fun. The horses, bulls, steers, and calves are thus all bred and raised especially for their spunk.   —Ray Raphael, *Edges*

At its best, as in this statement on rodeos, informal writing stays close to colloquial patterns. It becomes inexpressive and monotonous, however, when most of the sentences are short or loosely strung together.

To convey meaning when we speak, we depend on voice pitch and inflection. The baseball player above probably stressed particular words in the series of short sentences that conclude his statement. These resources in speech are not available to the writer. Written sentences therefore must be tighter than the fragmented or run-on sentences we sometimes speak. In our formal writing as in our formal speech, we give even more attention to precision and emphasis. When formal writing deals with ideas, it uses a large number of abstract words and words that are also chosen for their exactness:

> Lincoln was a pre-eminent example of that self-help which Americans have always so admired. He was not, of course, the first eminent American politican who could claim humble origins, nor the first to exploit them. But few have been able to point to such a sudden ascent from relative obscurity to high eminence; none has maintained so completely while scaling the heights the aspect of extreme simplicity; and none has combined with the attainment of success and power such an intense awareness of humanity and moral responsibility.
> —Richard Hofstadter, *The American Political Tradition*

The coordination of clauses in the first sentence of this formal passage is tighter than that in the statement on rodeos. The diction is also frequently abstract (*the aspect of extreme simplicity, the attainment of success and power, awareness of humanity and moral responsibility*) and the choice of words is exact (*ascent* rather than the informal *rise, high eminence* rather than *fame*). Formal writing, it should also be noted, sometimes depends on the passive voice more than informal writing does:

> Technological solutions to many formerly unremitting medical problems are at hand. Today, when penicillin, protein, and vaccines can be manufactured for pennies, no child should die from diseases, especially deficiency-related diseases, that can be relatively easily prevented or cured. To the extent that the quality of life is marred for so many of the world's people, the remedies are to be sought in expanded knowledge of human interactions. Profound socioeconomic adjustments could solve or ameliorate the overwhelming majority of distribution problems that cause the benefits of modern medical advances to be withheld from appalling numbers of the world's medically burdened populations. An appreciation of the impressive personal

efforts by the outstanding leaders we subsume as traditional
healers, coupled with knowledge of the tremendous obstacles
to survival that have been overcome through the biological
mechanisms of evolutionary selection, should contribute to an
attitude of optimism, indeed confidence, that the remaining
tasks, the social readjustments that lie ahead, should not be in-
surmountable. —Corinne Shear Wood, *Human Sickness and
Health*

An abstract subject such as success in politics invites a formal
style, a concrete subject like the rodeo an informal style; but
both subjects might be written about in informal and formal
language. Much depends on what style the writer believes is
suited to a particular audience or its expectations.

Much writing today avoids the extremes of highly formal or
highly informal English. General English is the term given to a
spoken and written standard that shares characteristics of both.
General English is much tighter than informal spoken English,
but it is looser than the formal sentences just quoted—conveying
the rhythm of ordinary speech, more often the rhythm of the active voice than the passive. It uses a plain vocabulary where
possible, depending on abstract and technical words when
simpler words will not express the intended ideas.

The Joan Didion essay on bureaucrats that follows illustrates
general English, and so do most of the essays in this book. Compare the baseball player's statement (p. 411) with the following
from Didion's essay:

Mere driving on the freeway is in no way the same as participating in it. Anyone can "drive" on the freeway, and many
people with no vocation for it do, hesitating here and resisting
there, losing the rhythm of the lane change, thinking about
where they came from and where they are going. Actual participants think only about where they are. Actual participation
requires a total surrender, a concentration so intense as to seem
a kind of narcosis, a rapture-of-the-freeway. *The mind goes clean.
The rhythm takes over.* A distortion of time occurs, the same
distortion that characterizes the instant before an accident. [em-
phasis added]

Didion varies these sentences to considerable effect. The italicized short sentences make the impact they do because Didion

uses them sparingly. Short sentences need not be as dramatic as these; the effect depends on the ideas they express.

At the same time, sentences that depart markedly from patterns of speech may sound stilted. In speaking, we usually begin with the main idea and add to it supporting details and other modifiers, or link the main idea to another as Didion does in the passage above:

> Anyone can "drive" on the freeway, and many with no vocation for it do, hesitating here and resisting there, losing the rhythm of the lane change, thinking about where they came from and where they are going.

Because so many spoken sentences open with the main clause, variation from this pattern catches the reader's attention:

> The closed door upstairs at 120 South Spring Street in downtown Los Angeles is marked OPERATIONS CENTER. In the windowless room beyond the closed door a reverential hush prevails. From six A.M. until seven P.M. in this windowless room men sit at consoles watching a huge board flash colored lights.

The second and third sentences—called *periodic* because the subject and verb of the main clause come at the end—catch our attention because of the dramatic build-up from the opening modifiers. Sentences such as these make their impact because Didion varies them to catch the pauses, interruptions, and nuances of talk.

Informal, formal, and general English use concrete and abstract words, specific and general ones. The passages quoted from Didion contain all of these. And writing at these three levels also contains metaphors and other figures of speech. In expressive writing like Annie Dillard's on the coming of spring (p. 478), metaphor dramatically expresses the special feeling and perceptions of the writer:

> This is the hoop of flame that shoots the rapids in the creek or spins across the dizzy meadows; this is the arsonist of the sunny woods. . . .

In informative writing, as in David R. Scott's description of his moon walk (p. 468), figurative language is often not so obvious:

The flowing moonscape, unmarred by a single jagged peak, reminds me of earth's uplands covered by a heavy blanket of fresh snow.

Every style has its hazards. Formal sentences that depart too far from colloquial English become hard to understand. Technical words or jargon are often essential in writing about technical subjects; usually only the special audience knows the meaning of these terms. The formal writer wants to be precise, but precision can become a fault as in the following sentence:

> But already at a point in economic evolution far antedating the emergence of the lady, specialized consumption of goods as an evidence of pecuniary strength had begun to work out in a more or less elaborate system.   —Thorstein Veblen, *Theory of the Leisure Class*

This overprecise sentence uses abstract, theoretical terms to state simple ideas. "Pecuniary strength" means nothing more than having money; "specialized consumption of goods" mean buying things because they look expensive. In colloquial English, people are "putting on the dog."

At the three levels, overused phrases can make writing sound stale. A phrase like "putting on the dog"—a popular colloquialism—loses its color in writing through overfamiliarity. We refer to phrases of this kind as clichés. A piece of writing may also seem too colorful—overcrowded with metaphor and other figures. But deciding what is overfamiliar or overcolorful is not easy. There are no rules for deciding what sentence style or kind of diction is appropriate to particular subjects or audiences. A sense of appropriateness comes only with wide reading and the awareness that writers achieve different effects with different means and in unpredictable ways.

Joan Didion

BUREAUCRATS

Joan Didion has had a varied career in writing since her graduation from the University of California at Berkeley in 1956. She has been an editor of *Vogue* and a columnist for *The Saturday Evening Post*. She reported on the Salvadoran civil war in *Salvador* (1983), and described southern Florida in the 1980s in *Miami* (1988). She has also written screenplays, numerous essays, and novels about contemporary American life including *Play It as It Lays* (1971), *The Book of Common Prayer* (1977), and *Democracy* (1984). "Bureaucrats" shows her concern with urban problems today and, in particular, her ironic view of the workings of government. It is reprinted from *The White Album* (1979), a collection of Didion's essays.

The closed door upstairs at 120 South Spring Street in 1
downtown Los Angeles is marked OPERATIONS CEN-
TER. In the windowless room beyond the closed door a
reverential hush prevails. From six A.M. until seven P.M. in
this windowless room men sit at consoles watching a huge
board flash colored lights. "There's the heart attack,"
someone will murmur, or "we're getting the gawk effect."
120 South Spring is the Los Angeles office of Caltrans, or
the California Department of Transportation, and the
Operations Center is where Caltrans engineers monitor
what they call "the 42-Mile Loop." The 42-Mile Loop is
simply the rough triangle formed by the intersections of the
Santa Monica, the San Diego and the Harbor freeways,
and 42 miles represents less than ten percent of freeway
mileage in Los Angeles County alone, but these particular
42 miles are regarded around 120 South Spring with a
special veneration. The Loop is a "demonstration system,"
a phrase much favored by everyone at Caltrans, and is part
of a "pilot project," another two words carrying totemic
weight on South Spring.

The Loop has electronic sensors embedded every half- 2
mile out there in the pavement itself, each sensor counting
the crossing cars every twenty seconds. The Loop has its
own mind, a Xerox Sigma V computer which prints out,

all day and night, twenty-second readings on what is and is not moving in each of the Loop's eight lanes. It is the Xerox Sigma V that makes the big board flash red when traffic out there drops below fifteen miles an hour. It is the Xerox Sigma V that tells the Operations crew when they have an "incident" out there. An "incident" is the heart attack on the San Diego, the jackknifed truck on the Harbor, the Camaro just now tearing out the Cyclone fence on the Santa Monica. "Out there" is where incidents happen. The windowless room at 120 South Spring is where incidents get "verified." "Incident verification" is turning on the closed-circuit TV on the console and watching the traffic slow down to see (this is "the gawk effect") where the Camaro tore out the fence.

As a matter of fact there is a certain closed-circuit aspect to the entire mood of the Operations Center. "Verifying" the incident does not after all "prevent" the incident, which lends the enterprise a kind of tranced distance, and on the day recently when I visited 120 South Spring it took considerable effort to remember what I had come to talk about, which was that particular part of the Loop called the Santa Monica Freeway. The Santa Monica Freeway is 16.2 miles long, runs from the Pacific Ocean to downtown Los Angeles through what is referred to at Caltrans as "the East–West Corridor," carries more traffic every day than any other freeway in California, has what connoisseurs of freeways concede to be the most beautiful access ramps in the world, and appeared to have been transformed by Caltrans, during the several weeks before I went downtown to talk about it, into a 16.2-mile parking lot.

The problem seemed to be another Caltrans "demonstration," or "pilot," a foray into bureaucratic terrorism they were calling "The Diamond Lane" in their promotional literature and "The Project" among themselves. That the promotional literature consisted largely of schedules for buses (or "Diamond Lane Expresses") and invitations to join a car pool via computer ("Commuter Computer") made clear not only the putative point of The Project, which was to encourage travel by car pool and bus, but also the actual point, which was to eradicate a central Southern California illusion, that of individual mobility, without anyone really noticing. This had not exactly worked out. "FREEWAY FIASCO," the *Los Angeles Times* was headlining page-one stories. "THE DIAMOND LANE: ANOTHER BUST BY CALTRANS." "CALTRANS PILOT EFFORT ANOTHER IN LONG LIST OF FAILURES." "OFFICIAL DIAMOND LANE STANCE: LET THEM HOWL."

All "The Diamond Lane" theoretically involved was reserving the fast inside lanes on the Santa Monica for vehicles carrying three or more people, but in practice this meant that 25 per cent of the freeway was reserved for 3 per cent of the cars, and there were other odd wrinkles here and there suggesting that Caltrans had dedicated itself to making all movements around Los Angeles as arduous as possible. There was for example the matter of surface streets. A "surface street" is anything around Los Angeles that is not a freeway ("going surface" from one part of town to another is generally regarded as idiosyncratic), and surface streets do not fall directly within the Caltrans domain, but now the engineer in charge of surface streets was accusing Caltrans of threatening and intimidating him. It appeared that Caltrans wanted him to create a "a confused and congested situation" on his surface streets, so as to force drivers back to the freeway, where they would meet a still more confused and congested situation and decide to stay home, or take a bus. "We are beginning a process of deliberately making it harder for drivers to use freeways," a Caltrans director had in fact said at a transit conference some months before. "We are prepared to endure considerable public outcry in order to pry John Q. Public out of his car. . . . I would emphasize that this is a political decision, and one that can be reversed if the public gets sufficiently enraged to throw us rascals out."

Of course this political decision was in the name of the greater good, was in the interests of "environmental improvement" and "conservation of resources," but even there the figures had about them a certain Caltrans opacity. The Santa Monica normally carried 240,000 cars and trucks every day. These 240,000 cars and trucks normally carried 260,000 people. What Caltrans described as its ultimate goal on the Santa Monica was to carry the same 260,000 people, "but in 7,800 fewer, or 232,200 vehicles." The figure "232,200" had a visionary precision to it that did not automatically create confidence, especially since the only effect so far had been to disrupt traffic throughout the Los Angeles Basin, triple the number of daily accidents on the Santa Monica, prompt the initiation of two lawsuits against Caltrans, and cause large numbers of Los Angeles County residents to behave, most uncharacteristically, as an ignited and conscious proletariat. Citizen guerrillas splashed paint and scattered nails in the Diamond Lanes, Diamond Lane maintenance crews expressed fear of hurled objects. Down at 120 South Spring the architects of the Diamond Lane had taken to regarding "the media" as the architects of their embarrassment, and Caltrans statements in the press had been cryptic and contradictory, reminiscent only of old communiqués out of Vietnam.

To understand what was going on it is perhaps necessary to have participated in the freeway experience, which is the only secular communion Los Angeles has. Mere driving on the freeway is in no way the same as participating in it. Anyone can "drive" on the freeway, and many people with no vocation for it do, hesitating here and resisting there, losing the rhythm of the lane change, thinking about where they came from and where they are going. Actual participants think only about where they are. Actual participation requires a total surrender, a concentration so intense as to seem a kind of narcosis, a rapture-of-the-freeway. The mind goes clean. The rhythm takes over. A distortion of time occurs, the same distortion that characterizes the instant before an accident. It takes only a few seconds to get off the Santa Monica Freeway at National-Overland, which is a difficult exit requiring the driver to cross two new lanes of traffic streamed in from the San Diego Freeway, but those few seconds always seem to me the longest part of the trip. The moment is dangerous. The exhilaration is in doing it. "As you acquire the special skills involved," Reyner Banham observed in an extraordinary chapter about the freeways in his 1971 *Los Angeles: The Architecture of Four Ecologies,* "the freeways become a special way of being alive . . . the extreme concentration required in Los Angeles seems to bring on a state of heightened awareness that some locals find mystical."

Indeed some locals do, and some nonlocals too. Reducing the number of lone souls careering around the East–West Corridor in a state of mechanized rapture may or may not have seemed socially desirable, but what it was definitely not going to seem was easy. "We're only seeing an initial period of unfamiliarity," I was assured the day I visited Caltrans. I was talking to a woman named Eleanor Wood and she was thoroughly and professionally grounded in the diction of "planning" and it did not seem likely that I could interest her in considering the freeway as regional mystery. "Any time you try to rearrange people's daily habits, they're apt to react impetuously. All this project requires is a certain rearrangement of people's daily planning. That's really all we want."

It occurred to me that a certain rearrangement of people's daily planning might seem, in less rarefied air than is breathed at 120 South Spring, rather a great deal to want, but so impenetrable was the sense of higher social purpose there in the Operations Center that I did not express this reservation. Instead I changed the subject, mentioned an earlier "pilot project" on the Santa Monica: the big electronic message boards that Caltrans had installed a year or two before. The idea was that traffic information transmitted from the Santa Monica to the Xerox Sigma V could be translated, here in the Operations Center, into suggestions to the driver, and flashed right back out to the Santa Monica. This operation, in that it involved telling drivers electronically what they already knew empirically, had the rather spectral circularity that seemed to mark a great many Caltrans schemes, and I was interested in how Caltrans thought it worked.

"Actually the message boards were part of a larger   10
pilot project," Mrs. Wood said. "An ongoing project in incident management. With the message boards we hoped to
learn if motorists would modify their behavior according
to what we told them on the boards."

I asked if the motorists had.   11

"Actually no," Mrs. Wood said finally. "They didn't   12
react to the signs exactly as we'd hypothesized they would,
no. *But.* If we'd *known* what the motorist would do . . .
then we wouldn't have needed a pilot project in the first
place, would we."

The circle seemed intact. Mrs. Wood and I smiled, and   13
shook hands. I watched the big board until all lights turned
green on the Santa Monica and then I left and drove home
on it, all 16.2 miles of it. All the way I remembered that I
was watched by the Xerox Sigma V. All the way the message boards gave me the number to call for CAR POOL
INFO. As I left the freeway it occurred to me that they
might have their own rapture down at 120 South Spring,
and it could be called Perpetuating the Department. Today
the California Highway Patrol reported that, during the
first six weeks of the Diamond Lane, accidents on the
Santa Monica, which normally range between 49 and 72
during a six-week period, totaled 204. Yesterday plans
were announced to extend the Diamond Lane to other
freeways at a cost of $42,500,000

Questions for Study and Discussion

1. What variations of sentence length do you find in paragraphs 1–6?
2. How many sentences in paragraphs 1–6 are built by addition
   of detail? How many are built by qualification and modification?
3. The greater the number of simple and compound sentences,
   the greater the informality of the essay. How informal is
   this essay?
4. Does Didion state her attitude toward Caltrans directly, or
   instead imply it through her details?

5. In what ways is the Los Angeles Freeway symbolic of Los Angeles life? Does Didion see the freeway as symbolic or representative of California or perhaps American life, generally?

Vocabulary Study

1. What is Didion saying about the word *verified* and the other forms of it she cites in paragraphs 2 and 3?
2. What points is she making about other special terms she discusses—for example, *surface street?*
3. Why does she use the word *proletariat* rather than *population* or *citizenry* in paragraph 6?
4. Why does she use the phrase *secular communion* instead of *being together*—"the only way of being together that Los Angeles has"—in paragraph 7?
5. Explain the italicized words:

    This operation, in that it involved telling drivers electronically what they already knew *empirically*, had the rather *spectral circularity* that seemed to mark a great many Caltrans schemes, and I was interested in how Caltrans thought it worked.

Suggestions for Writing

1. Use the traffic of your hometown or city to comment on its quality of life or atmosphere. Make your details as specific as you can.
2. Discuss an "improvement" that in your opinion has worsened the situation it was intended to make better. Describe the situation in detail.

Emphasis

Giving ideas exact emphasis requires attention to sentence co-ordination and subordination. When you *coordinate* you use the words *and, but, for, or, nor,* and *yet* to connect words, phrases, and clauses of the same weight and importance. The three opening clauses in the following sentence are independent and co-ordinate:

> The cold night had come, *and* Ukwane in the frosty grass was shivering, *yet* he sat for an hour keeping his patience, putting his hands into the cold blood of the springbok to trace veins to their source, prefacing all his answers with positive, qualifying remarks. —Elizabeth Marshall Thomas, *The Harmless People*

To stress a close relation between ideas, the writer may coordinate clauses with semicolons, with or without supporting or conjunctive adverbs like *however* and *furthermore* or adverbial phrases:

> For us, the cave paintings re-create the hunter's way of life as a glimpse of history; we look through them into the past. But for the hunter, I suggest they were a peep-hole into the future; he looked ahead. . . .
> . . . It is natural to come to astronomy straight from mathematics; after all, astronomy was developed first, and became a model for all the other sciences, just because it could be turned into exact numbers. —J. Bronowski, *The Ascent of Man*

When you *subordinate* you attach to independent clauses phrases and clauses that cannot stand alone. In the Thomas sentence above, the heavily stressed subordinate phrases that conclude the sentence contain specific details that explain the independent clauses:

Yet he sat for an hour keeping his patience, putting his hands into the cold blood of the springbok to trace veins to their source, prefacing all his answers with positive, qualifying remarks.

English sentences often reserve the end of the sentence for the most important idea or for new ideas and details. This end-focus is evident in the stress given final words in speaking:

My wife's parents live in NEW YORK.

Even if another word in the sentence is stressed, the final word still receives a degree of stress:

My WIFE'S parents live in NEW YORK (my wife's parents, not my own parents).

End-focus has important consequences for building sentences and varying them. It means that the speaker or writer can "load" the end of the sentence, adding ideas and details that cannot easily go at the beginning. You speak or write the following sentence without thinking about its structure:

(1) I know they won't come if they decide to go to Newark.

You would not say or write:

(2) That they won't come if they decide to go to Newark I know.

But you can open the sentence with a shorter complement:

(3) That they're coming I have no doubt.

Notice that the complement [*that*] *they won't come* in (1) is followed by a modifying subordinate clause (*if they decide to go to Newark*) and therefore cannot appear at the beginning of the sentence. The unmodified complement in (3)—*That he is coming*—can appear at the beginning. By contrast, phrasal modifiers can be added to the end of the sentence without difficulty:

A school of minnows swam by, each minnow with its small individual shadow, doubling the attendance, so clear and sharp in the sunlight. —E. B. White, "Once More to the Lake"

Most commonly we come to books with blurred and divided minds, asking of fiction that it shall be true, of poetry that it shall be false, of biography that it shall be flattering, of history that it shall enforce our own prejudices. —Virginia Woolf, "How Should One Read a Book?"

Compound sentences, which coordinate independent clauses to emphasize their connection, can run on indefinitely:

The height of the ginning season in that part of the country is early October, and in that time the loaded wagons are on the road before the least crack of daylight, the waiting is endless hours, and the gin is still pulsing and beating after dark. —James Agee, "Cotton"

This sentence might continue further. The familiar definition of a sentence as a complete thought is of no use in deciding when to end sentences of this kind. For the completeness of the thought lies in the mind of the speaker or writer, who seeks to emphasize each component idea and who alone knows when everything necessary has been said. At the same time, the emphasis or force diminishes for the reader if the sentence seems to run on or drift monotonously.

Richard P. Feynman

THE AMATEUR SCIENTIST

Richard P. Feynman was professor of Theoretical Physics at the California Institute of Technology, where he taught from 1950 until his death in 1988. Feynman was born in Far Rockaway, New York, in 1918, and studied at the Massachusetts Institute of Technology and Princeton University. From 1943 to 1946 he worked as a nuclear physicist at Los Alamos, New Mexico. In 1965 Feynman received the Nobel Prize in Physics for his contribution to quantum mechanics, which increased understanding of the fundamental forces of nature. *"Surely You're Joking, Mr. Feynman!"* is a collection of personal essays that form a memoir of his life. In the essay reprinted here from this collection, Feynman describes how he began to think and experiment like a scientist.

When I was a kid I had a "lab." It wasn't a laboratory in the sense that I would measure, or do important experiments. Instead, I would play: I'd make a motor, I'd 1 make a gadget that would go off when something passed a photocell, I'd play around with selenium; I was piddling around all the time. I did calculate a little bit for the lamp bank, a series of switches and bulbs I used as resistors to control voltages. But all that was for application. I never did any laboratory kind of experiments.

I also had a microscope and *loved* to watch things under the microscope. It took patience: I would get something under the microscope and I would watch it interminably. I saw many interesting things, like everybody sees—a diatom slowly making its way across the slide, and so on.

One day I was watching a paramecium and I saw something that was not described in the books I got in school—in college, even. These books always simplify things so the world will be more like *they* want it to be: When they're talking about the behavior of animals, they always start out with, "The paramecium is extremely simple; it has a simple behavior. It turns as its slipper shape moves through the water until it hits something, at which time it recoils, turns through an angle, and then starts out again."

It isn't really right. First of all, as everybody knows, the paramecia, from time to time, conjugate with each other—they meet and exchange nuclei. How do they decide when it's time to do that? (Never mind; that's not my observation.)

I watched these paramecia hit something, recoil, turn through an angle, and go again. The idea that it's mechanical, like a computer program—it doesn't look that way. They go different distances, they recoil different distances, they turn through angles that are different in various cases; they don't always turn to the right; they're very irregular. It looks random, because you don't know what they're hitting; you don't know all the chemicals they're smelling, or what.

One of the things I wanted to watch was what happens to the paramecium when the water that it's in dries up. It was claimed that the paramecium can dry up into a sort of hardened seed. I had a drop of water on the slide under my microscope, and in the drop of water was a paramecium and some "grass"—at the scale of the paramecium, it looked like a network of jackstraws. As the drop of water evaporated, over a time of fifteen or twenty minutes, the paramecium got into a tighter and tighter situation: there was more and more of this back-and-forth until it could hardly move. It was stuck between these "sticks," almost jammed.

Then I saw something I had never seen or heard of: the paramecium lost its shape. It could flex itself, like an amoeba. It began to push itself against one of the sticks, and began dividing into two prongs until the division was about halfway up the paramecium, at which time it decided *that* wasn't a very good idea, and backed away. 7

So my impression of these animals is that their behavior is much too simplified in the books. It is not so utterly mechanical or one-dimensional as they say. They should describe the behavior of these simple animals correctly. Until we see how many dimensions of behavior even a one-celled animal has, we won't be able to fully understand the behavior of more complicated animals. 8

I also enjoyed watching bugs. I had an insect book when I was about thirteen. It said that dragonflies are not harmful; they don't sting. In our neighborhod it was well known that "darning needles," as we called them, were very dangerous when they'd sting. So if we were outside somewhere playing baseball, or something, and one of these things would fly around, everybody would run for cover, waving their arms, yelling," A darning needle! A darning needle!" 9

So one day I was on the beach, and I'd just read this book that said dragonflies don't sting. A darning needle came along, and everybody was screaming and running around, and I just sat there. "Don't worry!" I said. "Darning needles don't sting!" 10

The thing landed on my foot. Everybody was yelling and it was a big mess, because this darning needle was sitting on my foot. And there I was, this scientific wonder, saying it wasn't going to sting me. 11

You're *sure* this is a story that's going to come out that 12
it stings me—but it didn't. The book was right. But I did
sweat a bit.

I also had a little hand microscope. It was a toy micro- 13
scope, and I pulled the magnification piece out of it, and
would hold it in my hand like a magnifying glass, even
though it was a microscope of forty or fifty power. With
care you could hold the focus. So I could go around and
look at things right out in the street.

When I was in graduate school at Princeton, I once 14
took it out of my pocket to look at some ants that were
crawling around on some ivy. I had to exclaim out loud,
I was so excited. What I saw was an ant and an aphid,
which ants take care of—they carry them from plant to
plant if the plant they're on is dying. In return the ants get
partially digested aphid juice, called "honeydew." I knew
that; my father had told me about it, but I had never
seen it.

So here was this aphid and sure enough, an ant came 15
along, and patted it with its feet—all around the aphid, pat,
pat, pat, pat, pat. This was terribly exciting! Then the juice
came out of the back of the aphid. And because it was
magnified, it looked like a big, beautiful, glistening ball,
like a balloon, because of the surface tension. Because the
microscope wasn't very good, the drop was colored a little bit from chromatic aberration in the lens—it was a
gorgeous thing!

The ant took this ball in its two front feet, lifted it off 16
the aphid, and *held* it. The world is so different at that scale
that you can pick up water and hold it! The ants probably
have a fatty or greasy material on their legs that doesn't
break the surface tension of the water when they hold it
up. Then the ant broke the surface of the drop with its
mouth, and the surface tension collapsed the drop right into his gut. It was *very* interesting to see this whole thing
happen!

In my room at Princeton I had a bay window with a 17
U-shaped windowsill. One day some ants came out on the
windowsill and wandered around a little bit. I got curious

as to how they found things. I wondered, how do they know where to go? Can they tell each other where food is, like bees can? Do they have any sense of geometry?

This is all amateurish; everybody knows the answer,   18
but *I* didn't know the answer, so the first thing I did was to stretch some string across the U of the bay window and hang a piece of folded cardboard with sugar on it from the string. The idea of this was to isolate the sugar from the ants, so they wouldn't find it accidentally. I wanted to have everything under control.

Next I made a lot of little strips of paper and put a fold   19
in them, so I could pick up ants and ferry them from one place to another. I put the folded strips of paper in two places: Some were by the sugar (hanging from the string), and the others were near the ants in a particular location. I sat there all afternoon, reading and watching, until an ant happened to walk onto one of my little paper ferries. Then I took him over to the sugar. After a few ants had been ferried over to the sugar, one of them accidentally walked onto one of the ferries nearby, and I carried him back.

I wanted to see how long it would take the other ants   20
to get the message to go to the "ferry terminal." It started slowly, but rapidly increased until I was going mad ferrying the ants back and forth.

But suddenly, when everything was going strong, I   21
began to deliver the ants from the sugar to a *different* spot. The question now was, does the ant learn to go back to where it just came from, or does it go where it went the time before?

After a while there were practically no ants going to   22
the first place (which would take them to the sugar), whereas there were many ants at the second place, milling around, trying to find the sugar. So I figured out so far that they went where they just came from.

In another experiment, I laid out a lot of glass micro-   23
scope slides, and got the ants to walk on them, back and forth, to some sugar I put on the windowsill. Then, by replacing an old slide with a new one, or by rearranging the slides, I could demonstrate that the ants had no sense

of geometry: they couldn't figure out where something was. If they went to the sugar one way, and there was a shorter way back, they would never figure out the short way.

It was also pretty clear from rearranging the glass slides   24
that the ants left some sort of trail. So then came a lot of easy experiments to find out how long it takes a trail to dry up, whether it can be easily wiped off, and so on. I also found out the trail wasn't directional. If I'd pick up an ant on a piece of paper, turn him around and around, and then put him back onto the trail, he wouldn't know that he was going the wrong way until he met another ant. (Later, in Brazil, I noticed some leaf-cutting ants and tried the same experiment on them. They *could* tell, within a few steps, whether they were going toward the food or away from it— presumably from the trail, which might be a series of smells in a pattern: A, B, space, A, B, space, and so on.)

I tried at one point to make the ants go around in a   25
circle, but I didn't have enough patience to set it up. I could see no reason, other than lack of patience, why it couldn't be done.

One thing that made experimenting difficult was that   26
breathing on the ants made them scurry. It must be an instinctive thing against some animal that eats them or disturbs them. I don't know if it was the warmth, the moisture, or the smell of my breath that bothered them, but I always had to hold my breath and kind of look to one side so as not to confuse the experiment while I was ferrying the ants.

One question that I wondered about was why the ant   27
trails look so straight and nice. The ants look as if they know what they're doing, as if they have a good sense of geometry. Yet the experiments that I did to try to demonstrate their sense of geometry didn't work.

Many years later, when I was at Caltech and lived in a   28
little house on Alameda Street, some ants came out around the bathtub. I thought, "This is a great opportunity." I put some sugar on the other end of the bathtub, and sat there the whole afternoon until an ant finally found the sugar. It's only a question of patience.

The moment the ant found the sugar, I picked up a   29
colored pencil that I had ready (I had previously done experiments indicating that the ants don't give a damn about
pencil marks—they walk right over them—so I knew I
wasn't disturbing anything), and behind where the ant
went I drew a line so I could tell where his trail was. The
ant wandered a little bit wrong to get back to the hole, so
the line was quite wiggly, unlike a typical ant trail.

When the next ant to find the sugar began to go back,   30
I marked his trail with another color. (By the way, he followed the first ant's return trail back, rather than his own
incoming trail. My theory is that when an ant has found
some food, he leaves a much stronger trail than when he's
just wandering around.)

This second ant was in a great hurry and followed,   31
pretty much, the original trail. But because he was going
so fast he would go straight out, as if he were coasting,
when the trail was wiggly. Often, as the ant was "coasting," he would find the trail again. Already it was apparent that the second ant's return was slightly straighter.
With successive ants the same "improvement" of the trail
by hurriedly and carelessly "following" it occurred.

I followed eight or ten ants with my pencil until their   32
trails became a neat line right along the bathtub. It's
something like sketching: You draw a lousy line at first;
then you go over it a few times and it makes a nice line
after a while.

I remember that when I was a kid my father would tell   33
me how wonderful ants are, and how they cooperate. I
would watch very carefully three or four ants carrying a little piece of chocolate back to their nest. At first glance it
looks like efficient, marvelous, brilliant cooperation. But if
you look at it carefully, you'll see that it's nothing of the
kind: They're all behaving as if the chocolate is held up by
something else. They pull at it one way or the other way.
An ant may crawl over it while it's being pulled at by the
others. It wobbles, it wiggles, the directions are all confused. The chocolate doesn't move in a nice way toward
the nest.

The Brazilian leaf-cutting ants, which are otherwise so   34
marvelous, have a very interesting stupidity associated
with them that I'm surprised hasn't evolved out. It takes
considerable work for the ant to cut the circular arc in order
to get a piece of leaf. When the cutting is done, there's a
fifty-fifty chance that the ant will pull on the wrong side,
letting the piece he just cut fall to the ground. Half the
time, the ant will yank and pull and yank and pull on the
wrong part of the leaf, until it gives up and starts to cut
another piece. There is no attempt to pick up a piece that
it, or any other ant, has already cut. So it's quite obvious,
if you watch very carefully, that it's not a brilliant business
of cutting leaves and carrying them away; they go to a leaf,
cut an arc, and pick the wrong side half the time while the
right piece falls down.

In Princeton the ants found my larder, where I had   35
jelly and bread and stuff, which was quite a distance from
the window. A long line of ants marched along the floor
across the living room. It was during the time I was doing
these experiments on the ants, so I thought to myself,
"What can I do to stop them from coming to my larder
without killing any ants? No poison; you gotta be humane
to the ants!"

What I did was this: In preparation, I put a bit of sugar   36
about six or eight inches from their entry point into the
room, that they didn't know about. Then I made those
ferry things again, and whenever an ant returning with
food walked onto my little ferry, I'd carry him over and put
him on the sugar. Any ant coming toward the larder that
walked onto a ferry I also carried over to the sugar. Eventually the ants found their way from the sugar to their
hole, so this new trail was being doubly reinforced, while
the old trail was being used less and less. I knew that after
half an hour or so the old trail would dry up, and in an
hour they were out of my larder. I didn't wash the floor;
I didn't do anything but ferry ants.

Comment

Feynman's essay seems like a long answer to a question he might have been asked while conversing with a friend; his sentences are colloquial in structure—a series of details or short explanatory phrases and clauses often are added to a base sentence; some clauses are compounded in a series, sometimes without verbal conjunctions:

> Instead I would play: I'd make a motor, I'd make a gadget that would go off when something passed a photocell, I'd play around with selenium; I was piddling around all the time.

Feynman is making a point through the details of the experiments he describes. Through these details the reader makes discoveries about Feynman.

Questions for Study and Discussion

1. What features make the sentences in paragraphs 32 and 33 colloquial—that is, suggestive of spoken English?
2. What implicit point is Feynman making about each of his various experiments? Is he making the same point in each instance?
3. Which of the author's personal qualities emerge in his narrative of these experiments? Are the experiments the cental focus of the essay, or is Feynman the experimenter the focus? How do you know?
4. Does Feynman leave you with the sense that he has more to tell about his amateur experiments and has merely broken off the narrative? Or does he conclude the essay informally or formally?
5. If you were writing a formal essay on experiments you performed as an adolescent, how different would your essay be in structure from Feynman's? What features in general make an essay formal?

Sentence Study

1. All but the first sentence in paragraph 1 consist of main clauses. Construct additional complex sentences by subordinating some of these main clauses. What change in emphasis occurs in your revision? Does the revision change Feynman's meaning?
2. Feynman coordinates a series of main clauses in the following sentences. Recast each sentence, combining these clauses or subordinating one or more. What change in emphasis occurs in your revision?
    a. "It took patience: I would get something under the microscope and I would watch it interminably." (paragraph 2)
    b. "I had a drop of water on the slide under my microscope, and in the drop of water was a paramecium and some "grass"—at the scale of the paramecium, it looked like a network of jackstraws." (paragraph 6)
    c. "Then the ant broke the surface of the drop with its mouth, and the surface tension collapsed the drop right into his gut." (paragraph 16)
3. Try to reduce the repetition of words in the following sentence:

    They go different distances, they recoil different distances, they turn through angles that are different in various cases; they don't always turn to the right; they're very irregular. (paragraph 5)

    What is gained or lost by your revision?
4. The concluding clause in the following sentence adds information about the larder. Speaking the sentence, we would probably raise our voice with *which* to show that it modifies *larder*. Revise the sentence so that *which* immediately follows *larder*:

    In Princeton the ants found my larder, where I had jelly and bread and stuff, which was quite a distance from the window. (paragraph 35)

    What problems did you meet in revising the sentence? Is your revision an improvement over Feynman's sentence?

Suggestions for Writing

1. Write about a series of related experiences that define your interests. Let the reader draw conclusions from your details. Don't draw these conclusions yourself.
2. Write a characterization of Feynman on the basis of what he tells you about his interests and how he presents them.

William Zinsser

JURY DUTY

William Zinsser was born in 1922 in New York City and has written much about life there in numerous articles and books. He attended Princeton University and later was a feature writer, film critic, and drama editor for the *New York Herald Tribune* and a columnist for *Look* and *Life*. Zinsser taught at Yale University from 1971 to 1979. His books include *Pop Goes America* (1966) and *On Writing Well*, 3rd ed. (1988).

Jury duty again. I'm sitting in the "central jurors' room" of a courthouse in lower Manhattan, as I do every two years, waiting to be called for a jury, which I almost never am. It's an experience that all of us have known, in one form or another, as long as we can remember: organized solitude.

The chair that I sit in is a little island of apartness. I sit there alone, day after day, and I go out to lunch alone, a stranger in my own city. Strictly, of course, I'm not by myself. Several hundred other men and women sit on every side, as closely as in a movie theater, also waiting to be called for a jury, which they almost never are. Sometimes we break briefly into each other's lives, when we get up to stretch, offering fragments of talk to fill the emptiness. But in the end each of us is alone, withdrawn into our newspapers and our crossword puzzles and our sacred urban privacy.

The room intimidates us. It is a dreary place, done in ³
thirties Bureaucratic, too dull to sustain more than a few
minutes of mental effort. On the subconscious level, however, it exerts a strong and uncanny hold. It is the universal waiting room. It is the induction center and the clinic;
it is the assembly hall and the office where forms are filled
out. Thoughts come unbidden there, sneaking back from
all the other moments—in the army, at camp, on the first
day of school—when we were part of a crowd and therefore lonely.

The mere taking of roll call by a jury clerk will summon ⁴
back the countless times when we have waited for our
name to be yelled out—loud and just a little wrong. Like
every person whose job is to read names aloud, the jury
clerk can't read names aloud. Their shapes mystify him.
They are odd and implausible names, as diverse as the
countries that they came from, but surely the clerk has met
them all before. *Hasn't* he? Isn't that what democracy—and
the jury system—is all about? Evidently not.

We are shy enough, as we wait for our name, without ⁵
the extra burden of wondering what form it will take. By
now we know most of the variants that have been imposed
on it by other clerks in other rooms like this, and we are
ready to answer to any of them, or to some still different
version. Actually we don't want to hear our name called
at all in this vast public chamber. It is so private, so vulnerable. And yet we don't want to *not* hear it, for only then
are we reassured of our identity, really certain that we are
known, wanted, and in the right place. Dawn over Camp
Upton, 1943: Weinberg, Wyzanski, Yanopoulos, Zapata,
Zeccola, Zinsser. . . .

I don't begin my jury day in such a retrospective state. ⁶
I start with high purpose and only gradually slide into
mental disarray. I am punctual, even early, and so is everybody else. We are a conscientious lot—partly because we
are so surrounded by the trappings of justice, but mainly
because that is what we are there to be. I've never seen
such conscientious-looking people. Observing them, I'm
glad that American law rests on being judged by our peers.

In fact, I'd almost rather be judged by my peers than judged by a judge.

Most of us start the day by reading. Jury duty is America's gift to her citizens of a chance to catch up on "good" books, and I always bring *War and Peace*. I remember to bring it every morning and I keep it handy on my lap. The only thing I don't do is read it. There's something about the room . . . the air is heavy with imminent roll calls, too heavy for tackling a novel that will require strict attention. Besides, it's important to read the newspaper first: sharpen up the old noggin on issues of the day. I'm just settling into my paper when the clerk comes in, around ten-twenty-five, and calls the roll ("Zissner?" "Here!"). Suddenly it is 1944 and I am at an army base near Algiers, hammering tin to make a hot shower for Colonel McCloskey. That sort of thing can shoot the whole morning.

If it doesn't, the newspaper will. Only a waiting juror knows how infinite the crannies of journalism can be. I read "Arrival of Buyers," though I don't know what they want to buy and have nothing to sell. I read "Soybean Futures," though I wouldn't know a soybean even in the present. I read classified ads for jobs that I didn't know were jobs, like "key-punch operators." What keys do they punch? I mentally buy 4bdrm 1½bth splt lvl homes w/fpl overlooking Long Island Sound and dream of taking ½ bath there. I read dog news and horoscopes ("bucking others could prove dangerous today") and medical columns on diseases I've never heard of, but whose symptoms I instantly feel.

It's an exhausting trip, and I emerge with eyes blurry and mind blank. I look around at my fellow jurors. Some of them are trying to work—to keep pace, pitifully, with the jobs that they left in order to come here and do nothing. They spread queer documents on their knees, full graphs and figures, and they scribble on yellow pads. But the papers don't seem quite real to them, or quite right, removed from the tidy world of filing cabinets and secretaries, and after a while the workers put the work away again.

Around twelve-forty-five the clerk comes in to make   10
an announcement. We stir to attention: we are needed!
"Go to lunch," he says. "Be back at two." We straggle
out. By now the faces of all my fellow jurors are familiar
(we've been here eight days), and I keep seeing them as
we poke around the narrow streets of Chinatown looking
for a restaurant that isn't the one where we ate yesterday.
I smile tentatively, as New Yorkers do, and they smile tentatively back, and we go our separate ways. By one-fifty-
five we are seated in the jurors' room again, drowsy with
Chinese food and American boredom—too drowsy, certainly, to start *War and Peace*. Luckily, we all bought the
afternoon paper while we were out. Talk about remote
crannies of journalism!

Perhaps we are too hesitant to talk to each other, to   11
invite ourselves into lives that would refresh us by being
different from our own. We are scrupulous about privacy—it is one of the better gifts that the city can bestow,
and we don't want to spoil it for somebody else. Yet within
almost every New Yorker who thinks he wants to be left
alone is a person desperate for human contact. Thus we
may be as guilty as the jury system of not putting our time
to good use.

What we want to do most, of course, is serve on a   12
jury. We believe in the system. Besides, was there ever so
outstanding a group of jurors as we, so intelligent and fair-
minded? The clerks have told us all the reasons why jurors
are called in such wasteful numbers: court schedules are
unpredictable; trials end unexpectedly; cases are settled at
the very moment when a jury is called; prisoners plead
guilty to a lesser charge rather than wait years for a trial
that might prove them innocent. All this we know, and in
theory it makes sense.

In practice, however, somebody's arithmetic is wrong,   13
and one of America's richest assets is being dribbled away.
There must be a better way to get through the long and
tragic list of cases awaiting a solution—and, incidentally,
to get through *War and Peace*.

Comment

Zinsser's opening paragraph illustrates important kinds of sentence emphasis. A brief phrase, "Jury duty again," serves as the opening topic sentence, contrasting with the two longer sentences that follow. The first of these adds qualifying clauses and a qualifying phrase to the opening main clause:

> I'm sitting in the "central jurors' room" of a courthouse in lower Manhattan, as I do every two years, waiting to be called for a jury, which I almost never am.

The second sentence—the concluding sentence of the paragraph —uses basically the same structure, but with an important difference:

> It's an experience that all of us have known, in one form or another, as long as we can remember: organized solitude.

A complement to the opening main clause of the sentence, the concluding phrase, *organized solitude,* gains emphasis at the end of the sentence. In many of his sentences Zinsser takes advantage of terminal emphasis. But he uses this effect sparingly. His sentences have the ring of spoken sentences, depending on coordination and occasionally italics to convey vocal inflection:

> They are odd and implausible names, as diverse as the countries that they came from, but surely the clerk has met them all before. *Hasn't* he? Isn't that what democracy—and the jury system—is all about?

Questions for Study and Discussion

1. Which sentences in paragraph 5 are coordinate only? How many sentences consist of one introductory main clause, and one or more subordinate clauses? Do any of the sentences join subordinate to coordinate clauses?
2. Paragraph 6 contains a series of short emphatic opening sentences. Does Zinsser maintain this kind of emphasis in the rest of the paragraph?
3. How different is paragraph 7 from paragraph 6 in sentence construction? What use does Zinsser make of ellipsis? How

much emphasis (through pitch and volume) should the parenthetical statements be given?

4. How much subordination do you find in paragraph 8? How many sentences are built through modification?
5. How does Zinsser establish a point of view and a dominant tone? Or do you find changes in tone throughout the essay?
6. Why would Zinsser "almost rather be judged by [his] peers than judged by a judge"?

Vocabulary Study

Write a sentence using each of the following pairs of words, and explain the difference between them. The first word in each pair is Zinsser's:

1. *fragments* (paragraph 2), parts
2. *intimidates* (paragraph 3), threatens
3. *bureaucratic* (paragraph 3), governmental
4. *uncanny* (paragraph 3), strange
5. *implausible* (paragraph 4), unconvincing
6. *vulnerable* (paragraph 5), weak
7. *scrupulous* (paragraph 11), careful
8. *bestow* (paragraph 11), give

Suggestions for Writing

1. Describe a waiting room and your feelings in it. Make your details specific, and use your description to make a comment about your general situation. Develop several of your sentences with modification, as Zinsser does. Where you can, combine coordinate clauses with subordinate phrases and clauses.
2. Analyze two of the final paragraphs of Zinsser's essay, showing how coordination and subordination are used to give emphasis to particular ideas.

Parallelism

Words, phrases, and clauses that are similar in structure and perform the same function in a sentence are said to be *parallel,* as indicated by the italicized words in the examples below:

> I have never seen a *maladroit, clumsy,* or *blundering* cat.
> —Lewis Thomas, "To Err Is Human" [parallel words]

> Everyone says, stay away from ants. They have no lessons for us; they are crazy little instruments, *inhuman, incapable of controlling themselves, lacking manners, lacking souls.* —Lewis Thomas, "The Tucson Zoo" [parallel words and phrases]

Sentences in a paragraph may be parallel in structure—in whole or in part:

> Science is undeniably hard. *Often, it can seem* quite boring. *It is unfortunately too often presented* as laws to be memorized instead of mysteries to be explored. *It is too often kept a secret* that science, like art, takes a well developed esthetic sense.
> —K. C. Cole, "Women and Physics"

Parallelism makes the reader aware of the similarity in ideas. If the ideas are not similar, the parallelism may seem awkward. Writers in the past sometimes made parts of sentences exactly parallel, using almost the same number of words in phrases and clauses. This kind of sentence sometimes occurs today in formal speeches, or addresses, like the following:

> Do not let us speak of darker days; let us rather speak of sterner days. These are not dark days: these are great days— the greatest days our country has ever lived. . . .
> —Winston S. Churchill, an address delivered on October 29, 1941

441

Modern writers favor a looser parallelism and may vary the length of parallel elements and vary the wording, to avoid a formal effect:

> He watched Martin slip the lens into his pocket, he sighed, he struggled for something else to say, and silently he lumbered into his bedroom. —Sinclair Lewis, *Arrowsmith*

> But if you cleaned the East River you could have ponds all over town, up and down the East Side of Manhattan anyway. If you lifted out the Empire State Building and the high structures nearby, you would have, instantly, an inland sea. A few holes bored in the right places would let water into the subways, and you'd have lovely underground canals all across to the Hudson, uptown to the Harlem River, downtown to the Battery, a Venice underground, without pigeons. —Lewis Thomas, "Ponds"

Rachel Carson

SUMMER'S END

Rachel Carson (1907–1964) is one of the great writers on nature. In her books *Under the Sea-Wind* (1941), *The Sea Around Us*, which received the National Book Award in 1951, and *The Edge of the Sea* (1955), she drew upon her experiences as an aquatic biologist at the Marine Biological Laboratory at Woods Hole, Massachusetts and, from 1936 to 1952, with the United States Fish and Wildlife Service. She is perhaps best known for her book *Silent Spring* (1962), which warned of the dangers of pesticides to the environment. The National Council of Women in the United States gave Carson its first "Woman of Conscience" citation in 1963. The section reprinted here from *Under the Sea-Wind* describes an island on the southeastern coast of the United States. Carson tells us that Ship's Shoal is a "point of land . . . where the sea had broken through the barrier island to the sound years before." Mullet Pond is "half encircled by marsh, between the eastern end of the dunes and the inlet beach."

It was September before the sanderlings, now in whitening plumage, ran again on the island beach or hunted Hippa crabs in the ebbing tide at the point of land called

1

Ship's Shoal. Their flight from the northern tundras had been broken by many feeding stops on the wide mud flats of Hudson Bay and James Bay and on the ocean beaches from New England southward. In their fall migration the birds were unhurried, the racial urge that drove them northward in the spring having been satisfied. As the winds and the sun dictated, they drifted southward, their flocks now growing as more birds from the north joined them, now dwindling as more and more of the migrants found their customary winter home and dropped behind. Only the fringe of the great southward wave of shore birds would push on and on to the southernmost part of South America.

As the cries of the returning shore birds rose once ₂ more from the frothy edge of the surf and the whistle of the curlews sounded again in the salt marshes, there were other signs of the summer's end. By September the eels of the sound country had begun to drop downstream to the sea. The eels came down from the hills and the upland grasslands. They came from cypress swamps where black-watered rivers had their beginnings; they moved across the tidal plain that dropped in six giant steps to the sea. In the river estuaries and in the sounds they joined their mates-to-be. Soon, in silvery wedding dress, they would follow the ebbing tides to the sea, to find—and lose—themselves in the black abysses of mid-ocean.

By September, the young shad, come from the eggs ₃ shed in river and stream by the spawning runs of spring, were moving with the river water to the sea. At first they moved slowly in the vaster currents as the sluggish rivers broadened toward their estuaries. Soon, however, the speed of the little fish, no longer than a man's finger, would quicken, when the fall rains came and the wind changed, chilling the water and driving the fish to the warmer sea.

By September the last of the season's hatch of young ₄ shrimp were coming into the sounds through the inlets from the open sea. The coming of the young was symbolic of another journey which no man had seen and no man could describe—a journey taken weeks before by the elder generation of shrimp. All through the spring and summer more and more of the grown shrimp, come to maturity at the age of a year, had been slipping away from the coastal waters, journeying out across the continental shelf, descending the blue slopes of undersea valleys. From this journey they never returned, but their young, after several weeks of ocean life, were brought by the sea into the protected inside waters. All through the summer and fall the baby shrimp were brought into the sounds and river mouths—seeking warm shallows where brackish water lay over muddy bottoms. Here they fed eagerly on the abundant food and found shelter from hungry fish in the carpeting eel grass. And as they grew rapidly, the young turned once more to the sea, seeking its bitter waters and its deeper rhythms. Even as the youngest shrimp from the last spawning of the season came through the inlets on each flood tide of September, the larger young were moving out through the sounds to the sea.

By September the panicles of the sea oats in the dunes   5
had turned a golden brown. As the marshes lay under the sun, they glowed with the soft greens and browns of the salt meadow grass, the warm purples of the rushes, and the scarlet of the marsh samphire. Already the gum trees were like red flares set in the swamps of the river banks. The tang of autumn was in the night air, and as it rolled over the warmer marshes it turned to mist, hiding the herons who stood among the grasses at dawn; hiding from the eyes of the hawks the meadow mice who ran along the paths they had made through the marshes by the patient felling of thousands of marsh-grass stems; hiding the schools of silversides in the sound from the terns who fluttered above the rolling white sea, and caught no fish until the sun had cleared away the mists.

The chill night air brought a restlessness to many fish   6
scattered widely throughout the sound. They were steely gray fish with large scales and a low, four-spined fin set on the back like a spread sail. The fish were mullet who

had lived throughout the summer in the sound and estuary, roving solitary among the eel grass and widgeon grass, feeding on the litter of animal and vegetable fragments of the bottom mud. But every fall the mullet left the sounds and made a far sea journey, in the course of which they brought forth the next generation. And so the first chill of fall stirred in the fish the feeling of the sea's rhythm and awakened the instinct of migration.

The chilling waters and tidal cycles of the summer's end brought to many of the young fish of the sound country, also, a summons to return to the sea. Among these were the young pompano and mullet, silversides and killifish, who lived in the pond called Mullet Pond, where the dunes of the barrier island fell away to the flat sands of the Ship's Shoal. These young fish had been spawned in the sea, but had found their way to the pond through a temporary cut earlier that year. 7

On a day when the full harvest moon sailed like a white balloon in the sky, the tides, which had grown in strength as the moon swelled to roundness, began to wash out a gully across the inlet beach. Only on the highest tides did the torpid pond receive water from the ocean. Now the beat of the waves and the strong backwash that sucked away the loose sand had found the weak place in the beach, where a cut had been made before, and in less time than it took a fishing launch to cross from the mainland docks to the banks a narrow gully or slough had been cut through to the pond. Not more than a dozen feet across, it made a bottleneck into which the surf rolled as the waves broke on the beach. The water surged and seethed as in a mill race, hissing and foaming. Wave after wave poured through the slough and into the pond. They dug out an uneven, corrugated bottom over which the water leaped and tobogganed. They spread out into the marshes that backed the pond, seeping silently and stealthily among the grass stems and the reddening stalks of the marsh samphire. Into the marshes they carried the frothy brown scud thrown off by the waves. The sandy foam filled the spaces 8 between the grass stalks so closely that the marsh looked like a beach thickly grown with short grass; in reality the grass stood a foot in water and only the upper third of the stalks showed above the froth.

Leaping and racing, foaming and swirling, the incoming flood brought release to the myriads of small fishes that had been imprisoned in the pond. Now in thousands they poured out of the pond and out of the marshes. They raced in mad confusion to meet the clean, cold water. In their excitement they let the flood take them, toss them, turn them over and over. Reaching mid-channel of the slough they leaped high in the air again and again, sparkling bits of animate silver, like a swarm of glittering insects that rose and fell, rose again and fell. There the water seized them and held them back in their wild dash to the sea, so that many of them were caught on the slopes of the waves and held, tails uppermost, struggling helplessly against the might of the water. When finally the waves released them they raced down the slough to the ocean, where they knew once more the rolling breakers, the clean sandy bottoms, the cool green waters. 9

How did the pond and the marshes hold them all? On they came, in school after school, flashing bright among the marsh grasses, leaping and bounding out of the pond. For more than an hour the exodus continued, with scarcely a break in the hurrying schools. Perhaps they had come in, many of them, on the last spring tide when the moon was a pencil stroke of silver in the sky. And now the moon had grown fat and round and another spring tide, a rollicking, roistering, rough-and-ready tide, called them back to the sea again. 10

On they went, passing through the surf line where the white-capped waves were tumbling. On they went, most of them, past the smoother green swells to the second line of surf, where shoals tripped the waves coming in from the open sea and sent them sprawling in white confusion. But there were terns fishing above the surf, and thousands of the small migrants went no farther than the portals of the sea. 11

Comment

Carson uses parallelism to highlight similar as well as contrasting actions, as in the following sentence from paragraph 1:

> As the winds and the sun dictated, they drifted southward, their flocks *now growing as more birds from the north joined them, now dwindling as more and more of the migrants found their customary winter home and dropped behind.* Only the fringe of the great southward wave of shore birds *would push on and on* to the southernmost part of South America. [italics added]

The parallel construction of the italicized participial phrases in the first sentence highlights the contrasting growth of the flocks of birds and their dwindling. The phrase *would push on and on* in the second sentence emphasizes the contrast with the birds who dropped from the migration. The parallelism of the following sentence from paragraph 5 allows Carson to combine a large number of contrasting actions and descriptive details without confusion or a loss of focus:

> The tang of autumn was in the night air, and as it rolled over the warmer marshes it turned to mist, *hiding the herons who stood among the grasses at dawn; hiding from the eyes of the hawks the meadow mice who ran along the paths they had made through the marshes by the patient felling of thousands of marshgrass stems; hiding the schools of silversides in the sound from the terns who fluttered above the rolling white sea, and caught no fish until the sun had cleared away the mists.* [italics added]

Occasionally Carson makes these elements similar in length as well as construction and wording:

> The water surged and seethed as in a mill race, hissing and foaming. [paragraph 8]

This balancing of sentence elements helps to convey the rhythms of nature that Carson wishes the reader to experience.

Questions for Study and Discussion

1. What in the behavior of the sanderlings, eel, shad, and other fish marks summer's end?

2. In what way is the coming of the young shrimp "symbolic of another journey"?
3. What changes in the weather and in the flora or vegetation of the island does Carson describe, and for what purpose?
4. What natural process is Carson describing in paragraphs 8, 9, and 10? Is she making a point about this process?

Sentence Study

Identify the parallel elements in the following sentences. What does the parallelism contribute to the clarity or effect of the sentence?

1. As the marshes lay under the sun, they glowed with the soft greens and browns of the salt meadow grass, the warm purples of the rushes, and the scarlet of the marsh samphire. [paragraph 5]
2. The fish were mullet who had lived throughout the summer in the sound and estuary, roving solitary among the eel grass and widgeon grass, feeding on the litter of animal and vegetable fragments of the bottom mud. [paragraph 6]
3. These young fish had been spawned in the sea, but had found their way to the pond through a temporary cut earlier that year. [paragraph 7]
4. On they went, most of them, past the smoother green swells to the second line of surf, where shoals tripped the waves coming in from the open sea and sent them sprawling in white confusion. [paragraph 11]

Suggestions for Writing

1. Describe a seasonal change in plant life and wild life you have observed in your town or city or a place you have visited. Organize your description to make a point. Let your reader discover the point or idea through the details of your description.
2. Describe changes in everyday life that occur in your neighborhood during a change of weather or change of season. Let your details make a point—perhaps a point about the people of your neighborhood or town.

Sentence Variety

Sentences need to be varied to avoid a sense of monotony. Thus, a series of short simple sentences like the following will soon lose the reader's attention:

> You are watching coal miners at work. You realize momentarily what different universes people inhabit. It is a sort of world apart down there. One can quite easily go through life without ever hearing about that world. Probably a majority of people would even prefer not to hear about it.

Few people think or write in such a disconnected way. Here is the actual version of the sentences above:

> Watching coal miners at work, you realize momentarily what different universes different people inhabit. *Down there* where coal is dug it is a sort of world apart *which* one can quite easily go through life without ever hearing about. Probably a majority of people would even prefer not to hear about it. — George Orwell, *The Road to Wigan Pier* [italics added]

Orwell varied his sentences probably as most writers do—without much conscious attention. The italicized connectives come naturally to us as we speak or write: it is the disconnection in the first version of the passage that is unnatural. Indeed, it takes some effort to write in so fragmented and disjointed a way. The rewritten sentences are not only monotonous but hard to understand because we must continually refocus our attention.

As a rule, the more varied the length and construction of our sentences, the less monotonous they are likely to be, and the more apparent the natural emphasis we wish to give our ideas. Notice the choices open to the writer in combining the following:

You are watching coal miners at work. You realize momentarily what different universes people inhabit.

Orwell might have written the following:

As you watch coal miners at work, you realize momentarily what different universes people inhabit.

You realize momentarily what different universes people inhabit, as you watch coal miners at work.

Watching coal miners at work makes one realize momentarily what different universes people inhabit.

These varied sentences achieve emphasis in different ways. In the first, the emphasis falls on the idea of different universes; in the second, on watching the miners at work. The third sentence gives the same emphasis to both ideas. Which sentence the writer chooses depends on what is emphasized in the whole paragraph or essay. As Orwell's paragraph shows, the choice can depend on making the connection of ideas clear.

Russell Baker

THE BEER CULTURE

Russell Baker was born in 1925 in Loudon County, in northern Virginia, and was raised in a Blue Ridge mountain community and later in Newark, New Jersey, and Baltimore, Maryland—very different worlds described in his autobiographical *Growing Up* (1982) and *The Good Times* (1989). Upon graduating from Johns Hopkins University in 1947, Baker began reporting for the *Baltimore Sun*. From 1954 to 1962 he reported on Washington and national politics for the *New York Times*. Since 1963 he has written a column for the *Times*. His many columns on national politics and American life— many of them humorous—have been collected in *This Is Depravity* (1980) and other books. In 1979 Baker received the Pulitzer Prize for Distinguished Commentary, and the Pulitzer Prize for Biography in 1983 for *Growing Up*.

The people of Beer World are named Buck, Mike, Al and Mac. There are no Algernons in Beer World, no Marmadukes, no Gaylords. Beer World has hair on its chest.

Yes, there are a few women in Beer World. They are 2
named Gladys, though there is one named Elvira. You
have seen the woman who brings a tray of beer to Buck,
Mike, Al and Mac while they are sitting in the beer parlor
in their mackinaws being rugged and jolly? Of course you
have seen her. That woman is Gladys.

You may also have seen Buck recently having his beer 3
at a distinctly sissified ski lodge in company with a lissome
young woman. That woman is Elvira. Buck sometimes
takes Elvira to these sissy places in order to experience the
perfection of beer without sweating.

Buck often feels guilty after these perspiration-free out- 4
ings with Elvira, for in Beer World it is man's duty to
heave and grunt until his pores open and let the honest
body juices cascade freely. Only then does he truly deserve
beer. Beer is the reward for manly toil in Beer World.

How often have you seen Buck, Mike, Al and Mac ex- 5
hausted at the end of an honest day's work on the firing
squad, sleeves rolled up, shirt collars opened, perspiration
dampening their cheeks as they labor to rid the world of
malcontents, looters and sissies—how often have you seen
them joyfully throw down their tools as the sun sets, embrace each other merrily and tramp over to Gladys's place
for their beer?

Now comes beer time. The beer has been created for 6
Buck, Mike, Al and Mac in recognition of their labor, in
recognition of all they do. The beer is for them. Not for
Algernon. Not for Marmaduke and Gaylord. Someone will
object that we never really see the boys putting in a full
day's work on the firing squad, that all we ever see are the
final few executions at sunset. But of course; in Beer
World, sunset is the only time of day. The sun stands eternally in the setting position. Shortly after Buck, Mike, Al
and Mac throw down their rifles, or their scythes or their
big tractor-trailers, and receive their beer from Gladys, they
tramp out into the sunset again and finish building a sky-
scraper so they can throw down their rivet guns and
march back to Gladys's place for another round of well-
earned beer.

Why does Buck occasionally sneak away to sissified 7
places with Elvira to drink his beer in dry clothing? Surely
Buck would rather be with Mike, Al and Mac arriving at
Beer World's cottage by the lake in their plaid fishing
shirts.

Of course, Buck would. It is much more fun racing to 8
the refrigerator with Mike, Al and Mac and discovering
four bottles of chilled beer than it is sitting across a table
from Elvira. Is Buck—let us phrase the question as delicately as possible—is Buck soft on women?

The question is often raised by Mike, Al and Mac when 9
they are all having dinner together in order to deserve a
beer, or jogging twenty miles together just at sunset in
order to earn the right really to enjoy a beer. Once they
even asked Doc—Beer World's psychiatrist—to put Buck on
the couch, give him a bottle of beer and find out if he was
really one of the boys.

Doc had just finished whipping a massive superego 10
down to size and was headed to Gladys's place for his beer
when he conducted the examination. He pronounced Buck
a perfectly normal beer guy with a slight woman problem.

It seems Buck had a mother, which is very rare in Beer 11
World. In his youth, "Old Moms," as Buck called her,
used to send him to the corner saloon to buy her what she
called "a bucket of suds." "Old Moms" had since been
deported under Beer World's rigid legal code, which denies
citizenship to most women, especially if, like "Old Moms,"
they sit around the house in dresses made from flour sacks
drinking beer out of tin buckets.

The law was necessary because people like "Old 12
Moms" created a bad image of Beer World, which wanted
to be viewed as a sweaty but clean-cut place full of boys
whose beer had fewer calories and whose mothers, if they
must have mothers, wouldn't be caught dead wearing
flour sacks. In short, Buck felt bad about the old lady's
deportation; when he took Elvira out for beer, he was
really taking out his mother who had learned to dress ex-
pensively and to drink her beer out of a glass.

Elvira actually despises beer and would much prefer a   13
drink with Amaretto in it, but doesn't dare order it for fear
Buck would accuse her of not being one of the boys and
walk out of her life forever. The women of Beer World do
not have much opportunity to get out for a good time.
Elvira has often asked Gladys to go out and have some
Amaretto with her, but Gladys is afraid that if the boys
learned about it they would call her a sissy.

Comment

Baker satirizes not just the characters and situations in beer ads
but also, in the phrase of Walker Gibson, their "tough talk."
Gibson characterizes tough talk through its "short sentences,
'crude' repetitions of words, simple grammatical structures with
little subordinating." Seeking a "tense intimacy with his assumed reader, another man who has been around," the tough
talker favors "colloquial patterns from oral speech and . . . a
high frequency of the definite article. He lets his reader make
logical and other connections between elements" (*Tough, Sweet,
and Stuffy*). Tough talk is marked by the monotony of its
sentences—the lack of variety that Baker is imitating.

Questions for Study and Discussion

1. The essay opens with three short simple sentences—all lack-
    ing modification. These illustrate one of the characteristics
    of Gibbon's "tough talk." What other paragraphs also con-
    tain relatively simple or short sentences, compound or com-
    plex sentences?
2. How much " 'crude' repetition of words" do you find
    throughout the essay?
3. How often does Baker depend on "colloquial patterns from
    oral speech" and a "high frequency of the definite article"?
4. In imitating the tough talker through the style of the essay,
    Baker is characterizing the tough-talking advertiser. What
    does he gain satirically in imitating the speech of this
    person?

5. What does the essay reveal about Baker's personality, out-look, and sense of humor?
6. What satirical points is Baker making not only about beer ads but also about the "beer culture"? Is the essay closer to social satire than to ethical satire (p. 374)?
7. How effective do you find the satire?

Vocabulary Study

Baker depends on connotation—the associations and emotional auras of words—to convey the tone and attitudes about the beer culture. What do the following words mean? What connotations do they convey?

1. *lissome* (paragraph 3)
2. *cascade* (paragraph 4)
3. *malcontents, sissies* (paragraph 5)
4. *massive superego, slight woman problem* (paragraph 10)
5. *Amaretto* (paragraph 13)

Suggestions for Writing

1. Write an essay analyzing another series of ads that depict a different kind of world or culture—perhaps that of sports car owners. Develop a thesis suggested by the similarities in these ads.
2. Use the same ads to write a satirical essay. Again, use the similarities in these ads to make your point. But do not state this point directly; let your descriptive details and tone convey it, as in Baker's satirical picture of "Beer World."

Concreteness

To make an idea *concrete* is to make it exist for the reader through the senses. The statement "That car's a beauty!" expresses a general attitude and feeling but nothing more. If we want readers to share our experience we must give particulars or details, as in this explanation of what California teenagers mean by the expression "low and slow, mean and clean":

> The car a lowrider drives—almost always a sedan produced by the General Motors Corporation—is also called a lowrider, or a ride. If it has been altered with conspicuous success—a multi-colored lacquer paint job, say, and metal-spoke wheels, and skimpy tires that seem to belong on a Datsun rather than a 1967 Chevrolet Impala, and a welded-chain steering wheel no bigger around than a 45-r.p.m. record—it is called a clean ride, or a bad ride. "Low and slow," lowriders sometimes say. "Mean and clean."   —Calvin Trillin and Edward Koren, "Low and Slow, Mean and Clean"

Not all abstract ideas can be expressed entirely through physical details. We can, however, show their application to experience, suggest how we came to the idea, or give a partial illustration, as in the following statement on ancient Egyptian burial practices:

> In Egypt, as has been said, the reality of the unseen world slowly overshadowed that of the seen, but invisible though it was, it remained substantial. The dead bodies must be preserved from returning to dust; they must be placed in tombs that were underground fortresses safe from disturbance; they must be surrounded by all the furnishings they had made use of in life.   —Edith Hamilton, *The Greek Way*

The idea has been made concrete. At the same time, we must be careful not to give more details than needed to make the idea clear. Writing can be so colorful—so crowded with details and descriptive words—that the reader is distracted from the main idea.

William G. Wing

CHRISTMAS COMES FIRST ON THE BANKS

William G. Wing was a veteran correspondent of the *New York Herald Tribune*. A specialist on natural resources and conservation, he has written for *Audubon Magazine*, the *New York Times*, and other periodicals. This evocative essay, based on a trip on a Gloucester, Massachusetts, trawler, shows how a popular subject can be written about freshly from a new and unusual point of view.

The Christmas sun rises first, in America, on trawler- 1
men fishing the undersea meadows of Georges Bank.

At the moment before sunrise a hundred miles east of 2
Cape Cod, the scene aboard a trawler is so unchanging it
can be imagined. The net has been hauled and streamed
again. The skipper is alone in the pilot house, surrounded
by the radio-telephone's racket and the green and amber
eyes of electronic instruments, instruments that are supposed to tell him not only where he is but where the fish
are, too. But this is only hope, not science. Despite the instruments, despite the boat's resemblance to a plow horse,
methodically criss-crossing the meadow, her men are not
engineers or farmers, but hunters who seek their prey in
the wilderness of the sea. The trawlermen are, in fact, the
last tribe of nomadic huntsmen left in the East.

The skipper is alone, then, with a huntsman's anxi- 3
eties: the whereabouts of the prey, the uncertainties of the
weather, the chances of hitting a good market. On deck
before him the men are processing the catch just brought
aboard. They sit in a circle of brilliance, the deck lights
reflecting from their yellow and Daybrite-orange oilskins
and from the brown curve of the riding sail above. They
sit on the edges of the pens, holding the big white and
silver fish between their knees, ripping with knives and
tearing with hands, heaving the disemboweled bodies into a central basket. Nothing is visible beyond the cone of

light but the occasional flash of a whitecap or comber.
There is much noise, though—wind and water and seabirds that have gathered in mobs for the feast of haulback.

There is an appropriateness to Christmas in this scene,   4
east of the sleeping mainland, so marked that it seems
quaint. The names of the trawlers themselves—*Holy Family,
Immaculate Conception, St. Mary, St. Joseph*—give the flavor.
On the engine room bulkhead of a trawler *Holy Cross*,
beyond the ugga-chugging Atlas diesel, is a painting of
Christ at Gethsemane. There is an appropriateness, too,
among the men. They share alike—equal shares of profit,
equal shares of danger. To work together in such small
quarters and stern conditions requires a graciousness of
spirit that is the essence of Christmas.

The sun is up and the pens are empty. As the deck is   5
hosed down and the trash fish pitchforked overboard, the
noise from the birds rises hysterically—barnyard sounds,
shrieks, whistles, klaxon horns. Now the birds can be seen
flying in a circle around the boat. Each can hold position
for only a few moments beside the point where the remains of fish are washing over. Then it falls astern and has
to come up to windward on the other side of the boat,
cross ahead and fall backward to the critical point. The
birds pumping up the windward side look like six-day
bicycle riders, earnest and slightly ridiculous, but when
they reach the critical point there is a miraculous moment
of aerobatics as the birds brake, wheel and drop in the
broken air.

Gulls snatch, gannets plunge, but the little kittiwakes   6
balance delicately, their tails spread like carved ivory fans.
There is a column of descending, shrieking birds, a scin-
tillating feathered mass. The birds revolving about the boat
have made themselves not only guests at the feast but have
formed the wreath as well.

Christmas Day has begun, but for the men it is time to   7
sleep. They hose each other off and then disappear
through the whaleback for a mug-up below. Boots and oilskins off, they will have a minute or two for a James Bond

novel or a crossword puzzle in the bunks, braced against the elevator motions of the hull, not hearing the sounds of Niagara outside. Then the instant unconsciousness that seamen and children know. The skipper alone remains awake, watching Christmas come.

Christmas came first to men on lonely meadows. It will come first again to the men on the lonely meadows offshore, fishing the Bank in boats wreathed by seabirds. 8

Comment

Wing tells us that he will seek to make the moment before the sun rises concrete: he will find images that convey the mood and experience of the moment. He does so in the details of the boat, the trawlermen, their relations—"equal shares of profits, equal shares of danger." The seabirds have an unexpected appropriateness, for they wreathe the boats in their circlings. Through careful selection of details, Wing succeeds in his purpose; through his description, he is able to make a point without stating it directly.

Questions for Study and Discussion

1. What point is Wing making through his description? Is it important to him where the Christmas sun first rises in America?
2. Is the order of details governed by space (moving from one part of the scene to another) or by time, or possibly both?
3. What details make the idea of Christmas in the essay concrete?
4. Is Wing saying that the life aboard the trawler and the relations between the men are different during the Christmas season or on Christmas Day?
5. How does Wing make transitions throughout the essay?
6. What is the point of the concluding comparison?

Vocabulary Study

For each of the following words, list at least two synonyms that suggest a more specific meaning or use. For example, *forecast* is more specific than *foretell* when referring to a weather prediction.

1. *large*
2. *small*
3. *dirty*
4. *clean*
5. *law*
6. *run*

Suggestions for Writing

1. Describe a scene at a particular moment—for example, the moment of impact in an automobile accident. Select details that contribute to a central impression, but do not state the impression directly.
2. Describe a day of work, showing how the season of the year affects you and your fellow workers. Use your description to develop a thesis.
3. Describe an unusual day in your life—one that perhaps was spent in an unusual setting, away from home. Stress those feelings and details that made the day unusual and memorable.

Elizabeth Janeway

WATER

Elizabeth Janeway is the author of numerous short stories and novels, including *Daisy Kenyon* (1945) and *Accident* (1964), and she has written about the role of women in various societies and the changes in women's lives in recent years. Her books on women include *Man's World, Woman's Place: A Study in Social Mythology* (1971), *Between Myth and Morning: Women Awakening* (1974), and *Powers of the Weak* (1980). Her essay on water, first published in *House and Garden* magazine, makes a number of abstract ideas concrete.

Water is a universal symbol. Tamed and trickling out of   1
the tap, softened and fluoridated, warmed in the boiler by
fires burning million-year-old oil, it is still not quite a com-
modity. Even for city dwellers some dim memory stirs
from time to time of those ancient eons when water or the
lack of it ruled everything—the sites of habitation, the paths
through the wilderness, the limits of hunting grounds,
famine and abundance, life and death. It can still shatter
human hopes and plans. Thirty years ago, the top soil in
the plain states rose into the sky and blew away. Men had
ploughed grazing land, counting on rain to bind the soil
where the tough grass roots had been cut, and the rain did
not come. A migration as great as that of the Mongols
poured out of the Dust Bowl toward California. Steinbeck,
in *The Grapes of Wrath*, recorded what happened to one bit
of flotsam on one stream of this Diaspora. Today, I read
in the papers, the Russians are ploughing the virgin
Siberian lands as, in the last century, we ploughed the
Dakotas. But the stubborn old gods of rivers and rains have
not yet submitted to Marxist-Leninist discipline. Disappointing harvests are reported.

Water. "It has caused more wars in the Middle East,"   2
writes Freya Stark in one of her brilliant travel books,
"than even religion." In the Middle East, that is quite a
feat. But there are historians who trace the breakdown of
the ancient civilizations along the Tigris, the Euphrates and
the Indus to wars and raiding parties which breached dams
and ruined irrigation and drainage systems. Whether the
cities fell first and the aqueducts and irrigation ditches
silted up through neglect, or whether they were
deliberately destroyed to strangle the cities, they have
never been rebuilt. Let us not imagine, in our smug pride
of modernity, that engineers have yet become more
powerful than statesmen, for even today, there is desert
where once there was fertile land. Civilization takes water
for granted, but that is civilization's mistake.

It's not a mistake, though, that will ever be made by   3
those who live past the limits of "city water." Amidst all
the denouncing of suburbia, let us give it credit for this:

suburban dwellers must face some of the old facts of life, of living and of weather. In the country, water comes out of a well—save for that blessed, lucky trickle which flows to a favored few from a gravity-fed spring (and that is a trickle which, in August, may dwindle disastrously). Civilization, of course, has changed the Old Oaken Bucket into an electric motor pumping so many gallons a minute to a cistern from an artesian well, but it has not changed the nature of the emotions that go with procuring this water, only bunched them together into patches of intensity with stretches of complacence in between. But when the power goes out in a storm, so does the water supply.

Where we used to live, seventy miles from New York, the power had a habit of failing before the telephone lines went. Why this should be, I don't know. But the prudence of the telephone company in locating its poles and stringing its wires allowed messages to get through from neighbor to neighbor before the telephone lines went down and silence followed darkness. Thus, a spreading rash of calls would ripple out from the center of casualty: "We've lost our power. If you still have yours, fill the bathtubs quick." Then the householder (or his wife, if he was a commuter who spent his days in an ivory tower in the city) would go into action and fill tubs and buckets and pots and pans against the drought to come. After one ice storm, the water famine lasted for a week in some parts of the township, and luckier folk invited their neighbors in for baths.

From time to time, as families grew in size or new houses went up with their demanding machines for washing clothes and dishes, new wells had to be dug. Then the drillers would come with their rig and thump away at the ancient granite beneath our green countryside, and the owners would groan and shake a little, too, at the dollars that each hour of thumping represented. There was water, the drillers would report encouragingly, but not yet quite enough, three gallons a minute, five gallons a minute—would they never find the level that would deliver the necessary eight gallons a minute? On and on they went, like persevering, unsuccessful disciples of Moses, smiting the rock. Once a friend of ours, in despair after weeks of fruitless pounding, called in a water dowser. Our friend is the founder of one of the oldest and most respected public opinion polls. It seemed quaintly appropriate to think of an old man with a hazel twig in his hands questioning every foot of the poll taker's land on its water content. At last he said, "Dig here," and they dug, and found water. Of course, it was simply luck—whatever that means.

Water. It is a universal symbol, I wrote, but a symbol 6
of what? Of birth and beginnings, as the scientists, the first chapter of Genesis and Dr. Freud all tell us? Life began in the sea, say the biochemists, when lightning discharges awoke, in the thin soup of almost life, some monstrous protein molecules which married each other: this is our most modern mythology. An older story tells us that the Spirit of God moved on the face of the waters even before His command created Light: which might, after all, be simply a more majestic way of describing the same event. As for Freud, when he had rummaged through enough people's heads and stitched thousands of fragments of dreams together, he came to the cautious conclusion that "to dream of being in water or passing through a stream often symbolized the act of birth." Which is a nice, pedantic, and quite useless conclusion, for it leaves us with another set of waters unexplained. What shall we make of "the bitter, salt, estranging sea," or the rivers of Styx and of Lethe, which are the rivers of death?

We must think again. Water can symbolize birth, as it 7
can symbolize death, but essentially its meaning is greater and simpler, and includes both. At the deepest level, water stands as the symbol of Change. Indeed, when St. John, in the Revelations, wished to describe the eternal landscape that would follow upon the Day of Judgment, he said, "There was no more sea." Changeless eternity could go no further.

Water is the present tense. It flows. It will not take a 8
shape of its own, but will fill indifferently any jug or pitcher or cup, and then flow out and on, indifferent still, forgetful and uninfluenced. Its strength is the strength of

movement. Even "still waters" must "run deep." If they do not, we distrust them and have made a pejorative word for such unnatural behavior—"stagnant," or standing. In New Mexico, the Indians believe that water can die. Mary Austin records the legend:

> At midnight drink no water
> For I have heard said
> That on the stroke of midnight
> All water goes dead.

Water is always now. It demands the present participle for its description—gushing, flowing, pouring, sprinkling. As every gardener knows, last week's soaking and next week's rain might as well not exist, unless we manage to string them together by constructing tanks and cisterns and reservoirs. Thirst is immediate. Water cannot be an event, it must be a presence. To make it so must be a primary concern of any stable society, great or small.   9

Modern man is astonishingly modest about his achievements. I am not at all sure that this is a healthy state of mind. Might we not be more confident of our ability to deal with our future problems if we took a bit more pride in our successful solutions to problems of the past? Modesty is all very well for individuals, but civic pride can give a community a sense of wholeness and of its obligations to its citizens. We have somehow lost the knack of celebrating deeds of greatness today, and are apt to go off to the beach on the Fourth of July, each family by itself, instead of taking a little time to remember our heroes and refresh our pride.   10

I would like to see more holidays, and as one of them I would like to propose a Festival of the Waters. It might well be held on St. Swithin's Day. I imagine pilgrimages to the Tennessee Valley, to Grand Coulee and to Boulder Dam. I think of holiday tours along the St. Lawrence Seaway, with river steamers full of bands and picnickers toasting all that good sense, engineering training and peace between nations have wrought there. The irrigated valleys of California could show off their wealth.   11

Above all, each city should offer thanks to its sani-   12
tary engineers, who might appear with an accompanying
guard of master plumbers—for even the grimmest nature
may sweeten a little once it feels itself appreciated. The
Mayor might read out the proud statistics citing the
number of years since typhoid or cholera claimed a victim
within his purlieus; and if the statistics should by any
chance not be proud, how quick the Mayor and the
Department of Sanitation would be to improve them! And
each year the ceremony would be crowned by the dedication of some new Wonder of Water: a handsome public
pool, or a fountain with a bit of green about it, shining and
leaping in the center of the city where passers-by could
refresh their eyes. Or a boat basin. Or a new wing on the
aquarium. Or—

But you see what I mean. Water is a universal symbol   13
because it is a universal need. As we live now, it is beyond
the power of the individual, in the vast majority of cases,
to satisfy this need on his own. Only men working together can build reservoirs and aqueducts and dams and
hydroelectric stations and sewage conversion plants and,
soon no doubt, great structures to desalt the sea and make
the desert blossom like the corn tassel and the alfalfa.

Our Festival of Waters, then, would be a holiday to   14
celebrate the things that men working together can achieve.
What could be more appropriate? For as we all know, the
just and the unjust both get wet when it rains and thirsty
when it does not. Too often, in the past, the just and the
unjust have preferred to disagree and to create deserts
rather than settle down and share out their water rights.
But now our engineering knowledge is growing with the
world's population, and with its need for water. Might not,
for once, new skills combine with new deeds? Might
not the just and the unjust decide to work together, literally for dear life? And might not these projects to control
the fluid strength and the eternal changeability of water
teach us something about controlling the fluid strength and
eternal changeability of human nature?

Comment

Elizabeth Janeway begins her reflective essay with an abstract statement, "Water is a universal symbol." Janeway makes this statement concrete through a wide range of examples drawn from cultural history, religion, psychology, and personal experience. Her essay is in fact an exploration of many symbolic meanings, not just one. In the course of her essay, Janeway states a number of problems associated with water; it is fitting, therefore, that she conclude by looking at possible solutions.

Questions for Study and Discussion

1. In paragraphs 1 and 2, does Janeway state what water symbolizes? Does she do so in describing the experiences of suburban people in pararaphs 3–5?
2. How do paragraphs 6 and 7 advance the discussion begun in paragraphs 1–5?
3. How did St. John use water to symbolize an abstract idea?
4. In paragraph 8, Janeway introduces another abstract idea: "Water is the present tense." How do the details of the paragraph make this idea concrete? How is this discussion related to the preceding paragraphs?
5. What topic does Janeway introduce in paragraph 10, and how is this topic related to the preceding discussion? How does she lead the reader back to her original thesis, restated in paragraph 13?
6. What problems has Janeway identified in the course of the essay, and what solutions does she propose in her concluding paragraph?

Vocabulary Study

To answer the following questions, you will need to consult dictionaries, encyclopedias, and other reference books in your college library:

1. What was the Diaspora, and how is Janeway using the term in paragraph 1. What does she mean in the same paragraph by the word *flotsam?*

2. What is the difference between an aqueduct and an irrigation ditch (paragraph 2)?
3. What kinds of wells and springs does Janeway describe in paragraph 3?
4. To what biblical event is Janeway referring in paragraph 5? To what other biblical events and passages does she refer, and why?
5. In what mythology do the rivers of Lethe and Styx occur (paragraph 6)? What mythological significance did these rivers have?
6. Why might a water festival be fitting on St. Swithin's day (paragraph 11)?

Suggestions for Writing

1. Illustrate an idea about water in Janeway's essay from personal experience and observation, or state and illustrate an idea of your own.
2. Water plays a prominent role in "Dover Beach," "To Marguerite—Continued," and other poems of Matthew Arnold. Analyze one of these poems in a short essay, focusing on Arnold's symbolic use of water.

Figurative Language

Much of our language is *figurative* in departing from the literal meaning of words—sometimes without our realizing it is. Certain figures of speech that once called a picture to mind may have become stale. Here are a few examples:

blaze of glory   drunk with power   hard as nails

"Blaze of glory" is a *metaphor*—a figure of speech in which one thing is talked about as if it were something else. The metaphor does not tell us that glory is like a fire: it speaks of glory as if it were. "Drunk with power" is also a metaphor: it specifies that power acts like an intoxicant. "Hard as nails" makes the comparison directly through the word *as*, and we therefore call it a *simile*. Another important figure of speech is *personification*, which gives animate or human qualities to something inanimate or nonhuman:

The tree *cowered* in the storm.

Figurative language is a valuable way of conveying our feelings about an object or experience.

In exposition and argument, figurative language can make an idea or attitude concrete and persuasive. It can be unobtrusive, and at other times it can be dramatic, as in this description by a surgeon of one of the tools of his art:

The scalpel is in two parts, the handle and the blade. Joined, it is six inches from tip to tip. At one end of the handle is a narrow notched prong upon which the blade is slid, then snapped into place. Without the blade, the handle has a blind, decapitated look. It is helpless as a trussed maniac. But slide on the blade, click it home, and the knife springs instantly to life. It is headed now, edgy, leaping to mount the fingers for the gallop to its feast. —Richard Selzer, *Mortal Lessons*

Metaphor, simile, and personification here are combined in a highly effective way; the description conveys the excitement of the surgeon as he holds the scalpel and prepares to use it.

David R. Scott

WHAT IS IT LIKE TO WALK ON THE MOON?

David R. Scott was born in San Antonio, Texas, in 1932, where his father was stationed as an Air Force brigadier general. Educated at West Point and MIT, Scott served in the Air Force as a jet pilot, and in 1963 began his training as an astronaut. He was one of the three who piloted the *Endeavour*, in the Apollo 15 mission to the moon, entering lunar orbit on July 29, 1971. Scott explored the lunar surface with James B. Irwin, while Alfred Worden remained in the command ship. The *Endeavour* returned to earth on August 7. The essay reprinted here gives a vivid account of his experiences on the moon, and shows how figurative language can serve in exposition.

Sixty feet above the moon, the blast of our single 1 rocket churns up a gray tumult of lunar dust that seems to engulf us. Blinded, I feel the rest of the way down "on the gauges." With an abrupt jar, our lunar module, or LM, strikes the surface and shudders to rest. We have hit our target squarely—a large amphitheater girded by mountains and a deep canyon, at the eastern edge of a vast plain.

As Jim Irvin and I wait for the dust to settle, I recall 2 the twelve revolutions we have just spent in lunar orbit aboard our Apollo 15 spaceship *Endeavour*. Each two hours found us completing a full circuit of earth's ancient satellite—one hour knifing through lunar night, then sunrise and an hour of daylight. As we orbited, I found a particular fascination in that sector of the darkened moon bathed in earthshine. The light reflected by our planet illuminates the sleeping moon much more brightly than moonlight silvers our own night. The mountains and crater rims are clearly seen.

I will always remember *Endeavour* hurtling through that 3 strange night of space. Before us and above us stars spangled the sky with their distant icy fire; below lay the moon's far side, an arc of impenetrable blackness that blotted the firmament. Then, as our moment of sunrise approached, barely discernible streamers of light—actually the glowing gases of the solar corona millions of miles away—played above the moon's horizon. Finally the sun exploded into our view like a visual thunderclap. Abruptly, completely, in less than a second, its harsh light flooded into the spaceship and dazzled our eyes.

As we looked into the early lunar morning from *Endeavour*, the moonscape stretched into the distance, everything the color of milk chocolate. Long angular shadows accentuated every hill, every crater. As the sun arched higher, the plains and canyons and mountains brightened to a gunmetal gray, while the shadows shrank. At full lunar noontide, the sun glared down upon a bleached and almost featureless world.

Now we have come to rest on the moon, and the last of the dust settles outside the LM. We throw the switches that convert this hybrid vehicle from spacecraft to dwelling. Thus begin our 67 hours of lunar residence. We are on a still and arid world where each blazing day and each subfreezing night stretch through 355 earth hours. We have landed in the bright morning of a moon day. When we depart, the sun will not have reached zenith.

It is sobering to realize that we are the only living souls on this silent sphere, perhaps the only sentient beings in our solar system not confined to earth. Though we have slipped the bonds of our home planet, we remain earthmen. So we keep our clocks set to Houston time and gear our lives to the 24-hour cycle we have always known.

Opening the top hatch for a preliminary reconnaisance, I peer out at a world seemingly embalmed in the epoch of its creation. Each line, each form blends into the harmonious whole of a single fluid sculpture. Craters left by "recent" meteorites—merely millions of years ago—stand out, startlingly white, like fresh scar tissue against the soft beige of the undulating terrain.

I steal a moment and glance straight up into the black sky where the crystalline sphere of earth—all blue and white, sea and clouds—gleams in the abyss of space. In that cold and boundless emptiness, our planet provides the only glow of color. For 30 minutes my helmeted head pivots above the open hatch as I survey and photograph the wonderland of the lunar surface. The incredible variety of landforms in this restricted area (on the moon, the horizon lies a scant mile and a half from a viewer) fills me with pleasant surprise. To the south an 11,000-foot ridge rises above the bleak plain. To the east stretch the hulking heights of an even higher summit. On the west a winding gorge plunges to depths of more than 1,000 feet. Dominating the northeastern horizon, a great mountain stands in noble splendor almost three miles above us. Ours is the first expedition to land amid lunar mountains. Never quickened by life, never assailed by wind and rain, they loom still and serene, a tableau of forever. Their majesty overwhelms me.

Eight years' training in lunar geology makes me instantly aware of intriguing details. A dark line like a bathtub ring smudges the bases of the mountains. Was it left by the subsiding lake of lava that filled the immense cavity of Palus Putredinis, on the fringes of Mare Imbrium, billions of years ago? Mare Imbrium, on whose edge we have landed, stretches across the face of the moon for some 650 miles. The celestial projectile that excavated it must have been huge—perhaps as much as 50 miles across—and it slammed into the moon with a velocity many times greater than that of a rifle bullet.   9

When we descend the ladder of the LM and step onto the moon's surface, Jim and I feel a gratifying sense of freedom. For five days we have been crammed into the tight confines of the spacecraft that brought us here. Now, all at once, we regain the luxury of movement. But, we quickly discover, locomotion on the moon has its own peculiar restrictions. At one-sixth of earth's gravity, we weigh only a sixth our normal poundage. Our gait quickly evolves into a rhythmic, bounding motion that possesses all the lightness and ease of strolling on a trampoline.   10

At the same time, since the mass of our bodies and personal gear—and hence, our inertia—remains unchanged,   11 starting and stopping require unusual exertion. I learn to get under way by thrusting my body forward, as though I were stepping into a wind. To stop, I dig in my heels and lean backward.

To fall on the moon—and I did several times—is to re- 12 discover childhood. You go down in slow motion, the impact is slight, the risk of injury virtually nil. Forsaking the adult attitude that regards a fall not only as a loss of dignity but also a source of broken bones, the moon walker— like a child—accepts it as yet another diversion. Only the clinging moon dust, the untoward demand on the oxygen supply occasioned by the exertion of getting up, pall the pleasure of a tumble. Personally I find the one-sixth gravity of the moon more enjoyable than the soothing weightlessness of space. I have the same sense of buoyancy, but the moon provides a reassuringly fixed sense of up and down.

As we unload and begin to assemble our equipment— 13 including the battery-powered four-wheeled Rover that will carry us across the moonscape at a jaunty six or so miles an hour—I gaze around at the plains and mountains that have become our world. My eyes trace a curiously contoured, totally alien wasteland. I scale the lofty mountains and feel a strange, indescribable emotion: No naked eye has ever seen them; no foot has ever trod them. I am an intruder in an eternal wilderness.

The flowing moonscape, unmarred by a single jagged 14 peak, reminds me of earth's uplands covered by a heavy blanket of fresh snow. Indeed, the dark-gray moon dust— its consistency seems to be somewhat between coal dust and talcum powder—mantles virtually every physical feature of the lunar surface. Our boots sink gently into it as we walk; we leave sharply chiseled footprints.

Color undergoes an odd transformation here. Every- 15 thing underfoot or nearby is gray, yet this hue blends gradually into the uniform golden tan that characterizes distant objects. And this small spectrum moves with the walker. Most of the scattered rocks share the same gray tint as the dust, but we find two that are jet black, two of pastel green, several with sparkling crystals, some coated with glass, and one that is white. As we advance, we are surrounded by stillness. No wind blows. No sound echoes. Only shadows move. Within the space suit, I hear the reassuring purr of the miniaturized machines that supply vital oxygen and shield me from the blistering 150°F. surface heat of lunar morning.

Any of a thousand malfunctions in a space suit or the 16 LM could condemn an astronaut to swift death. Yet we have a quiet confidence in our own abilities, and boundless faith in the engineers and technicians who have fashioned the ingenious devices that transport and sustain us in space. Often, in the course of my stay on the moon, I recall the words of American poet Edwin Markham: ''There is a destiny which makes us brothers; none goes his way alone.''

At first we experience a troubling deception with per- 17 spective. Without the familiar measuring sticks of our native planet—trees, telephone poles, clouds, and haze—we cannot determine whether an object stands close at hand or at a considerable distance, or whether it is large or small. Gradually our eyes learn to cope with the craters—mammoth, medium, and minuscule—that dot virtually every inch of the surface. And gradually the moon becomes a friendlier place. A thought occurs to me: Would human beings born on the moon be able to find their way among the trees and clouds of earth?

Each excursion on the lunar surface is planned to last 18 seven hours, almost to the limit of a space suit's life-sustaining capabilities. We dig and drill into the surface, gather rocks and soil, take endless photographs. The photographs, it seems to me, provide us with a testament that transcends time, for we may be photographing the distant past of our own planet. The Rover functions impeccably as we ride from site to site, accumulating fragments of history. We bounce and pitch across omnipresent chuckholelike craters. The motion exactly resembles that of a small boat in a rough sea; so does the physical effect. Incredible as it seems, in the arid environment of the moon, seasickness could become an occupational hazard.

After each of our expeditions, we climb—sapped of en-   19
ergy—back into the LM. With its oxygen and food and
water, it is a tiny artificial earth that comforts us in the
void. Removing our space suits and attending to our
housekeeping chores consumes two hours. For the first
twenty minutes we are conscious of a pervasive odor,
similar to that of gunpowder, from the moon dust we have
tracked in. Our air-purifying system soon dispels the acrid
scent, but the fine, adhesive dust clings to everything. Back
on earth, no amount of cleaning will convert our space
suits from the gray hue acquired on the moon to their once
pristine and sparkling white.

The better to sleep, we create the illusion of night. We   20
place opaque shades over the windows of the LM to exclude the harsh sunlight reflected from the moon's surface.
Then we go through all the homey activities of sunset on
earth, even to snapping on overhead lights. When finally
we switch them off, we settle into hammocks. On earth,
I have always found hammocks uncomfortable. But here
my 30-pound body adapts marvelously to the canvas cres-
cent, and I easily fall into dreamless sleep.

Bounding along in the Rover on our third and final ex-   21
pedition, we begin to feel fully at home in our new habitat. The craters now seem familiar and help us gauge
distances. And we venture across the horizon—the first
astronauts ever to do so—without anxiety. Should the
sophisticated Rover navigation system fail, we have a small
cardboard sun compass fashioned by a technician in
Houston—a frail instrument much shriveled by the savage
lunar sunlight and coated with moon dust—that will give
us our bearings. But our newfound confidence stems less
from instruments than from the fact that we have come to
know and understand our surroundings.

On our return we even dare a shortcut. The Rover   22
bounces between undulations and crater walls that mask
our view of the LM for long minutes, but we emerge on
target. Arriving at the LM, I experience a sense of impend-
ing loss. Soon I will leave the moon, probably forever. And,
in a peculiar way, I have come to feel a strange affection
for this peaceful, changeless companion of the earth.

As I mount the ladder for the last time, I halt and 23
glance back at the Rover. It seems poised and ready for its
next task. And poised in that same eager attitude it could
remain for thousands, perhaps millions of years—a driver-
less vehicle lost in the loneliness of this lifeless realm.
Beside it, like staunch sentinels through the long millenniums, will hulk the LM descent stage and the assorted
equipment of our mission. The vacuum of space, which
knows only negligible decay, will confer upon all of it—
even to the footprints we have left in the undrifting dust—a
permanence akin to immortality.

The thought haunts us that the end of the Apollo 24
flights may mark man's last visit to the moon for a long
time. American manned exploration of deep space is
scheduled for an indefinite hiatus. Most scientists have
already suggested that, when it resumes, all effort should
concentrate upon reaching Mars and beyond. So our lunar
artifacts—bypassed in the race to the planets—could remain
undisturbed for eternity.

Clutching the ladder, I raise my eyes from the now- 25
familiar moonscape to earth, glowing in the black heavens
—that incredibly vivid sphere, so blue, so beautiful, so be-
loved. And so bedeviled: by ecological balances gone awry,
by scattered starvation, by a shortage of energy that may
motivate us to seek sources beyond our earth. Our Apollo
crew believes that a technology capable of exploring space
can and will help resolve such problems. We feel a sense
of pride in the accomplishments of our program, yet we
cannot escape a sense of deep concern for the fate of our
planet and our species. This concern has led us to add certain items to the equipment we are leaving on the moon.
The sum of these articles, we hope, will form a résumé
of our era in the continuing story of the human race.

In eons to come, should astronauts from the deeps of 26
space—from other solar systems in other galaxies—pass this
way, they may find our spoor, our abandoned gear. A
plaque of aluminum affixed to the deserted LM descent
stage portrays the two hemispheres of our planet; upon it
are engraved the name of our spacecraft, the date of our

mission and a roster of the crew. From these data, the equipment, and even the dimensions of our footprints, intelligent beings will readily deduce what kind of creatures we were and whence we came. We leave a piece of fauna—a falcon feather—and of flora—a four-leaf clover.

In a little hollow in the moon dust we place a stylized   27
figurine of a man in a space suit and beside it another metal plaque bearing the names of the 14 spacemen—Russians and Americans—who have given their lives so that man may range the cosmos. Finally we deposit a single book: the Bible.

Our mission ends in fatigue and elation. Amazing suc-   28
cess has rewarded the first extended scientific expedition to the moon. After debriefing and helping in the analyses of our findings, our crew disbands.

Now, two years later, I continue to work in the Lyn-   29
don B. Johnson Space Center near Houston. Frequently I reflect upon those three most memorable days of my life. Although I can reconstruct them virtually moment by moment, sometimes I can scarcely believe that I have actually walked on the moon.

Occasionally, while strolling on a crisp autumn night   30
or driving a straight Texas road, I look up at the moon riding bright and proud over the clouds. My eye picks out the largest circular splotch on the silvery surface: Mare Imbrium. There, at the eastern edge of that splotch, I once descended in a spaceship. Again I feel that I will probably never return, and the thought stirs a pang of nostalgia. For when I look at the moon I do not see a hostile, empty world. I see the radiant body where man has taken his first steps into a frontier that will never end.

Comment

To describe an experience entirely new to human beings, Scott must refer to experiences with which we are familiar. Some of his experiences are exactly like those on earth; for example, the movement of the Rover across the lunar surface "exactly resembles that of a small boat in a rough sea; so does the physical effect." To fall on the moon is to feel as we did as children, and Scott gives examples of that kind of feeling. But not every feeling and experience has an exact equivalent on earth. As his frequent resort to simile shows, we depend on figurative language to express new experiences, feelings, and insights. "Beside it, like staunch sentinels through the long millenniums, will hulk the LM descent stage and the assorted equipment of our mission."

Questions for Study and Discussion

1. To what does Scott implicitly compare the weightlessness experienced on the lunar surface? What other such experiences does he describe through comparisons?
2. What sights not previously experienced by human beings does he describe, and how does he? How does figurative language help him to make these experiences vivid?
3. What aspects of the total experience does he stress the most?
4. Had he been writing to an audience of future astronauts, how might the description and exposition have been different?
5. Does Scott develop a thesis, or instead describe an experience without drawing conclusions?

Vocabulary Study

1. Explain how Scott uses the following words figuratively:
   a. *blotted, dazzled* (paragraph 3)
   b. *shrank* (paragraph 4)
   c. *embalmed* (paragraph 7)
   d. *alien* (paragraph 18)
   e. *radiant* (paragraph 30)
2. The phrase "the shadows *shrank*" is an example of personification: the inanimate shadows are given animate or human qualities. What other examples of personification do you find in the essay?

3. Metaphors that do not immediately call a picture to mind or strike us as being comparisons are sometimes called "submerged" or "buried" metaphors:

   So we keep our clocks set to Houston time and *gear* our lives to the 24-hour cycle we have always known.

   Find several examples of such metaphors in the essay.
4. Use your dictionary to investigate the etymology of the following words—that is, their origin:
   a. *firmament* (paragraph 3)
   b. *reconnaissance* (paragraph 7)
   c. *mantles* (paragraph 14)
   d. *mammoth* (paragraph 17).

Suggestions for Writing

1. Describe a recent experience in several paragraphs, in as literal a language as possible. Then rewrite one of these paragraphs, substituting metaphorical for literal language where possible.
2. Narrate and describe an experience that would be strange to a particular audience. Assume that this audience knows nothing about the circumstances, equipment, or world of this experience, and therefore needs them explained or described. Focus on those aspects of the experience that you consider most significant or revealing.

Annie Dillard

UNTYING THE KNOT

In *Pilgrim at Tinker Creek* Annie Dillard (p. 108) describes her life at Tinker Creek, in the Roanoke Valley in Virginia's Blue Ridge. Dillard tells us in the opening chapter of the book: "It's a good place to live; there's a lot to think about. The creeks—Tinker and Carvin's—are an active mystery, fresh every minute." Later in the book, Dillard comments on the act of seeing: "Seeing is of course very much a matter of verbalization. Unless I call attention to what passes before my eyes, I simply won't see it. It is, as Ruskin says, 'not merely unnoticed, but in the full, clear sense of the world, unseen.'" The act of seeing is one of the themes of the following chapter from *Pilgrim at Tinker Creek.*

Yesterday I set out to catch the new season, and instead I found an old snakeskin. I was in the sunny February woods by the quarry; the snakeskin was lying in a heap of leaves right next to an aquarium someone had thrown away. I don't know why that someone hauled the aquarium deep into the woods to get rid of it; it had only one broken glass side. The snake found it handy, I imagine; snakes like to rub against something rigid to help them out of their skins, and the broken aquarium looked like the nearest likely object. Together the snakeskin and the aquarium made an interesting scene on the forest floor. It looked like an exhibit at a trial—circumstantial evidence—of a wild scene, as though a snake had burst through the broken side of the aquarium, burst through his ugly old skin, and disappeared, perhaps straight up in the air, in a rush of freedom and beauty.

The snakeskin had unkeeled scales, so it belonged to a nonpoisonous snake. It was roughly five feet long by the yardstick, but I'm not sure because it was very wrinkled and dry, and every time I tried to stretch it flat it broke. I ended up with seven or eight pieces of it all over the kitchen table in a fine film of forest dust.

The point I want to make about the snakeskin is that, when I found it, it was whole and tied in a knot. Now there have been stories told, even by reputable scientists, of snakes that have deliberately tied themselves in a knot to prevent larger snakes from trying to swallow them—but I couldn't imagine any way that throwing itself into a half hitch would help a snake trying to escape its skin. Still, ever cautious, I figured that one of the neighborhood boys could possibly have tied it in a knot in the fall, for some whimsical boyish reason, and left it there, where it dried and gathered dust. So I carried the skin along thoughtlessly as I walked, snagging it sure enough on a low branch and ripping it in two for the first of many times. I saw that thick ice still lay on the quarry pond and that the skunk cabbage was already out in the clearings, and then I came home and looked at the skin and its knot.

The knot had no beginning. Idly I turned it around in   4 my hand, searching for a place to untie; I came to with a start when I realized I must have turned the thing around fully ten times. Intently, then, I traced the knot's lump around with a finger: it was continuous. I couldn't untie it any more than I could untie a doughnut; it was a loop without beginning or end. These snakes *are* magic, I thought for a second, and then of course I reasoned what must have happened. The skin had been pulled inside-out like a peeled sock for several inches; then an inch or so of the inside-out part—a piece whose length was coincidentally equal to the diameter of the skin—had somehow been turned right-side out again, making a thick lump whose edges were lost in wrinkles, looking exactly like a knot.

So. I have been thinking about the change of seasons.   5 I don't want to miss spring this year. I want to distinguish the last winter frost from the out-of-season one, the frost of spring. I want to be there on the spot the moment the grass turns green. I always miss this radical revolution; I see it the next day from a window, the yard so suddenly green and lush I could envy Nebuchadnezzar down on all fours eating grass. This year I want to stick a net into time and say "now," as men plant flags on the ice and snow and say, "here." But it occurred to me that I could no more catch spring by the tip of the tail than I could untie the apparent knot in the snakeskin; there are no edges to grasp. Both are continuous loops.

I wonder how long it would take you to notice the regular recurrence of the seasons if you were the first man on earth. What would it be like to live in open-ended time broken only by days and nights? You could say, "it's cold again; it was cold before," but you couldn't make the key connection and say, "it was cold this time last year," because the notion of "year" is precisely the one you lack. Assuming that you hadn't noticed an orderly progression of heavenly bodies, how long would you have to live on earth before you could feel with any assurance that any one particular long period of cold would, in fact, end? "While the earth remaineth, seedtime and harvest, and cold and heat, and summer and winter, and day and night shall not cease": God makes this guarantee very early in Genesis to a people whose fears on this point had perhaps not been completely allayed.

It must have been fantastically important, at the real beginnings of human culture, to conserve and relay this vital seasonal information, so that the people could anticipate dry or cold seasons, and not huddle on some November rock hoping pathetically that spring was just around the corner. We still very much stress the simple fact of four seasons to school children; even the most modern of modern new teachers, who don't seem to care if their charges can read or write or name two products of Peru, will still muster some seasonal chitchat and set the kids to making paper pumpkins, or tulips, for the walls. "The people," wrote Van Gogh in a letter, "are very sensitive to the changing seasons." That we are "very sensitive to the changing seasons" is, incidentally, one of the few good reasons to shun travel. If I stay at home I preserve the illusion that what is happening on Tinker Creek is the very newest thing, that I'm at the very vanguard and cutting edge of each new season. I don't want the same season twice in a row; I don't want to know I'm getting last week's weather, used weather, weather broadcast up and down the coast, old-hat weather.

But there's always unseasonable weather. What we think of the weather and behavior of life on the planet at any given season is really all a matter of statistical probabilities; at any given point, anything might happen. There is a bit of every season in each season. Green plants—deciduous green leaves—grow everywhere, all winter long, and small shoots come up pale and new in every season. Leaves die on the tree in May, turn brown, and fall into the creek. The calendar, the weather, and the behavior of wild creatures have the slimmest of connections. Everything overlaps smoothly for only a few weeks each season, and then it all tangles up again. The temperature, of course, lags far behind the calendar seasons, since the earth absorbs and releases heat slowly, like a leviathan breathing. Migrating birds head south in what appears to be dire panic, leaving mild weather and fields full of insects and seeds; they reappear as if in all eagerness in January, and poke about morosely in the snow. Several years ago our October woods would have made a dismal colored photograph for a sadist's calendar: a killing frost came before the leaves had even begun to brown; they dropped from every tree like crepe, blackened and limp. It's all a chancy, jumbled affair at best, as things seem to be below the stars.

Time is the continuous loop, the snakeskin with scales endlessly overlapping without beginning or end, or time is an ascending spiral if you will, like a child's toy Slinky. Of course we have no idea which arc on the loop is our time, let alone where the loop itself is, so to speak, or down whose lofty flight of stairs the Slinky so uncannily walks.

The power we seek, too, seems to be a continuous loop. I have always been sympathetic with the early notion of a divine power that exists in a particular place, or that travels about over the face of the earth as a man might wander—and when he is "there" he is surely not here. You can shake the hand of a man you meet in the woods; but the spirit seems to roll along like the mythical hoop snake with its tail in its mouth. There are no hands to shake or edges to untie. It rolls along the mountain ridges like a fireball, shooting off a spray of sparks at random, and will not be trapped, slowed, grasped, fetched, peeled, or aimed. "As for the wheels, it was cried unto them in my hearing, O wheel." This is the hoop of flame that shoots the rapids in the creek or spins across the dizzy meadows; this is the arsonist of the sunny woods: catch it if you can.

Comment

Metaphor is particularly appropriate to the ideas of this essay. Dillard uses the knotted snakeskin as a metaphor for existence. She makes her point directly: she can no more "catch spring by the tip of the tail" than she can untie the knot—"there are no edges to grasp. Both are continuous loops." She builds carefully to this statement, her full meaning emerging in the details of her account. The open feeling of spring stands for a larger experience: the sense of "open-ended time." Dillard wants to see the world anew at each moment, though she knows that experiences repeat themselves. Having explored these ideas, she can finish her analogy—"Time is the continuous loop"—and she thinks also of a divine power that is everywhere always. It is the oneness and at the same time the variousness of nature that she seeks to express through figurative language.

Questions for Study and Discussion

1. The power of nature, and its openness, are symbolized in many ways in the essay. Through what metaphor is it symbolized at the end?
2. Dillard moves from ordinary experience to the extraordinary. What words and phrases suggest the extraordinary and mysterious qualities of life as the essay proceeds? Which of these words and phrases are figurative?
3. What use does Dillard make of the Bible (Daniel 4:25) in paragraph 5?
4. In how many ways is the knotted snakeskin used in the essay? That is, how many references do you find to entanglement and overlapping?

5. Why can Dillard not "catch spring by the tip of the tail" (paragraph 5)? What point is she making through this metaphorical statement?
6. How does the author characterize herself through her response to the snakeskin and the world of Tinker Creek?
7. What use does Dillard make of personification?

Vocabulary Study

Write a paraphrase of the final paragraph, translating similes, metaphors, and other figures of speech into literal language.

Suggestions for Writing

1. Write about your feelings and thoughts concerning a season of the year. Focus your discussion on an object you associate with this season. You may want to explore the various qualities of the object and what these tell you about the season.
2. Develop one of the ideas of the essay from your point of view and personal experience.

Tone

The tone of a statement expresses the attitude or feeling of a speaker or writer. The tone of the following statement on zoos is immediately clear:

> Just what sort of instruction do they radiate, and what is its value? I have never been able to find out. The sober truth is that they are no more educational than so many firemen's parades or displays of skyrockets, and that all they actually offer to the public in return for the taxes spent upon them is a form of idle and witless amusement, compared to which a visit to a penitentiary, or even to a State Legislature in session, is informing, stimulating, and ennobling. —H. L. Mencken, "Zoos"

Mencken's blunt statement expresses his astonishment and exasperation. He says exactly what he means—in contrast to this ironic statement in which the writer implies more in his opening sentence than he actually says:

> Already architectural designers are toiling to find ways out of the technical trap represented by sealed buildings with immovable glass, ways that might let in some of the naturally cool air outside. Some have lately come up with a remarkable discovery: the openable window. Presumably, that represents progress. —Frank Trippett, "The Great American Cooling Machine"

The designers of sealed buildings, the writer implies, are not very bright if they are making so obvious a discovery as the openable window. The final comment is openly sarcastic.

Many statements are harder to interpret, particularly in writing. If you heard a person exclaim "What a tragedy!", you would know immediately from the tone of voice whether the person is expressing pain, anger, sarcasm, wonder, or bewilderment. If you came upon the same exclamation in a piece of writing, you would examine its context or setting to discover the writer's tone. Trippett's opening statement seems straightforward when read out of context. Reading the statement in its context, you realize that Trippett has depended on surprise. Ironic statements often say the opposite of what we expect to hear: "He has a great future behind him." Ironic situations surprise us in the same way: "The firehouse burned to the ground."

In writing your own essays, you often adopt a tone without giving it consideration. In looking at your draft, you may need to revise the tone and clarify ambiguous words or statements, as well as your feelings or attitude, perhaps stating them directly rather than implying them.

William Aiken

HANGING OUT AND LOOKING GOOD

William Aiken is a poet, essayist, and social critic who teaches poetry at the University of Lowell in Massachusetts. He has published articles in the *Wall Street Journal* and the *Christian Science Monitor*, where his essay reprinted here appeared in 1984. Provincetown and Truro are towns on Cape Cod, Massachusetts.

My son, Matthew, has just turned 15 and arrived at that time when children like to hang out where people are cheerful. As you may know, that is not home.   1

The days of selling home-picked berries at the beach are gone. (I kept him at that for three years, but he objected to my taking half the profits.) Now he wants to work with stainless-steel machines—dishwashers and gas pumps. No more of this berry-basket stuff.   2

In the course of my recent belated education I have learned that 15-year-olds will clean up houses as a surprise for pleasant strangers, but they don't want to clean the house for me. They go for holistic personalities, which they find at ice cream parlors or in houses down the street.   3

During this new age of the public persona the big trick is not to grow fretful. You want to project a smiley face, pretend you're an aerobics teacher. It gets hard.

Fifteen is the time when kids are too young to drive, and yet they want to go certain places. You may not want them to go, but you don't want them to hitchhike, either. As a result of such dilemmas you begin to perfect various levels of grumpiness. As Matthew pops out his plans for any given day I keep thinking there is something he should be doing around the house, but I can't think what it might be. 4

I was going over his new summer schedule, scratching my head as my mind drifted back to my own vivid past raising chickens. After pumping gas for six hours in the morning he figures the rest of the day is his, so he's off to *town:* to dive for quarters off MacMillan Wharf, go waterskiing in Provincetown Harbor, walk around town pricing silver bracelets, have a slice of pizza, and join the breakdancers at Union Square. 5

Listening blankly to his adventures, I feel I'm in some kind of parental limbo of the '80s: almost ready to go out and have a good time—but not quite. I still find myself waiting by the phone and can't really seem to set out for anywhere. I watch the underlying happiness of my 15-year-old as he scales the heights of adolescence, and I keep thinking maybe he'll drop me a rope. But as he wanders farther and farther from his backyard I become more and more homebound. I have begun to take up stamp collecting again. I do these little garbage things around the house. 6

One day I decided to slip into a disguise and follow my son up to Provincetown. I have some costumes from the '50s that I still occasionally wear, and I was going over these in my closet, confident that in Provincetown no one would notice. The last time I walked down Commercial Street there was a man dressed as a lobster in front of the Wreck Club who kept an eye on passers-by through his claws. No one paid any attention. Besides, I have this underlying certainty that no young person has looked at me for years. 7

So I got to town, parked my car, and walked down to   8
the center. Nothing much seemed to be happening, just
people moving along in short pants and sequins. As I
looked around through my new reflecting glasses I noticed
a ring of young people in front of the Town Hall playing
hackensack—popping this leather thing around on their
feet. Suddenly I realized that one of them was my son.
Dressed in a mesh T-shirt, he was playing hackensack in
front of the Town Hall.

There they all were—all his friends—with their smiles   9
and their faces and their stainless-steel presences. And
there I was, all bent over in my tattered overcoat, dreaming of lobster suits. It suddenly occurred to me that while
I was in disguise, my 15-year-old had decided to go
public. Like a small corporation that had gotten itself
together and become a dazzling new entry on the Exchange, he was "hanging out and looking good." He saw
me and waved. There are certain things a disguise will
never cover.

I walked back to my car, which I had left at a food-   10
store where there's free parking for customers, and a nine-
year-old says, "That'll be $3, mister." "Your store didn't
have any Sure-Gel so I had to go downtown," I say.
"That'll be $3."

I pay up and drive slowly back to Truro. It was almost   11
time for my walk in the marsh.

Comment

Aiken writes humorously about his relationship to his fifteen-
year-old son. The tone of his essay is shaped by his attitude
toward his son and also toward his audience—by the relationship that he establishes in his opening paragraph. This audience
is a general one, needing some details but not others about
Matthew and his world. Aiken's gentle humor arises from
the understatement of his feelings, particularly at the end. This
understatement is one source of the quiet irony that characterizes the whole essay.

Questions for Study and Discussion

1. Irony is possible when the writer and the audience share certain experiences and facts. What does Aiken assume his audience knows about the towns of Cape Cod, Massachusetts? What other facts and what experiences does he assume his audience possesses? In general, what shared ironies does Aiken develop in the whole essay?
2. How would you define the attitude and feelings of Aiken toward Matthew and his world? What are his feelings at the end of the essay—on the Provincetown street and in the foodstore parking lot?
3. Is Aiken developing a thesis or merely describing personal experiences and feelings?
4. How would you characterize the writer of these experiences? What qualities of personality and outlook emerge in the telling of what happened?

Vocabulary Study

What do the following words, phrases, and sentences contribute to the tone of the essay?

1. *my recent belated education, a smiley face* (paragraph 3)
2. *some kind of parental limbo of the '80s* (paragraph 6)
3. *stainless-steel presences, "hanging out and looking good"* (paragraph 9)

Suggestions for Writing

1. Write about experiences with a younger or older brother or sister or relative that define your relationship. Don't state this relationship directly. Let your details reveal it.
2. Aiken ends his essay with an embarrassing experience. Write about an embarrassment of your own and its consequences. Use the episode to make a point about yourself or people in general.

Hilary DeVries

REAL YUPPIES

Hilary DeVries, a staff writer for the *Christian Science Monitor*, graduated from Ohio Wesleyan University in 1976. She received her M.A. in Creative Writing from Boston University in 1981. In 1983 she was named Magazine Writer of the Year by the New England Women's Press Association. The term *yuppie* became popular in the 1984 presidential election through its association with the primary candidate Senator Gary Hart. DeVries writes humorously about her efforts to join the ranks of yuppies.

Yup. I was proud not to be saddled with an acronym, 1 pleased that I nimbly sidestepped the plethora of life-style manuals—"The Official Preppy Handbook," "Real Women Don't Pump Gas," and the rest of that know-thyself paperback pack. I was poised in the face of Woodstock's 15th anniversary; I had spent the Age of Aquarius trying to ace English in a public high school in Illinois.

Yet, despite my best efforts to avoid being pegged to a 2 generational trait, I find the term "Yuppie" not only unwithered but, like so much gourmet wheat germ, still sprouting, even though Gary Hart, the true Yuppie hero, has come and gone.

If I am to believe what I hear during the waning days 3 of this campaign, I remain a political wooee, an assimilator of food processors, and unbearably upwardly mobile— the latter tips me into yet another socioeconomic category, that of the Yumpie, or "young upwardly mobile professional," in layman's lingo.

Much of this is news to me, not to mention my par- 4 ents. As far as I can tell, I still write rent-controlled rent checks every month and coddle along a car that is my college graduation present.

But in a sociological nutshell, it seems that we baby- 5 boomers have come of age—not by virtue of our achievements, rather by the extent of our style. Make that Style. Brunch has become a rite of passage and an MBA an almost requisite coat of arms.

Apparently we of the Me generation have decided that, 6
if we can't have it all, we can at least have it all First
Class—a sort of "I strive, therefore I am." Our goals lie
somewhere in the realm of inputtable data: a six-figure
salary, live-in help, and the ability to snare the best tables
at the city's top restaurants. All of it apparently reflects our
insatiable taste for the good life.

As a newly christened Yuppie—an unutterably pert 7
term to my way of thinking—I find my native tongue has
undergone some rehabbing. "Mesquite" and "dhurrie"
are all linguistically right on, at least for the moment, unlike the already déclassé "Fettuccine Alfredo," "network-
ing," and "cash machine." No one has to tell Yuppies the
times, they are a-changing. An appetite for affluence is
now the unwritten acme of good taste—a far cry from the
creeds of beads and flowers hippies.

Hence, as a true YUP, I will never, according to certain 8
codes of behavior, drink anything instant, cancel reserved
tennis court time, or pay cash. I am supposed to be too
busy patronizing those restaurants displaying a requisite
amount of ferns, brass and marble, where I never eat
macaroni and cheese or tuna on white. I am too busy stok-
ing up on sushi, gravlax, and gourmet chocolates.

And there is more to this way of life style. 9

I am supposed to do aerobics in the morning, jog at 10
noon, and meet at the health club after work. I am meant
to work—better if I can "bill"—60-plus hours a week. But
I must never tire and while away the down time in front
of the TV. Excuse me, but I think I hear my arugula calling.

If my furniture doesn't float in my loft, if my cookware 11
(and it must be "cookware," not pots and pans) doesn't
require copper cleanser or a small loan to finance, if I do
not possess multiple vinegars or a particular make of German car, I will be suspected of being out of step. Or,
more's the pity, I will miss becoming my own role model.

Yet, in a braver moment, I cannot resist testing the 12
waters. I had successfully brunched in the past, so I picked
the yuppiest restaurant I could find and blithely booked a
table for four. On the site of a humble eatery where I had

previously reveled in plates of meat loaf, mashed potatoes, and brown gravy whenever I felt nostalgic for Mom-type cooking, I picked my way into a stark art deco wonder in order to see if I wore my socioeconomic label well. If I could hold my own with those who knew their way around a wedge of Brie.

I was in for trouble the minute I crossed the polished 13 threshold. Getting a meal here turned out to be as intimidating as applying for a bank loan or country club membership. The menu was as elliptical as a French symbolist poem—perfectly designed to make one feel simple-minded should a particular quail item need explication. Maybe I wasn't a true blue Yuppie after all. Not that I trembled in the face of ''lightly oiled pasta,'' but others in the place seemed so at home, as if they had been weaned on warm lamb salad and not Bosco. My quartet stumbled through the ordering process, selecting the most familiar dishes with a relief not felt since getting out of grad school. It looked like a long evening.

Ironically, rescue came in the form of our busboy, a 14 pleasant-looking lad who had geometrically shaped hair, wore an earring, and clearly noticed our consternation. As he refilled water glasses and passed out plates of bread and ceramic tubs of pale butter, he murmured without our even asking, ''Land o' Lakes served in a ramekin.'' It was a clear tone of self-mockery totally out of synch with the industrial carpeting and bird-of-paradise flower arrangements. I glanced up. Sure enough, there was a wry twinkle in the busboy's eye not quite obscured by the new-wave coiffure.

Comment

Hilary DeVries defines the Yuppie through a series of humorous examples of the codes Yuppies obey, the games they play, the restaurants they patronize, and the food they eat. But being a Yuppie is more than the sum of what Yuppies do. Being a Yuppie is a state of mind that DeVries must attain. She tries to convey that state of mind and also her anxiety that she is missing the Yuppie style.

Questions for Study and Discussion

1. The Yuppie is materialistic, DeVries shows. But does the Yuppie want to acquire things for their own sake, or does acquisition satisfy other needs?
2. What other attitudes characterize the Yuppie, and how does DeVries illustrate them?
3. What does DeVries mean by the satirical statement, ''I will miss becoming my own role model'' (paragraph 11)? What other popular phrases like *role model* does she satirize?
4. What words or phrases suggest Yuppie talk? What is the tone of the presentation of these words and phrases?
5. Is DeVries suggesting at the end that she has succeeded in becoming a Yuppie? Or has she failed? What is the tone of the conclusion? Does her tone change in the course of the essay, or does she maintain the same tone throughout the essay?

Vocabulary Study

1. DeVries depends on the connotations or associations of words to convey the feeling and style that mark the Yuppie. Give the denotative and connotative meanings of the following words—that is, the things the words represent, the feelings and images these words convey. Then discuss what they contribute to the humor or satire of the essay: *brunch, gourmet chocolates, aerobics, arugula, Bosco, cookware, new-wave coiffure.*
2. The phrases *Woodstock's 15th anniversary* and *Age of Aquarius* are references to a rock concert in Woodstock, New York, in 1969, and to a song in the 1960s musical *Hair,* ''This is the dawning of the Age of Aquarius.'' Use the *New York Times Index* and other reference sources to explain these references in the essay.

Suggestions for Writing

1. Describe your own comical efforts to join the ranks of a fashionable group of people. Choose words that give the reader the sense of what you experienced and felt.

2. Define one of the following or a similar slang or faddish word through the connotations or associations the word has for you. Where possible, illustrate the association through images or brief episodes as DeVries does. Use your discussion to make a point about these associations or uses:
   a. funky
   b. jazzy
   c. macho
   d. nerdy

Frank Deford

BEAUTY AND EVERLASTING FAITH— LOCAL LEVEL

The sports writer and novelist Frank Deford attended Princeton University, where he edited *The Daily Princetonian* and the humor magazine *The Tiger*. For many years a senior writer for *Sports Illustrated*, he has written on numerous sports, including tennis, basketball, and roller derbies. His books include *Cut 'n' Run* (1973), *The Owner* (1976), and *Alex: The Life of a Child* (1983). In the following section from his book on the Miss America contest, *There She Is* (1971), Deford describes preliminary interviews in the local contest in Wilson, North Carolina, for the state title. The chapter from which this section is taken focuses on Doris Smith and Judi Brewer, who became finalists for first and second place. The veteran judges of the contest have long-standing memories of earlier winners; one of them mentions Jeanne Swanner, Miss North Carolina of 1963, who sometimes helps to conduct local contests.

The judging formally begins with the Saturday lunch- 1 eon at the Heart of Wilson Motel. Dr. Vincent Thomas, the head of the judges' committee, welcomes all the judges, and is himself thereafter always introduced as "Dr. Vincent," by Jerry Ball, the well-known "dean of beauty-pageant judges." Jerry has sent two state queens on to become Miss America, and judged in states as far away as Alaska. Jerry is joined on the jury by Mrs. Judy Cross, who was Most Photogenic at Miss North Carolina a few years ago, and by Mrs. Marilyn Hull, a former Miss New Jersey. She is married, as so many beauty queens are, to an athlete. Her husband is Bill Hull, a former Kansas City Chief. The other two judges are Jim Church, chairman of the board of the North Carolina Jaycees, and Bob Logan, Charlotte sales manager for Fabergé, the beauty products concern. It is a hot-shot panel for any local Pageant.

The eight contestants keep a wary eye out as they sit   2
down to lunch and make sure to reach for the correct implements. The judges, however, show no interest whatsoever in what eating tools are being utilized. They are genial and pleasant; the girls could be dispensing peas with a knife for all they seem to care about such formalities.

Doris's hat tumbles off. She does not realize it has   3
gone, which is not surprising, since hats are as foreign to these girls as bustles or U.S. Army fatigues would be. Judi has a hat on for exactly the second time in her life. The first time was when she was in another beauty pageant. There are speeches and everyone in attendance is introduced. Then the room is cleared, and a table set up for the judges at the far end. It is time for the serious interviewing. Officially, the girls in any *Miss America* Pageant are not graded on their interviews. Actually, it is the underside of the iceberg that determines the winner.

The girls are directed to another room where, one by   4
one, they will be funneled toward the judges. Following an interview, the contestant will proceed on to another room for a sort of debriefing. The judges arrange themselves and pour coffee. The men must concentrate to do their best, for the South Carolina–Duke basketball game is just starting on TV, and their hearts all lie there. Jerry Ball presides in the middle, like a Chief Justice, a leader among equals, and everyone agrees that there will be no set order to the questioning, just "catch as catch can."

Dr. Thomas sits at the other end of the room with a   5
stop watch. Jerry says, "All right, Dr. Vincent, bring in the first young lady." The girls have been assigned an order in which they will present their talents in the show; they visit the judges in the same order. Rita Deans is first. Like

all the others, she has her little hat on and carries a handbag, and she walks, as she has been taught, in the proper manner. This is an unfamiliar gait for all the girls and makes them resemble the little dogs on the Ed Sullivan Show, who have outfits on, are balanced precariously on their hind feet, and take desperate little steps to keep from pitching forward.

Rita, seated, is straightforward and demure. She assures the panel that her fourteen-year Sunday School record is not in any danger of being jeopardized by a victory tonight. The judges spring what is considered as a controversial question: what does Rita think of coed college dormitories? Rita thinks awhile. "Well, I haven't formed an opinion about that," she finally says. Mrs. Butner has instructed the girls to answer that way whenever they feel that they are unsure of an answer. The judges nod and agree that Rita would be unwise, indeed, to venture into unknown philosophical territory.

Sharon Shackleford is next. Talkative anyway, she seems especially garrulous when juxtaposed to Rita. "You've got to pull the plug on her," a judge says upon her departure. Wendy Formo, the third contestant, makes the best approach of all. Over six feet tall, she cannot help walking like a normal person. Also, she shuffles a question about Vice President Agnew beautifully, and the panel is obviously impressed. "It reminds you," Jim Church says. "I always liked that Jeanne Swanner."

Bob Logan asks, "What time is it?"

Jerry answers, "About the end of the first quarter."

Peggy Murphy, recovered from the flu, is next, and for her, the judges reach back for a classic old standard of a question: what kind of person do you think you are yourself? There is one stock answer to this question, which every girl ever in a beauty pageant has always provided. In so many words, it is: that I am naturally a shy, thoughtful person, but I love a good time on occasion. Also, I am nuts about people. Peggy is close enough.

The interviewing is now halfway through, so the judges stand and reach for some coffee. Doris comes in.

She is in yellow, with a matching handbag that she sets on the rug by the side of her chair. She banters back the usual polite preliminaries, and then one of the judges asks her if she believes there is a generation gap. "Yes, I definitely believe there is one," Doris replies firmly. All the judges sit up and cock their heads. The regular answer to this question is that there certainly isn't one around my house, where everyone works to understand each other better. Doris proceeds. "Ours is the first generation brought up with the threat of the hydrogen and atom bombs, and the first generation to have grown up with television as a major force in our lives. I really don't even believe it is surprising that there is a gap. Maybe we should only be surprised that there is not more of one."

The judges nod sagely, and to test her further, pull   12
another old chestnut out of the fire. All right, what about coed dorms? Doris backs down here; she comes out with the company line. "It may be fine for other people," she says, "but I can certainly see enough of the opposite sex on dates and other things." Doris has inserted a proper amount of righteous indignation in her voice by the end of her speech. The judges draw a breath, relieved not to have a genuine revolutionary on their hands. They are spent, though, so they ask her if she has any questions for them.

Gay Butner has informed the girls that they may be   13
faced with this request, and to have a question on standby. "Yes," Doris says, "I'd like to know why you're still interested in judging. Does it keep you closer to our generation and help close the gap for you?" Yes, the judges agree, yes, it certainly works that way for them.

Time is up; the panel smiles and thanks her; and Doris   14
is hardly out of the door when Jerry slams his hand down. "She came through like 'Gangbusters,'" he exclaims. "She took everything we threw at her and came right back."

"A live cookie," Jim Church says.   15

Vince Thomas goes to fetch Judi. She comes in, smil-   16
ing broadly, wearing her aunt's bright orange sleeveless dress. She talks enthusiastically, almost conversationally,

from the moment she deposits herself in the chair before
the judges. It is as if she has been doing this all her life.
Judi is restrained only by what she keeps reminding herself, to keep her hands anchored in her lap and not to say
"you know." She is bright and cheery and carries the
judges along with her. "Learn to gain control over the interview," Gay has told all the girls. "Give a brief answer,
then lead into another area that you particularly like to talk
about."

That advice was like giving Judi a license to steal. She   17
and all the other modern Southern belles are born and bred
in this briar patch. In Atlantic City a few months later,
Phyllis George, Judi's temperamental and verbal kin, bab-
bled on with such dazzle about her pet crab and her dog
that the most serious thing that the judges found time to
ask her was whether or not she liked beer—and Phyllis
even side-stepped that one, and went rambling right on,
absolutely stunning the judges from start to finish of the
interview. Judi's footwork is proportionately as good at the
Heart of Wilson Motel, but she slows down and twice permits the judges time to reach into the portfolio of controversial questions.

First, they want to know if Judi endorses drugs. Well,   18
she doesn't. Then Marilyn Hull remembers Doris. "Do you
think there is a generation gap?" she asks. Judi pauses but
for a second, then replies: "I don't think there's any more
gap now than there's ever been." The judges nod, and
then they want to know if she might have a question for
them.

Judi has come loaded for that bear. "What is your idea   19
of a Miss Wilson?" she rips back at them.

A girl with poise, the judges solemnly agree.   20

"Now, do you have any other question you would like   21
to ask us?" Jerry asks. This is a formality, like drop-over-
some-time-and-see-us, but Judi tears into it at face value.
"Do you think there is a generation gap?" she asks.
Marilyn fields the answer, uneasily, and this time Jerry
does not ask Judi if she has another question to ask. "I'm
afraid Dr. Vincent is signaling that our time is up," he

informs her. Judi thanks everyone and leaves. As soon as
she is out of the room, the judges start marveling about her
performance. "Imagine," one says, "we asked if she had
another question, and she did." There is a first time for
everything.

They are still chuckling at Judi's effervescence as Rose   22
Thorne comes in. She expresses a solid opposition to coed
dorms, and then Connie Whisenant finishes up by voicing
displeasure at those college students who had participated
in the Vietnam Moratorium.

Outside the room Doris and Judi are already compar-   23
ing notes. It is immediately obvious to each that her rival
was not disappointed; at the least, neither felt she had
done poorly. Judi is stunned to learn, though, that Doris
has actually said that there is a generation gap. Was she
right? Was that the correct answer that the judges were
fishing for? Anyway, it only reinforces Judi's growing opinion. By the time she goes home to put her hair up in
curlers, and to affix false eyelashes for the first time in her
life, Judi Brewer is absolutely convinced that Doris Smith
is the only thing that stands between her and Miss Wilson
1970.

Comment

Deford's attitude toward Miss America is suggested by his opening comment in the book: "Maligned by one segment of
America, adored by another, misunderstood by about all of it,
Miss America still flows like the Mississippi, drifts like amber
waves of grain, sounds like the crack of a bat on a baseball,
tastes like Mom's apple pie, and smells like dollar bills." Deford
is obviously concerned with the values the contest represents.
In the section reprinted here, he is direct about how the contest
affects the participants. "Over six feet tall," he says about
Wendy Formo, "she cannot help walking like a normal person."
And he has similar things to say about how the young women
act on the advice of Mrs. Butner, a woman from Rocky Mount
who has been tutoring them. Another important indication of

tone is the incongruity he stresses. Deford need not comment directly on the young women. His sympathy for them shapes his attitude and therefore his tone; so does his complex attitude toward the contest and the idea of "Miss America." Tone is revealed unmistakably in exaggeration as in understatement— if the author prefers not to state his or her attitude directly. The details selected for emphasis can be equally revealing.

Questions for Study and Discussion

1. How does Deford's choice of details stress the incongruous? How do his comparisons to Army fatigues, bustles, and little dogs make the incongruities vivid to us? What is the tone of these statements and comparisons?
2. Does Deford express or imply the same attitude towards all the girls in the contest? To what extent is his sympathy toward them qualified by his attitude toward the values represented by or implied in the contest?
3. What are those values, and what details best reveal them?
4. How sympathetic is Deford toward the judges? Is it his view that the panel is "hot-shot," or is he giving someone's opinion of it?
5. What does Deford mean by the statement that "it is the underside of the iceberg that determines the winner"? How does he illustrate the statement?
6. Does Deford resort to understatement or irony, or does he depend solely on the details to create tone? Does the essay have an overall tone, or does the tone vary?
7. How does he establish and maintain a consistent point of view in the whole essay?
8. What are your feelings toward the contestants and the judges? How much were they shaped for you by Deford?

Vocabulary Study

Identify words and phrases that you would classify as slang (such as "hot-shot") and determine their use in the essay, in particular their contribution to the overall tone. If this slang is no longer current, suggest how the statements might be reworded to convey the same tone.

Suggestions for Writing

1. Describe a contest in which you participated. Focus on the behavior and attitude of the judges or the participants, and use your discussion to reveal your attitude toward the contest. Choose vivid details that best reveal the values represented by or implied in the contest.
2. Discuss what you think Deford is saying or implying about the contest. Consider his details about the judges as well as about the contestants.
3. Rewrite a part of this essay from the point of view of one of the contestants. Allow her attitude toward the judges and the contest itself to emerge in the details she selects and the feelings she expresses.

Usage

Each of us has a formal and informal vocabulary. We use each vocabulary on different occasions, often without much thought. On formal occasions like weddings, funerals, and job interviews, we use a vocabulary different from that at home or with friends. Though judgments about vocabulary vary from one group of people or one part of the country to another, people usually agree on what is extremely formal and informal—the language of insurance policies and that of television comedy and sports writing, for example.

Consider the following formal and informal statements:

> Increasingly, then, the critical function must be added to the traditional triumvirate of teaching, research, and public service. Criticism must be seen not as the price to be paid for the services of higher education, but as one of the most crucial of these services. As our century progresses, as our society and the world become more complex, as the pace of social change accelerates, higher education that is not eminently critical will be increasingly useless. More and more, our society and the world will need young men and women who have not only assimilated the past and made themselves familiar with the present, but who have become articulate, informed, and thoughtful critics of both. —Kenneth Keniston, "Youth and Dissent"

He sailed up to me, and then cut to my left for the sidelines, with a little grunt, and I could hear the *shu-shu* of his football trousers as he went by, and the creak of his shoulder pads. —George Plimpton, *Paper Lion*

The vocabulary of the first passage is formal—abstract words and phrases like *critical function* and *assimilated the past* expressing

501

abstract ideas. In the second passage, the colloquial or everyday conversational phrases like *sailed up* and *cut to my left* contribute to the informality.

Vocabulary and sentence structure work together to make a piece of writing formal or informal. In the first passage the tight parallelisms and the periodic sentence that builds to the core idea (*As our century progresses*) creates a highly formal effect. In the second the loose coordination is characteristic of everyday informal conversation. However, formal English is not limited to ideas, nor is informal English limited to concrete experiences. Formal English often deals with specific concrete ideas and experience and uses a simple vocabulary. Informal English often deals with ideas in concrete language and in sentences containing looser parallelism.

Slang and jargon associated with particular jobs or activities are found in informal speech and writing. Slang consists of colorful, usually short-lived expressions peculiar to a group of people. Jargon consists of the technical words specific to a trade or profession. Assembly-line workers and telephone and automobile repairmen have their own special language—in particular, special terms and expressions. So have teenagers, jazz musicians, college professors, and baseball fans. This special language is less common in formal speech and writing, mainly because the audience for that writing is usually a general one. Expressions associated with rock music will be understood by a special audience of rock fans, but a general audience will need an explanation.

As in Art Buchwald's following comic series of letters, awareness of usage often begins when a piece of writing creates an unintended impression or effect. Unless you know your audience will be a special one, you will do best to think of it as general—representing many backgrounds and interests. This advice bears especially on diction, for vocabulary gives readers the most trouble—especially inexact, ambiguous words and phrases and empty, hackeneyd expressions or clichés.

Art Buchwald

JOB HUNTING

Art Buchwald was born in Mount Vernon, New York, in 1925, and was educated at the University of Southern California. During the Second World War he served in the Marine Corps. He has written for many newspapers; his satirical columns have been collected into many books, including *I Never Danced at the White House* (1973) and *Whose Rose Garden Is It Anyway?* (1989). His chief target has been the Washington scene but he has also written about contemporary social problems.

Vice President of Development
Glucksville Dynamics
Glucksville, California

DEAR SIR,

I am writing in regard to employment with your firm. I have a BS from USC and PhD in physics from the California Institute of Technology.

In my previous position I was in charge of research and development for the Harrington Chemical Company. We did work in thermonuclear energy, laser beam refraction, hydrogen molecule development, and heavy-water computer data.

Several of our research discoveries have been adapted for commercial use, and one particular breakthrough in linear hydraulics is now being used by every oil company in the country.

Because of a cutback in defense orders, the Harrington Company decided to shut down its research and development department. It is for this reason I am available for immediate employment.

Hoping to hear from you in the near future, I remain

Sincerely yours,
EDWARD KASE

DEAR MR. KASE,

We regret to inform you that we have no positions available for someone of your excellent qualifications. The truth of the matter is that we find you are "overqualified" for any position we might offer you in our organization. Thank you for thinking of us, and if anything comes up in the future, we will be getting in touch with you.

Yours truly,
MERRIMAN HASELBALD
Administrative Vice-President

Personnel Director
Jessel International Systems
Crewcut, Mich.

DEAR SIR,

I am applying for a position with your company in any responsible capacity. I have had a college education and have fiddled around in research and development. Occasionally we have come up with some moneymaking ideas. I would be willing to start off at a minimal salary to prove my value to your firm.

Sincerely yours,
EDWARD KASE

DEAR MR. KASE,

Thank you for your letter of the 15th. Unfortunately we have no positions at the moment for someone with a college education. Frankly it is the feeling of everyone here that you are "overqualified," and your experience indicates you would be much happier with a company that could make full use of your talents.

It was kind of you to think of us.

HARDY LANDSDOWNE
Personnel Dept.

To Whom It May Concern
Geis & Waterman Inc.
Ziegfried, Ill.

DERE SER,
I'd like a job with your outfit. I can do anything you want me to. You name it Kase will do it. I ain't got no education and no experience, but I'm strong and I got moxy an I get along great with people. I'm ready to start any time because I need the bread. Let me know when you want me.

Cheers
EDWARD KASE

DEAR MR. KASE,
You are just the person we have been looking for. We need a truck driver, and your qualifications are perfect for us. You can begin working in our Westminister plant on Monday. Welcome aboard.

CARSON PETERS
Personnel

Comment

Buchwald is not writing in his own person in these letters, but we do hear him indirectly—in the language he has given the correspondents. Buchwald's humor arises in the changes we see in Kase's letters and in the situation itself. Humor must develop out of real problems in the world we know: we will not find humor long in invented qualities and situations. Those problems may be serious—the problem Buchwald deals with is a serious one today. We can laugh with Buchwald because we are laughing not at Kase but at ourselves and at a current social problem.

Questions for Study and Discussion

1. How do Kase's letters change in language? What are the most important changes? What changes do you notice in sentence structure?
2. What situation is the source of Buchwald's humor? Is he satirizing this situation—that is, trying to correct it through ridicule?
3. What do Kase and his correspondents reveal about themselves in the impressions they give of themselves?

Vocabulary Study

Find substitutes for the formal diction in the letters to Kase. Discuss how their substitution would change the humor or point of the letters.

Suggestions for Writing

1. Write three letters of application for the same job. Change your language to give a different impression of yourself. Use these letters to make a satirical point, as Buchwald does.
2. Write an exchange of letters like Buchwald's, satirizing a current social problem through them. Fit the language of each letter to the character and attitude of the writer.

The New Yorker

THESE PAST FEW WEEKS

The New Yorker publishes fiction, poetry, criticism, and the social and political commentary of leading American writers. John Hersey's *Hiroshima*, Rachel Carson's *Silent Spring*, and Jonathan Schell's *The Fate of the Earth* first appeared in the magazine. Each issue opens with a section titled "The Talk of the Town"—a collection of short sketches and commentaries written by the staff. E. B. White wrote many of these, and so have John Updike and Lillian Ross. This comment on the state of the nation appeared in 1977 and refers to issues and events of the day, including negotiations over the Panama Canal.

These past few weeks, we have turned our attention to the newspapers in a manner not habitual with us—asking, as we read, the hard question "How are we—all of us—doing?"

We have not, it seems, done well. We have failed to live up to our advance billing. We have failed to come to terms with economic and philosophical reality. We have failed to pass litmus tests, to build up players through the farm system, to spend money where it will do the most good, to follow our gut instincts, to comply, to come face to face with what's beyond the French Quarter; failed to see the big picture, to correct oversights; failed to develop a unified approach, monitor progress, work miracles; failed to obtain access to the sea

We went too far. We threw away unique opportunities. We wasted all our energy on the Canal, giving little or no attention to outdoor lighting. We mistook rudeness and self-righteousness for leadership, yielded to lawlessness, gave tangibles for intangibles. We met behind closed doors, and disagreed on the question of seating. We brooded. We were obsessed with style rather than substance. We declined to lead the diamond jack and allow it to ride. We indulged in excessive snacking, quibbled over which expenditures belonged in the numerator, and cried disaster over each new Supreme Court decision. We tolerated "excused" absences and bad things done badly. We hushed up incidents, galvanized the opposition, made four straight unforced errors, and fought on a dozen battlefields at once. We carried loyalties past the point of good sense and sought round-the-clock companionship from cronies and assistants. We rushed to judgment.

We failed to identify enormous problems, apparently   4
intractable problems, chronic problems, and major problems. We denied that there are problems. We were unable to cope with problems that should have been anticipated. We were reluctant to adopt known solutions.

We held to old and narrow concepts. We shamelessly   5
recycled ideas, and curtailed their flow. We made archaic rules, heretical assertions, unnecessarily sharp statements.

We continued to believe that millionaires are mental   6
giants, to allow the proliferation of pirated tapes and discs, and to engage in a constant drive to "communicate" which has created a modern-day Tower of Babel.

But we were not completely at fault. We had to deal   7
with snags, slumps, impasses, summary uprootings, slights, dilution. There were erosions, declines, transitions, reversals, slouchings toward and fallings behind, inescapable aftermaths.

There were various outbreaks.   8

All the while, we were being asked to assume added   9
costs, hobbling costs, hidden costs: the hidden costs of Empire, the hidden costs of rigidity.

We were subject to the pendulum effect and the rip-   10
ple effect. We were beset by lawyers, hopeless fogies and mossbacks, the Rockefellers, and uninformed persons.

We were prey to forces: the herd instinct, the liberal   11
legacy, the division of the self against itself, the politics of barbarism, the new cult of age, machismo, post-Watergate morality, containerization and fragmentation, the breakup of the nuclear family, a debauched culture, post-recession jitters, creeping annexation, defeatism, human folly, Snowbelt-Sunbelt chauvinism, and the movement from mod to punk.

We want to do better. But, looking ahead, we see a 12
confusing mosaic of goals and means. We see historical
tensions and the convergence of a multitude of strands in
American political life. We see last straws. We see a national preoccupation with the past, and we see the future,
which has a way of catching up with you.

Comment

In this comment from the "Talk of the Town," the writer summarizes the phrases used by newspapers in 1977 to characterize
the nation. The writer does not directly express approval or
disapproval of this characterization or the language used. The
reader instead discovers the writer's attitude in the tone of the
comment and the presentation.

Questions for Study and Discussion

1. Does the writer share the opinions and judgments quoted?
    Have the newspapers satisfactorily answered the question,
    "How are we—all of us—doing?"
2. Does the writer approve of the words and phrases used by
    the newspapers to describe the nation? How do you know?
3. Is the tone of the column neutral and objective, sarcastic,
    amused, angry, or approving? Does the tone vary?

Suggestions for Writing

1. Examine several recent issues of one or two newspapers and
    magazines to make a list of words and phrases used by col-
    umnists and editorialists to describe the nation today. Com-
    ment on these words and phrases in an essay of your own.
2. Examine other "Talk of the Town" columns in the *New
    Yorker.* Then discuss whether you hear the same voice or
    different voices in these columns. Characterize the voice
    that you hear.

Joan Didion

ON KEEPING A NOTEBOOK

Joan Didion's earlier essay on the California Department of
Transportation (p. 416) illustrates her interest in how Americans live
and work. Didion looks at how people talk about themselves and
their work; she is interested in how they dress, and the setting in
which she observes them. The details recorded in her notebooks
often find their way into novels and essays, but Didion wonders in
this essay about stray details for which she has not found a use.

"'That woman Estelle,'" the note reads, "'is partly the 1
reason why George Sharp and I are separated today.' *Dirty
crepe-de-Chine wrapper, hotel bar, Wilmington RR, 9:45 a.m.
August Monday morning.*"

Since the note is in my notebook, it presumably has 2
some meaning to me. I study it for a long while. At first
I have only the most general notion of what I was doing
on an August Monday morning in the bar of the hotel
across from the Pennsylvania Railroad station in Wilmington, Delaware (waiting for a train? missing one? 1960?
1961? why Wilmington?), but I do remember being there.
The woman in the dirty crepe-de-Chine wrapper had come
down from her room for a beer, and the bartender had
heard before the reason why George Sharp and she were
separated today. "Sure," he said, and went on mopping
the floor. "You told me." At the other end of the bar is a
girl. She is talking, pointedly, not to the man beside her
but to a cat lying in the triangle of sunlight cast through
the open door. She is wearing a plaid silk dress from Peck
& Peck, and the hem is coming down.

Here is what it is: the girl has been on the Eastern 3
Shore, and now she is going back to the city, leaving the
man beside her, and all she can see ahead are the viscous
summer sidewalks and the 3 a.m. long-distance calls that
will make her lie awake and then sleep drugged through
all the steaming mornings left in August (1960? 1961?). Because she must go directly from the train to lunch in New

York, she wishes that she had a safety pin for the hem of the plaid silk dress, and she also wishes that she could forget about the hem and the lunch and stay in the cool bar that smells of disinfectant and malt and make friends with the woman in the crepe-de-Chine wrapper. She is afflicted by a little self-pity, and she wants to compare Estelles. That is what that was all about.

Why did I write it down? In order to remember, of 4 course, but exactly what was it I wanted to remember? How much of it actually happened? Did any of it? Why do I keep a notebook at all? It is easy to deceive oneself on all those scores. The impulse to write things down is a peculiarly compulsive one, inexplicable to those who do not share it, useful only accidentally, only secondarily, in the way that any compulsion tries to justify itself. I suppose that it begins or does not begin in the cradle. Although I have felt compelled to write things down since I was five years old, I doubt that my daughter ever will, for she is a singularly blessed and accepting child, delighted with life exactly as life presents itself to her, unafraid to go to sleep and unafraid to wake up. Keepers of private notebooks are a different breed altogether, lonely and resistant rearrangers of things, anxious malcontents, children afflicted apparently at birth with some presentiment of loss.

My first notebook was a Big Five tablet, given to me by 5 my mother with the sensible suggestion that I stop whining and learn to amuse myself by writing down my thoughts. She returned the tablet to me a few years ago; the first entry is an account of a woman who believed herself to be freezing to death in the Arctic night, only to find, when day broke, that she had stumbled onto the Sahara Desert, where she would die of the heat before lunch. I have no idea what turn of a five-year-old's mind could have prompted so insistently "ironic" and exotic a story, but it does reveal a certain predilection for the extreme which has dogged me into adult life; perhaps if I were analytically inclined I would find it a truer story than any I might have told about Donald Johnson's birthday party or the day my cousin Brenda put Kitty Litter in the aquarium.

So the point of my keeping a notebook has never been, 6
nor is it now, to have an accurate factual record of what
I have been doing or thinking. That would be a different
impulse entirely, an instinct for reality which I sometimes
envy but do not possess. At no point have I ever been able
successfully to keep a diary; my approach to daily life
ranges from the grossly negligent to the merely absent, and
on those few occasions when I have tried dutifully to
record a day's events, boredom has so overcome me that
the results are mysterious at best. What is this business
about "shopping, typing piece, dinner with E, depressed"?
Shopping for what? Typing what piece? Who is E? Was
this "E" depressed, or was I depressed? Who cares?

In fact I have abandoned altogether that kind of point- 7
less entry; instead I tell what some would call lies. "That's
simply not true," the members of my family frequently tell
me when they come up against my memory of a shared
event. "The party was *not* for you, the spider was *not* a black
widow, *it wasn't that way at all."* Very likely they are right,
for not only have I always had trouble distinguishing between what happened and what merely might have happened, but I remain unconvinced that the distinction, for
my purposes, matters. The cracked crab that I recall having for lunch the day my father came home from Detroit
in 1945 must certainly be embroidery, worked into the day's
pattern to lend verisimilitude; I was ten years old and would
not now remember the cracked crab. The day's events
did not turn on cracked crab. And yet it is precisely that
fictitious crab that makes me see the afternoon all over again,
a home movie run all too often, the father bearing gifts, the
child weeping, an exercise in family love and guilt. Or that
is what it was to me. Similarly, perhaps it never did snow
that August in Vermont; perhaps there never were flurries
in the night wind, and maybe no one else felt the ground
hardening and summer already dead even as we pretended
to bask in it, but that was how it felt to me, and it might
as well have snowed, could have snowed, did snow.

How it felt to me: that is getting closer to the truth about 8
a notebook. I sometimes delude myself about why I keep

a notebook, imagine that some thrifty virtue derives from preserving everything observed. See enough and write it down, I tell myself, and then some morning when the world seems drained of wonder, some day when I am only going through the motions of doing what I am supposed to do, which is write—on that bankrupt morning I will simply open my notebook and there it will all be, a forgotten account with accumulated interest, paid passage back to the world out there: dialogue overheard in hotels and elevators and at the hat-check counter in Pavillon (one middle-aged man shows his hat check to another and says, "That's my old football number"); impressions of Bettina Aptheker and Benjamin Sonnenberg and Teddy ("Mr. Acapulco") Stauffer; careful *aperçus* about tennis bums and failed fashion models and Greek shipping heiresses, one of whom taught me a significant lesson (a lesson I could have learned from F. Scott Fitzgerald, but perhaps we all must meet the very rich for ourselves) by asking, when I arrived to interview her in her orchid-filled sitting room on the second day of a paralyzing New York blizzard, whether it was snowing outside.

I imagine, in other words, that the notebook is about 9 other people. But of course it is not. I have no real business with what one stranger said to another at the hat-check counter in Pavillon; in fact I suspect that the line "That's my old football number" touched not my own imagination at all, but merely some memory of something once read, probably "The Eighty-Yard Run." Nor is my concern with a woman in a dirty crepe-de-Chine wrapper in a Wilmington bar. My stake is always, of course, in the unmentioned girl in the plaid silk dress. *Remember what it was to be me:* that is always the point.

It is a difficult point to admit. We are brought up in the 10 ethic that others, any others, all others, are by definition more interesting than ourselves; taught to be diffident, just this side of self-effacing. ("You're the least important person in the room and don't forget it," Jessica Mitford's governess would hiss in her ear on the advent of any social occasion; I copied that into my notebook because it is only recently that I have been able to enter a room without hearing some such phrase in my inner ear.) Only the very young and the very old may recount their dreams at breakfast, dwell upon self, interrupt with memories of beach picnics and favorite Liberty lawn dresses and the rainbow trout in a creek near Colorado Springs. The rest of us are expected, rightly, to affect absorption in other people's favorite dresses, other people's trout.

And so we do. But our notebooks give us away, for 11 however dutifully we record what we see around us, the common denominator of all we see is always, transparently, shamelessly, the implacable "I." We are not talking here about the kind of notebook that is patently for public consumption, a structural conceit for binding together a series of graceful *pensées*; we are talking about something private, about bits of the mind's string too short to use, an indiscriminate and erratic assemblage with meaning only for its maker.

And sometimes even the maker has difficulty with the 12 meaning. There does not seem to be, for example, any point in my knowing for the rest of my life that, during 1964, 720 tons of soot fell on every square mile of New York City, yet there it is in my notebook, labeled "FACT." Nor do I really need to remember that Ambrose Bierce liked to spell Leland Stanford's name "£eland $tanford" or that "smart women almost always wear black in Cuba," a fashion hint without much potential for practical application. And does not the relevance of these notes seem marginal at best?:

> In the basement museum of the Inyo County Courthouse in Independence, California, sign pinned to a mandarin coat: "This MANDARIN COAT was often worn by Mrs. Minnie S. Brooks when giving lectures on her TEAPOT COLLECTION."

> Redhead getting out of car in front of Beverly Wilshire Hotel, chinchilla stole, Vuitton bags with tags reading:

MRS LOU FOX
HOTEL SAHARA
VEGAS

Well, perhaps not entirely marginal. As a matter of 13
fact, Mrs. Minnie S. Brooks and her MANDARIN COAT pull
me back into my own childhood, for although I never
knew Mrs. Brooks and did not visit Inyo County until I
was thirty, I grew up in just such a world, in houses clut-
tered with Indian relics and bits of gold ore and ambergris
and the souvenirs my Aunt Mercy Farnsworth brought
back from the Orient. It is a long way from that world to
Mrs. Lou Fox's world, where we all live now, and is it not
just as well to remember that? Might not Mrs. Minnie S.
Brooks help me to remember what I am? Might not Mrs.
Lou Fox help me to remember what I am not?

But sometimes the point is harder to discern. What 14
exactly did I have in mind when I noted down that it cost
the father of someone I know $650 a month to light the
place on the Hudson in which he lived before the Crash?
What use was I planning to make of this line by Jimmy
Hoffa: "I may have my faults, but being wrong ain't one
of them"? And although I think it interesting to know
where the girls who travel with the Syndicate have their
hair done when they find themselves on the West Coast,
will I ever make suitable use of it? Might I not be better off
just passing it on to John O'Hara? What is a recipe for
sauerkraut doing in my notebook? What kind of magpie
keeps this notebook? *"He was born the night the Titanic went
down."* That seems a nice enough line, and I even recall
who said it, but is it not really a better line in life than it
could ever be in fiction?

But of course that is exactly it: not that I should ever 15
use the line, but that I should remember the woman who
said it and the afternoon I heard it. We were on her terrace by the sea, and we were finishing the wine left from
lunch, trying to get what sun there was, a California winter
sun. The woman whose husband was born the night the

Titanic went down wanted to rent her house, wanted to go back to her children in Paris. I remember wishing that I could afford the house, which cost $1,000 a month. "Someday you will," she said lazily. "Someday it all comes." There in the sun on her terrace it seemed easy to believe in someday, but later I had a low-grade afternoon hangover and ran over a black snake on the way to the supermarket and was flooded with inexplicable fear when I heard the checkout clerk explaining to the man ahead of me why she was finally divorcing her husband. "He left me no choice," she said over and over as she punched the register. "He has a little seven-month-old baby by her, he left me no choice." I would like to believe that my dread then was for the human condition, but of course it was for me, because I wanted a baby and did not then have one and because I wanted to own the house that cost $1,000 a month to rent and because I had a hangover.

It all comes back. Perhaps it is difficult to see the value   16
in having one's self back in that kind of mood, but I do see it; I think we are well advised to keep on nodding terms with the people we used to be, whether we find them attractive company or not. Otherwise they turn up unannounced and surprise us, come hammering on the mind's door at 4 a.m. of a bad night and demand to know who deserted them, who betrayed them, who is going to make amends. We forget all too soon the things we thought we could never forget. We forget the loves and the betrayals alike, forget what we whispered and what we screamed, forget who we were. I have already lost touch with a couple of people I used to be; one of them, a seventeen-year-old, presents little threat, although it would be of some interest to me to know again what it feels like to sit on a river levee drinking vodka-and-orange-juice and listening to Les Paul and Mary Ford and their echoes sing "How High the Moon" on the car radio. (You see I still have the scenes, but I no longer perceive myself among those present, no longer could even improvise the dialogue.) The other one, a twenty-three-year-old, bothers me more. She was always a good deal of trouble, and I suspect she will

reappear when I least want to see her, skirts too long, shy to the point of aggravation, always the injured party, full of recriminations and little hurts and stories I do not want to hear again, at once saddening me and angering me with her vulnerability and ignorance, an apparition all the more insistent for being so long banished.

It is a good idea, then, to keep in touch, and I sup- 17 pose that keeping in touch is what notebooks are all about. And we are all on our own when it comes to keeping those lines open to ourselves: your notebook will never help me, nor mine you. *"So what's new in the whiskey business?"* What could that possibly mean to you? To me it means a blonde in a Pucci bathing suit sitting with a couple of fat men by the pool at the Beverly Hills Hotel. Another man approaches, and they all regard one another in silence for a while. "So what's new in the whiskey business?" one of the fat men finally says by way of welcome, and the blonde stands up, arches one foot and dips it in the pool, looking all the while at the cabaña where Baby Pignatari is talking on the telephone. That is all there is to that, except that several years later I saw the blonde coming out of Saks Fifth Avenue in New York with her California complexion and a voluminous mink coat. In the harsh wind that day she looked old and irrevocably tired to me, and even the skins in the mink coat were not worked the way they were doing them that year, not the way she would have wanted them done, and there is the point of the story. For a while after that I did not like to look in the mirror, and my eyes would skim the newspapers and pick out only the deaths, the cancer victims, the premature coronaries, the suicides, and I stopped riding the Lexington Avenue IRT because I noticed for the first time that all the strangers I had seen for years—the man with the seeing-eye dog, the spinster who read the classified pages every day, the fat girl who always got off with me at Grand Central—looked older than they once had.

It all comes back. Even that recipe for sauerkraut: even 18 that brings it back. I was on Fire Island when I first made that sauerkraut, and it was raining, and we drank a lot of bourbon and ate the sauerkraut and went to bed at ten, and I listened to the rain and the Atlantic and felt safe. I made the sauerkraut again last night and it did not make me feel any safer, but that is, as they say, another story.

Comment

In this reflective essay on keeping a notebook, Didion asks a question similar to one Virginia Woolf asks about her diary (p 132). Writing a diary or keeping a notebook seems to have an obvious purpose—to keep a record of daily thoughts and events. But, in reading some of her notebook entries, Didion realizes that she never has been able to keep a diary, and keeps a notebook for another purpose entirely. The essay is an exploration of that purpose.

Questions for Study and Discussion

1. Does Didion claim to remember all of the details she gives about the woman in the Wilmington bar? Or is she inventing these details in seeking to understand why she noted the episode? Does Didion come to understand why she wrote the notebook entry?
2. Referring to another entry, Didion states: "In fact I have abandoned altogether that kind of pointless entry; instead I tell what some would call lies." What does she mean by a "lie," and why does she prefer to tell one?
3. What reasons for keeping a notebook does Didion reject in paragraph 8, and why does she?
4. According to paragraphs 11–13, why is the "meaning" of a detail or an entry difficult to determine? Does Didion say or imply that it is never possible to determine the meaning?
5. Why is it valuable "to keep on nodding terms with the people we used to be" (paragraph 16)? When does Didion want to forget one of the people she has been?
6. Are Didion's sentences formal or informal in structure, or do you find a mix of the two? Do you find a mix in her choice of words?

Vocabulary Study

Explain the use Didion makes of the following words and phrases:

1. *crepe-de-Chine* (paragraph 1)
2. *compulsive, inexplicable, malcontents, presentiment* (paragraph 4)
3. *analytically inclined* (paragraph 5)
4. *embroidery, verisimilitude* (paragraph 7)
5. *diffident, self-effacing* (paragraph 10)
6. *structural conceit, pensées, indiscriminate and erratic assemblage* (paragraph 11)
7. *marginal* (paragraph 13)
8. *river levee, improvise, recriminations, apparition* (paragraph 16)
9. *cabaña* (paragraph 17)

Suggestions for Writing

1. Didion makes a personal discovery in the course of exploring why she keeps a notebook. Describe a discovery you made about yourself under similar circumstances, perhaps on coming upon a letter you did not send or a note to yourself on a forgotten matter.
2. Each of us has a different way of writing an essay—from the initial preparation to its completion. Describe your own way of writing and what it reveals about your personal habits or way of performing a job.

Glossary

allusion: An indirect reference to a presumably well-known literary work or an historical event or figure. The phrase "the Waterloo of his political career" is a reference to Napoleon's disastrous defeat at the Battle of Waterloo in 1815. The allusion implies that the career of the politician under discussion has come to a dramatic end.

analogy: A point-by-point comparison between two unlike things or activities (for example, comparing writing an essay to building a house) for the purpose of illustration or argument. Unlike a comparison (or contrast), in which the things compared are of equal importance, analogy exists for the purpose of illustrating or arguing the nature of one of the compared things, not both.

antithesis: The arrangement of contrasting ideas in grammatically similar phrases and clauses (*The world will little note, nor long remember, what we say here, but it can never forget what they did here* —Lincoln, *Gettysburg Address*). See *parallelism*.

argument: Proving the truth or falseness of a statement. Arguments are traditionally classified as *inductive* or *deductive*. See *deductive argument* and *inductive argument*. Argument can be used for different purposes in writing. See *purpose*.

autobiography: Writing about one's own experiences, often those of growing up and making one's way in the world. The autobiographical writings of Mary E. Mebane and Maya Angelou describe their childhood in the South.

balanced sentence: A sentence containing parallel phrases and clauses of approximately the same length and wording. (*You can fool all the people some of the time, and some of the people all the time, but you cannot fool all the people all of the time.* —Lincoln).

cause and effect: Analysis of the conditions that must be present for an event to occur (*cause*) and of the results or consequences of the event (*effect*). An essay may deal with causes or with effects only.

classification and division: *Classification* arranges individual objects into groups or classes (Jonathans, Winesaps, Golden Delicious, and Macintoshes are types of apples). *Division* arranges a broad class into subclasses according to various principles (the broad class *apples* can be divided on the basis of their color, use, variety, or taste). There are as many divisions as principles of division or subclassification.

cliché: A once-colorful expression made stale through overuse (*putting on the dog, mad as a wet hen*).

coherence: The sense, as we read, that the details and ideas of a work connect clearly. A paragraph or essay that does not hold together seems incoherent.

colloquialism: An everyday expression in speech and informal writing. Colloquialisms are not substandard or "illiterate" English. They are common in informal English and occur sometimes in formal English.

comparison and contrast: The analysis of similarities and differences between two or more persons, objects, or events (A and B) for the purpose of a relative estimate. The word *comparison* sometimes refers to the analysis of similarities and differences in both A and B. *Block comparison* presents each thing being compared as a whole (that is, if the comparison is between A and B, then features a, b, c of A are discussed as a block of information, then features a, b, c, of B are compared to A in their own block of information). *Alternating comparison* presents the comparable features one by one (a, a, b, b, c, c).

complex sentence: A sentence consisting of one main or independent clause, and one or more subordinate or dependent clauses. (*The rain began when she stepped outside*).

compound sentence: A sentence consisting of coordinated independent clauses (*She stepped outside and then the rain began*).

compound-complex sentence: A sentence consisting of two or more main or independent clauses and at least one subordinate or dependent clause (*She stepped outside as the rain began, but she did not return to the house*).

concrete and abstract words: Concrete words refer to particular objects, people, and events (Benedict Arnold, Franklin Delano Roosevelt, the Rocky Mountains); abstract words refer to general shared qualities (treason, courage, beauty). Concrete writing makes abstract ideas perceptible to the senses through details and images.

concreteness: Making an idea exist through the senses. Writing can be concrete at all three levels—informal, general, and formal. See *concrete and abstract words*.

connotation: Feelings, images, and ideas associated with a word. Connotations change from reader to reader, though some words probably have the same associations for everybody.

context: The surrounding words or sentences that suggest the meaning of a word or phrase. Writers may dispense with formal definition if the context clarifies the meaning of a word.

coordinate sentence: A sentence that joins clauses of the same weight and importance through the conjunction *and, but, for, or, nor,* or *yet,* or through semicolons; sometimes followed by conjunctive adverbs (*however, therefore, nevertheless, in fact*).

deductive argument: Reasoning from statements assumed to be true or well-established factually. These statements or assumptions are thought sufficient to guarantee the truth of the inferences or conclusions. In formal arguments they are called premises. A valid argument reasons correctly from the premises to the conclusion. A sound argument is true in its premises and valid in its reasoning. See *enthymeme, syllogism.*

definition: Explaining the current meaning of a word through its etymology or derivation, its denotation, or its connotations. Denotative or "real" definitions single out a word from all other words (or things) like it by giving *genus* and *specific difference.* Connotative definitions give the associations people make to the word. See *connotation.*

description: A picture in words of people, objects, and events. Description often combines with narrative and it may serve exposition and persuasion.

division: See *classification and division.*

enthymeme: A deductive argument that does not state the conclusion or one of the premises directly. The following statement is an enthymeme: *Citizens in a democracy, who refuse to register for the draft, are not acting responsibly.* The implied premise is that the responsible citizen obeys all laws, even repugnant ones.

essay: A carefully organized composition that develops a single idea or impression or develops several related ideas or impressions. The word sometimes describes a beginning or trial attempt which explores the central idea or impression instead of developing it completely.

example: A picture or illustration of an idea, or one of many instances or occurrences that is typical of the rest.

exposition: An explanation or unfolding or setting forth of an idea, usually for the purpose of giving information. Exposition is usually an important part of persuasive writing. Example, process analysis, causal analysis, definition, classification and division, and comparison and contrast are forms of exposition.

expressive writing: Essays, diaries, journals, letters, and other kinds of writing which present personal feelings and beliefs for their own sake. The expressive writer is not primarily concerned with informing or persuading readers.

figure of speech: A word or phrase that departs from its usual meaning. Figures of speech make statements vivid and capture the attention of readers. The most common figures are based on similarity between things. See *metaphor, personification, simile.* Other figures are based on relationship. See *allusion. Metonymy* refers to a thing by one of its qualities (*the Hill* as a reference to the United States Congress). *Synecdoche* refers to a thing by one of its parts (*wheels* as a reference to racing cars). Other figures are based on contrast between statements and realities. See *irony.* Related to irony is *understatement,* or saying less than is appropriate ("Napoleon's career ended unhappily at Waterloo"). *Hyperbole* means deliberate exaggeration ("crazy about ice cream"). *Paradox* states an apparent contradiction ("All great truths begin as blasphemies" —G. B. Shaw). *Oxymoron,* a kind of paradox, joins opposite qualities into a single image (*lake of fire*).

focus: The limitation of subject in an essay. The focus may be broad, as in a panoramic view of the mountains, or it may be narrow, as in a view of a particular peak. For example, a writer may focus broadly on the contribution to scientific thought of scientists from various fields, or focus narrowly on the achievements of astronomers or chemists or medical researchers, or focus even more narrowly on the achievements of Albert Einstein as representative of twentieth-century science.

formal English: Spoken and written English, often abstract in content, with sentences tighter than spoken ones, and an abstract and sometimes technical vocabulary. See *general English* and *informal English.*

general English: A written standard that has features of informal and formal English and avoids the extremes of both. See *formal English* and *informal English.*

image: A picture in words of an object, a scene, or a person. Though visual images are common in writing, they are not the only kind. Images can also be auditory, tactile, gustatory, and olfactory. Keats's line "With beaded bubbles winking at the brim" appeals to our hearing and taste as well as to our sight. His phrase "coming muskrose" appeals to our sense of smell. Images help to make feelings concrete.

implied thesis: The central idea of the essay, suggested by the details and discussion rather than stated directly. See *thesis.*

inductive argument: Inductive arguments reason from particulars of experience to general ideas—from observation, personal experience, and experimental testing to probable conclusions. Inductive arguments make predictions on the basis of past and present experience. An argumentative analogy is a form of inductive argument because it is based on limited observation and experience and therefore can claim probability only. Analysis of causes and effects, like statistical analysis, is inductive when used in argument.

"inductive leap": Making the decision that sufficient inductive evidence (personal experience, observation, experimental testing) exists to draw a conclusion. Sometimes the writer of the argument makes the leap too quickly and bases his conclusions on insufficient evidence.

informal English: Written English, usually concrete in content, tighter than the loose sentences of spoken English, but looser in sentence construction than formal English. The word "informal" refers to the occasion of its use. A letter to a friend is usually informal; a letter of application is usually formal. See *formal English* and *general English*.

irony: A term generally descriptive of statements and events. An ironic statement says the opposite of what the speaker or writer means, or implies that something more is meant than is stated, or says the unexpected (*He has a great future behind him*). An ironic event is unexpected or is so coincidental that it seems impossible (*The firehouse burned to the ground*).

jargon: The technical words of a trade or profession (in computer jargon, the terms *input* and *word processor*). Unclear, clumsy, or repetitive words or phrasing, sometimes the result of misplaced technical words (*He gave his input into the decision process*).

loose sentence: A sentence that introduces the main idea close to the beginning and concludes with a series of modifiers (*The car left the expressway, slowing on the ramp and coming to a stop at the crossroad*). See *periodic sentence*.

metaphor: An implied comparison which attributes the qualities of one thing to another (the word *mainstream* to describe the opinions or activities of most people).

mixed metaphor: The incongruous use of two metaphors in the same context (*The roar of protest was stopped in its tracks*).

narrative: The chronological presentation of events. Narrative often combines with description and it may serve exposition or persuasion.

order of ideas: The presentation of ideas in a paragraph or an essay according to a plan. The order may be *spatial*, perhaps moving from background to foreground, or from top to bottom, or from side to side; or the order may be *temporal* or chronological (in the order of time). The presentation may be in the order of *importance*, or if the details build intensively, in the order of *climax*. The paragraph or essay may move from *problem* to *solution* or from the *specific* to the *general*. Some of these orders may occur together—for example, a chronological presentation of details that build to a climax.

parallelism: Grammatically similar words, phrases, and clauses arranged to highlight similar ideas (*There are neighborhoods of nations. . . . There are streets where, on January nights, fires burn on every floor of every house. . . . There are meadows and fields* —Mark Helprin). See *antithesis*.

paraphrase: A rendering of a passage in different words that retain the sense, the tone, and the order of ideas.

periodic sentence: A sentence that builds to the main idea (*Building speed as it curved down the ramp, the car sped into the crowded expressway*). See *loose sentence*.

personification: Giving animate or human qualities to something inanimate or inhuman (The sun *smiled* at the earth).

persuasion: The use of argument or satire or some other means to change thinking and feeling about an issue.

point of view: The place or vantage point from which an event is seen and described. The term sometimes refers to the mental attitude of the viewer in narrative. Mark Twain's *Huckleberry Finn* narrates the adventures of a boy in slave-owning Missouri from the point of view of the boy, not from that of an adult.

premise: See *syllogism*.

process: An activity or operation containing steps usually performed in the same order. The process may be mechanical (changing a tire), natural (the circulation of the blood), or historical (the rise and spread of a specific epidemic disease such as bubonic plague at various times in history).

purpose: The aim of the essay as distinguished from the means used to develop it. The purposes or aims of writing are many; they include expressing personal feelings and ideas, giving information, persuading readers to change their thinking about an issue, inspiring readers to take action, giving pleasure. These purposes may be achieved through description, narrative, exposition, or argument. These means may be used alone or in combination, and an essay may realize more than one purpose.

reflection: An essay that explores ideas without necessarily bringing the exploration to completion. The reflective essay can take the form of a loosely organized series of musings or tightly organized arguments.

satire: Ridicule of foolish or vicious behavior or ideas for the purpose of correcting them. *Social satire* concerns foolish but not dangerous behavior and ideas—for example, coarse table manners, pretentious talk, harmless gossip. George Bernard Shaw's "Arms and the Man" is a social satire. *Ethical satire* attacks vicious or dangerous behavior or ideas—religious or racial bigotry, greed, political corruption. Mark Twain's *Huckleberry Finn* is an ethical satire.

simile: A direct comparison between two things (*A growing child is like a young tree*). See *figure of speech, metaphor.*

simple sentence: A sentence consisting of a single main or independent clause and no subordinate or dependent clauses (*The rain started at nightfall*).

slang: Colorful and sometimes short-lived expressions peculiar to a group of people, usually informal in usage and almost always unacceptable in formal usage (*nerd, goof off*).

style: A distinctive manner of speaking or writing. A writing style may be plain in its lack of metaphor and other figures of speech. Another writing style may be highly colorful or ornate.

subordinate clause: A clause that completes a main clause or attaches to it as a modifier (She saw *that the rain had begun; When it rains,* it pours).

syllogism: The formal arrangement of premises and conclusion of a deductive argument. The premises are the general assumptions or truths (*All reptiles are cold-blooded vertebrates, All snakes are reptiles*) from which necessary conclusions are drawn (*All snakes are cold-blooded vertebrates*). This formal arrangement helps to test the validity or correctness of the reasoning from premises to conclusion. See *deductive argument.*

symbol: An object that represents an abstract idea. The features of the symbol (the fifty stars and thirteen horizontal stripes of the American flag) suggest characteristics of the object symbolized (the fifty states of the Union, the original confederation of thirteen states). A sign need not have this representative quality: a green light signals "go," and a red light "stop" by conventional agreement.

thesis: The central idea that organizes the many smaller ideas and details of the essay.

tone: The phrasing or words that express the attitude or feeling of the speaker or writer. The tone of a statement ranges from the angry, exasperated, and sarcastic, to the wondering or approving. An ironic tone suggests that the speaker or writer means more than the words actually state.

topic sentence: Usually the main or central idea of the paragraph that organizes details and subordinate ideas. Though it often opens the paragraph, the topic sentence can appear later—in the middle or at the end of the paragraph.

transition: A word or phrase (*however, thus, in fact*) that connects clauses and sentences. Parallel structure is an important means of transition.

unity: The connection of ideas and details to a central controlling idea of the essay. A unified essay deals with one idea at a time.

✧

Copyrights and Acknowledgments

Index

See the Glossary, pp. 520–27, for additional definitions of key terms and others not listed here.